T0185056

Communications in Computer and Information Science 1246

More information about this series at http://www.springer.com/series/7899

Claudio Parente · Salvatore Troisi ·
Antonio Vettore (Eds.)

R3 in Geomatics: Research, Results and Review

First International Workshop
in memory of Prof. Raffaele Santamaria
on R3 in Geomatics: Research, Results and Review, R3GEO 2019
Naples, Italy, October 10–11, 2019
Revised Selected Papers

Springer

Editors
Claudio Parente (iD)
Parthenope University of Naples
Naples, Italy

Salvatore Troisi (iD)
Parthenope University of Naples
Naples, Italy

Antonio Vettore (iD)
University of Padova
Padua, Italy

ISSN 1865-0929   ISSN 1865-0937 (electronic)
Communications in Computer and Information Science
ISBN 978-3-030-62799-7   ISBN 978-3-030-62800-0 (eBook)
https://doi.org/10.1007/978-3-030-62800-0

This Springer imprint is published by the registered company Springer Nature Switzerland AG
The registered company address is: Gewerbestrasse 11, 6330 Cham, Switzerland

Preface

The First International Workshop R3 in Geomatics: Research, Results and Review (R3GEO 2020), was held in Naples at the Parthenope University of Naples, Italy, during October 10–11, 2019. This event was dedicated to the memory of Raffaele Santamaria (1950–2017), Italian Professor of Geomatics and Director of the Department of Sciences and Technologies (DiST) at Parthenope University of Naples (2013–2017). In his honor, the event was focused on Geomatics, the "discipline concerned with the collection, distribution, storage, analysis, processing, and presentation of geographic data or geographic information" (Standard Technical Committee ISO/TC 211).

According to the Declaration on Geomatics by the Italian Ministry of Education University and Research (MIUR), the contents of the scientific disciplines concern the acquisition, return, analysis, and management of metric or thematic data relating to the surface of the Earth, or portions of it, including the urban environment, infrastructures, and architectural heritage, identified by their spatial location and qualified by detection accuracy. The disciplines included in this scientific sector are: Geodesy (physical, geometric, and spatial), Topography, Photogrammetry (aerial and terrestrial), Cartography, Remote Sensing (by satellite, airplane, and close-range), Navigation (space, air, sea, and land), and Geographic Information Systems (GIS). The application areas concern, in particular, the study of the global and local reference systems, the instruments and methods of detection, control, monitoring of the territory, of the structures, and cultural heritage, the processing of measurement data, the production and updating of cartography, topographic databases, layout of works and infrastructures, mobile systems for surveying, Global Navigation Satellite System (GNSS), digital terrain and surface models (DTMs and DSMs), management and sharing of multidimensional, and multi-time geographic information.

The workshop was organized to remark on the recent developments in Geomatics and the submission of high quality abstracts was encouraged. Every contribution received (first as an abstract and then, if approved, as an article) was subjected to a rigorous single-blind review process. At the start, 39 of the submitted abstracts were accepted. Each submitted article received at least three reviews from the Scientific Committee and additional reviewers. Then authors were invited to revise their contribution. After revision was received, each paper was resubmitted to the review process. Ultimately, of the 39 papers submitted, 29 (74.4%) were accepted for publication, of which 27 (93.1%) included at least 12 pages (full papers). All Scientific Committee members were assembled from different countries and they made the workshop truly international in scope.

The papers were grouped according to the topics they addressed. For instance, three thematic areas were identified for the proceedings: GNSS and Geodesy, Photogrammetry and Laser Scanning, and GIS and Remote Sensing.

The support for the conference was provided by the International Society for Photogrammetry and Remote Sensing (ISPRS), the Association of the Italian University professors and researchers of Geomatics (Associazione Universitari di Topografia e Cartografia, AUTEC) two Italian Scientific Associations named, respectively, Società Italiana di Fotogrammetria e Topografia (SIFET) and Associazioni Scientifiche per le Informazioni Territoriali e Ambientali (ASITA), and the Parthenope Univesity of Naples.

We would like to thank the organization staff, the members of the Scientific Committee, and reviewers. They worked very hard in reviewing papers and making valuable suggestions for the authors to improve their work. We would also like to express our gratitude to the external reviewers, for providing extra help in the review process, and the authors for contributing their research results to the workshop. We would like to extend our sincere thanks to the Rector of the Parthenope University of Naples, Prof. Alberto Carotenuto, and the Director of the DiST, Prof. Giorgio Budillon, for encouraging and supporting the event, as well as the DiST technical staff, especially Mr. Francesco Peluso, for the workshop website construction. Special thanks go to Springer for technically supporting and publishing the proceedings.

July 2020   Claudio Parente
                                                    Salvatore Troisi
                                                    Antonio Vettore

Organization

Scientific Committee Chairs

Claudio Parente	Parthenope University of Naples, Italy
Salvatore Troisi	Parthenope University of Naples, Italy
Antonio Vettore	University of Padova, Italy

Scientific Committee

Vladimiro Achilli	University of Padova, Italy
Fernando J. Aguilar Torres	University of Almeria, Spain
Maurizio Barbarella	University of Bologna, Italy
Giovanni Battista Benciolini	University of Trento, Italy
Barbara Betti	Polytechnic University of Milan, Italy
Gabriele Bitelli	University of Bologna, Italy
Alessandro Capra	University of Modena and Reggio Emilia, Italy
Mauro Caprioli	Polytechnic University of Bari, Italy
Mattia Crespi	Sapienze University of Rome, Italy
Fabio Crosilla	University of Udine, Italy
Naser El-Sheimy	University of Calgary, Canada
Vassilis Gikas	National Technical University of Athens, Greece
Ayman Habib	Purdue University, USA
Allison Kealy	RMIT University, Australia
Eva Malinverni	Polytechnic University of Marche, Italy
Ambrogio Manzino	Polytechnic of Turin, Italy
Fabio Radicioni	University of Perugia, Italy
Fabio Remondino	Fondazione Bruno Kessler, Italy
Günther Retscher	Vienna University of Technology, Austria
Fernando Sansò	Polytechnic University of Milan, Italy
Charles Toth	The Ohio State University, USA

Session Chairs

Valerio Baiocchi	Sapienza University of Rome, Italy
Riccardo Barzaghi	Polytechnic University of Milan, Italy
Alberto Cina	Polytechnic of Turin, Italy
Ambrogio Manzino	Polytechnic of Turin, Italy
Andrea Masiero	University of Padova, Italy
Claudio Parente	Parthenope University of Naples, Italy
Giuseppina Prezioso	Parthenope University of Naples, Italy
Salvatore Troisi	Parthenope University of Naples, Italy
Andrea Vallario	Parthenope University of Naples, Italy
Antonio Vettore	University of Padova, Italy

Additional Reviewers

Emanuele Alcaras
Antonio Angrisano
Valerio Baiocchi
Vincenzo Barrile
Oscar R. Belfiore
Ludovico G. A. Biagi
Gabriella Caroti
Domenica Costantino
Paolo Dabove
Gino Dardanelli
Silvio Del Pizzo
Donatella Dominici
Massimo Fabris
Ugo Falchi
Francesco Fassi
Margherita Fiani
Salvatore Gaglione
Stefano Gandolfi
Francesca Giannone
Valentina A. Girelli

Francesca Guastaferro
Andrea M. Lingua
Mauro Lo Brutto
Emanuele Mandanici
Andrea Masiero
Federica Migliaccio
Massimiliano Pepe
Andrea Piemonte
Marco Piras
Giuseppina Prezioso
Giovanni Pugliano
Umberto Robustelli
Domenico Sguerso
Aurelio Stoppini
Eufemia Tarantino
Grazia Tucci
Giuseppina Vacca
Andrea Vallario
Domenico Visintini
Luca Vittuari

Contents

Photogrammetry and Laser Scanning

GIS and Remote Sensing

Short biography

 **Raffaele Santamaria** Born on 2 May 1950 in Naples (Italy), Raffaele Santamaria graduated in Nautical Sciences at Naval University Institute of Naples and became full Professor of Geomatics (Topography and Cartography) at the Parthenope University of Naples. First he held the role of dean of the Faculty of Sciences and Technologies (2005–2013) and then of director of the Department of Sciences and Technologies at the same University (2013–2017). He also carried out teaching activities at the Federico II University of Naples, Faculty of Engineering, where he was a teacher of Topography.

He was the Coordinator of the PhD Course in Geodetic and Topographical Sciences for the three-year period 2006–2008. In the next years, he took part in the teaching staff of the Doctoral program in "Geomatics, Navigation and Geodesy" and of the Doctoral program in "Sciences Applied to the Sea, the Environment and the Territory" of the same University.

In 1994 he was director of the post-graduate Master in Marine Sciences and Engineering at the Naval University Institute of Naples.

He was member of the Commission for the National Radio Navigation Plan, and scientific manager of the European consortium for research named MED-TEAM (Maritime Engineering Development and Trans Mediterranean Environmental Awareness and Management) of the European Commission (EU).

He participated in numerous research projects relating to Cartography, Navigation, Geographic Information System (GIS), Global Positioning System (GPS), Global Navigational Satellite System (GNSS), and Remote sensing, presenting the results of his studies and applications in national and international conferences. He was involved in the study of orbits and constellations of artificial satellites for selective coverage of the earth's surface. He conducted research activities funded by ASI (Italian Space Agency) on the reduction of ionospheric and multipath errors to improve accuracy in RTK (Real Time Kinematic) GPS applications, with particular attention to navigational ones.

He was scientific responsible of numerous research projects in the geodetic, topo-cartographic and remote sensing fields. Particularly, he was National Coordinator of two projects funded by the Italian Ministry of Education University and Research (MIUR): the PRIN 2008 project entitled "WEBGIS and innovative remote sensing techniques for safeguarding against territorial and environmental risks" as well as the PRIN 2010–11 project entitled "Innovative and emerging geomatics techniques of survey, remote sensing (by airplane, satellite, UAV) and WEBGIS for risk mapping in real-time and the prevention of environmental damage".

He was the author of more than one hundred works presented at national and international conferences and/or published in national and international journals. At age 67, he died in Naples in June 2017, mourned by family and friends, many of whom had been his pupils.

GNSS and Geodesy

Positioning Domain Assessment of Multi Constellation Dual Frequency Lowcost Receivers in an Highly Degraded Scenario

Umberto Robustelli$^{(\boxtimes)}$ ⓘ, Matteo Cutugno ⓘ,
and Giovanni Pugliano ⓘ

Parthenope University of Naples, Naples, Italy
{umberto.robustelli,matteo.cutugno,
giovanni.pugliano}@uniparthenope.it

Abstract. The objective of this paper is to test in a degraded environment the performances of two different type of low-cost GNSS receivers. The first one is a typical low-cost hardware: the u-blox ZED-F9P GNSS module interfaced with u-center evaluation and a commercial front-end while the second one is a *Software-Defined Receiver* (SDR) software developed by Centre Tecnològic Telecomunicacions Catalunya coupled with a Nuand BladeRF x40. In order to investigate the performance of the hardware involved we applied our analysis to the measurements captured in a strong multipath scenario. Four different tests have been carried out employing the two receivers and coupled with two different antennas. Results achieved shows that the employment of the more performing antenna leads to better positioning results. The DRMS (Distance Root Mean Square) of horizontal position errors decreases of about the 54% and the 40% for the SDR and the u-blox, respectively.

Nonetheless, the Nuand bladeRF shows poor positioning results with respect to those obtained with u-blox. The results achieved shows that Nuand is not yet suitable for surveying purposes. The reason resides in the poor quality of the reference clock of the on-board oscillator that doesn't assure an appropriate stability.

Keywords: SDR · u-blox ZED-F9P · Nuand blade RF · Low cost · GNSS-SDR

1 Introduction

The objective of this paper is to test in a degraded environment the performances of two different type of low-cost GNSS receivers: a u-blox ZED-F9P GNSS module interfaced with u-center evaluation software and a commercial front-end (Nuand BladeRF x40) drived by a *Software Defined Receiver* (SDR) approach by using GNSS-SDR, an open source code developed by Centre Tecnològic Telecomunicacions Catalunya (CTTC). In order to achieve this goal we employed two GNSS active antennas of different quality. The tests were conducted in an urban-canyon site such as the Directional center of Naples where the presence of tall skyscrapers not only limits the satellites availability but also results in a strong multipath interference caused by

© Springer Nature Switzerland AG 2020
C. Parente et al. (Eds.): R3GEO 2019, CCIS 1246, pp. 3–15, 2020.
https://doi.org/10.1007/978-3-030-62800-0_1

signals reflection from facades of buildings. The two antennas were placed in a site with known coordinates. Once the performance assessment was carried out the results obtained with the u-blox and those obtained with Nuand were compared.

SDR technology is a continuous evolving topic following its birth in the mid-1980 s, growing side-by-side with new developments in related hardware technologies (processor power, serial busses, signal processing techniques and SDR chipsets). Some important advances were achieved by Akos in [1] and Borre in [2]. Nowadays there are some software solutions in GNSS positioning following this approach. Ledvina et al. proposed a 12-channel real time GPS L1 software receiver achieving an accuracy of 10 m [3]. In 2006 Borre and Akos published [4] a keystone book where the authors discuss different GPS receiver architectures based on software defined radio techniques. A promising software receiver capable of acquire, process and compute navigation solution for different kind of constellations (GPS, Glonass and Galileo) is GNSS-SDR, developed by CTTC, where in [5] and in [6] has been described the software architecture design providing details about its implementation, targeting a multiband, multisystem GNSS receiver. Other interesting studies on low-cost software receivers can be found in [7–10]. For the extreme customization capabilities, *Software defined receivers* are the best candidates for different applications regarding inertial navigation systems for vehicles [11], drone navigation [12] and GNSS reflectometry (GNSS-R) [13].

In the low cost receiver context an increasingly role will be played by smartphone receivers that are becoming more and more performing as shown in [14] and [15].

Moreover, in order to increase precision and accuracy, a key-role can be also played by CORS networks as shown in [16] and [17].

In 2019 Cutugno et al. [18] tested GNSS-SDR using the same hardware in different sky view conditions. Results achieved demonstrated that a key to get better results both in positioning accuracy and satellites tracking, is the antenna quality.

Following previous research, this work is focused on the performance comparison between a low-cost SDR and a low-cost hardware receiver.

During the signal acquisition stage u-center software stores a binary file in a proprietary format (.ubx). To obtain the RINEX files useful for post-processing computations, we use the RTKlib GNSS software suite. In details RTKconv utility was used. At this stage we experienced the impossibility to completely convert the files with the Graphic User Interface (GUI) of RTKconv. Indeed, in the outputted RINEX (Receiver INdependent EXchange format) files the observations related to E5b signal were not logged. To overcome this problem we employed the command line interface (CUI) of RTKconv. Once we obtained the RINEX files we were able to post-process the data with RTKpost package obtaining the position solution with a single point algorithm. SDR is a very useful tool since it is capable of extreme customization allowing user to access, visualize and modify signal acquisition, signal tracking and signal processing blocks. The software used (GNSS-SDR) allows user to store both the intermediate frequency (IF) data and the RINEX files. In this test we chose to use the latter strategy, thus the output of the acquisition were RINEX files post-processed with a Single Point

Position approach using RTKpost utility. In both computations, we used the same RTKpost parameters. In particular, the positioning mode has been set in single mode, the elevation mask to 15°, the ionosphere correction has been made by using broadcasted Klobuchar parameters while troposphere correction used is based on Saastamoinen model. Finally, the satellite ephemeris [29, 30] were downloaded from the Crustal Dynamics Data Information System (CDDIS) site where are stored the product archive of Multi-GNSS Experiment (MGEX) projects [19, 20].

2 Experimental Setup

2.1 Acquisition Scenario

In order to investigate the performance of the hardware involved we applied our analysis to the measurements captured in a strong multipath scenario. Four different tests were carried out employing two receiver and two antennas. As shown in Fig. 1, the data acquisition was carried out in Directional Center, a business area in the center of Naples, on the 25th and 27th of September 2019 during a thirty minutes surveying session for each acquisition.

This is a difficult environment in which the receivers are surrounded by buildings. It can be seen as a typical example of an urban canyon where many GNSS signals are

Fig. 1. Acquisition scenario: Directional Center site (Napoli).

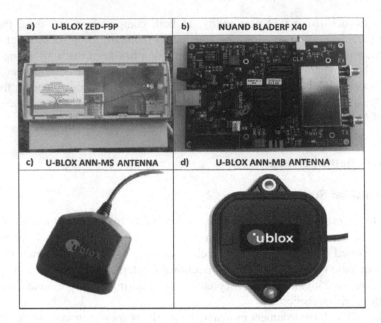

Fig. 2. Hardware tested: a) ZED-F9P module, b) Nuand BladeRF x40, c) u-blox ANN-MS active antenna, d) u-blox ANN-MB active antenna.

strongly degraded by multipath effects or blocked by skyscrapers as showed in [21–23]. The analysis was performed for all visible satellites of GPS and Galileo constellations during the whole observation periods. In order to evaluate the absolute performance positioning of the tested receivers, the survey was carried out on a precise point of known coordinates. For sake of clarity the main features of the tests are shown in Table 1.

Table 1. Tests main features.

	Receiver	Antenna
TEST A	SDR	ANN-MS
TEST B	SDR	ANN-MB
TEST C	u-blox ZED F9P	ANN-MS
TEST D	u-blox ZED F9P	ANN-MB

2.2 Hardware Setup

The hardware tested in this paper consist in two different receivers. The first one, as shown in Fig. 2, is a low-cost GNSS receiver assembled by *Educabile s.r.l,* an innovative start-up based in Naples. The receiver relies on the ZED-F9P u-blox high precision GNSS module. The ZED-F9P GNSS module is a GNSS receiver able to receive and track multiple GNSS systems. Owing to the multi-band RF front-end architecture, all four major GNSS constellations (GPS, GLONASS, Galileo and Bei-Dou) plus QZSS satellites can be received simultaneously. All satellites in view can be processed to provide an RTK navigation solution when used with correction data.

The second receiver tested is a SDR where the hardware consisted in a front end, in particular the Nuand bladeRF x40, a low-cost USB 3.0 Software Defined Radio, able to tune up from 300 MHz to 3.8 GHz; so, potentially, it can provide access to all of the frequency used by GNSS satellites (L1, L2 and L5). Its price is about 400 $. The keystone features of a front-end for satellite positioning application is the stability of the reference clock. The board tested here has a precision of 1 PPM and it's factory calibrated within 1 Hz of 38.4 MHz reference. The board is equipped with a Field Programmable Gate Array (FPGA) that provides the interface between the firmware and RF transceiver. This FPGA has single-cycle access embedded memory, hard 18×18 multipliers for dedicated DSP and many general logic elements ready to be programmed. For the tests carried out with the SDR we use the same data of [15]. The front-end has been connected to a notebook via USB 3.0.The notebook is equipped with a intel i7 microprocessor with 16 Gb of RAM running a stable release of Ubuntu 16.04. The hardware needed was completed by a low-cost GNSS antenna and a bias-tee. Two different antennas have been tested. First, we employ the ANN-MS u-blox GNSS active antenna; subsequently the ANN-MB antenna, a Multi-band, high precision GNSS active antenna, was tested. In Table 2 are shown the main features of the active u-blox GNSS antennas employed. As previously said these antennas were low-cost ones where the latter being more expensive seems to show better performances with respect to the former. Lastly, the hardware configuration was completed by a bias-tee, needful to provide external gain to the antenna, feeded by 5 V provided via a USB port (Table 3).

Table 2. Antennas characteristics.

	ANN-MS L1 band	ANN-MB L1 band
Frequency [MHz]	1555–1605	1559–1606
Impedance [Ohm]	50	50
Peak gain [dBic]	Min.4	Typ.3.5
Gain(no cable)[dB]	29	25–31
Noise figure [dB]	0.9	2.8
DC voltage [V]	2.7–5.5	3–5
Polarization	RHCP	RHCP
Price [€]	15	55

2.3   Software Setup

The ZED-F9P is fully configurable with UBX configuration interface keys. The configuration in the receiver's RAM holds the current configuration, which is used by the receiver at run-time.

The configuration interface and the available keys are fully described in the ZED-F9P Interface Description in [24].

The module, linked with the processing unit via USB, lets the user obtain his position, either in real time or in post-processing, making use of the last release of U-center, a GNSS evaluation software useful for evaluation, performance analysis and configuration of u-blox GNSS receivers.

As previously said the software chosen for this tests is GNSS-SDR, an open source project hosted on *github.com*, developed by CTTC in [5], that implements a complete global navigation satellite system software defined receiver in C++. It performs signal acquisition and tracking of the available satellite signals, decodes the navigation message and computes the observables needed by positioning algorithms, which ultimately compute the navigation solution. In this experiment we set up SDR to store Intermediate Frequency (IF) signal. The data storage requirement depends on the received signal bands and number of bits used to represent each digital sample. In particular, we experienced that the space needed to store raw data for L1 frequency packed in complex samples, with real and imaginary parts of type float, was ~1 GB for every minute of acquired data. After the acquisition step IF data were post-processed in order to achieve pseudorange measurements lastly used to compute single point position solution.

3   Results

The carrier-to-noise density C/N0 output by a receiver provides an indication of the accuracy of the tracked satellite GNSS observations and the noise density as seen by the receiver's front-end. It also indicates the level of noise present in the measurements. These values are stored in RINEX files. The lower the signal-to-noise ratio the worse the quality of the measurements. Figure 3 shows the mean of C/N0 values for each tracked satellite between signal acquisition with ANN-MS antenna (blue bars) and ANN-MB antenna (red bars). The C/N0 is lower for the ANN-MS antenna compared to the better one. This is due to the limited performance of former antenna with respect to latter one.

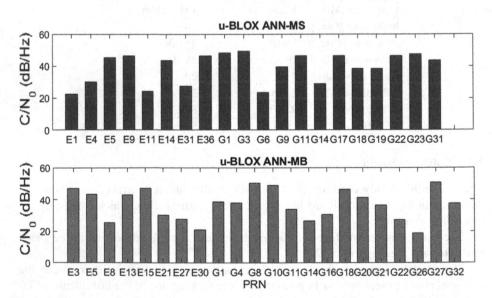

Fig. 3. Mean of C/N0 values on L1 frequency comparison for u-blox receiver between ANN-MS and ANN-MB antennas. Blue bars represent values for ANN-MS, red represent values for ANN-MB. (Color figure online)

In Fig. 4 are shown the skyplots for the four tests carried out. It is clear that TEST C and TEST D, those related to u-blox, allows to track more satellites with respect to the tests related to the SDR (TEST A and TEST B).

In Fig. 5 are shown the plots of the number of satellites tracked and the values of the Horizontal Dilution of Precision (HDOP).

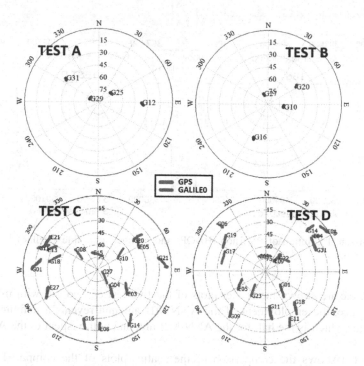

Fig. 4. Skyplots of the tests conducted

In Fig. 6.a is shown the scatter plot of the horizontal error components for the SDR tested; the blue dots represent the error of the computed positions made with the ANN-MS antenna while the red ones refer to the ANN-MB antenna. As one can notice the better antenna allows to achieve more fixes. Moreover, the value of the DRMS of horizontal position errors achieved with enhanced antenna is about 30% less of that obtained using worst antenna.

Figure 6.b Shows the comparison of the scatter plots obtained with ANN-MS antenna for the two tested receivers. It can be noticed that the SDR reveals better performances; indeed the DRMS of horizontal position errors is 22% less of the same value of the u-blox receiver.

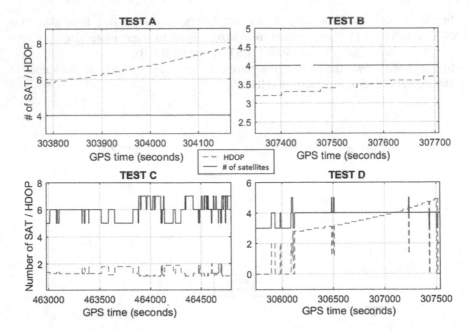

Fig. 5. Horizontal Dilution of Precision (HDOP) and number of visible satellites for the four tests conducted.

In Fig. 6.c are shown the scatter plots of the two test carried out with u-blox. As one can notice, the employment of the ANN-MB antenna reveals a definitely better DRMS value which is the half for the ANN-MB antenna with respect to the ANN-MS one.

Figure 6.d shows the comparison of the scatter plots of the computed position errors when employing the ANN-MB antenna. The blue dots represent the position error components of the SDR while the red ones stand for the u-blox computed position errors. This test show that the DRMS for the u-blox receiver is 17% less than the same indicator for SDR.

In Fig. 7 are shown East, North and Up error components of the SDR with ANN-MS antenna. The values of the root mean squares are 21.78 m for the East component, 30.88 m for the North component and 25.90 m for the Up one.

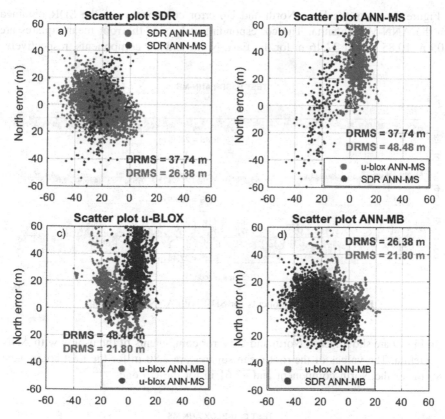

Fig. 6. Panel a: Performance comparison for SDR with different antennas. Panel b: Performance comparison for ANN-MS with different receivers. Panel c: Performance comparison for u-BLOX with different antennas Panel d: Performance comparison for ANN-MB with different receivers. (Color figure online)

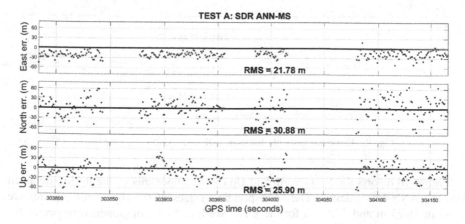

Fig. 7. Error components for SDR with ANN-MS antenna.

Figure 8 reports the East, North and Up error components of the SDR obtained with the ANN-MB antenna. The corresponding values of the root mean squares are 24.05 m 10.85 m and 27.46 m for the East, North and Up components, respectively.

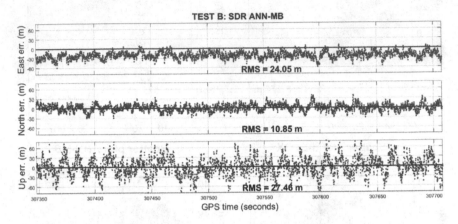

Fig. 8. Error components for SDR with ANN-MB antenna

In Fig. 9 are shown East, North and Up error components of the u-blox with ANN-MS antenna. The values of the root mean squares are 7.80 m for the East component, 47.85 m for the North component and 43.61 m for the Up one.

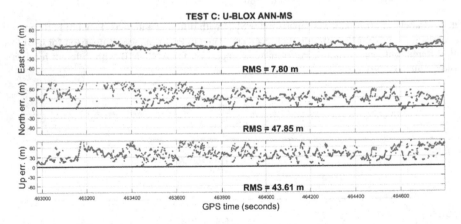

Fig. 9. Error components for u-BLOX with ANN-MS antenna.

Figure 10 reports the East, North and Up error components of the u-blox obtained with the ANN-MB antenna. The corresponding values of the root mean squares are 13.95 m 16.75 m and 57.92 m for the East, North and Up components, respectively.

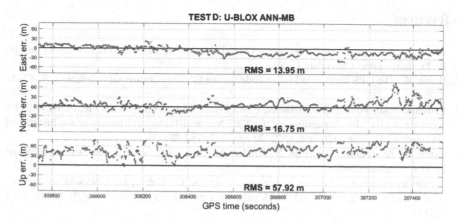

Fig. 10. Error components for u-blox with ANN-MB antenna.

Table 3. Summary table of the performance of single-point positioning for all the tests conducted.

	RMS east [m]	RMS north [m]	RMS up [m]	DRMS [m]
TEST A	21.78	30.88	25.90	37.74
TEST B	24.05	10.85	27.46	26.38
TEST C	7.80	47.85	43.61	48.48
TEST D	13.95	16.75	57.92	21.80

4 Conclusions

The single point positioning performance assessment of two low-cost front-ends have been presented. Achieved results show that, in both cases, the employment of the more performing antenna leads to better positioning results. Indeed, the horizontal DRMS decreases of about the 30% and the 55% for the SDR and the u-blox, respectively.

Nonetheless, the Nuand bladeRF has shown poor positioning results when compared to u-blox. These results aren't suitable for surveying purposes, so far. The reason resides in the poor reference clock of the on-board oscillator that doesn't assure an appropriate stability; indeed, clocks are the fundamental components of the GNSS receiver architecture [25, 26, 27, 28]. From the software point of view, the performances could be improved by adjusting the DLL and PLL bandwidth parameters. From the hardware point of view, one could employ a different board with a better clock stability of at least 0.5 PPM or recalibrate the bladeRF with an external clock reference.

Acknowledgements. The hardware receiver relying on u-blox ZED-P9F module was assembled and configured by Educabile s.r.l. We are most grateful for this contribution.

References

1. Akos, D.: A software radio approach to Global Navigation Satellite System receiver design. Ph.D. thesis, Ohio Univeristy (1997)
2. Borre, K.: The GPS easy suite Matlab code for the GPS newcomer. GPS Solutions **7**, 47–51 (2003)
3. Ledvina, B.M., Powell, S.P., Kintner, P.M., Psiaki, M.L.: A 12-channel real-time GPS L1 software receiver. In: Proceedings of the 2003 National Technical Meeting of the Institute of Navigation, Anaheim, CA, USA, 22–24, pp. 767–782 (2003)
4. Borre, K., Akos, D.M., Bertelsen, N., Rinder, P., Jensen, S.H.: A Software-Defined GPS and Galileo Receiver (2007)
5. Fernández-Prades, C., Arribas, J., Closas, P., Avilés, C., Esteve, L.: GNSS-SDR: an open source tool for researchers and developers. In: Proceedings of the 24th ION GNSS 2011 (2011)
6. Fernández-Prades, C., Arribas, J., Esteve, L., Pubill, D., Closas, P.: An open source Galileo E1 software receiver. In: NAVITEC (2012). https://doi.org/10.1109/NAVITEC.2012. 6423057
7. Anghileri, M., et al.: Performance evaluation of a multi–frequency GPS/Galileo/SBAS software receiver. In: Proceedings of ION GNSS 2007, pp. 2749–2761 (2007)
8. Fantino, M., Molino, A., Nicola, M.: N–Gene GNSS receiver: benefits of software radio in navigation. In: Proceedings of ENC-GNSS 2009 (2009)
9. Li, X., Akos, D.: Implementation and performance of clock steering in a software GPS L1 single frequency receiver. J. Inst. Navig. **57**, 69–85 (2010)
10. Luo, Y., et al.: Research on time-correlated errors using Allan variance in a Kalman filter applicable to vector-tracking-based GNSS software-defined receiver for autonomous ground vehicle navigation. Remote Sens. **11**, 1026 (2019). https://doi.org/10.3390/rs11091026
11. Angrisano, A., Petovello, M., Pugliano, G.: Benefits of combined GPS/GLONASS with low-cost MEMS IMUs for vehicular urban navigation. Sensors **12**(4), 5134–5158 (2012). https://doi.org/10.3390/s120405134
12. Bae, T.S.: Network-based RTK performance for drone navigation. E3S Web Conf. **94**, Article no. 01006 (2019). https://doi.org/10.1051/e3sconf/20199401006
13. Rover, S., Vitti, A.: GNSS-R with low-cost receivers for retrieval of antenna height from snow surfaces using single-frequency observations. Sensors (Switz.) **19**(24), Article no. 5536 (2019). https://doi.org/10.3390/s19245536
14. Dabove, P., Di Pietra, V.: Towards high accuracy GNSS real-time positioning with smartphones. Adv. Space Res. **63**(1), 94–102 (2019). https://doi.org/10.1016/j.asr.2018.08. 025
15. Robustelli, U., Baiocchi, V., Pugliano, G.: Assessment of dual frequency GNSS observations from a Xiaomi Mi 8 android smartphone and positioning performance analysis. Electronics (2019). https://doi.org/10.3390/electronics8010091
16. Pepe, M.: CORS architecture and evaluation of positioning by low-cost GNSS receiver. Geodesy Cartography **44**(2), 36–44 (2018). https://doi.org/10.3846/gac.2018.1255
17. Dardanelli, G., Lo Brutto, M., Pipitone, C.: GNSS CORS network of the University of Palermo: design and first analysis of data. Geographia Technica **15**(1/2020), 43–69 (2020). https://doi.org/10.21163/GT_2020.151.05
18. Cutugno, M., Robustelli, U., Pugliano, G.: Testing a GNSS software receiver for end-user utilization. In: 2019 IMEKO TC 2019 International Workshop on Metrology for the Sea: Learning to Measure Sea Health Parameters, MetroSea 2019, pp. 92–97 (2020)

19. Rizos, C., Montenbruck, O., Weber, R., Neilan, R., Hugentobler, U.: The IGS MGEX experiment as a milestone for a comprehensive multi-GNSS service. In: Proceedings of the ION 2013 Pacific PNT Meeting, Honolulu, Hawaii (2013)
20. Montenbruck, O., et al.: The multi-GNSS experiment (MGEX) of the international GNSS service (IGS). Achievements, prospects and challenges. Adv. Space Res. **59**, 1671–1697 (2017)
21. Robustelli, U., Pugliano, G.: GNSS code multipath short time Fourier transform analysis. Navigation **65**, 353–362 (2018). https://doi.org/10.1002/navi.247
22. Robustelli, U., Pugliano, G.: Code multipath analysis of Galileo FOC satellites by time-frequency representation. Appl. Geomatics **11**(1), 69–80 (2018). https://doi.org/10.1007/s12518-018-0241-3
23. Pugliano, G., Robustelli, U., Rossi, F., Santamaria, R.: A new method for specular and diffuse pseudorange multipath error extraction using wavelet analysis. GPS Solutions **20**(3), 499–508 (2015). https://doi.org/10.1007/s10291-015-0458-0
24. U-blox: ZED-F9P UBX 18010802 R04 Integration Manual. u-blox.com (2019)
25. Bruggemann, T.S., Greer, D.G., Walker, R.A.: Chip scale atomic clocks: benefits to airborne GNSS navigation performance. In: International Global Navigation Satellite Systems Society Symposium (2006)
26. Thongtan, T., Tirawanichakul, P., Satirapod, C.: Precise receiver clock offset estimations according to each global navigation satellite systems (GNSS) timescales. Artif. Satell. **52**, 99–108 (2017)
27. Misra, P.: The role of the clock in a GPS receiver. In: GPS World, pp. 60–66 (1996)
28. Cutugno, M., Robustelli, U., Pugliano, G.: Low-cost GNSS software receiver performance assessment. Geosciences **10**, 79 (2020). https://doi.org/10.3390/geosciences10020079
29. Robustelli, U., Benassai, G., Pugliano, G.: Signal in space error and ephemeris validity time evaluation of Milena and Doresa Galileo satellites. Sensors **19**(8), 1786 (2019)
30. Robustelli, U., Benassai, G., Pugliano, G.: Accuracy evaluation of Doresa and Milena Galileo satellites broadcast ephemerides. In: 2018 IEEE International Workshop on Metrology for the Sea, Learning to Measure Sea Health Parameters (MetroSea), pp. 217–221. IEEE (2018)

Statistical Comparison Between Different Approaches to GNSS Single-Frequency Data Processing for Meteorological Applications

Alessandra Mascitelli[1]([✉]) [iD], Andrea Gatti[2] [iD], Eugenio Realini[2] [iD], and Giovanna Venuti[1] [iD]

[1] GEOlab – Geomatics and Earth Observation Laboratory, Department Civil and Environmental Engineering, Politecnico di Milano, Milan, Italy
alessandra.mascitelli@polimi.it
[2] Geomatics Research & Development s.r.l., Lomazzo, CO, Italy

Abstract. The use of low-cost GNSS stations for meteorological applications requires the modeling of ionospheric errors. Although low-cost dual-frequency receivers are now available, current ones are still missing the L2 frequency and this prevents the availability of iono-free observations. This second frequency can be predicted by exploiting dual-frequency data collected by existent geodetic receivers according to different techniques. This paper presents a quality assessment of three different algorithms for synthetic L2 observations reconstruction, evaluating the impact on the Zenith Total Delay estimation. The three algorithms were applied to reconstruct the L2 frequency of a target geodetic receiver of EUREF Network. The differences between the ZTDs obtained from dual frequency observations and those obtained from L1 observations and synthetic L2 observations derived from the three different methods are computed to assess the quality of the reconstruction algorithms. The differences show good performances of the three methods with an overall accuracy ranging between 0.1 cm and 1 cm when the corrections are computed from geodetic stations at distances up to 65 km from the target one. Some considerations on the advantages and limits of the three compared techniques conclude the paper.

Keywords: GNSS · ZTD · Single-frequency receivers · Ionospheric corrections

1 Introduction

Knowledge of precipitable water vapor variations in space and time is a fundamental aspect of atmospheric analyses. A useful contribution in this sense can be given by the Zenith Total Delay (ZTD) derived from Global Navigation Satellite System (GNSS) data processing.

Dry air and water vapor molecules in the troposphere affect GNSS signals by lowering their propagation velocities with respect to vacuum [1].

© Springer Nature Switzerland AG 2020
C. Parente et al. (Eds.): R3GEO 2019, CCIS 1246, pp. 16–26, 2020.
https://doi.org/10.1007/978-3-030-62800-0_2

A diminished speed results in a time delay in the signal propagation along the satellite–receiver path, which, multiplied by the vacuum speed of light, adds an extra distance, referred to as delay, to the satellite–receiver geometrical one.

The tropospheric delay, due to the dry air and water vapor molecules, is just one out of many other systematic errors affecting GNSS observations that must be accounted for in order to achieve sub-centimeter accuracy positions. Nevertheless, it is possible to use this delay as a source of information; in this case, the contribution of dry air and water vapor to the total delay is separated and estimated in the zenith direction.

This leads to the definition of three delay parameters: ZTD (zenith total delay), ZHD (zenith hydrostatic delay) and ZWD (zenith wet delay), related by the equation:

$$ZHD + ZWD = ZTD \tag{1}$$

If, from the positioning point of view, the tropospheric delay is just a systematic error to be removed, its estimation makes GNSS a useful system for the remote sensing of the troposphere water vapor content, opening the way to the application of GNSS to meteorology [2, 3, 8–10].

The advantage of using GNSS technology for meteorology lies both in the system reliability and in the high number of GNSS receivers available in several countries. Networks of geodetic receivers allow for the maintenance of national reference systems as well as for enabling rapid surveying applications. However, the inter-distances between the receivers in such networks are too loose for meteorological applications.

In this respect, the availability of low-cost receivers is promising. They could be used to shorten the inter-distances of existing geodetic networks, to better meet the requirements of meteorological applications. They could be also installed in areas where the geodetic networks are still missing, as it happens in developing countries. The possibility to efficiently correct the observations for the ionospheric effects for those single frequency receivers has therefore become crucial.

The present research has the purpose of analyzing three methods for ionospheric correction of single-frequency receivers and evaluate their impact on ZTD computation.

The three methods, shortly described in the following, were applied to the M0SE GNSS station, a geodetic receiver part of EUREF Network. This station ZTDs were evaluated by using its dual frequency observations (L1 and L2), obtaining a reference time series, and by using the observed L1 and the L2 reconstructed by applying the three methods. The differences between the time series were used to assess the accuracy of the applied ionospheric corrections.

The methods work in similar ways. The missing frequency observations of the single frequency receiver (SFR) to each of the satellites in view are reconstructed by exploiting the observations to the same satellites collected by dual frequency reference receivers (DFR) surrounding the target. This is done by computing for each satellite in common between SFR and DFR, temporal differences of geometry free (L4) observations.

Those quantities depend only on the ionospheric delay which behaves quite smoothly in space. They can be therefore predicted to obtain the ionospheric delay temporal difference of the target. The way in which the prediction is performed distinguishes the different methods. Once the prediction is performed, the L4 combination is first obtained and then the L2 reconstructed by using the predicted L4 and the observed L1 of the target station.

The first method, called "A New Ground Based Augmentation Strategy (ANGBAS)", was developed at the Sapienza University of Rome [5, 9]. For each satellite in view, epoch-by-epoch, the algorithm computes the time variation of the ionospheric delay of the geodetic class receiver nearest to the target. By using a mapping function, the time variations are projected in the zenith direction. The zenithal variation is then used as a prediction of the target ionospheric delay time variation. This variation is then projected back in the target-satellite direction and used to reconstruct the corresponding geometry free and L2 frequency.

The second one is the "Satellite-specific Epoch-differenced Ionospheric Delay (SEID)" algorithm developed at GFZ, Germany [4]. This algorithm requires at least three reference stations simultaneously seeing the same satellite tracked by the target receiver. The estimation is done by using a first-degree polynomial interpolating the time variations computed from these reference receivers. The time variations of ionospheric delays are expressed as a linear function of the ionospheric pierce point (IPP) position, i.e., by the longitude and latitude of the intersection between the considered signal path and a thin reference layer at 350 km altitude. When more than three dual frequency receivers are available, a least squares interpolation is performed.

The third method, that we will call goSEID, is the default implementation of the SEID approach integrated in the goGPS open source software [6]. This algorithm can work with one or more reference receivers. It takes up the principles of SEID, but with two main distinctions. First, the time variation ionospheric delays of the reference stations are mapped onto the zenith direction; secondly, the first-degree polynomial interpolation is replaced by a simple mean weighted with the inverse of the angular distance between the reference and target IPP.

All processing was handled with the beta release of goGPS software, version 1.0, written on the basis of older releases [7] by using a new batch least-squares engine and applying the precise point positioning method [12].

2 Data Processing

The test described in the paper was carried out on a time period of two consecutive days, May 11th–12th, 2014 and performed on a study area located in Lazio region in Italy.

Six geodetic receivers nearby Rome were considered (i.e. Fig. 1): M0SE from EUREF Permanent GNSS Network was used as target station; while ROUN (35 m from M0SE), RMPO (19 km from M0SE), FIUM (25 km from M0SE), VALM (38 km from M0SE) and CVTV (65 km from M0SE), belonging to Lazio Region Permanent Network, were used as reference stations.

GPS only observations were employed. Starting from dual frequency observational files of the reference receivers, the three methods were applied to M0SE to reconstruct its L2 observations.

Fig. 1. Employed dual-frequency receivers map

2.1 Geometry-Free Combination Application

First of all, the Geometry-Free combination of the L1 and L2 observations of the M0SE was evaluated for each satellite in view. It is easy to show that this combination compares with the integral of the time variations of the ionospheric delays, evaluated from the predicted values, obtained by applying the three different techniques under study.

Results obtained by comparing the observed geometry free and the synthetic one through the application of ANGBAS are shown in Fig. 2. The method was applied using as reference dual frequency receivers located at increasing distance (35 m, 25 km, 38 km and 65 km) from the single frequency receiver. The plot shows the increasing noise of the method as the distance of the single-frequency receiver from the reference, taken into consideration for each case, increases.

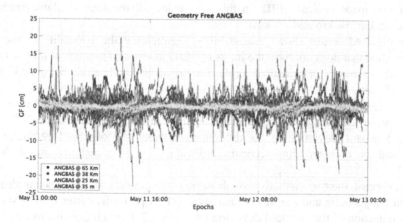

Fig. 2. Geometry free output obtained by ANGBAS

The SEID algorithm produced the result given in Fig. 3. In this case, as explained before, it was necessary to use at least three receivers to reconstruct the target L2 observations. To have redundancy, it was opted for four receivers (in this case a least squares interpolation is applied) located at 19 km, 25 km, 38 km and 65 km. Note that the station at 19 km was used instead of the close station of ROUN, which produces a numerical nonstable solution. This is one of the limits of SEID approach, the others being related to the availability of the data from each single reference station, their geometry and the presence of cycle slips. Moreover, at least three geodetic receivers are necessary and not always, neither everywhere, this is possible.

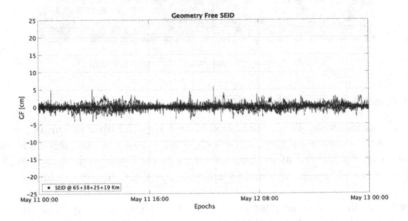

Fig. 3. Geometry free output obtained by the original SEID

The last application regarded the goSEID model, Fig. 4. We first made a comparison with ANGBAS, by using only one receiver at time, at increasing distance (35 m, 25 km, 38 km and 65 km) from the single-frequency device. A second comparison was made against SEID, in this case using all the four available receivers (19 km, 25 km, 38 km and 65 km).

The obtained results show great stability, highlighting the versatility of the proposed method that does not have the limits of SEID in terms of number of receivers and shows improvements in statistical terms, for the same application, compared to the ANGBAS method.

Both ANGBAS and goSEID were first used, by exploiting one geodetic receiver only, to reconstruct the geometry free combination of the target receiver (M0SE).

The Standard Deviation of the differences between the observed geometry free values and the corresponding reconstructed values for each distance are shown in Table 1.

As expected, the two methods provide decreasing accuracy with increasing distance between the geodetic and the M0SE stations. goSEID performs better than ANGBAS (with a reduction of the standard deviation by a factor 2/3) when this distance is larger or equal to 25 km. The Standard deviations of the differences of both ANGBAS and

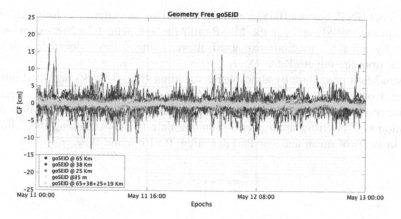

Fig. 4. Geometry free output obtained by the goSEID

Table 1. Geometry free difference standard deviation values

Method	Standard deviation [cm]
ANGBAS @35 m	0.7
ANGBAS @25 km	1.7
ANGBAS @38 km	2.4
ANGBAS @65 km	3.5
SEID @ 65 + 38 + 25 + 19 km	0.7
goSEID @35 m	0.7
goSEID @25 km	1.1
goSEID @38 km	1.6
goSEID @65 km	2.3
goSEID @ 65 + 38 + 25 + 19 km	0.6

goSEID methods, exploiting one geodetic station only, compare with the SEID standard deviation, only when the geodetic station is really close to the target one.

The two approaches differ by the software used for reconstructing the L2 frequency. In the case of ANGBAS a python script is used to generate a new RINEX file containing the synthetic L2, then processed by goGPS PPP. In the case of goSEID the approach is integrated into the goGPS workflow. The better results obtained with goSEID could be ascribed to the finer data preprocessing performed before the reconstruction (e.g. outlier and cycle slip detection and removal).

2.2 Atmospheric Sounding Validation

In the second phase the PPP technique [12], undifferenced phase observation processing, was applied to daily processing sessions, and the ionospheric free combination was used in order to estimate ZTD values for each epoch. For what concerns the ancillary products (ephemeris and clocks), precise products provided by the

International GNSS Service (IGS) were employed. This procedure was followed for the dual-frequency M0SE and for the M0SE with the synthetic L2 observations reconstructed by the three methods explained above, using receiver located at different distances from the target (Table 1).

A validation procedure by atmospheric sounding (Fig. 5) was conducted only for the output obtained by the observed dual-frequency RINEX, which is that used as reference result. In this case the procedure implemented in goGPS software allowed the calculation of ZTD from atmospheric sounding data [6, 11] obtaining the following results in terms of mean and standard deviation: 0.51 cm and 0.77 cm.

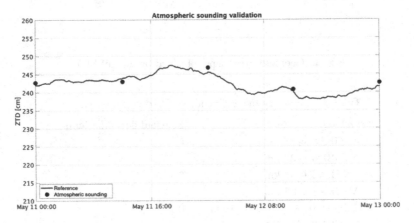

Fig. 5. Dual-frequency GNSS-ZTD validation by atmospheric sounding

2.3   Zenith Total Delay Data

Reconstructed dual frequency data were processed to obtain zenith total delay estimates. In Fig. 6, Fig. 7 and Fig. 8 it is possible to observe respectively the ZTD values obtained employing the three methods for synthetic L2 reconstruction.

In Fig. 6 outputs related to ANGBAS L2 reconstruction method, applied using receivers at different distances from the target, are given. In this case five lines are available in the plot, each of the colored line represents the result in term of ZTD obtained using the four different devices located at different distance from M0SE, whereas the black line identifies the reference solution obtained using M0SE dual frequency observations.

In Fig. 7 the result related to SEID, using the four stations (RMPO, FIUM, VALM and CVTV) to reconstruct L2, is shown.

Figure 8 represents the results obtained through the use of goSEID; in this case the four stations configuration involved RMPO (19 km), FIUM (25 km), VALM (38 km) and CVTV (65 km) receivers too. As already said, RMPO at 19 km, was used in-stead of ROUN station, due to the numerical instability that this close-by station produces on SEID. The use of one receiver at time involves the ROUN (35 m), FIUM, VALM and CVTV devices.

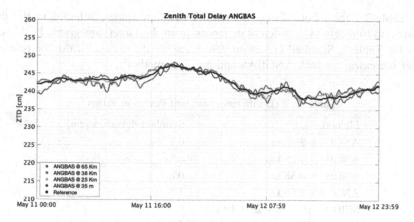

Fig. 6. Zenith Total Delay obtained by ANGBAS model

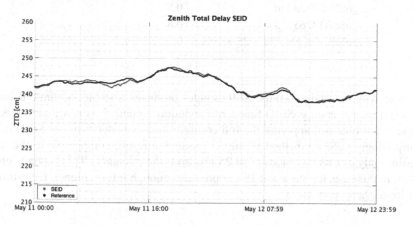

Fig. 7. Zenith Total Delay obtained by SEID model

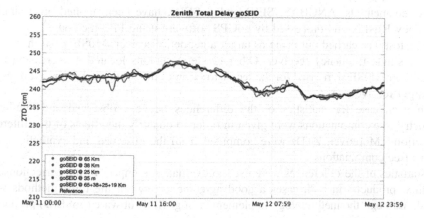

Fig. 8. Zenith Total Delay obtained by goSEID model

In Table 2 Zenith Total Delay Standard Deviation values, referred to the three methods and to receivers at different distances from the target, are given. In this case too, as for Table 1, Standard Deviation values rise as the distance from the reference receiver increases, for both ANGBAS and goSEID methods.

Table 2. ZTD difference standard deviation values

Method	Standard deviation [cm]
ANGBAS @35 m	0.1
ANGBAS @25 km	0.5
ANGBAS @38 km	0.8
ANGBAS @65 km	1.1
SEID @ 65 + 38 + 25 + 19 km	0.4
goSEID @35 m	0.1
goSEID @25 km	0.4
goSEID @38 km	0.5
goSEID @65 km	0.8
goSEID @ 65 + 38 + 25 + 19 km	0.2

In line with the above results, SEID model produces a stable, accurate solution. Anyway, if we focus on goSEID Standard Deviation outputs, it is possible to observe how the result obtained applying the full configuration is better than the SEID one.

Surprisingly goSEID method is able to produce a result, comparable to the SEID one, using only one receiver located at 25 km from the reference. This depends on the fact that, in this case, the station at 25 km provides enough information to the estimates of the ionospheric correction.

3 Conclusion

The three methods, ANGBAS, SEID and goSEID, have been applied on a single-frequency RINEX and processed by goGPS software using PPP method.

The test was carried out using as target a geodetic receiver, M0SE, used in turn as dual or single frequency receiver. Other geodetic stations located at increasing distances from M0SE were used for the reconstruction of the synthetic L2 observations of the target receiver.

In each case the statistics of the differences between observed and synthetic geometry free combinations were given in order to quantify the effects of the different corrections. Moreover, ZTDs were computed from the observed and synthetic ionosphere free combinations.

Statistics of the differences were used to evaluate the impact of the corrections on the final products. In both cases a good agreement between the three methods was found, although the methodology implemented in goGPS software (goSEID) produced always better results, both in terms of geometry free and ZTD difference standard deviations.

The reason can be found in the fact that this method is the result of a reasonable combination of the strengths of the two previous methods (ANGBAS and SEID). Indeed, the use of more than one receiver, where available, in an optimal configuration for the target RINEX reconstruction (see Fig. 1), shows a solution improvement.

Using only one device for the reconstruction of the synthetic L2 observations, the solution degrades with increasing distance.

Also, in particular study areas (e.g. sub-Saharan Africa), where ionospheric condition is peculiar and receivers management is complicated, the use of a unique receiver could be the only available choice. In this sense further analyses will be performed also taking into account critical conditions.

However, by the results obtained in this study, it is possible to say that where no more than one geodetic receiver is available, within 60 km distance, the application of goSEID can provide a good solution, the standard deviation of the ZTD differences with respect to the dual frequency case being below the cm level (Fig. 8).

References

1. Bevis, M., Businger, S., Herring, T.A., Rocken, C., Anthes, R.A., Ware, R.H.: GPS meteorology: remote sensing of atmospheric water vapor using the global positioning system. J. Geophys. Res. Atmos. **97**, 15787–15801 (1992)
2. Campanelli, M., et al.: Precipitable water vapour content from ESR/SKYNET sun–sky radiometers: Validation against GNSS/GPS and AERONET over three di_erent sites in Europe. Atmos. Measur. Tech. **11**, 81–94 (2018)
3. D'Adderio, L.P., Pazienza, L., Mascitelli, A., Tiberia, A., Dietrich, S.: A Combined IR-GPS satellite analysis for potential applications in detecting and predicting lightning activity. Remote Sens. **12**(6), 1031 (2020)
4. Deng, Z., et al.: Retrieving tropospheric delays from GPS networks densified with single frequency receivers. Geophys. Res. Lett. **36**(19), L19802 (2009)
5. Fortunato, M., Mascitelli, A., Mazzoni, A., Crespi, M.: A new ground based augmentation strategy for centimetric PPP solution with GNSS single frequency receiver. In: EGU General Assembly Conference Abstracts, vol. 20, p. 9187 (2018)
6. Gatti, A., Tagliaferro, G., Realini, E.: goGPS 1.0 OPEN edition: a new software based on a multi-GNSS undifferenced, uncombined processing engine for PPP and network adjustment. [online] goGPS Project 2020. https://gogps-project.github.io. Accessed Mar 2020
7. Herrera, A.M., Suhandri, H.F., Realini, E., Reguzzoni, M., de Lacy, M.C.: goGPS: open-source MATLAB software. GPS Solutions **20**(3), 595–603 (2015). https://doi.org/10.1007/s10291-015-0469-x
8. Mascitelli, A.: New Applications and Opportunities of GNSS Meteorology. La Sapienza University, Rome (2020)
9. Mascitelli, A., et al.: Data assimilation of GPS-ZTD into the RAMS model through 3D-Var: preliminary results at the regional scale. Meas. Sci. Technol. **30**, 055801 (2019)
10. Sguerso, D., Labbouz, L., Walpersdorf, A.: 14 years of GPS tropospheric delays in the French-Italian border region: comparisons and first application in a case study. Appl. Geomatics **8**, 13–25 (2016)

11. Vedel, H., Mogensen, K., Huang, X.: Calculation of zenith delays from meteorological data comparison of NWP model, radiosonde and GPS delays. Phys. Chem. Earth Part A. **26**(6–8), 497–502 (2001)
12. Zumberge, J.F., Heflin, M.B., Jefferson, D.C., Watkins, M.M., Webb, F.H.: Precise point positioning for the efficient and robust analysis of GPS data from large networks. J. Geophys. Res. Solid Earth **102**(B3), 5005–5017 (1997)

Precipitable Water Vapor Content from GNSS/GPS: Validation Against Radiometric Retrievals, Atmospheric Sounding and ECMWF Model Outputs over a Test Area in Milan

Alessandra Mascitelli[1](✉) , Stefano Barindelli[1] ,
Eugenio Realini[2] , Lorenzo Luini[3] , and Giovanna Venuti[1]

[1] GEOlab – Geomatics and Earth Observation Laboratory, Department Civil and
Environmental Engineering, Politecnico di Milano, Milan, Italy
alessandra.mascitelli@polimi.it
[2] Geomatics Research & Development s.r.l., Lomazzo, CO, Italy
[3] DEIB – Dipartimento di Elettronica, Informazione e Bioingegneria, Politecnico
di Milano, Milan, Italy

Abstract. The availability of atmospheric water vapor content observations, with high temporal and spatial resolution, proved to have a high impact in the prediction of heavy rain events obtained from numerical weather prediction models. Several techniques can be applied to derive such observations. Some of them are well consolidated, some others are still under development. The focus of this work is to provide a statistical assessment of the consistency between four different techniques for water vapor monitoring, and specifically for precipitable water vapor (PWV) retrieval: radiometer-derived, European Centre for Medium-Range Weather Forecasts (ECMWF) meteorological model derived, GNSS-derived and atmospheric sounding derived PWV. An overview of the data processing needed to estimate such parameter in the four cases is given to highlight how the corresponding PWV is related to the actual atmospheric water vapor content. Time series of PWV obtained with the different methods are compared for a case study in Milan, over a period of one year (March 1st, 2018–February 11th, 2019). A four-channel Ka-band/W-band radiometer located in the main campus of Politecnico di Milano is employed in association with a GNSS dual-frequency receiver (MILA), part of a regional network and installed in the same campus, 280 m far from the radiometer. GNSS data are processed by the goGPS software, applying a precise point positioning strategy. A comparison with atmospheric sounding (Milano-Linate station, located at about 6 km from the GNSS receiver), as well as with PWV derived from the ECWMF model (operational products), is also given. Results show a good agreement between the outputs of the four different data sources confirming GNSS as a valid alternative to the well consolidated techniques and opening the way to its synergistic use with co-located radiometers.

Keywords: PWV · Radiometer · GNSS meteorology · Validation

© Springer Nature Switzerland AG 2020
C. Parente et al. (Eds.): R3GEO 2019, CCIS 1246, pp. 27–34, 2020.
https://doi.org/10.1007/978-3-030-62800-0_3

1 Introduction

Precipitable Water Vapor (PWV) represents the total atmospheric water vapor contained in a vertical column above a specific sensor. It is a fundamental variable in many atmospheric processes like raindrops formation and it is a key component of the Earth-atmosphere energy balance.

The estimation of this quantity is of interest for different meteorological applications, e.g. its assimilation into numerical weather prediction models [13, 16], nowcasting of intense rain events [4, 23, 24, 29], heavy rainfall monitoring and related lightning activity [3, 9, 25].

In this respect, due to its high variability [7], it is important to estimate PWV with high temporal and spatial resolution.

Different sensors and methods are available to this aim and it is useful to evaluate the consistency between their outputs [10, 17, 19].

In this research work, a statistical analysis of the comparison between PWV values obtained through different techniques is given.

More precisely, microwave radiometer PWV values are compared with Global Navigations Satellite System (GNSS), atmospheric sounding derived PWV measurements and ECMWF operational model values [18].

One of the goals of the experiment is to understand if the radiometer data can be corrected for atmospheric water vapor effect by using external sources.

The experiment was conducted using a GNSS dual-frequency receiver (MILA), part of the Piedmont-Lombardy regional network SPIN, located at a distance of 280 m from a four-channel Ka-band/W-band radiometer; both instruments are located in the main campus of Politecnico di Milano.

The atmospheric sounding is referred to the Linate radiosonde (ID 16080, launched from the Linate airport in Milan, at a distance of about 6 km from the MILA station).

The validation test was carried out through a time period of about one year, from March 1st, 2018 to February 11th, 2019, in order to consider seasonal variations and instruments consistency on a long-term basis.

2 Equipment and Methodology

2.1 Radiometer

In the absence of scattering, which occurs in rain-free conditions, under the hypothesis of local thermodynamic equilibrium [28], the PWV (as well as the Integrated Cloud Liquid Water Content, ILWC) can be estimated from brightness temperature measurements using at least two channels, one of which (f_1) must be mainly sensitive to water vapor, and the other one (f_2) more to the liquid water content in clouds. To this aim, first the total path attenuation at frequency f_i (for a link with elevation angle θ) is calculated from the brightness temperature T_B as:

$$A(f_i, \theta) = 10\log_{10}\left(\frac{T_{mr}(f_i, \theta) - T_C}{T_{mr}(f, \theta) - T_B(f, \theta)}\right) \tag{1}$$

where $T_C = 2.73$ K is the cosmic background temperature and $T_{mr}(f_i, \theta)$ is the so-called mean radiating temperature [14]. Monthly values of T_{mr} can be calculated by regressing the results obtained from 10 years of Linate Airport radiosonde-derived vertical profiles of pressure (P), relative humidity (RH) and temperature (T) used as input first to the Teknillinen KorkeaKoulu (TKK) cloud detection method [22] and then to the Liebe MPM93 mass absorption model [12]. In non-rainy conditions, $A(f_i, \theta)$ can also be written as:

$$A(f_i, \theta) = A_{OX}(f_i, \theta) + a_V(f_i)PWV(\theta) + a_L(f_i)ILWC(\theta) \tag{2}$$

In (2), $A_{OX}(f_i, \theta)$ is the mean monthly path attenuation due to oxygen at frequency f_i, while $a_V(f_i)$ and $a_L(f_i)$ are the monthly water vapor and liquid water mass absorption coefficients; all these quantities (whose values are not reported here for the sake of brevity) have been calculated by resorting again to the Linate Airport RAOBS data coupled with the TKK and MPM93 models [14]. The two unknowns PWV and ILWC can be retrieved by using (1) for both radiometric channels $(f_1 = 23.84$ GHz and $f_2 = 31.4$ GHz) and by solving the resulting system of two equations, thus yielding:

$$PWV(\theta) = a_0 + a_1 A(f_1, \theta) + a_2 A(f_2, \theta) \tag{3}$$

$a_0 = -0.0298$, $a_1 = 53.626$ and $a_2 = -32.488$ are function of A_{OX} (f_i, θ), $a_V(f_i)$ and $a_L(f_i)$.

2.2 GNSS Receivers

Dry air and water vapor molecules in the troposphere affect GNSS signals by lowering their propagation velocities with respect to vacuum [6, 21].

A diminished speed results in a time delay in the signal propagation, which adds an extra distance to the satellite–receiver geometrical one. From the positioning point of view, this delay is just one of systematic errors to be removed, but it is possible to consider this parameter as a tool for the sounding of atmospheric water vapor content [15].

To estimate this parameter, different strategies can be applied; in this work the precise point positioning (PPP) strategy [30], implemented in the goGPS software [11] was selected.

The ionosphere-free linear combination of dual-frequency phase observations collected by a geodetic receiver (MILA) at 30 s rate, were used to estimate both coordinates and ZTD values. The geodetic receiver is a TOPCON NET-G3A (GPS + GLONASS) equipped with a TPSCR.G3 TPSH antenna.

As for satellite orbits and clocks, precise products provided by the International GNSS Service (IGS) were used.

PWV patterns were obtained from ZTD values [1, 6, 8], based on weather station data of pressure and temperature, after applying adjustments related to the altitude difference between the weather sensors and the GNSS receiver [2, 5, 20, 26].

2.3 Raobs

Radiosondes are sensors that measure the vertical profile of meteorological variables like pressure, temperature, relative humidity and wind. The instruments are carried into air up to heights of about 35 km by weather balloons filled with hydrogen or helium.

During the ascent phase, they transmit by radio altitude, latitude, longitude and all the meteorological collected data to a ground receiver. Since are quite expensive, the main drawback is that, usually, radiosonde data are collected worldwide twice a day at 12:00 UTC and 00:00 UTC.

The radiosondes analysis involves the study of some thermodynamic variables which indicate the potential predisposition of the atmosphere to the onset of weather phenomena.

One of the parameters provided by the radiosondes is the PWV [27] that can be compared with that obtained by other techniques.

2.4 ECMWF Model

ECMWF produces operational ensemble-based analyses and predictions that describe the range of possible scenarios and their likelihood of occurrence [18].

In this study the operational values of temperature, pressure and relative humidity, delivered every 6 h, with a horizontal resolution of $0.1° \times 0.1°$ and referred to 140 vertical layers, were used in order to compute PWV values according to [formula].

These values (related to the grid knot position: Lat. 45.5, Lon. 9.2) were finally compared with radiometer outputs.

3 Output Comparison

A comparative analysis of the results provided by the different instruments was performed on a dataset of about one year (March 1st, 2018–February 11th, 2019) to highlight the seasonal behavior of PWV.

This was carried out through a statistical analysis on the differences between radiometer PWV and those obtained by GNSS, radiosounding (RAOBS) and ECWMF model (operational products).

Table 1 summarizes the results of the statistical comparison of the difference between the radiometer and the three other sources of PWV values. The radiometer tends to underestimate PWV values, but the differences have a standard deviation that is below 2 mm for every case.

The high variability in the number of samples used for each case is due to the significantly different measurement rates of the four techniques: the ECMWF model values are available every 6 h, radiosondes are launched from Linate station every 12 h, GNSS PWV is computed every 30 s and radiometer PWV every second. It is also

Table 1. Statistics of the comparisons between PWV values derived from different sources, in terms of minimum (min) and maximum (max) differences, mean difference (mean) and standard deviation (std)

Statistics	RAD – GNSS	RAD – ECMWF	RAD – RAOBS
# samples	347135	1040	529
min [mm]	−8	−7	−6
max [mm]	5	5	5
mean [mm]	−1	−1	−1
std [mm]	1	2	1

worth reminding that PWV estimates from the radiometer are reliable only under rain free conditions, i.e. approximately 93% of the yearly time in Milan.

Although the statistical comparison shows a good agreement between the values of the different sensors, a further analysis on the time series of differences was performed, to highlight patterns related to seasonal variations.

Figure 1 shows the differences between radiometer and GNSS PWV. These differences increase during seasons with higher water vapor content (i.e. spring and summer).

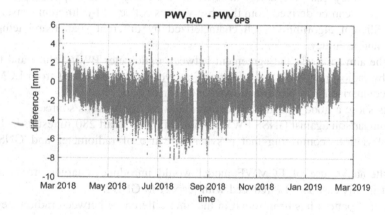

Fig. 1. Time series of differences between radiometer PWV values and GNSS PWV values

This pattern can be noticed also from the boxplot in Fig. 2: monthly means of the differences reach their peaks in July and August.

Data gaps are associated to the lack of radiometer values during rainy days.

The seasonal effect might be due to the use of monthly values of $T_{mr}(f_i,\theta)$ in (1): the results could be likely further improved by employing proper relationships to estimate $T_{mr}(f_i,\theta)$ as a function of the ground values of temperature and relative humidity, which are available with high temporal resolution (1 s).

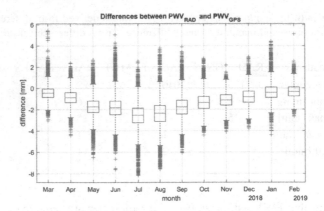

Fig. 2. Boxplot of monthly differences between radiometer PWV values and GNSS PWV values

4 Conclusion

Atmospheric water vapor observations are important for a variety of applications, like numerical weather prediction model assimilation or extreme rain events nowcasting.

Moreover, they can give useful insights for the study of atmospheric processes. Values of PWV can be derived from the observations collected by different sensors, by applying different algorithms, each characterized by different spatial and temporal resolution and accuracy.

With the aim to assess the agreement between radiometer PWV values and those retrieved by radiosonde, GNSS observations, as well as those derived from ECMWF model, a comparison was performed over one year of data.

Results show a good statistical agreement between the various sources.

The comparison against GNSS PWV from a station far apart 280 m results in 1 mm standard deviation, confirming that a synergistic use of radiometer and GNSS is feasible.

The alternative use of ECMWF model would introduce a larger error, as the agreement in this case is 50% reduced with respect to GNSS.

A seasonal pattern has been found in the time differences between radiometer and the other techniques, which could be likely reduced by using a more complex retrieval algorithm, for the radiometer PWV values, involving additional input data (e.g. ground values of temperature and pressure).

References

1. Askne, J., Nordius, H.: Estimation of tropospheric delay for microwaves from surface weather data. Radio Sci. **22**(03), 379–386 (1987)
2. Bai, Z., Feng, Y.: GPS water vapor estimation using interpolated surface meteorological data from Australian automatic weather stations. J. Glob. Positioning Syst. **2**(2), 83–89 (2003)

3. Barindelli, S., Realini, E., Venuti, G., Fermi, A., Gatti, A.: Detection of water vapor time variations associated with heavy rain in northern Italy by geodetic and low-cost GNSS receivers. Earth, Planets and Space **70**(1), 1–18 (2018). https://doi.org/10.1186/s40623-018-0795-7

4. Benevides, P., Catalao, J., Miranda, P.M.A.: On the inclusion of GPS precipitable water vapour in the nowcasting of rainfall. Nat. Hazards Earth Syst. Sci. **15**, 2605–2616 (2015)

5. Berberan-Santos, M.N., Bodunov, E.N., Pogliani, L.: On the barometric formula. Am. J. Phys. **65**(5), 404–412 (1997)

6. Bevis, M., Businger, S., Herring, T.A., Rocken, C., Anthes, R.A., Ware, R.H.: GPS meteorology: remote sensing of atmospheric water vapor using the Global Positioning System. J. Geophys. Res. Atmos. **97**(D14), 15787–15801 (1992)

7. Campanelli, M., et al.: Precipitable water vapour content from ESR/SKYNET sun–sky radiometers: validation against GNSS/GPS and AERONET over three different sites in Europe. Atmos. Meas. Tech. **11**(1), 81–94 (2018)

8. Davis, J.L., Herring, T.A., Shapiro, I.I., Rogers, A.E.E., Elgered, G.: Geodesy by radio interferometry: effects of atmospheric modeling errors on estimates of baseline length. Radio Sci. **20**(6), 1593–1607 (1985)

9. D'Adderio, L.P., Pazienza, L., Mascitelli, A., Tiberia, A., Dietrich, S.: A combined IR-GPS satellite analysis for potential applications in detecting and predicting lightning activity. Remote Sens. **12**(6), 1031 (2020)

10. Fionda, E., Cadeddu, M., Mattioli, V., Pacione, R.: Intercomparison of integrated water vapor measurements at high latitudes from co-located and near-located instruments. Remote Sens. **11**(18), 2130 (2019)

11. Herrera, A.M., Suhandri, H.F., Realini, E., Reguzzoni, M., de Lacy, M.C.: goGPS: open-source MATLAB software. GPS Solutions **20**(3), 595–603 (2015). https://doi.org/10.1007/s10291-015-0469-x

12. Liebe, H.J., Hufford, G.A., Cotton, M.G.: Propagation modelling of moist air and suspended water/ice particles at frequencies below 1000 GHz. In: AGARD 52nd Specialists' Meeting of the EM Wave Propagation Panel, Palma De Maiorca, Spain (1993)

13. Lagasio, M., et al.: Effect of the ingestion in the WRF model of different Sentinel-derived and GNSS-derived products: analysis of the forecasts of a high impact weather event. Eur. J. Remote Sens. **52**, 1–18 (2019)

14. Luini, L., Riva, C., Capsoni, C., Martellucci, A.: Attenuation in non-rainy conditions at millimeter wavelengths: assessment of a procedure. IEEE Trans. Geosci. Remote Sens. **45**(7), 2150–2157 (2007)

15. Mascitelli, A.: New Applications and Opportunities of GNSS Meteorology. Sapienza Università di Roma (2020)

16. Mascitelli, A., et al.: Data assimilation of GPS-ZTD into the RAMS model through 3D-Var: preliminary results at the regional scale. Meas. Sci. Technol. **30**(5), 055801 (2019)

17. Niell, A.E., et al.: Comparison of measurements of atmospheric wet delay by radiosonde, water vapor radiometer, GPS, and VLBI. J. Atmos. Oceanic Technol. **18**(6), 830–850 (2001)

18. Owens, R.G., Hewson, T.D.: ECMWF Forecast User Guide. ECMWF, Reading (2018). https://doi.org/10.21957/m1cs7h

19. Pacione, R., et al.: GPS meteorology validation and comparisons with ground-based microwave radiometer and mesoscale model for the Italian GPS permanent stations. Phys. Chem. Earth Part A. **26**(3), 139–145 (2001)

20. Realini, E., Sato, K., Tsuda, T., Manik, T.: An observation campaign of precipitable water vapor with multiple GPS receivers in western Java, Indonesia. Prog. Earth Planet. Sci. **1**(1), 17 (2014)

21. Saastamoinen, J.: Contributions to the theory of atmospheric refraction. Bull. Géodésique (1946–1975) **107**(1), 13–34 (1973)
22. Salonen, E., Uppala, W.: New prediction method of cloud attenuation. Elect. Lett. **27**(12), 1106–1108 (1991)
23. Sangiorgio, M., et al.: Improved extreme rainfall events forecasting using neural networks and water vapor measures. In: Proceedings of the 6th International Conference on Time Series and Forecasting, pp. 820–826 (2019)
24. Sangiorgio, M., et al.: A comparative study on machine learning techniques for intense convective rainfall events forecasting. In: Advances in Time Series and Forecasting. Springer, Cham (2020). Stage of publication (accepted)
25. Sapucci, L.F., Machado, L.A., de Souza, E.M., Campos, T.B.: Global positioning system precipitable water vapour (GPS-PWV) jumps before intense rain events: a potential application to nowcasting. Meteorol. Appl. **26**(1), 49–63 (2019)
26. Ssenyunzi, R.C., et al.: Variability and accuracy of zenith total delay over the east african tropical region. Adv. Space Res. **64**, 900–920 (2019)
27. Vedel, H., Mogensen, K.S., Huang, X.Y.: Calculation of zenith delays from meteorological data comparison of NWP model, radiosonde and GPS delays. Phys. Chem. Earth Part A. **26** (6–8), 497–502 (2001)
28. Westwater, E.R., Guiraud, F.O.: Ground-based microwave radiometric retrieval of precipitable water vapor in the presence of clouds with high liquid content. Radio Sci. **15**, 947–957 (1980)
29. Zhao, Q., Liu, Y., Ma, X., Yao, W., Yao, Y., Li, X.: An improved rainfall forecasting model based on GNSS observations. IEEE Trans. Geosci. Remote Sens. **58**, 4891–4900 (2020)
30. Zumberge, J.F., Heflin, M.B., Jefferson, D.C., Watkins, M.M., Webb, F.H.: Precise point positioning for the efficient and robust analysis of GPS data from large networks. J. Geophys. Res.: Solid Earth **102**(B3), 5005–5017 (1997)

A Fuzzy Logic-Based Weighting Model for GNSS Measurements from a Smartphone

Anna Innac[1]([✉]) [ID], Antonio Angrisano[2] [ID], Salvatore Gaglione[1] [ID], and Antonio Maratea[1] [ID]

[1] Department of Sciences and Technologies,
Parthenope University of Naples, Naples, Italy
{anna.innac, salvatore.gaglione,
antonio.maratea}@uniparthenope.it
[2] G. Fortunato University, Benevento, Italy
a.angrisano@unifortunato.eu

Abstract. GNSS navigation is critical in unfavourable scenarios, where the solution can be degraded by errors such as multipath reflections and weak geometries caused by obstacles surrounding the receiver. Nonetheless, the influence of the errors can be reduced defining an adequate quality measure for each signal and, consequently, using weights inversely related to the quality of the received signals. In this paper, a quality index, obtained from the fuzzy integration of various features of the received signals and leveraged to weight each measure in a Weighted Least Square (WLS) estimation process, is validated on measurements coming from a High Sensitivity receiver embedded in a smartphone. The main objective is to validate a fuzzy control designer provided by the authors in a previous work using raw data from a smartphone to compute the navigation solution and to extend its application to the multi-GNSS constellation case. The performance of the tested weighting strategy is evaluated in the position domain and in comparison with another weighting method. GNSS real data have been collected through a smartphone located in typical urban canyon environment, and processed in Single Point Positioning. Results show an evident enhancement obtained from the application of the fuzzy logic to obtain a proper weight to be assigned to GNSS observables reproducing a stochastic model similar to the reality.

Keywords: GNSS · Weighting model · Fuzzy logic

1 Introduction

In signal-degraded environments (i.e. urban canyons, dense vegetation environments or indoors) the presence of obstacles can limit the satellite availability [1], worsening observation geometry, and in the extreme condition compromising the positioning solution computation. GNSS signals can also be reflected by obstructions surrounding the user, so producing the multipath and NLOS (Not-Line-Of-Sight) phenomena and, by consequence, introducing large measurement errors (blunders).

C. Parente et al. (Eds.): R3GEO 2019, CCIS 1246, pp. 35–46, 2020.
https://doi.org/10.1007/978-3-030-62800-0_4

Recently, smartphones come equipped with low-cost high-sensitivity (HS) GNSS receivers, which are used in a variety of location-based services (LBS) and also by the geodetic community for static survey requiring high-precision performance [2]; it is acknowledged that HS receivers are able to detect weaker signals in difficult environments and provide in average more measurements than conventional receivers [3]. However, in those conditions, HS GNSS measurements are biased and noisy due to low-power signals being drowned into noise and multipath effects, strongly degrading the accuracy of the estimated position.

Several techniques are able to reduce the negative consequences of large blunders in urban scenarios [4] exploiting weights inversely related to the quality of the received signal. In this context, several authors have shown the importance of the stochastic model, especially for high-accuracy applications [5–7]; indeed, several independent variables have been proposed as quality indices: essentially the satellite elevation, Signal-to-Noise Ratio (SNR) and combinations of them [8–10]. A description of several indicators for GPS observation quality can be found in [11–13].

Starting from measurements of an HS GNSS receiver embedded in a smartphone, in this paper, a method based on fuzzy logic to set the weighting matrix in a Weighted Least Squares estimation process is proposed.

Fuzzy logic is an evolution of Boolean logic with a continuum of truth values instead of just two alternatives; it allows to model problems in which imprecise data must be handled or in which the rules of inference are formulated in a very general way, making use of diffuse categories [14].

Fuzzy logic has been of widespread use in several applications, varying from controlling consumer electronics or medical devices, to decision-support systems, and more [15, 16]. Fuzzy logic has been also applied in the GNSS context to enhance the position estimation accuracy, especially when GNSS is used in critical conditions (urban canyons, dense vegetation environments or indoor). In [17] fuzzy logic is used to improve GPS data processing applying it to different contexts such the selection of the satellites and quality assessment of GPS processing results. In [18] first the Adaptive Neuro-Fuzzy Inference System (ANFIS) is applied to generate the best Fuzzy Inference System (FIS) and then the weighting model obtained from ANFIS is modified and fine-tuned by hand to build the final fuzzy system; the final designed fuzzy controller computes the weights to be assigned to GPS pseudorange (PR) measurements integrating in an implicitly nonlinear way two indicators of the signal quality: satellite elevation angle and SNR.

In this paper, the fuzzy system proposed in [18] is applied for the stochastic modelling of GNSS PR measurements to enhance the positioning accuracy on data coming from an HS GNSS receiver embedded in a smartphone. The model is based only on two input variables to be fuzzified that are satellite elevation and Signal-to-Noise Ratio (SNR). At first, the considered quality measures of the received signals are fuzzified and integrated, then a rule base is used to obtain an aggregated fuzzy weight, finally defuzzified in a numerical value representing the weight to be assigned to GNSS measurements [18].

To test the adopted fuzzy weighting technique, GNSS real data are processed in Single Point Positioning (SPP) using PR observables. A static test is carried out with a smartphone Xiaomi Mi 8 placed in an urban scenario, in order to challenge the weighting model in harsh conditions. The proposed method is compared with a weighting model that adopts the same quality indicators, performing the accuracy analysis in the position domain.

The paper is organized as follows: in Sect. 2 the importance of a proper GNSS stochastic model and the weighting strategy used for the comparison are discussed; in Sect. 3 the main concepts of Fuzzy set theory are outlined and the adopted fuzzy controller is described in detail. Subsequently, in Sect. 4 the experimental setup and the results of the static test are summarized and Sect. 5 concludes the paper.

2   GNSS Stochastic Model

The computation of positions using GNSS observations requires two important steps: to define the relationship between the unknown parameters and the measurements, and choose the stochastic model indicating the uncertainty of the measurement model [19]. Several authors have highlighted the importance of selecting an adequate stochastic model [5–7], primarily when higher accuracy performance are required. The parameter estimation used for positioning can only produce reasonable results if the stochastic model resembles reality [20].

Several errors resulting from atmospheric delays, orbit effects and multipath interferences can affect GNSS measures, in a different way for each satellite: for this reason, it is not possible to assume that all observations have equal weights. For example, from literature it is well-known that measurements received from satellite at high elevation or with higher values of Carrier-to-Noise density power ratio (C/N$_0$) are less subject to large errors due to multipath or ionospheric/tropospheric delays. To this purpose, scientific literature describes several independent variables as indicators of quality: criterions based on satellite elevation, SNR and combinations of them [9, 21] have been widely considered.

The Weighted Least Squares (WLS) is adopted in this work as estimation technique. The WLS solution is computed as follow:

$$\underline{\Delta x} = \left(H^T W H\right)^{-1} H^T W \underline{z} \tag{1}$$

where $\underline{\Delta x}$ is the vector containing the corrections to the receiver position and the receiver clock bias, $\underline{z}$ is the vector containing the difference between actual and predicted PR, H is the design matrix, W is the weighting matrix. Then, the navigational solution $\underline{\hat{x}}$ is computed updating the predicted position with the corrections vector as:

$$\underline{\hat{x}} = \underline{x}_0 + \underline{\Delta x} \tag{2}$$

where $\underline{x}_0$ includes the approximate position and clock offset.

The weighting matrix W is defined as the inverse of the PR error covariance matrix, denoted as R:

$$W = R^{-1} \tag{3}$$

Assuming uncorrelated measurements, R is a diagonal matrix and considering uncorrelated measurements, it is defined as:

$$R = diag\left(\left[\sigma_1^2, \ldots, \sigma_i^2, \ldots, \sigma_n^2\right]\right) \tag{4}$$

with σ_i^2 indicating the error variance of the i-th PR and n is the number of satellites used for the solution computation.

To verify the performance of the adopted fuzzy controller in the weighting matrix computation (as described in Sect. 3.1), a variance model proposed in [21] is used in the baseline configuration. In detail, the variance of the i-th satellite is expressed as:

$$\sigma_i^2 = \begin{cases} \frac{1}{sin^2(El_i)} \Gamma_i & if \ C/N_0 < s_1 \\ 1 & if \ C/N_0 \geq s_1 \end{cases} \tag{5}$$

where

$$\Gamma_i = 10^{-\frac{C/N_0 - s_1}{B}} \left[\left(\frac{A}{10^{-\frac{s_0 - s_1}{B}}} - 1 \right) \frac{C/N_0 - s_1}{s_0 - s_1} + 1 \right] \tag{6}$$

and s_1 indicates the threshold after which the measurements are considered good and the assigned weights is equal to 1. The constant values s_1, s_0, B and A are chosen from [21]. This model is named as SPELW in the next sections.

3 Fuzzy Logic

In the middle 1960s Lotfi Zadeh proposed the fuzzy logic as a rule-based decision-making methodology to be used in expert systems and process control, aimed at emulating the heuristic, rule-of-thumb approach of human reasoning [22]. Expert's knowledge can be modeled in complex systems thanks to fuzzy logic that is based on a higher level of abstraction rather than exact mathematical formulas and rigorous implications.

In a fuzzy controller, numerical input variables are mapped to numerical outputs using fuzzified linguistic variables, indicating some property (for example, the "SNR", or the "satellite elevation" for GNSS measurements) and terms (e.g., "high" and "low"), instead of numbers, while the properties are transferred using rules rather than formulas [15, 16].

To design a controller, two concepts need to be introduced: the linguistic variable (LV) and the linguistic term (LT). A LV indicates a measurable concept (i.e. SNR or satellite elevation) delineating its domain, while a LT, that is a fuzzy set, quantifies that concept (for example "low", "medium" or "high"). For example, a numerical variable like "temperature" may have a range from 0 to 30 °C – its domain – and fuzzy sets defined on it – categories – may be low ("low temperature"), normal ("medium temperature") and high ("high temperature"). Most notably one single temperature value can belong to more than one category with a different degree: fuzzy sets normally overlap.

After the definition of LVs and LTs, the fuzzification process is applied to delineate a set of overlapping categories (fuzzy sets) on the variable domain, and for each of them a membership function (MF) $\mu(x)$, which assigns a value between 0 and 1 to each element x of the domain to that category. So, the degree of belonging of x to C is indicated by the membership value of an element x to a category C: membership values equal to 0 and 1 indicate, respectively, the fully exclusion and inclusion of the element x in the set while values of μ between 0 and 1 indicate partial membership [23]. To be used in a fuzzy controller, each numerical input variable needs to be fuzzified determining the shape and the parameters of the membership functions. Several shapes of membership functions exist (i.e. triangular, trapezoidal, Gaussian, etc.)

Once the input variables are fuzzified, it is necessary to determine the fuzzy rules that are IF-THEN statements involving LVs and LTs, logically linked by OR/AND connectives. The rules are based on expert's knowledge about the application context. A collection of fuzzy rules need to be interpreted using two steps: an implication operator is applied and the obtained results are then aggregated. More detail about the interpretation of the fuzzy rules can be found in [22, 24].

The final step is defuzzification, consisting in the reverse transformation used to obtain a single numerical value from the aggregated fuzzy outputs. Several criteria can be used for the defuzzification of the fuzzy outputs (i.e. center of gravity, maximum-height or the average of support).

3.1 Fuzzy Controller Design for GNSS Weighting Model

In order to estimate the quality of GNSS PR measurements used in the Position, Velocity and Time (PVT) algorithm, the Matlab® Fuzzy Logic Toolbox is used to create the adopted fuzzy controller as described in [18]. Briefly, the input LVs are the SNR and elevation angle for each satellite that are fuzzified using, respectively, five and six LTs and trapezoidal MFs (labelled "very low", "low", "medium", "high", "very high" and "extremely high"); while the output LV is the weight (varying from 0 to 1) representing the ith diagonal element of the weighting matrix W, characterized by five triangular and one trapezoidal functions. The range and shape for each MF are defined as those ones obtained by the authors in the previous work in which they are fine-tuned manually after the analysis of the validation datasets collected in signal degraded scenarios.

Furthermore, the fuzzy controller is based on twenty-six rules created considering the two input and one output LVs and assuming that a satellite at low elevation or with a low SNR value (C/N_0) can be subject to large errors due to multipath or ionospheric/tropospheric effects. For the interpretation of the fuzzy rules, the implication operator uses the minimum function, the aggregator uses the maximum, while the defuzzification is done computing the centroid of the aggregated area. In this way, the weighting coefficients are obtained and used in the WLS technique for the estimation of the position solution processing the observed GNSS PRs in SPP algorithm. In particular, GPS and Galileo measurements are equally weighted, while GLONASS PRs are empirically down-weighted by a factor of 4 due to its lower accuracy compared to GPS or Galileo systems. The PVT algorithm is developed in the MatLab® environment as detailed in [25, 26] and belongs to a Toolbox developed by PANG [27].

4   Tests and Results

A data collection in static mode was performed on 25th of June 2019 for about thirty minutes with a sampling rate of 1 s. The smartphone Xiaomi Mi 8 was used to collect GPS, GLONASS and Galileo measurements using the app RINEX ON, an android application, to log raw GNSS measurements. A Broadcom 47755 dual-frequency GNSS chip is embedded in Mi 8, which is able to track GPS L1 C/A, GLONASS L1, BeiDou (BDS) B1, QZSS L1, Galileo (GAL) E1, GPS L5, Galileo E5a and QZSS L5 signals [28]. In the static campaign, the smartphone was located at Centro Direzionale of Naples (Italy), where the presence of skyscrapers guarantees the typical signal-degraded scenario. Figure 1 provides an overview of the environment characteristic, in which the red marker represents the reference position and where the smartphone was located.

Fig. 1. Data collection environment

In Fig. 2, the number of GNSS visible satellites during the session are shown. The number of GNSS visible satellites ranges between 13 and 19, with an average of 17.3. In detail, the mean of visible GPS satellites is equal to 8.1 reaching a maximum value of 9 satellites, while GLONASS and Galileo visibility is characterized by a mean value of, respectively, 4.3 and 4.9 with a maximum equal to 5 satellites.

The use of a high-sensitivity receiver and the combination of different GNSS satellites makes possible a higher satellite availability is high even if the scenario

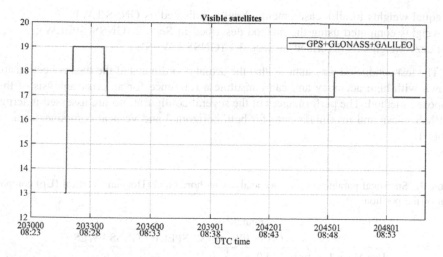

Fig. 2. Number of visible GNSS satellites during the data collection starting from 8:26 a.m. to 8:56 a.m. on 25th of June 2019

characteristics. In addition, also GNSS satellite geometry appears to be good since the PDOP (Position Dilution of Precision) varies from a minimum of 1.2 to a maximum of 1.5 with a mean equal to 1.4 as shown in Fig. 3 where the PDOP trend is plotted as function of the time.

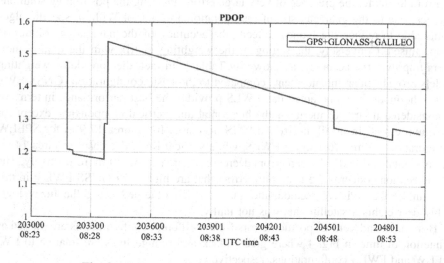

Fig. 3. GNSS PDOP behavior during the data collection

Three GNSS (GPS + Glonass + Galileo) configurations are analysed, characterized by a different weighting matrix computation (as described previously):

- equal weights to all measurements (briefly indicated as GNSS EW);
- weights computed using the method described in Sect. 2 (GNSS SPELW);
- Fuzzy weights as described in Sect. 3.1 (GNSS FWLS).

The test conducted was static so that the actual coordinates of the data collection are known with high accuracy and can constitute a reference for an error analysis of the proposed method. The performances of the several configurations are assessed in terms of RMS, mean and maximum error for both horizontal and vertical components, as in Table 1.

Table 1. Statistical parameters for error analysis on horizontal (Hor) and vertical (Up) component of the position

KPI	Configurations		
	GNSS EW	GNSS SPELW	GNSS FWLS
Hor Mean Err. [m]	25.0	15.2	12.8
Up Mean Error [m]	77.1	49.6	29.8
Hor RMS [m]	30.6	17.9	16.1
Up RMS [m]	92.7	54.3	40.5
Hor Max Error [m]	117.0	59.2	79.9
UP Max Error [m]	367.9	136.8	205.4

From the table, the presence of very large errors affecting the positioning solutions emerges, due to the characteristic of the operational scenario. Without specific algorithms able to reduce the blunder effects, the accuracy of the navigation solution is compromised. Conversely, the setting of the weighting matrix with the quality indicators improves the accuracy, as shown by Table 1. In fact, the considered weighting models provide clear enhancements compared to the basic configuration (GNSS EW).

Furthermore, it can be noted that FWLS provides the best performance in terms of all considered figures of merit for the horizontal and vertical components, except for maximum errors. In detail, horizontal RMS decreases from circa 17.9 m for SPELW configuration to circa 16.1 m for FWLS, while vertical RMS decreases of circa 14 m; the horizontal and vertical mean errors decrease of circa 2 and 20 m, respectively. The only exception concerns the maximum errors that are higher for GNSS FWLS: in this case, unlike the SPELW method, the quality index obtained using the fuzzy logic highly de-weights a satellite that it is not faulty.

Horizontal and vertical position errors for the different configurations are plotted as a function of time in Fig. 4 where green, black and orange lines are relative to EW, SPELW and FWLS configurations, respectively.

The results summarized in Table 1 are confirmed by the subplots: FWLS provides the best behavior compared to the other configurations for the horizontal and vertical components. Contrarily, it is evident that the highest errors affect the EW configuration since equal weights are assigned to all measurements, including the blunders,

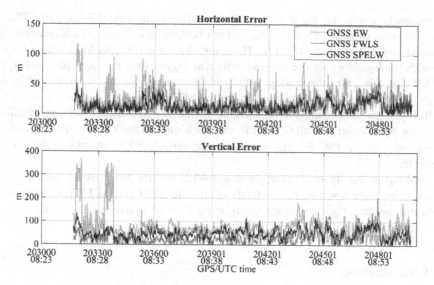

Fig. 4. Horizontal and Vertical Errors as a function of time for Equal Weights, SPELW, and Fuzzy weights for the GNSS configuration

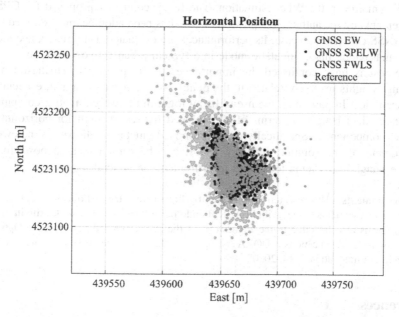

Fig. 5. Horizontal position solutions obtained using Equal Weights, the SPELW method, and the Fuzzy Logic process for GNSS configuration (Color figure online)

consequently degrading the solution. Additionally, comparing FWLS and SPELW configurations, evident enhancements, on both horizontal and vertical components, are obtained using Fuzzy logic (FWLS). However, there are few epochs in which FWLS provides horizontal errors (i.e. around 8:50 am) higher than the ones obtained using SPELW: in this case, the quality index obtained using the fuzzy logic highly de-weights a blunder-free measurement unlike the SPELW method.

In Fig. 5 the green points are relative to the horizontal position solutions obtained assigning equal weights to all GNSS PR, the black ones to the SPELW method and the orange ones to the FWLS. The red point represents the known coordinates of the reference.

Looking at the figure, it emerges that FWLS has the best overall performance, however, both the resulting point clouds relative to SPELW and FWLS are concentrated around the origin (reference truth), even if some sparse measurements are not well weighted, degrading the horizontal solution.

5   Conclusions

This research provides a validation on commodity hardware of an innovative methodology used to compute the weights of PR measurements in order to reduce the effects of signal distortions and biases. The idea is based on the fuzzy logic to set the weighting matrix in the WLS estimation. The fuzzy controller proposed for GPS PR measurements by the authors in a previous work, has been adopted and extended to the multi-GNSS constellation case. Its performances are evaluated using real data collected with a smartphone placed in static mode in a typical urban canyon scenario.

The results have confirmed the importance of an appropriate stochastic model assigning weights inversely related to the quality of the received signal, especially in harsh scenarios. In particular, the use of fuzzy logic in the weight matrix computation provides evident benefits in terms of all analysed figures of merit for horizontal and vertical components. Specifically, the proposed method allows a noteworthy enhancement of the solution accuracy and it can be candidate as a powerful and effective weighting schema for GNSS measurements in general.

Acknowledgments. This research is supported by Italian Ministry of Education and Research funding basic research activities with FFABR (Fondo per il Finanziamento delle Attività Base di Ricerca) and is also included in the framework of the project DORA (Deployable Optics for Remote Sensing Applications). DORA is part of National Operational Program entitled "Research and Innovation 2014–2020".

References

1. Ackermann, S., Angrisano, A., Del Pizzo, S., Gaglione, S., Gioia, C., Troisi, S.: Digital surface models for GNSS mission planning in critical environments. J. Surv. Eng. **140**(2), 04014001 (2014). https://doi.org/10.1061/(ASCE)SU.1943-5428.0000119
2. Schwieger, V: Sensitivity GPS-an availability, reliability and accuracy test. In: Proceedings on FIG Working Week, Stockholm (2008)

3. Wieser, A., Gaggl, M., Hartinger, H.: Improved positioning accuracy with high-sensitivity GNSS receivers and SNR aided integrity monitoring of pseudo-range observations. In: Proceedings of the ION GNSS 2005 of The Institute of Navigation, Long Beach, CA, 13–16 September, pp 1545–1554 (2005)
4. Angrisano, A., Maratea, A., Gaglione, S.: A resampling strategy based on bootstrap to reduce the effect of large blunders in GPS absolute positioning. J. Geodesy 92(1), 81–92 (2017). https://doi.org/10.1007/s00190-017-1046-6
5. Han, S.: Quality control issues relating to instantaneous ambiguity resolution for real-time GPS kinematic positioning. J. Geodesy 71(7), 351–361 (1997)
6. Barnes, B.J., Ackroyd, N., Cross, P.A.: Stochastic modelling for very high precision real-time kinematic GPS in an engineering environment. In: Proceedings of FIG XXI International Conference, 21–25 July, Brighton, UK, Commission 6, pp. 61–76 (1998)
7. Wang, J.: Stochastic assessment of the GPS measurements for precise positioning. In: Proceedings of the GPS ION 1998 of The Institute of Navigation, Nashville, Tennessee, 15–18 September, pp 81–89 (1998)
8. Brunner, F.K., Hartinger, H., Troyer, L.: GPS signal diffraction modelling: the stochastic SIGMA-δ model. J. Geodesy 73(5), 259–267 (1999)
9. Satirapod, C.: A review of stochastic models used in static GPS positioning technique. In: 25th ACRS & 1st ASC, 22–26 November 2004, Thailand (2004)
10. Luo, X., Mayer, M., Heck, B.: Improving the stochastic model of GNSS observations by means of SNR-based weighting. In: Sideris, M.G. (ed.) Observing our Changing Earth. International Association of Geodesy Symposia, vol. 133, pp. 725–734. Springer, Heidelberg (2009). https://doi.org/10.1007/978-3-540-85426-5_83
11. Euler, H.J., Goad, C.C.: On optimal filtering of GPS dual frequency observations without using orbit information. J. Geodesy 65(2), 130–143 (1991)
12. Petovello, M.G., Cannon, M.E., Lachapelle, G.: Benefits of using a tactical-grade IMU for high-accuracy positioning. Navigation 51(1), 1–12 (2004). https://doi.org/10.1002/j.2161-4296.2004.tb00337.x. Journal of the Institute of Navigation
13. Angrisano, A., Gaglione, S., Del Core, G., Gioia, C.: GNSS reliability testing in signal-degraded scenario. Int. J. Navig. Obs. (2013). https://doi.org/10.1155/2013/870365
14. Zadeh, L.: Fuzzy Sets, Fuzzy Logic, and Fuzzy Systems: Selected Papers by Lotfi A Zadeh, vol. 6. World Scientific, Singapore (1996)
15. Ross, T.J.: Fuzzy Logic with Engineering Applications, 2nd edn. Wiley, New York (2004)
16. Syed, S., Cannon, E.: Map-aided GPS navigation: linking vehicles and maps to support location-based services. GPS World 16(11), 39–44 (2005)
17. Takagi, T., Sugeno, M.: Fuzzy identification of systems and its applications to modeling and control. IEEE Trans. Syst. Man Cybern. 15, 116–132 (1985)
18. Gaglione, S., Angrisano, A., Innac, A., Del Pizzo, S., Maratea, A.: Fuzzy logic applied to GNSS. Measurement 136, 314–322 (2019)
19. Leick, A., Rapoport, L., Tatarnikov, D.: GPS Satellite Surveying, 4th edn. Wiley, New York (2015)
20. Wieser, A., Brunner, F.K.: SIGMA-F: variances of GPS observations determined by a Fuzzy system. In: Proceeding of the IAG2001 Scientific Assembly, Budapest (2001)
21. Realini, E., Reguzzoni, M.: GoGPS: open source software for enhancing the accuracy of low-cost receivers by single-frequency relative kinematic positioning. Meas. Sci. Technol. 24(11), 115010 (2013). https://doi.org/10.1088/0957-0233/24/11/115010
22. Zadeh, L.A.: Fuzzy sets. Inf. Contr. 8(3), 338–353 (1965)
23. Innac, A.: Fuzzy techniques applied to GNSS for quality assessment and reliability testing in difficult signal scenarios. Ph.D. Thesis (2017)
24. Klir, G., Yuan, B.: Fuzzy Sets and Fuzzy Logic, vol. 4. Prentice Hall, New Jersey (1995)

25. Angrisano, A., Gaglione, S., Gioia, C., Massaro, M., Robustelli, U.: Assessment of NeQuick ionospheric model for Galileo single-frequency users. Acta Geophys. **61**(6), 1457–1476 (2013). https://doi.org/10.2478/s11600-013-0116-2
26. Gaglione, S., Angrisano, A., Gioia, C., Innac, A., Troisi, S.: NeQuick Galileo version model: Assessment of a proposed version in operational scenario. In: International Geoscience and Remote Sensing Symposium (IGARSS), November 2015, pp. 3611–3614 (2015). https://doi.org/10.1109/igarss.2015.7326603
27. Angrisano, A., Gaglione, S., Crocetto, N., Vultaggio, M.: PANG-NAV: a tool for processing GNSS measurements in SPP, including RAIM functionality. GPS Solutions **24**(1), 1–7 (2019). https://doi.org/10.1007/s10291-019-0935-y
28. Robustelli, U., Baiocchi, V., Pugliano, G.: Assessment of dual frequency GNSS observations from a Xiaomi Mi 8 Android smartphone and positioning performance analysis. Electronics **8**(1), 91 (2019)

Educational Experiences for Geomatics Scientific Dissemination

Domenico Sguerso[1] , Elena Ausonio[1,2] , Bianca Federici[1] ,
Ilaria Ferrando[1(✉)] , Sara Gagliolo[1] , and Stefania Viaggio[1]

[1] Geomatics Laboratory, Department of Civil, Chemical and Environmental
Engineering (DICCA), University of Genoa, Genoa, Italy
ilaria.ferrando@edu.unige.it
[2] Department of Mechanical, Energy, Management and Transportation
Engineering (DIME), University of Genoa, Genoa, Italy

Abstract. The present work aims to illustrate the experience in geomatic dissemination, gained by actively participating and contributing to seminars, lectures and educational workshops, applying both traditional and innovative teaching methods. The main focus is on two educational workshops: one on altitude, its measurement techniques, issues and the evolution of the instrumentation employed; the second on photogrammetry applied to various environments and scenarios, such as securing buildings and ruins in emergencies or underwater analyses, mapping and surveying of coral reefs. In both workshops, the authors begin by capturing the attention with simple examples of every-day experiences related to the workshop's main theme, then give explanations using posters, videos, simple games and practical experiences that can improve understanding. The authors scientific dissemination highlights the concrete application of Geomatics in every-day life and enhances the audience emotional involvement. The workshops' main goal is to stimulate the audience curiosity to understand the basic concepts, starting from intuitive considerations and questions from the audience itself. This allows the introduction of the main concepts of Geomatics and highlights its full potential.

Keywords: Scientific dissemination · Didactic experimentation · Innovative teaching · Public involvement · Learning-by-doing

1 Introduction

In addition to teaching and research, the first and second fundamental and central missions of a university, which provide education and new knowledge, the "third mission" is a task aimed at generating knowledge outside academia to benefit social, cultural and economic development. It requires openness to the socio-economic context, exercised both through the economic exploitation of knowledge produced by research to promote economic growth, and through cultural and educational activities to promote the application and enhancement of knowledge as a contribution to the

---

The original version of this chapter was revised: The name of the author Stefania Viaggio has been corrected. The correction to this chapter is available at https://doi.org/10.1007/978-3-030-62800-0_30

C. Parente et al. (Eds.): R3GEO 2019, CCIS 1246, pp. 47–60, 2020.
https://doi.org/10.1007/978-3-030-62800-0_5

social well-being[1]. Focusing on the social context, it contemplates all the activities that allow the University to have a direct interaction with society, widening audiences other than university students and the scientific community. The considerable involvement of the participants in the proposed educational activities can help on the one hand the teachers to conciliate scientific dissemination with didactic experimentation [1–3] and on the other hand the audience to learn with emotional involvement.

Many technologies and concepts from Geomatics are increasingly employed in every-day life also by non-skilled users, who should have at least an introduction to the basic working principles of what they are deploying. Educational events are even more worthy from this perspective. Thus, the researchers' interest is focused on disseminating scientific concepts to enhance knowledge in the easiest and most suitable way to the audience target [4], but without trivializing.

This paper is aimed to illustrate the authors' experiences in Geomatic dissemination, through the description of the proposed activities, their temporal, conceptual and procedural evolution, together with their impact on the audience (Sect. 2); the lessons learned and final remarks conclude the paper (Sect. 3).

2   Experiences of Geomatics Dissemination

Since 2012, the University of Genoa's Geomatics Laboratory has been involved in cultural festivals and events proposing and organizing educational workshops, for children 5–18 (*UniversiKids*[2]), students from primary, middle and secondary schools (Sea Festival - *Festival del Mare*, Genoa, Italy[3]), and the general public (White Night of Savona, Italy - *Notte Bianca di Savona*), seminars for citizens (*Pint of Science*[4], Science on Wednesdays organized by the Genoa Aquarium Friends - *Mercoledì Scienza degli Amici dell'Acquario*[5]), university students, university of the third age students and professionals.

At present, the two most significant and successful workshops concern altitude measurement and photogrammetry. The first introduces the theme of measuring altitude, with the concepts of altimetric reference frame and the difficulties related to its determination. The latter illustrates stereovision and photogrammetry principles, their application to practical case studies and experiences, and some examples of photogrammetric surveys and their products. The main goal of both workshops is to spark audience curiosity, trigger understanding of basic concepts, promoting intuitive considerations and questions from the audience itself.

From an organizational point of view, the two workshops have several points in common in their structure, even if the topics are substantially different. Both contemplate a theoretical part, where the objectives and motivations are introduced by

---

[1] http://www.anvur.it/attachments/article/882/8.Rapporto%20ANVUR%202013_UNI~.pdf.
[2] http://kids.unige.it/.
[3] http://festivaldelmare.unige.it/.
[4] https://pintofscience.it/.
[5] https://www.amiciacquario.ge.it/.

using posters, videos, and explanations to clarify the main concepts. A more practical part follows, including short experiments and experiences accompanied by a full scientific explanation.

The key features of the workshops are the scalability and adaptability, both in terms of time usage and of public needs, interests and competences. In fact, according to the authors' experience, the same structure is applicable and effective in case the workshops have a predefined time schedule (i.e. a defined time in which the experience must begin and end, with an eventual previous reservation) or allow a continuous free access to the workshop location, and the experience evolves according to the people present at the time. Moreover, it is adaptable in function of the target audience, modifying the complexity of the terminology, from a more technical-scientific one to a common vocabulary, which is more appropriate to facilitate the understanding of young participants. Both workshops have been an opportunity to explore innovative teaching, by means of both unusual tools and interaction with people, especially with children, who often inspire different ways of communicating and interacting.

The workshops have given secondary school students the opportunity to acquire work experience through University internships (*Alternanza Scuola-Lavoro*[6], AS-L). Students have given useful contributions both proposing clever ways of introducing the topics and actively cooperating in the organization and in the management of the workshops. One of the outcomes of the AS-L students work is the realization of workshops booklets, which are distributed to the workshop participants as souvenirs in addition to pins and stickers reporting the Geomatics Laboratory's logo. Moreover, during the workshop activities, the entire staff wears a t-shirt carrying the same Geomatics Laboratory's logo, to be clearly recognizable.

The Geomatics Laboratory's Facebook page[7] is the most recent activity of dissemination, set-up in July 2019 to post pictures of past workshops and didactic experiences and to advertise upcoming educational events. Furthermore, it has been enriched with staff presentations, in order to share information about the research activity that each member is carrying out, in addition to pictures and description of present and past surveys and geomatic work. Up to now, the page has about 150 followers who actively comment and interact with reactions to post updates.

Finally, the authors participated as speaker to several conferences and seminars, addressed to various target audiences: the general public, university students and university of the third age students, professionals, and academics. The conferences dedicated to academia, including also students and professionals, became a showcase for advancements in research and were characterized by a specialist, technical style and language, whereas the ones addressed to the general public target audience employed a simpler and more educational approach.

More details of the mentioned didactic experience are given below: Sect. 2.1 is about the involvement of work experience secondary students (AS-L) in workshop activities, whereas Sects. 2.2 and 2.3 are dedicated to a more accurate description of the Altitude and Photogrammetry workshops, respectively.

---

[6] http://www.istruzione.it/alternanza/.

[7] https://www.facebook.com/LaboratorioGeomaticaUnige/.

2.1 Involvement of Secondary School Students in Work Experience Placements (AS-L)

Work experience placements (AS-L) is an innovative way of teaching, helping students to enrich their knowledge acquired at school through practical experience to test their attitudes and to orient their learning process in order to shape their own working future. This is a cultural change in the Italian school system, embracing European good practice within the Italian socio-cultural context.

A week long training period consisting in both theoretical and practical parts on geomatic topics related to the workshops preceded workshop activities. The AS-L students showed interest and curiosity in expanding their knowledge of the subjects, parts of which were not covered by their school curriculum. The workshop experience allowed AS-L students to understand the importance of careful planning and organization, allowing them to personally have direct contact with an audience and improve their communication, teamwork, problem-solving and creativity skills. Furthermore, after a short oral presentation of the planned workshop activities and one day of training on Geomatics through lectures with the aid of projection slides (Fig. 1), the AS-L students were asked to conceptualize and realize two booklets to distribute to the workshop participants.

Fig. 1. Pre-workshop training with AS-L secondary school students. A theoretical lesson to introduce reference systems (left). Practical demonstration to execute a photogrammetric survey (right).

Students carried out the task working in small groups, autonomously deciding how to structure the booklets and their contents. They identified three easy and well-known games: figure colouring, word search and connect-the-dots, and adapted them to the workshop topics. They decided to place the figure colouring game on the front cover of the booklet together with the workshop title. The word search and the connect-the-dots games were placed inside and a diploma was inserted on the back cover as a workshop participation souvenir (Fig. 2), which was well received by the younger audiences.

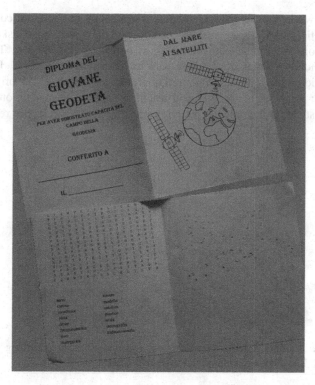

Fig. 2. Front and back cover of the Altitude booklet (top) and inside left and right pages of the Photogrammetry booklet (bottom).

For the Altitude workshop word search game the students selected significant key words: e.g. altitude, levelling rod, mean sea level and tide gauge. For the Photogrammetry workshop: drone, orthophoto, photogrammetry and three-dimensional model. For the figure colouring and connect-the-dots games they drew objects related to the topics of the events and to an important tool in the field of altitude measuring and photogrammetry, respectively. The proposed geomatic training was successful, because the AS-L students were able to understand the theoretical lessons, to identify key words and main survey objects, and to elaborate the concepts learnt. This type of activity is similar to the Problem-based learning (PBL) teaching strategy [5], where a group of students acquires and develops knowledge and skills, problem-solving abilities, teamwork, analysing real-life tasks, such as the realization of the booklets in the present case. In this way, the entire educational process is centred on the students [6], who feel to be an active part of the learning process, relying on their own resources, previous knowledge, critical thought, and ability to gather and transmit the learned concepts. The authors left the AS-L students free to work by themselves, helping them in some difficult parts of study and elaboration. In this way, the authors did not act as passive viewers, but their main role was to be advisors and facilitators of the AS-L students group, according to [7].

During the workshops, the AS-L students were mainly in charge of conducting the practical activities, typically related to games, but they were also asked to try to perform the more theoretical part after a short period of observation. This leads to follow the authors' belief that "the best way to learn is by teaching". In Fig. 3 the learning pyramid by the National Training Laboratories (Bethel, USA), originated from [8], is depicted: on the right some typical teaching methods are listed, on the left, the corresponding students' knowledge retention rates after two weeks are reported.

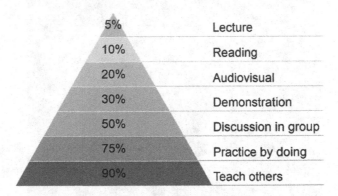

Fig. 3. National Training Laboratories learning pyramid. Teaching-learning methods and average students' knowledge retention rates after two weeks.

In order to be able to teach others, the AS-L students needed the already mentioned knowledge-transfer (in form of lecture with visual support), which was enriched by their own experience of group study, discussion and practice during the realization of the booklets. This teaching strategy demonstrated to be effective in the considered scenario.

The change in the pedagogical approach and method in teaching in higher education, that some European Universities have implemented, highlights the importance of captivating students in concrete problems as active actors. One example is Aalborg University, that since its inception in 1974, has used PBL teaching model as a common approach to teaching geomatic subjects like photogrammetry, remote sensing and laser scanning [7].

2.2   The Altitude Workshop

The Altitude workshop was first created in March 2017 within a scientific event organized by the University of Genoa with a wide educational workshop programme for schools and nurseries with children age range 4-14[8]. The aim of the workshop is to

---

[8] http://www3.dicca.unige.it/ita/eventi/ventimilalaboratori/.

explain the concept of altitude and its measuring methods and techniques. The Altitude workshop has been used in other three major events: *UniversiKids* (January 2018) and *Festival del Mare* (May 2018 and May 2019). In each edition, the target audience was made up of children and young people up to 18 years old.

Over the years, all the experimented activities were subdivided into two teaching units: a more theoretical approach to the presented notions and a subsequent practical application. In the first editions, the main concepts were introduced via slides. The audience was invited to sit in a semicircle in front of the projection, in order to focus the attention on the authors' explanations. Since May 2018, the same concepts of the presentation have also been displayed in four 70 × 100 cm posters, a highly effective visual medium for a freer and quicker visit of the exhibition for the passing public.

From the beginning of the workshop, the authors introduce the definition of altitude as the vertical distance of an object from a well-known reference level, called level zero, which is generally identified with the mean sea level. Some of the highest peaks in the world are then mentioned, and the question arises: "How is it possible to obtain a unique altitude value with tides and melting glaciers?". Concerning tides, the known cases of Mont Saint-Michel in Normandy in the North of France, with the highest tides in continental Europe, up to 15 m difference between low and high water and those in the Venetian lagoon are mentioned, to attract the audience's attention and generate curiosity and enthusiasm, especially in children. With the aim of involving the public as deeply as possible, the inevitable question arises: "How is the average sea level measured?". This question is followed by a description of the tide gauge, using a schematic representation of its functioning principles, consisting of a float operating in a stilling well, to dampen oscillations due to waves and reminding the audience that one of the first tide gauges was installed in Ponte Morosini, in the port of Genoa in 1910. The importance of the Ponte Morosini tide gauge is underlined by explaining that its measurements, progressively detected and processed by the Italian Navy Hydrographic Institute, are used to establish the mean sea level reference for Italy, on which the altitude determination of each point of the Italian territory depends. Moving from average sea level to mountain peaks, the authors inform the public about the existence of an Italian high-precision levelling network and about the various mechanisms that have been used to measure altitude in recent centuries, at any point on the Earth's surface.

The final segment of the workshop consists in several interactive game sessions, often carried out in parallel, which involve participants in understanding the basic height-measurement instrumentation operating principles. A table is organized with graduated pencils or straws, specifically designed and realized to simulate a level, which is suitable for calculating the height of a LEGO® tower or mountain, built by the workshop participants (Fig. 4).

Fig. 4. Practical demonstration of measuring altitude with self-built "topographic levels" made by AS-L work-experience secondary school students.

Another engaging activity is to perform a measurement using a real level and a levelling rod. This part of the workshop is highly appreciated by younger audiences and is an opportunity to expand the conceptual knowledge of measuring and to explain how levelling measures are performed with a topographic instrument.

The last game of the workshop concerns global positioning by means of the Global Navigation Satellite System (GNSS) technique. Four people play the role of three satellites and one of a receiver. The receiver is connected with a first satellite by means of a ribbon of a certain length. The receiver tries to understand if his/her position could be univocally determined with this single information. Then a new ribbon is added to connect a new satellite to the receiver, as long as the position is fixed (Fig. 5).

Fig. 5. The "Satellites-Receiver" game performed by AS-L work experience students and secondary school students.

2.3 Photogrammetry Workshop

The Photogrammetry workshop was firstly conceived in June 2017 and addressed to the general public in occasion of a large all-night series of events in Savona, with a main focus on photogrammetric surveys for post-seismic scenarios. Subsequently it was repeated in another five educational events in Liguria: *UniversiKids* (January 2018), *Aspettando Orientamento* (April 2018), *Festival del Mare* (May 2018 and 2019) and *Giovedì in Musica* (July 2019), with young audiences made up of children, final-year secondary school students about to enrol in University, school pupils (age 6–16) and the general public, respectively.

The main topic progressively moves from the vital contribution of the photogrammetric survey techniques in emergency scenarios, to the application of geodesy to maritime, coastal and underwater surveys, varying in accordance to the main theme of the event in which it is performed. On the contrary, the theoretical part is kept almost identical in all events.

The workshop starts from the experiences of the audience in the every-day vision of a 3D environment, creating curiosity about the principles and the techniques on which they are based. During the workshop, the authors illustrate anaglyph 3D stereoscopic images as the starting point of 3D cinema, focusing on how they are obtained and why stereovision is perceived only using special lenses. An on-site demonstration of ana-glyph image creation through the freeware software Anaglyph Maker ver. 1.08 [9] increases the interactivity of the workshop experience. Red and blue 3D glasses are made available and everyone can experience the anaglyph visualization with a video, images and posters.

Moving from 3D vision to photogrammetry, the collinearity equations and absolute orientation are explained using a hand-made wooden structure (the "Collinearity structure"): two panels represent likewise images, connected to the structure base by means of collinearity rays, linking three GCPs (Ground Control Points) with their corresponding image points. The model helps with the introduction of the main photogrammetric terminology and definitions, keeping the audience focused and facilitating understanding (Fig. 6).

Fig. 6. Photogrammetry workshop set-up: 3D anaglyph images on the (left), "Collinearity structure" (centre) and a photogrammetry video (right).

Therefore, following the more theoretical part, a live demonstration of a photogrammetric survey is carried out, to illustrate the different phases of a survey and to introduce the processing methods and products, i.e. point clouds, meshes and orthophotos.

Respectively from May 2018 and May 2019, the 3D printed model of Casalbagliano Castle (Alessandria, Italy) and of Vernazzola beach (Genoa, Italy) enriched the workshop, thus permitting the audience to observe the outcome of a real photogrammetric survey. As an additional product deriving from a photogrammetric survey, in the editions of April 2018, May 2018 and May 2019, augmented reality was introduced, through a mobile app designed and created by one of the authors. The app is intended to share the information related to a survey: image number and preview for each camera position for the Unmanned Aerial Vehicle (UAV) used for the survey; coordinate points and their measurement uncertainties, number of received satellites and quality indices of the GCPs surveyed with the GNSS technique.

The most radical change to the workshop's organization took place during its last edition (July 2019), when the "Collinearity structure" was substituted by a new structure, constituted by a sand-box and a support for a projector. The Vernazzola beach model is now contained in the sand-box to simulate the emerged part of a beach, while real sand is placed into it to represent the sea floor (Fig. 7). A special hand-made metallic structure holds a projector, which is used as an educational tool, together with the sand-box itself. The entire structure which substitutes the "Collinearity structure" attracts the public's attention. The sand-box is covered with a lid onto which images are projected to explain the main aspects of the workshop (anaglyph images, 3D vision and photogrammetry principles). Then, the lid is removed and the contour lines are projected onto the beach model, as depicted in Fig. 7.

Fig. 7. Photogrammetry workshop set-up: sand-box and contour line projection.

When there is time and/or a strongly interested group, the experience of a photogrammetric survey of a small sand tower is proposed, to demonstrate that the photogrammetric products, mainly the point cloud, can help in evaluating the amounts of volume. Comparing the computed volume with the previously known also gives the opportunity to introduce the themes of accuracy, precision and their assessment.

Note that the different phases of the survey, such as the image shooting, the processes and analysis to evaluate the contour lines and the volume of the tower, are obtained in near real-time by a collaborator during the workshop.

While the participants are focused on the central part of the stand, two monitors on each side show videos describing different significant applications of the photogrammetric survey for people passing-by. In the last event, one video showed UAV photogrammetry acquisition after the earthquakes in Central Italy in 2016 and 2017 [11, 12]; the other presented an example of underwater survey to measure coral reefs in the Maldives [13].

Post-seismic surveys in Central Italy mainly addressed cultural and historical buildings, which were considerably damaged or mostly destroyed. In such a treacherous situation, a quick and accurate survey is needed to support the survey campaign planning for securing sites and to document the state of the remaining structures. The criteria and guidelines described in [11, 12] were applied to the case studies of the Civic Tower and the Co-Cathedral of Santa Maria Argentea in Norcia, surveyed on behalf of the Italian Ministry of Cultural Heritage Activities and Tourism (MiBACT). These surveys were preliminary to the design of the safety operations commissioned by MiBACT. The video shown in the Photogrammetry workshop describes the different phases of the survey (planning and acquisition) and data processing, together with some tools used to share the survey results, also to inexperienced users.

The second monitor shows a video taken during a scientific cruise in the Maldives [14]. It illustrates the captivating underwater environment of colourful coral and fish, and it focuses on the operations performed to achieve *in situ* measurements of the coral reef using traditional techniques. The final part of the short video deals with photogrammetric post-processing imagery, helpful in reducing diving time and, in parallel, in enlarging the scale of the survey by producing a reliable 3D model from images. The biologists involved in the scientific cruise, affiliated to the Department of Earth, Environment and Life Sciences (DiSTAV) of the University of Genoa, had been trained to take suitable pictures (in terms of shooting geometry, and image quality, resolution and overlapping) for the photogrammetric workflow, with good results. These activities are intended to check the health of the coral reef, stressed by the rise of sea temperature and consequent bleaching phenomenon, that are well-known problems even for an unskilled audience.

3 Lessons Learned and Future Perspectives

This paper aims to highlight the importance of scientific dissemination both to improve the traditional classroom approach and to raise the interest of untrained people, in particular young audiences. The main goal of the workshops is to make an audience curious to understand the basic concepts of Geomatics, starting from intuitive considerations and questions from the audience itself, leading to a full introduction on the potential, practical application and usefulness of Geomatics.

The workshops were the perfect occasion to explain to a wide number of people what Geomatics is, also starting from their perceptions and intuitions deriving from every-day life on which Geomatics may have a strong impact. Figure 8 depicts which disciplines are included in Geomatics and the theoretical basis on which Geomatics relies: mathematics, physics, astronomy, physical geodesy and informatics to name a few [10].

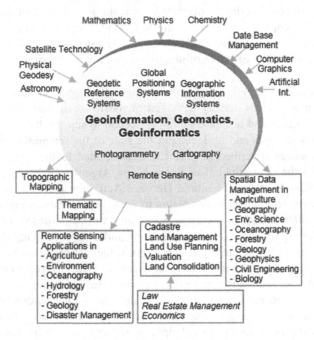

Fig. 8. What is Geomatics?

It was noticeable from the previously mentioned educational and didactic experiences that the audience had a strong desire to take an active part in the learning process. In fact, workshops and other educational activities in general, and those related to Geomatics, must be focused on the public needs: pragmatic and comprehensible language, practical examples, clear explanations, close to the social needs and high emotional involvement. These are the continuous challenges in scientific research and didactics, and these events surely allow to test the effectiveness and the quality of the ongoing work. Moreover, the coupling of the "third mission" activities with secondary school pupil work experience AS-L placements through University internships creates a virtuous cycle between different teaching methods and techniques to share research achievements.

The teaching method tested during the experience with the AS-L students mainly focused on learning-by-doing with PBL strategies, together with the double aspect of individual/collective and collaborative study. The authors believe that the same strategies are applicable with University students, organizing group activities. In fact, the transformation of the teaching method should be based on underlining the importance of Geomatics aspects in real life, and the consequent necessity to shape engineers with strong transversal skills: self-regulation, problem solving, effective communication, working in team, quality and modelling [6].

The demonstration of the continuous and progressive experimentation in teaching strategies is the evolution of the workshops over time. It does not entirely depend on the different event themes, but also on experience in the field, derived from both surveys and previous workshop editions. Such experience leads to modify, add and integrate new activities within the workshops, with a continue focus on public needs, to raise awareness of the importance that metric information has in society. In this perspective and as a future development, a short feedback survey will be carried out at the end of each event, which will help to further improve the workshop activities. Primarily, curiosity and questions are always fundamental starting points for the improvement of educational strategies, remarking that "the more important way to learn is by teaching".

Acknowledgements. The authors wish to thank all the work experience *Alternanza Scuola-Lavoro* students for their enthusiastic participation to the workshop activities; Davide Burlando for the construction of the support structure for the Photogrammetry workshop; Sandro Macrì of Department of Architecture and Design (DAD) of University of Genoa and Federico Briano for the 3D printed models of the Vernazzola beach and Casalbagliano Castle, respectively; Dr. Virginia Giannelli for the language revision of the manuscript.

References

1. Jian, W., Jing-xiang, G., Chang-hui, X.: Discovery learning and its application in geomatics education. In: 5th International Conference on Computer Science & Education, pp. 1614–1617. IEEE, Hafei, China (2010)
2. Kosmatin Fras, M., Grigillo, D.: Implementation of active teaching methods and emerging topics in photogrammetry and remote sensing subjects. Int. Arch. Photogram. Remote Sens. Spat. Inf. Sci. **XLI-B6**, 87–94 (2016)
3. Martín-Romero, J.L., et al.: Virtual reality immersive of geomatic techniques learning. In: 10th International Conference on Education and New Learning Technologies, pp. 7177–7181 (2018)
4. Tucci, G., Parisi, E.I., Conti, A., Corongiu, M., Fiorini, L., Panighini, F.: Educational and training experiences in Geomatics: tailored approaches for different audience. Int. Arch. Photogram. Remote Sens. Spat. Inf. Sci. **XLII-2/W11**, 1097–1104 (2019)
5. Barrows, H.S., Tamblyn, R.M: Problem-Based Learning: An Approach to Medical Education. Springer, New York (1980)
6. Al-Nasr, A.B.A.A.: Role of engineering design in enhancing ABET outcomes of engineering programs at Taif university. Int. J. Appl. Sci. Technol. **6**, 9–15 (2017)
7. Höhle, J.: Project-based learning in geomatics at Aalborg University. In: König, G., Lehmann, H., Köhring, R. (eds.) Tools and Techniques for e-Learning, Proceedings of the ISPRS working group VI/1-VI/2, Institute of Geodesy and Geoinformation Science, Technische Universität Berlin (2005)

8. Dale, E.: Audio-Visual Methods in Teaching. The Dryden Press, New York (1946)
9. Anaglyph Maker ver. 1.08. https://www.stereoeye.jp/index_e.html. Accessed 17 Sep 2019
10. Konecny, G.: Recent global changes in geomatics education. Int. Arch. Photogram. Remote Sens. Spat. Inf. Sci. **XXXIV(6/CVI)**, 9–14 (2002)
11. Gagliolo, S., et al.: Use of UAS for the conservation of historical buildings in case of emergencies. Int. Arch. Photogram. Remote Sens. Spat. Inf. Sci. **XLII(5/W1)**, 81–88 (2017)
12. Gagliolo, S., et al.: Parameter optimization for creating reliable photogrammetric models in emergency scenarios. Appl. Geomat. **10**(4), 501–514 (2018). https://doi.org/10.1007/s12518-018-0224-4
13. Sguerso, D., et al.: 3D photogrammetric surveys on coral reefs in the Maldives. In: IMEKO TC19 International Workshop on Metrology for the Sea, pp. 292–297 (2020)
14. Montefalcone, M., Morri, C., Bianchi, C.N.: Long term change in bioconstruction potential of Maldivian coral reefs following extreme climate anomalies. Glob. Change Biol. **24**, 5629–5641 (2018)

Use of CORS Time Series for Geodynamics Applications in Western Sicily (Italy)

Claudia Pipitone[1] , Gino Dardanelli[1(✉)] , Mauro Lo Brutto[1] ,
Valentina Bruno[2] , Mario Mattia[2] , Francesco Guglielmino[2] ,
Massimo Rossi[2] , and Giovanni Barreca[3]

[1] Department of Engineering, University of Palermo, Palermo, Italy
{claudia.pipitone02, gino.dardanelli,
mauro.lobrutto}@unipa.it
[2] Istituto Nazionale di Geofisica e Vulcanologia, Osservatorio Etneo,
Catania, Italy
{valentina.bruno, mario.mattia, francesco.guglielmino,
massimo.rossi}@ingv.it
[3] Dipartimento di Scienze Geologiche, Biologiche ed Ambientali,
Università degli Studi di Catania, Catania, Italy
g.barreca@unict.it

Abstract. In the last few decades, the use of GNSS Continuously Operating Reference Station (CORS) networks allowed improving the accuracy of real-time positioning and post-processing positioning. In this way, several applications have been performed including remote sensing, agriculture, cultural heritage and geodynamics studies. The latter have been developed analysing CORS time-series and consistent data over long periods were needed to validate the results. In Italy, specifically in Sicily, two CORS networks were be used to monitor the geodynamics motions: the Istituto Nazionale di Geofisica e Vulcanologia (INGV) GNSS CORS network in the eastern part and the University of Palermo (UNIPA) GNSS CORS network in the western part. In this research, preliminary results of time series about geodynamics motions of the western part of Sicily have been presented. In particular, the time series of the UNIPA GNSS CORS network have been analyzed over time by using the static positioning, over a period of approximately 5 years. Results showed a linear trend for all CORS time series, according to literature. An innovative methodology, the static Precise Point Positioning (PPP) has been also tested, to determine the time series of one CORS and compare the results with the static solution. The comparison between the two methodologies (static and PPP) demonstrated the capabilities of PPP technique with benefits in terms of costs and time.

Keywords: Time series · CORS · GNSS data · PPP data · Geodynamic

© Springer Nature Switzerland AG 2020
C. Parente et al. (Eds.): R3GEO 2019, CCIS 1246, pp. 61–76, 2020.
https://doi.org/10.1007/978-3-030-62800-0_6

1   Introduction

In the last few years, the role of GNSS Continuously Operating Reference Station (CORS) time series for geodynamics studies has been extensively analysed. Since 1990s, many authors have used GNSS CORS to demonstrate the capabilities of the network processing about precursory and aftershock seismic deformations detection [1].

Simons et al. [2] detected the GPS velocity field in Southeast Asia, for 10 years, using data collected from more than 100 sites mainly located in Indonesia, Malaysia, Thailand, Myanmar, Philippines and Vietnam. Additional research analysed the earthquakes in Turkey, in Southwest Anatolia by using 44 GNSS CORSs, over a wide period. The analysis aimed to detect the velocity field and the effects after the earthquakes in 2007 [3]. In Turkey, another research has been performed to detect the tectonic plate's motions by Uzel et al. [4].

Recently, both GNSS and InSAR techniques have been used to detect crustal deformations in Beijing. The results have been analysed by using more than 30 CORSs and 50 SAR images for 6 years from 2012 to 2017 [5].

Several works have also analysed the capabilities of the Precise Point Positioning (PPP), based on the use of a single receiver's information [6, 7]. Yamamoto et al. [8], for example, have tested the Real-Time Kinematic-GPS processing (RTK-GPS) for crustal deformation monitoring involving satellite mobile phone and comparing different strategies based on the use of all ultra-rapid, rapid, and final orbits for post-processed PPP. After the Van earthquake (Eastern Anatolia-Turkey), in 2011, Altiner et al. [9] involved GPS data of 1 s high-rate of the permanent stations belonging to the Turkey GNSS CORS network to determine the displacements of 11 stations by using PPP technique.

The same technique has been involved to analyse 1 Hz rate observations of more than 200 GNSS CORSs in Taiwan and surrounding islands, recording data during the Tohoku earthquake in 2011. The aim was the estimation of the absolute position of the receivers [10].

In 2014, Lou et al. [11] have shown the results of dynamic displacements after comparing 50 Hz and 1 Hz GPS data for kinematic-PPP analysis recorded during the Lushan earthquake (2013). Better results, in terms of accuracy, have been found with 50 Hz data, recorded by the Crustal Movement Observation Network of China (CMONOC) and nearby stations.

Gandolfi et al. [12] in 2016, applied an innovative methodology to obtain PPP solutions in the International Terrestrial Reference System (ITRS) involving local parameters from 14 stations within the Helmert transformation.

Hung et al. [13] analysed the solutions from kinematic positioning derived from four GNSS software (TRACK, RTKLIB, GIPSY, VADASE) to detect the seismic waveforms and the co-seismic displacements.

Recently, Jasim et al. [14] analysed the Arabian tectonic plate motion for approximately 10 years using the freely available GNSS-PPP software from the Canadian Geodetic Survey of Natural Resources Canada (CSRS). The results, in agreement with other studies available in literature, were able to detect the velocity and the direction of the tectonic plate motion.

In southern Italy (Sicily), a project for the installation and control of a GNSS CORS network (Rete Integrata Nazionale GPS - RING) has been set up by Istituto Nazionale di Geofisica e Vulcanologia (INGV) [15]. This GNSS CORS network is located on the east side of Sicily and is only used for geodynamics monitoring. Thus, in 2007, the University of Palermo (UNIPA) developed a research project to guarantee the presence of several permanent stations also in the western side and set up the UNIPA GNSS CORS network. This network was mainly developed for real-time and post-processing positioning but it was also used for geodynamics studies.

This research aims to shows the results of a time series analysis of UNIPA GNSS CORS network for geodynamics studies. In particular, the CORS time series have been analysed over ~5 years by using static positioning.

An innovative methodology has been also tested to analyse the time series of a UNIPA reference station. The comparison between the two processing approaches (static and PPP) showed the capability of the latter to obtain reliable results with benefits in terms of costs and time.

2   UNIPA GNSS CORS Network

UNIPA GNSS CORS network consists of eight permanent stations far away from each other from 22 to 83 km, evenly distributed on the western side of Sicily and carried out since 2007 as part of a research project by the University of Palermo.

Fig. 1. UNIPA GNSS CORS network.

The network was developed after preliminary analyses about the area to be covered. In particular, recommendations about the minimum number of stations to be installed and the distances between the stations were considered. The tests performed by Grejner-Brzezinska et al. [17] considering different distances between the permanent stations, revealed that the best configuration is achieved with distances within 50–80 km. Then, preliminary studies have been carried out on data availability, quality check and geodetic framework, as showed by Dardanelli et al. [16].

The GNSS CORSs were installed in Palermo (PALE), Campobello di Mazara (CAMP), Termini Imerese (TERM), Trapani (TRAP), Agrigento (AGRI), Partinico (PART), Prizzi (PRIZ) and Caltanissetta (CALT) (Fig. 1).

The reference stations are equipped with Topcon NET-G3 GPS and GLONASS receivers and TPSCR3 GGD with CONE antennas. The Topcon software TopNET was used for real-time network corrections and Receiver Independent Exchange Format (RINEX) data analysis. Data from the International GNSS Service (IGS) CORS of Noto, Cagliari, Matera and Lampedusa have been used for the geodetic framework. The *a-priori* precisions of the IGS CORSs were 2 mm and 4 mm for the planimetric and the height components, respectively. The weekly solutions have been determined from the daily solutions, applying the double differences (DD). Other parameters have been also considered for each CORS as the quality data, the cycle-slips, the ambiguity phase, the standard deviation of the float and the final solutions, the percentage (%) of fixed ambiguities.

Six reference stations from the UNIPA GNSS CORS network have been included and computed in the new version of the Italian GPS dynamic permanent network called Rete Dinamica Nazionale (RDN) ver. 2. Since 2009, the RDN was developed with 100 CORSs throughout the national territory by the Istituto Geografico Militare Italiano (IGMI). Few years later, in 2014, the IGMI replaced the failed stations with other CORSs; new processing of the CORS coordinates was updated to the epoch 2014.4. This process allowed the realization of a new RDN version (RDN ver. 2), including only 80 stations (Fig. 2).

The UNIPA GNSS CORS network has been validated for different purposes: use of Mobile Mapping System (MMS) for integrated survey [18], land and structure monitoring, *e.g.* dams [19–21], geological analyses [22] and more recently for geodynamic analyses (combining geodetic and InSAR techniques) to detect active faults in south-western Sicily [23].

3   UNIPA GNSS CORS Network Processing Strategy

The UNIPA GNSS CORS network time series were processed using three different software: Network Deformation Analysis (NDA), RTKLIB and GAMIT/GLOBK.

The coordinates of the reference stations have been computed with NDA in IGS08 (International GNSS Service, epoch 2008.0) and ETRF2000 (European Terrestrial Reference Frame, epoch 2008.0); results were statistically analysed to remove outliers and residual noise. In NDA the tropospheric and the ionospheric errors have been modelled by using the Saastamoinen [24] and Niell [25] mapping functions and the Klobuchar model [26] respectively. The influence of the ocean loadings has been also considered, involving the corrections by Schwiderski's model [27]. The precise ephemerides and the antenna phase centre position from the International GNSS Service (IGS) were employed. Also, the time range and the cut-off angle were set to 30 s and 10°, respectively. Additional parameters, as the Earth's Rotation Parameter (ERP) and the ephemerides of the sun and the moon, were also used for the analysis. The Least Squares Ambiguity Decorrelation Adjustment (LAMBDA) method was used to fix the phase ambiguity [28]. To estimate the final solution, the wide-lane observable estimating the Wide-lane ambiguity and then, the ionospheric-free observables estimating the remaining narrow-lane ambiguity were also used.

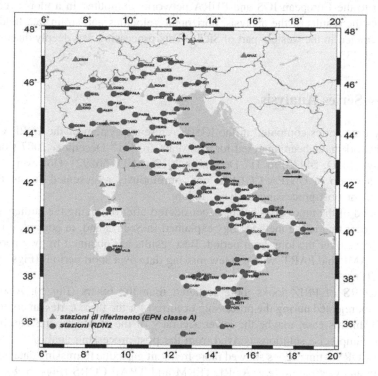

Fig. 2. RDN ver. 2 CORS network (from Maseroli, 2015).

The other processing was performed using the freely available software RTKLIB ver. 2.42 and, in particular, with the RTKPOST routine [29]. The software includes algorithms for the analysis of GPS, GLONASS, Galileo, QZSS, BeiDou and SBAS satellite constellations. Specifically, the analysis focused on static PPP positioning. Although the main problem of this method is the long convergence time of the parameters, by using multi-GNSS constellation, less computational time and high accuracy can be achieved. The GOT4.7 model has been performed for the ocean tides, according to Zawadzki et al. [30]. Also, the solutions with GDOP (Geometric Dilution of Precision) values higher than 30 have been rejected, and the cut-off angle (10°) used with NDA software was set. The ionospheric delay was reduced and removed using the ionosphere free-linear combination of phase-carrier and code. The satellites orbits and clocks corrections have been applied using the precise products provided by the IGS. Other parameters have been set according to the static post-processing analysis by NDA software. Also, in this case, the results were statistically analysed to remove outliers and residual noises; to show the tendency of the long-term displacements, a simple moving average (SMA) has been applied over a moving window. The suitable length of the moving window was determined by testing different time lengths.

The dataset from 2008 to 2016 of UNIPA GNSS CORS network was also processed using the GAMIT/GLOBK software [31, 32] and IGS precise ephemerides. As discussed in Barreca et al. [23], the post-processing included other permanent stations belonging to the European IGS and EURA networks computed in a global reference system. As the results of the analysis, horizontal velocities and strain rate fields have been determined in the western part of Sicily. This processing was deeply discussed by Bruno et al. [33].

4 Time-Series Analysis

The daily time series computed in the IGS08 reference system of the UNIPA GNSS CORS network have been analysed for ~5 years from 1st December 2007 (Modified Julian Days, MJD: 54435) to 31st December 2012 (MJD: 56292). However, the time series of a group of UNIPA CORS is not continuously represented due to missing acquisitions or post-processing analysis' failure.

The trend of the time series has been considered after removing the outliers and the residuals according to the methodology explained in Sect. 3 and, in general, it is linear for all CORSs over the long-term period. Best results are obtained by two permanent stations, CAMP and PART, with just few missing data over short periods (Figs. 3 and 4, respectively).

The CORS of PRIZ looks more scattered than the others (Fig. 5). Also, some blunders not rejected during the processing occurred for the three cartesian components (X, Y, Z). In this case, maybe the lower accuracy of the measurements can be associated with imprecise solutions derived from the post-processing analysis.

Some CORSs' time series showed more frequent gaps due to missing data and post-processing analysis failure, *e.g.* AGRI, TERM and TRAP CORS (Figs. 6–8).

PALE CORS' time series shows an evident scattered behavior at the beginning of the analysed period, due to an electromagnetic problem occurred by the first days of 2008 (from MJD 54437 to MJD 54497) (Fig. 9). Indeed, during the data acquisition, a temporal electromagnetic disturbance occurred for this station, influencing the quality of the GNSS signal.

Preliminary, in 2006, to avoid electromagnetic disturbances from other signals, the site has been monitored by Agenzia Regionale per la Protezione Ambientale (ARPA, Regional Agency for the Environmental Protection) for three weeks using the monitoring station PMM8055. Results did not show any relevant interference on GNSS activities, as reported in Fig. 12a. Later, in 2007, since the time series of PALE CORS has been monitored, the analysis of GNSS signal revealed a strong interference on L2, probably due to a Global System for Mobile Communications (GSM) repeater installed nearby the CORS ($\sim$1 km). The analysis revealed a disturbance on a single frequency (1300.4 MHz) close to those used for GNSS analysis (1217−1260 MHz) (Fig. 12b).

In 2008, the problem was solved and further analyses managed by ARPA, confirmed the absence of any electromagnetic disturbance on the site (Fig. 12c). Indeed, since MJD 55498 (2nd of February 2008) the time series has shown a well-defined linear trend by the end of the analysis.

Most critical results were obtained for CALT station. Specifically, the time series has shown a long gap, from MJD 55727 to MJD 56079 (Fig. 10). In this period, indeed, data was not recorded because the permanent station was not active.

Only for this station, after MJD 56079 (6th January 2012), a jump occurred for the three cartesian coordinates (X, Y, Z) after changing the materialization site of the antenna (CALT2), approximately far 1.5 km from the previous one (CALT1). Also, at the beginning of the time series, data was missing because the station acquired data since MJD 54510 (14th February 2008).

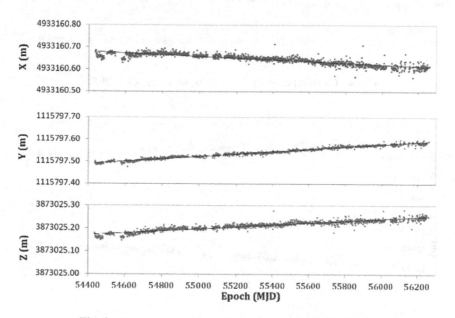

Fig. 3. Cartesian coordinates' time series of CAMP CORS.

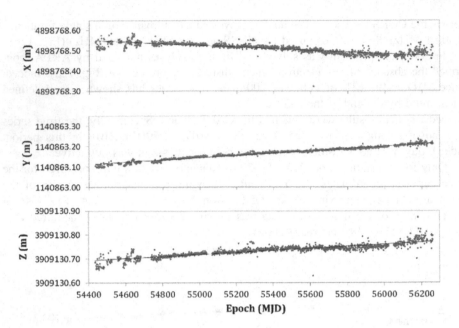

Fig. 4. Cartesian coordinates' time series of PART CORS.

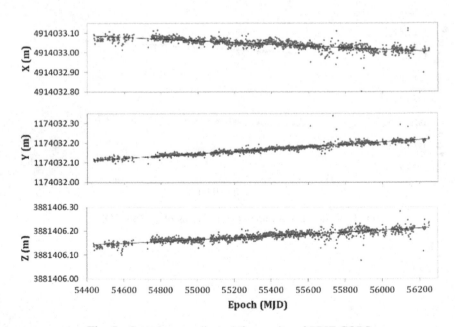

Fig. 5. Cartesian coordinates' time series of PRIZ CORS.

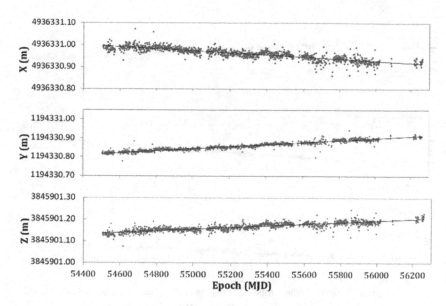

Fig. 6. Cartesian coordinates' time series of AGRI CORS.

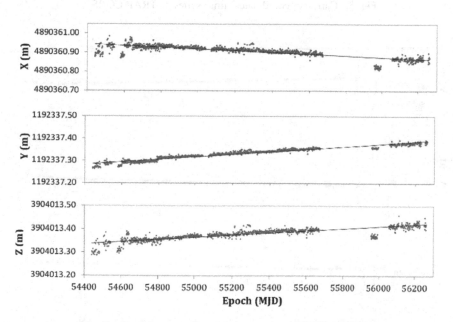

Fig. 7. Cartesian coordinates' time series of TERM CORS.

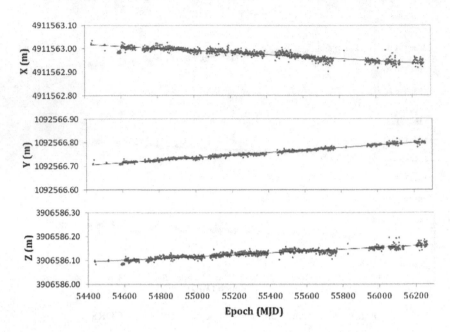

Fig. 8. Cartesian coordinates' time series of TRAP CORS.

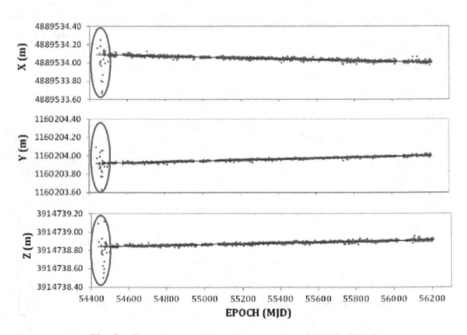

Fig. 9. Cartesian coordinates' time series of PALE CORS.

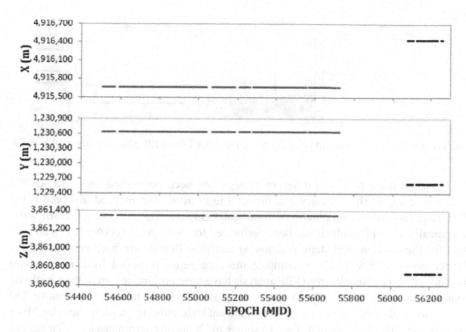

Fig. 10. Cartesian coordinates' time series of CALT CORS.

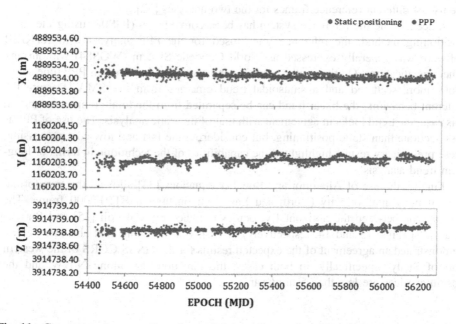

Fig. 11. Comparison between Cartesian coordinates' time series of PALE CORS with static and PPP positioning.

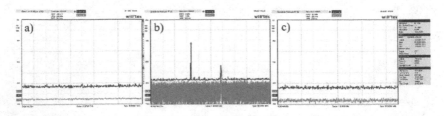

Fig. 12. Interference Vs time in OCT 2006 (a), DEC 2007 (b), FEB 2008 (c), from left to right.

Based on these results, a different strategy has been performed on PALE CORS dataset to compare the accuracy and the long term trend. The method involved is the PPP, requiring lower computational time and freely available open-source software. Specifically, the PPP analysis has been performed for ~ 10 years (2008−2017), already used for the conventional static positioning analysis. Results are here presented for a shorter period (2008−2012) to compare the time series retrieved by using the two methods (Fig. 11). Results from PPP analysis have been preliminary smoothed applying a simple moving average (SMA) over a temporal moving window (~ 1 month). The long-term trend of the series emerged from the analysis, although it is characterized by a marked scattering. In particular, Fig. 12 shows for X and Z coordinates a similar pattern between the two time series with differences of few millimeters and also the two trends look in agreement. The differences between the two representations are probably due to the use of different reference frames for the two analyses [12].

Indeed, while the reference system has been correctly set (IGS08) using the static positioning method, the reference frame used for the PPP analysis with RTKLIB software was generally expressed as World Geodetic System (WGS84) without any other specifications. On the contrary, for Y component, the behavior of PPP time series looks more scattered and a sinusoidal trend emerges from the SMA. Despite the different behaviors, the linear trend can be separated from the total component and, in this case, the trend looks in agreement with that of the static analysis. The use of PPP is less accurate than static positioning, but considering the fast and low-cost processing, these preliminary results highlighted the capabilities of the technique in terms of long-term trend analysis.

Finally, the use of Altamimi and Boucher equations [34] allowed the transformation of horizontal velocity (North and East components) in ETRF2000 frame. The comparison between the horizontal velocities obtained by Maseroli [35] and Barreca et al. [23] (Figs. 13 and 14, respectively), in terms of directions and absolute values, demonstrated an agreement of the expected results for the GNSS CORS of the western part of Sicily. Specifically, in both cases, the directions are along N-NW and the absolute values are less than 5 mm/year.

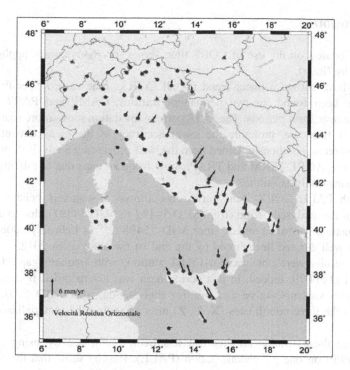

Fig. 13. Horizontal GPS velocities (from Maseroli, 2015).

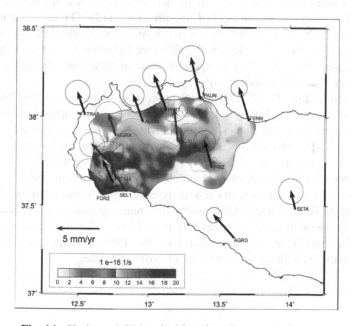

Fig. 14. Horizontal GPS velocities (from Barreca et al., 2020).

5 Conclusions

This study focused on the use of CORS time series for geodynamics applications in western Sicily (Italy).

Results have shown a linear trend for all CORSs time series. Specifically, best results have been found for two permanent stations, CAMP and PART with few missing data over short periods. The PRIZ permanent station looks more scattered than the others; in this case, probably the lower accuracy of the measurements may be related to imprecise solutions obtained from the post-processing analysis. Some CORSs time series, *e.g.* AGRI, TERM and TRAP, show frequent gaps due to missing data and post-processing analysis failure.

Although PALE CORS' time series has shown a scattered behaviour at the beginning of the analysed period (from MJD 54437 to MJD 54497), due to a temporal electromagnetic disturbance on L2, since MJD 55498 (2nd of February 2008) the time series has a well-defined linear trend by the end of the analysis in 2012.

Critical results were obtained for CALT station, with frequent gaps, from MJD 55727 to MJD 56079. Indeed, in this period data was not recorded because the permanent station was not active and just for this station, after MJD 56079, a jump occurred for the three coordinates (X, Y, Z) after changing the materialization site of the antenna.

Based on these results, another test has been performed by using a different approach (PPP) on one permanent station (PALE). Results show that the time series along X and Z coordinates have a similar behavior with the static solution; indeed the two solutions differ few millimeters and also the two trends look in agreement. The differences between the two behaviors are probably due to the use of different reference frames for the analyses, according to Gandolfi et al. [12]. On the contrary, for Y component, the behaviour of PPP time series looks more scattered and a sinusoidal trend emerges from the SMA. Despite the different behaviours, the linear component can be separated from the total component and, in this case, the trend looks in agreement with that of the static analysis.

Finally, results from GNSS CORS post-processing belonging to UNIPA network confirmed an agreement between the different analyses computed with different strategies. In particular, the values obtained from the above mentioned studies by Barreca et al. [23] confirmed the residual velocities, referred to the European plate obtained by the development of the RDN published by Maseroli [35] because directions were along N-NW and absolute values were less than 5 mm/year.

Of course, further improvements and analyses need to be involved to validate the results of all UNIPA GNSS CORS using different methodologies. Currently, the comparison between the two time series determined with different strategies referred to PALE CORS, highlighted the capabilities of the PPP technique for GNSS post-processing analyses, with benefits in terms of costs and time.

References

1. Bock, Y., et al.: Detection of crustal deformation from the Landers earthquake sequence using continuous geodetic measurements. Nature **361**(6410), 337–340 (1993)
2. Simons, W.J.F., et al.: A decade of GPS in Southeast Asia: Resolving Sundaland motion and boundaries. J. Geophys. Res. Solid Earth, **112**(6) (2007). art. no. B06420
3. Gulal, E., et al.: Tectonic activity inferred from velocity field of GNSS measurements in Southwest of Turkey. Acta Geodaetica et Geophysica **48**(2), 109–121 (2013)
4. Uzel, T., Eren, K., Gulal, E., Tiryakioglu, I., Dindar, A.A., Yilmaz, H.: Monitoring the tectonic plate movements in Turkey based on the national continuous GNSS network. Arab. J. Geosci. **6**(9), 3573–3580 (2013)
5. Hu, L., et al.: Research on the crustal deformation characteristics in Beijing using InSAR and GNSS technology. Int. Arch. Photogramm. Remote Sens. Spat. Inf. Sci. **42**(3), 559–564 (2018)
6. Wübbena, G., Schmitz, M., Bagge, A.: PPP-RTK: precise point positioning using state-space representation in RTK networks. In: Proceedings of the 18th International Technical Meeting of the Satellite Division of the Institute of Navigation, pp. 2584–2594. ION GNSS 2005, USA (2005)
7. Teunissen, P.J.G., Odijk, D., Zhang, B.: PPP-RTK: results of CORS network-based PPP with integer ambiguity resolution. J. Aeronaut. Astronaut. Aviat. **42**(4), 223–230 (2010)
8. Yamamoto, J., et al.: Real time GPS processing utilizing satellite communications - toward more reliable real-time crustal deformation monitoring under a situation of ground communication failure. J. Geod. Soc. Jpn. **59**(4), 133–145 (2013)
9. Altiner, Y., Söhne, W., Güney, C., Perlt, J., Wang, R., Muzli, M.: A geodetic study of the 23 October 2011 Van, Turkey earthquake. Tectonophysics **588**, 118–134 (2013)
10. Hung, H.-K., Rau, R.-J.: Surface waves of the 2011 Tohoku earthquake: observations of Taiwan's dense high-rate GPS network. J. Geophys. Res. Solid Earth **118**(1), 332–345 (2013)
11. Lou, Y., Zhang, W., Shi, C., Liu, J.: High-rate (1-Hz and 50-Hz) GPS seismology: application to the 2013 Mw 6.6 Lushan earthquake. J. Asian Earth Sci. **79**, 426–431 (2014)
12. Gandolfi, S., Tavasci, L., Poluzzi, L.: Improved PPP performance in regional networks. GPS Solutions **20**(3), 485–497 (2015). https://doi.org/10.1007/s10291-015-0459-z
13. Hung, H.-K., et al.: GPS seismology for a moderate magnitude earthquake: lessons learned from the analysis of the 31 October 2013 ML 6.4 Ruisui (Taiwan) earthquake. Ann. Geophys. **60**(5) (2017). art. no. S0553
14. Jasim, Z.N., Alhamadani, O.Y.M., Mohammed, M.U.: Investigation the Arabian tectonic plate motion using continuously operating reference stations. Int. J. Civ. Eng. Technol. **9**(13), 419–429 (2018)
15. Avallone, A., et al.: The RING network: improvements to a GPS velocity field in the central Mediterranean. Ann. Geophys. **53**(2), 39–54 (2010)
16. Grejner-Brzezinska, D.A., Kashani, I., Wielgosz, P.: On accuracy and reliability of instantaneous network RTK as a function of network geometry, station separation, and data processing strategy. GPS Solutions **9**(3), 212–225 (2005)
17. Dardanelli, G., Lo Brutto, M., Pipitone, C.: GNSS CORS network of the university of Palermo: design and first analysis of data. Geogr. Tech. **15**(1), 43–69 (2020)
18. Dardanelli, G., Paliaga, S., Allegra, M., Carella, M., Giammarresi, V.: Geomatic applications tourban park in palermo. Geogr. Tech. **10**(1), 28–43 (2015)

19. Dardanelli, G., La Loggia, G., Perfetti, N., Capodici, F., Puccio, L., Maltese, A.: Monitoring displacements of an earthen dam using GNSS and remote sensing. In: Proceedings of the SPIE 9239, Remote Sensing for Agriculture, Ecosystems, and Hydrology XVI, 923928, 21 October 2014. SPIE, Amsterdam (2014)
20. Dardanelli, G., Pipitone, C.: Hydraulic models and finite elements for monitoring of an earth dam, by using GNSS techniques. Period. Polytech. Civ. Eng. **61**(3), 421–433 (2017)
21. Pipitone, C., Maltese, A., Dardanelli, G., Lo Brutto, M., La Loggia, G.: Monitoring water surface and level of a reservoir using different remote sensing approaches and comparison with dam displacements evaluated via GNSS. Remote Sens. **10**(1), 71 (2018). art. no. 71
22. Stocchi, P., et al.: A stalactite record of four relative sea-level highstands during the middle Pleistocene transition. Quatern. Sci. Rev. **173**, 92–100 (2017)
23. Barreca, G., et al.: An integrated geodetic and InSAR technique for the monitoring and detection of active faulting in southwestern Sicily. Ann. of Geophys. **63**(SE101), 1–11 (2020)
24. Saastamoinen, J.: The use of artificial satellites for geodesy. Atmospheric correction for troposphere and stratosphere in radio ranging of satellites. Henriksen, S.W., Mancini, A., Chovitz, B.H. (eds.): AGU, Washington, USA (1972)
25. Niell, A.E.: Global mapping functions for the atmosphere delay at radio wavelengths. J. Geophys. Res. **101**, 3227–3246 (1996)
26. Klobuchar, J.A.: Ionospheric effects on GPS. In: Global Positioning System: Theory and Applications. American Institute of Aeronautics and Astronautic, Reston (1996)
27. Schwiderski, E.W.: On charting global ocean tides. Rev. Geophys. **18**, 243–268 (1980)
28. Teunissen, P.J.G., Kleusberg, A.: GPS for Geodesy, 2nd edn. Springer, Berlin (1998). https://doi.org/10.1007/978-3-642-72011-6
29. Takasu, T., Kubo, N., Yasuda, A.: Development, evaluation and application of RTKLIB: a program library for RTK-GPS. In: GPS/GNSS Symposium (2007)
30. Zawadzki, L., et al.: Investigating the 59-day error signal in the mean sea level derived from TOPEX/Poseidon, Jason-1, and Jason-2 data with FES and GOT ocean tide models. IEEE Trans. Geosci. Remote Sens. **56**(6), 3244–3255 (2018)
31. Herring, T.A., King, R.W., Floyd, M.A., McClusky, S.C.: GAMIT Reference Manual. GPS Analysis at MIT, Massachusetts Institute of Technology, Cambridge (2015)
32. Herring, T.A., Floyd, M.A., King, R.W., McClusky, S.C: GLOBK Reference Manual. Global Kalman filter VLBI and GPS analysis program, Massachusetts Institute of Technology, Cambridge (2015)
33. Bruno, V., Mattia, M., Aloisi, M., Palano, M., Cannavò, F., Holt, W.E.: Ground deformations and volcanic processes as imaged by CGPS data at Mt. Etna (Italy) between 2003 and 2008. J. Geophys. Res. **117**, B07208 (2012)
34. Boucher, C., Altamimi Z.: Memo: Specifications for reference frame fixing in the analysis of EUREF GPS campaign; 18-05-2011, Version 8. 2011. http://etrs89.ensg.ign.fr/memo-V8.pdf (2011). Accessed 16 April 2020
35. Maseroli, R.: Evoluzione del Sistema Geodetico di Riferimento in Italia: la RDN2. Bollettino della Associazione Italiana di Cartografia **2015**(153), 19–44 (2015)

Performances and New Aspects of Multi-GNSS, Dual Frequency and Low-Cost Receivers in Harsh Urban Environments

Marco Piras⬤, Paolo Dabove(✉)⬤, and Nives Grasso⬤

DIATI Department, Politecnico di Torino,
Corso Duca degli Abruzzi 24, 10129 Turin, Italy
{marco.piras,paolo.dabove,nives.grasso}@polito.it

Abstract. Traditionally, multi-constellation and multi-frequency chipsets were only adopted on geodetic receivers, considering the high costs and limited number of mass applications. Nowadays, with a wide range of constellations available, satellite navigation has opened up to many civilian domains like navigation and positioning, surveying and mapping, weather prediction, mobile satellite communications, smart technologies, etc. Currently, many geodetic receivers are available and they can provide highly accurate results up to millimetre level. In addition, there are several low-cost solutions, which are able to work in multi-constellation and multi-frequencies domain. Usually the accuracy of receivers, especially low-cost ones, is not very high in harsh urban environment due to low visibility of satellites, frequent signal blockages and increasing multipath effects. In this paper the accuracy and the reliability of multi-GNSS (GPS/GLONASS/BeiDou/Galileo), low-cost single and dual frequency receivers are investigated and analysed for kinematic positioning. Different datasets have been collected by single (Emlid Reach GNSS) and dual frequency GNSS receivers (i.e. Tersus Precis BX306 and Piksi multi GNSS) in a harsh urban environment and then analysed using real time and post-processed solutions. This work shows that under suitable conditions, mass-market sensors could be a valid alternative to a more expensive receiver for many environmental applications.

Keywords: Multi-GNSS · Low-cost receivers · Harsh urban environments · High accuracy · Real time kinematic (RTK)

1 Introduction

High-accuracy positioning with low-cost GNSS receivers always remain an issue for many application fields such as precise agriculture, unmanned aerial vehicles (UAV), mobile mapping, landslide monitoring etc. Currently many types of GNSS receivers are available in the market ranging from geodetic triple frequency and multi constellation to low-cost mass-market single frequency and single constellation receivers. An accuracy of centimetre level can be obtained with low-cost and single frequency GNSS receivers in real-time positioning using Continuous Operating Reference Stations

© Springer Nature Switzerland AG 2020
C. Parente et al. (Eds.): R3GEO 2019, CCIS 1246, pp. 77–90, 2020.
https://doi.org/10.1007/978-3-030-62800-0_7

(CORSs) whereas in sub-centimetre after post-processing (Dabove et al. 2014). Low-cost and dual frequency receivers are also available which can utilize both frequencies (L1 and L2) to remove errors due to atmospheric (e.g. ionosphere) and environmental (e.g. multipath) conditions and an accuracy up to cm level can be obtained after correctly resolving the carrier-phase integer ambiguities. Some past researches (Skournetou and Lohan 2011; Carcanague et al. 2013; He et al. 2014) have shown that rapid ambiguity resolution (AR) can be achieved better in open sky conditions with dual-frequency GNSS receivers as compare to single frequency receivers. With the rapid development of multi-GNSS systems (Montenbruck et al. 2014), the performance of real-time kinematic (RTK) positioning using low-cost single-frequency receivers and antennas can be improved considerably due to the more satellite visibility and better spatial geometry (Teunissen et al. 2013; Odolinski et al 2014; Odolinski and Teunissen 2017; Li et al. 2017).

Positioning and tracking of people and transport vehicles by the GNSS sensors experienced a major expansion in recent years, especially after the launch of smart mobile phones which have already built-in GNSS receiver. The reason for using GNSS systems in many devices is very obvious: it increases the availability of maximum satellites in most parts of the world, which makes accurate position measurements more likely, and at the same time it enables the receiver to exclude poor signal satellites and to improve the accuracy and reliability of positioning (Takac et al. 2005; Takac and Walford 2006; Dvorkin and Karutin 2006).

Many people are now familiar with GNSS devices used for applications like road navigation, ships navigation in sea, surveying and mapping etc. The roots of GNSS technology are in the radio-navigation systems like Long Range Navigation (LORAN), which was developed for the navigation of ships and aircrafts. Many researches were conducted in the past for the improvement of positioning accuracy with GNSS signals (Valeev et al. 2014), problems due to obstructions (Yamamoto et al. 2008), improvement of time to first fix (Low and Law 2015) etc. Although the GNSS technology uses satellites and their signals for positioning and navigation, there are many differences among the available GNSS sensors like number of frequencies used from the satellites, or the satellites tracked from different constellations i.e. GPS, GLONASS, BeiDou, Galileo etc. The capability to correct position calculations from systems like Satellite-Based Augmentation Systems (SBAS) and RTK techniques are also different for GNSS sensors.

Theoretically, single frequency GNSS receivers are less precise as compared to the dual frequency GNSS receivers. Normally single frequency receivers allow to obtain an accuracy of a few meters in real-time performing a stand-alone positioning while up to centimetres if network corrections, provided by CORSs, are considered (Dabove et al. 2018). Regarding post-processing of the raw data, it is possible to obtain an accuracy of few cm by considering a Virtual RINEX (Receiver Independent Exchange Format) data which is generated by the network software that manages the CORSs network (Cina et al. 2014a, b).

The main goal of this research is to test and analyse the performances of some new recent single and dual frequency low-cost mass-market GNSS receivers in order to understand their accuracy, precision and use towards mass-market applications like navigation, UAV and pedestrian purposes. All three receivers tested are able to apply differential corrections broadcasted by a software that manages CORSs network and to collect raw data (carrier-phase, pseudoranges and Doppler measurements) in their internal memory or an external device (i.e. laptop). In this paper only a kinematic test has been carried out, using a cargo bike. All tests have been supported by the services provided by a CORSs network.

The paper is organized as follows: after this introduction, Sect. 2 describes the receivers and other instruments used to evaluate the performance of different GNSS receivers, Sects. 3 and 4 describe the sites selected for kinematic tests and the obtained results respectively, while Sect. 4 concludes this paper.

2 Material and Instruments

In order to test the performances of the low-cost, multi-constellation, single and dual frequency mass-market GNSS receivers, three different receivers are considered: Precis-BX306 by Tersus GNSS, Swift Multi Piksi GNSS by Swift Navigation and Reach RTK by EMLID. The characteristics of these instruments are shown in Table 1.

The Tersus BX306 is a low-cost and dual frequency GNSS RTK board for cm level positioning: it provides raw measurements which can be integrated with autopilots and inertial navigation units. Currently, it supports three constellations (GPS L1/L2, GLONASS G1/G2, and BeiDou B1/B2) to improve the continuity and reliability of the RTK solution even in harsh urban environments. Piksi Multi is another low-cost, dual frequency and high-performance GNSS receiver ready for RTK technology in order to reach cm-level positioning accuracy. Piksi Multi is an ideal candidate to integrate with different applications due to its robustness, fast position solution upgrade and small form factor. Multi-constellation and multi-band support enables Piksi Multi to offer fast RTK convergence times. Emlid Reach is a single frequency and multi-constellation RTK GNSS receiver which can be integrated with many civilian applications, it relies on RTK technology to deliver cm-level accuracy. Reach runs a modified version of an open-source processing software called RTKLIB (2018) (http://www.rtklib.com/) written by Tomoji Takasu. Previously a separate computer was required to run RTKLIB, but now all RTKLIB features are available directly on Reach. As available in bibliography (Manzino and Dabove 2013; Cina et al. 2014a, b), GNSS antenna plays an important role in order to reach high performance of positioning in particular working with mass-market receivers. It is fundamental both to reduce the noise and to increase the signal quality, under this condition, AX3702 mini survey antenna was selected for Tersus BX-306 and Piksi Multi GNSS receivers, its characteristics can be seen in Table 2. This antenna has internal multi-path-rejection board which eliminates multi-path interference errors and it also has a multi-feed design to minimize influence of multipath errors and superposition of phase center and geometrical center.

Table 1. Characteristics of Tersus BX-306, Swift Multi Piksi and Emlid Reach GNSS Receivers.

GNSS Receivers	Tersus Precis BX-306	Swift Multi Piksi	EMLID Reach
Images			
Price	$1,699.00	$595.00	$235.00
Power Consumption	3.5 W	2.9 W	1 W
Weight	23g	20g	20g
Constellations	GPS L1/L2, GLONASS G1/G2, BeiDou B1/B2	[a] GPS L1/L2, GLONASS G1/G2, BeiDou B1/B2, Galileo E1/E5b, QZSS L1/L2	GPS L1/QZSS L1, GLONASS G1, Galileo E1, SBAS
Position update rate	1Hz-20Hz	1Hz-20Hz	1Hz-14Hz
Raw data format	Tersus Binary Protocol (TRS)	Swift Binary Protocol (SBP)	UBX format/ RINEX2.X, RINEX3.X
Corrections type	RTCM 2.x/3.x/CMR/CMR+	RTCM 2.x/3.x/CMR/CMR+	RTCM 2.x/RTCM 3.x

[a] Hardware is ready for GPS, GLONASS, BeiDou, Galileo and QZSS signals but current firmware can process GPS and GLONASS signals only (1 June 2018)

Then a signal splitter is used to split signals coming from this GNSS antenna and distribute in both dual frequency GNSS receivers i.e. Tersus Precis BX306 and Swift Multi Piksi. Another patch antenna was also installed on the top of a cargo bike for single frequency GNSS receiver Emlid reach.

Table 2. Characteristics of GNSS Antenna AX3702 from Tersus.

GNSS Antenna	**AX3702**
Image	
Price	$160.00
Gain	5.5 dBi
Weight	374 g
Constellations	GPS L1/L2, GLONASS G1/G2, BeiDou B1/B2

3 Test Site

The area chosen for the RTK test was the 'Crocetta' District in Turin, northwest of Italy (Fig. 1). This area is predominantly residential, located in the semi-central location of the City, and characterized by the presence of commercial facilities, as well as public places and services, such as schools. This test site was selected for the presence of different kind of features like buildings, narrow streets, roads and tall trees to make it represent a harsh urban scenario.

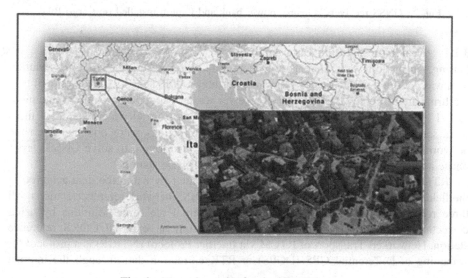

Fig. 1. Map of test site for the kinematic test.

The described test was carried out on July 2018. For this paper data was collected from all the receivers considering only the RTK approaches, because the static analyses have been performed in many different papers available in literature (Cina et al. 2014a, b; Jackson et al. 2018; Sridhara et al. 2015; Manurung et al. 2019; Zhang et al. 2019). The dataset was collected on June 17, 2018 in Turin, close to the Politecnico di Torino (Turin, NW Italy).

3.1   RTK Positioning Solution

The Cargo bike was selected for the kinematic test as it was easy to install all GNSS receivers and antennas on it. A laptop was fixed on the cargo bike to initiate and record the data from all three GNSS receivers as shown in Fig. 2.

Both dual frequency GNSS sensors are connected to the laptop through USB interface whereas the single frequency GNSS receiver was connected through a Wi-Fi hotspot. A power bank with capacity of 15000 mAh was also fixed in the cargo bike to provide power to the receivers.

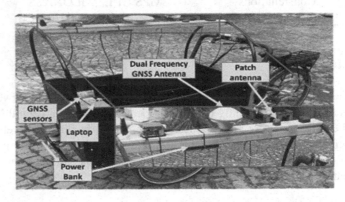

Fig. 2. GNSS receivers, antenna, power bank and Laptop installed on Cargo Bike.

3.1.1   Real Time Solution Data Analysis

During kinematic test, a reference trajectory was followed and the real time solution data was collected with a rate of 1 Hz from all three GNSS sensors. At the time of test, the firmware of Tersus BX-306 GNSS receiver was not supporting solution rate more than 1 Hz so for the comparison of position solutions from all receivers, all of them were set to have 1 solution every second. The corrections were obtained from the network of reference stations for accurate real-time positioning to solve GNSS carrier phase ambiguities between the rover and permanent base station.

RTK allows to obtain a precise satellite positioning by using the data acquired in the field from GNSS receiver and the data by the GNSS network reference stations. All three receivers used for this test can provide internal real time solutions by using corrections through NTRIP server/caster/clients from an external CORS reference station. Networked Transport of RTCM via Internet Protocol (NTRIP) is a protocol for streaming of Differential GPS (DGPS) or RTK correction data through the internet using TCP/IP. The NTRIP server sends out the corrections data to an NTRIP caster with very low latency and the NTRIP client receives it. To get internet service, a cell phone network having a good and reliable coverage in the test area was used. SPIN GNSS network, an interregional GNSS Positioning Service of the Piemonte and Lombardia regions of Italy (http://www.spingnss.it/spiderweb/frmIndex.aspx) (SPIN GNSS 2018), was used to get base corrections with both constellations GPS and GLONASS. SPIN GNSS network is an indispensable infrastructure to support satellite measurements directly in the territory, in respect of well-known precision and linked to the European Geodetic Reference System ETRS89-ETRF2000 (Altamimi 2010). The setup was different for each GNSS receiver to get corrections from the base station. Tersus-BX306 GNSS receiver does not support built-in NTRIP client feature so a Bluetooth module and a smartphone was used for this purpose. NTRIP client app was installed on the smartphone which allowed to report the location manually or auto-matically. In automatic mode, the client reads the National Marine Electronics Asso-ciation (NMEA) GGA data from the receiver and sends it to the NTRIP caster, therefore the receiver has to output NMEA GGA sentences accordingly. Alternatively, in case of failure to report the user location, latitude and longitude can be sent manually to the NTRIP caster. For Swift GNSS receiver, the NTRIP caster streamed the base station data to the STRSVR application of the RTKLIB software, which is streamed to the receiver via an USB port, where it is combined with the raw receiver observations to create an internal RTK solution.

To control the Reach RTK module, a web-based app ReachView was installed on the smartphone. It can work on any device with a browser without an internet con-nection. ReachView is hosted on the Reach receiver itself and can be accessed via Wi-Fi connection, which makes it compatible with any operating system like Windows, Linux, Android etc. ReachView supports built-in NTRIP feature to transfer GNSS corrections over Internet and for this purpose any public service or private caster can be used.

After the collection of real time solutions computed by internal RTK engines of Piksi multi, Emlid Reach and Tersus GNSS receivers, solutions were plotted in Google Earth as shown in Fig. 3. The Tersus GNSS manufacturer claims a 60 s time to first fix which it achieves easily even with the longer baseline most of the time, performing better than the Piksi Multi and Emlid Reach GNSS receivers which often took 90 s or more to find its first fix solution. The Cargo bike was moved around the test site in a loop for a period of 8–10 min to perform kinematic positioning.

In order to evaluate the quality of positioning, standard deviation has been con-sidered, comparing the solutions with respect to the reference trajectory obtained in an independent way (using traditional topographic surveys). The mean, maximum and minimum standard deviation was analyzed and computed for all three GNSS receivers, in North, East and Up coordinates as shown in Fig. 4.

Fig. 3. RTK solutions from all 3 GNSS receivers plotted on Google Earth.

The mean standard deviations of North, East and Up components for both dual frequency GNSS receivers are better than the single frequency GNSS receiver. Tersus BX-306 has the best precision in RTK positioning as the mean standard deviation values are around 1–3 cm for horizontal whereas around 8 cm for vertical component. Even if the data was collected in a harsh urban environment with tall buildings, trees and low visibility of sky, the precision of real-time solutions of both single and dual frequency GNSS are still in centimeters.

In the RTK positioning, one of the key point to obtain the best accuracy is to fix the carrier phase ambiguities to integer numbers. This is possible only considering a statistical method also known as ratio test (Cina et al. 2014a, b). High values of ratio, e.g. greater than 3, indicates that the chosen solution is at least 3 times better than the next most likely solution and the solution can be declared as "fixed"; otherwise, if the value of ratio is between 0 and 3 then the solution will be defined as "float". Figure 5 shows the percentage of Fix, Float and Single (no differential corrections are applied) solutions during the RTK positioning test.

As it can be observed from Fig. 5 that the Piksi Multi receiver was able to fix the ambiguity phase at 96% and Tersus BX-306 at 86% of the epochs. Emlid reach had the minimum percentage (2%) of fix solutions in real time as it was single frequency GNSS receiver and was not able to remove ionospheric errors like other two dual frequency receivers.

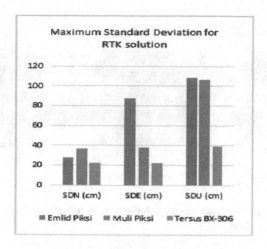

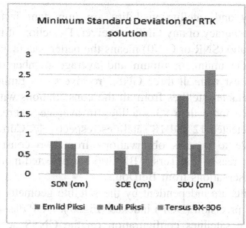

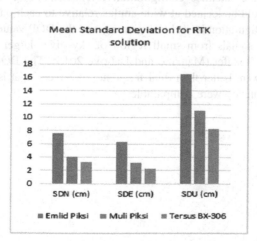

Fig. 4. Maximum, minimum and mean standard deviation values with RTK solutions obtained from GNSS receivers.

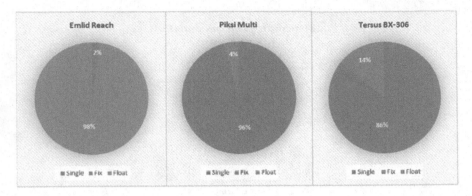

Fig. 5. Percentage fix, float and single solutions with GNSS receivers using continuous ambiguity resolution method.

Satellite geometry and satellite visibility are important factors that plays an important role in the accuracy of any GNSS receiver. Detection of more satellites with good signal to noise ratio (SNR or C/N0) means the better accuracy in the positioning. Figure 6 shows the maximum, minimum and average number of satellites visible during the kinematic test with all three GNSS receivers. As Emlid reach can detect satellites from all available satellites from all the constellations with single frequency only so it has detected more than 23 satellites in average whereas Piksi Multi and Tersus BX-306 has detected 12 and 18 satellites respectively. Currently, the firmware of Piksi Multi is able to process observations from two constellations GPS and GLONASS, that is the reason that Tersus BX-306 has detected more satellites because it can also process observations from BeiDou.

The obtained results are independent by the satellite geometry distribution, represented by Dilution of precision (DOP) indexes (Fig. 7). DOP describes the geometric strength of the visible satellites configuration on the GNSS accuracy. Ideally, the visible satellites should be located at wide angles relative to each other. The geometry of such satellite configuration is said to be strong and the DOP values are low (Tahsin et al. 2015). GNSS signals from small region of sky gives larger DOP values, and position accuracy will suffer (Manzino and Dabove 2013). The DOP values of single frequency receiver were better than dual frequency receivers, that is why accuracy of single and dual frequency were comparable.

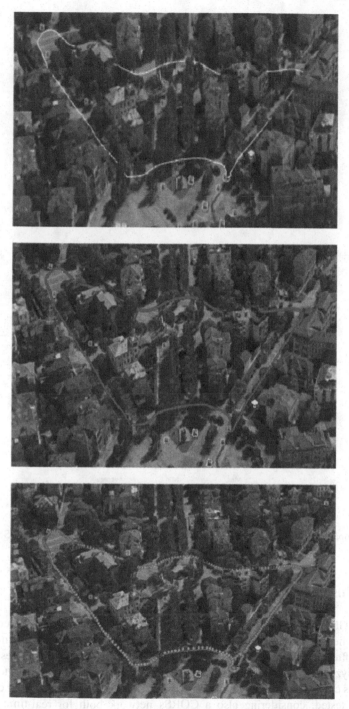

Fig. 6. RTK solutions from all 3 GNSS receivers plotted on google earth (Tersus RTK solution upward, Piksi RTK solution in centre, Emlid Reach RTK solution below).

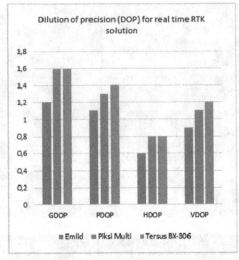

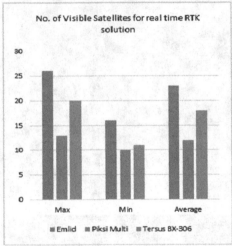

Fig. 7. Comparison of DOP (top) and Satellites Visibility (bottom) from three GNSS Receivers for RTK test.

4   Conclusions

Nowadays GNSS positioning is available almost everywhere and it is required for many application fields such as precise agriculture, mobile mapping and landslide monitoring. With the diffusion of multi-frequency GNSS mass-market devices, it is interesting to test and to analyze their performances in terms of accuracy, precision and use towards the applications cited. Three different receivers that are able to apply differential corrections have been tested, considering also a CORSs network both for real-time and post-processing applications. In the first case the differential corrections have been requested in order to perform a fixed positioning, trying to reach an accuracy of few cm in real-time, while in the latter case raw data (carrier-phase, pseudoranges and Doppler measurements) have been collected and stored in their internal memory or an external device (i.e. laptop). Different tests have been carried out considering the kinematic approach: a cargo bike has been used to perform a dynamic test in a sub-urban area of the Turin (Italy) road network. All tests have been supported by the services provided by a CORSs network: considering the NRTK corrections the mean standard deviation for Emlid Reach, Piksi Multi and Tersus GNSS receivers were 17, 11 and 8 cm respectively for vertical component and in the range of 2–3 cm for both dual frequency and 5–8 cm for single frequency GNSS receivers if the horizontal standard deviations is considered. About the percentage of FIX solutions, the range varies from about 2% up to 96% in function of the ambiguity resolution method considered for NRTK positioning. In this case, it is possible so conclude that the "Fix and hold" procedure is very useful for static surveys, because it allows to have a better estimation of the ambiguities, while for kinematic purposes it is preferable to consider the "continuous" method, because it allows to reduce the possibility to have a "false fixing". These methods do not depend from the receiver and kind of frequencies considered. This work has also showed that under suitable conditions, single-frequency mass-market GNSS sensors could be considered as valid alternative to more expensive receivers, for many environmental applications.

Acknowledgements. The authors would like to thank prof. Horea Bendea for his contribution to assembling the instruments on Cargo bike and Ansar Abdul Jabbar for helping during data collection.

References

Altamimi, Z.: ITRF2008 and transformation to ETRF2000. In: EUREF Symposium (2010)

Carcanague, S., Julien, O., Vigneau, W., Macabiau, C.: Low-cost single-frequency GPS/GLONASS RTK for road users. In Proceedings of the ION 2013 Pacific PNT Meeting, Honolulu, HI, USA, 23–25 April 2013; pp. 168–184 (2013)

Cina, A., Dabove, P., Manzino, A., Piras, M.: Network real time kinematic (NRTK) positioning-description, architectures and performances. In: Satellite Positioning-Methods, Models and Applications, pp. 23–45. InTech Publishing (2014)

Cina, A., Dabove, P., Manzino, A.M., Piras, M.: Augmented positioning with CORSs network services using GNSS mass-market receivers. In: 2014 IEEE/ION Position, Location and Navigation Symposium-PLANS 2014, pp. 359–366. IEEE (2014)

Dabove, P., Cina, A., Manzino, A.M.: Single-frequency receivers as permanent stations in GNSS networks: precision and accuracy of positioning in mixed networks. In: Cefalo, R., Zieliński, J., Barbarella, M. (eds.) New Advanced GNSS and 3D Spatial Techniques. LNGC. Springer, Cham (2018). https://doi.org/10.1007/978-3-319-56218-6_8

Dabove, P., Manzino, A.M., Taglioretti, C.: GNSS network products for post-processing positioning: limitations and peculiarities. Appl. Geomat. **6**(1), 27–36 (2014). https://doi.org/10.1007/s12518-014-0122-3

Dvorkin, V., Karutin, S.: GLONASS: Current Status and Perspectives. In Proceedings of the 3rd ALLSAT Open Conference, Hannover, Germany, 22 June 2006

He, H., Li, J., Yang, Y., Xu, J., Guo, H., Wang, A.: Performance assessment of single- and dual-frequency BeiDou/GPS single-epoch kinematic positioning. GPS Solut. **18**(3), 393–403 (2014)

Jackson, J., Davis, B., Gebre-Egziabher, D.: A performance assessment of low-cost RTK GNSS receivers. In: 2018 IEEE/ION Position, Location and Navigation Symposium (PLANS), Monterey, CA, 2018, pp. 642–649 (2018)

Li, T., Zhang, H., Niu, X., Gao, Z.: Tightly-coupled integration of Multi-GNSS single-frequency RTK and MEMS-IMU for enhanced positioning performance. Sensors 17, 2462 (2017)

Low, Z.N., Law, C.L.: Improving time to first fix for GPS receivers, 07 April 2015

Manurung, P., Pramujo, H., Manurung, J.B.: Development of GNSS receiver for mobile CORS with RTK correction services using cloud server. E3S Web Conf. 94, 01010 (2019)

Manzino, A.M., Dabove, P.: Quality control of the NRTK positioning with mass-market receivers. In: Global Positioning Systems: Signal Structure, Applications and Sources of Error and Biases, pp. 17–40 (2013)

Montenbruck, O., et al.: IGS-MGEX: Preparing the ground for multi-constellation GNSS science. Inside GNSS 9, 42–49 (2014)

Odolinski, R., Teunissen, P.J.G.: Low-cost, high-precision, single-frequency GPS–BDS RTK positioning. GPS Solut. 21(3), 1315–1330 (2017). https://doi.org/10.1007/s10291-017-0613-x

Odolinski, R., Teunissen, P.J.G., Odijk, D.: Combined BDS, Galileo, QZSS and GPS single-frequency RTK. GPS Solut. 19(1), 151–163 (2014). https://doi.org/10.1007/s10291-014-0376-6

RTKLIB. http://www.rtklib.com/. Accessed 15 May 2018

Skournetou, D., Lohan, E.-S.: Comparison of single and dual frequency GNSS receivers in the presence of ionospheric and multipath errors. In: Giambene, G., Sacchi, C. (eds.) PSATS 2011. LNICST, vol. 71, pp. 402–410. Springer, Heidelberg (2011). https://doi.org/10.1007/978-3-642-23825-3_35

SPIN GNSS Network. https://www.spingnss.it/. Accessed 15 May 2018)

Sridhara, H.S., Kubo, N., Kikuchi, R. Single-frequency multi-GNSS RTK positioning for moving platform. In Proceedings of the 2015 International Technical Meeting of the Institute of Navigation, pp. 26–28 (2015)

Tahsin, M., Sultana, S., Reza, T., Hossam-E-Haider, M.: Analysis of DOP and its preciseness in GNSS position estimation. In 2015 International Conference on Electrical Engineering and Information Communication Technology (ICEEICT), pp. 1–6. IEEE (2015)

Takac, F., Hilker, C., Kotthoff, H., Richter, B.: Combining measurements from multiple global navigation satellite systems for RTK applications. In Proceedings of International Symposium on GPS/GNSS, Hong Kong, China, 8–10 December 2005 (2005)

Takac, F., Walford, J.: Leica system 1200—high performance GNSS technology for RTK applications. In: Proceedings of the 19th International Technical Meeting of the Satellite Division of the Institute of Navigation (ION GNSS 2006), Fort Worth, TX, 26–29 September 2006, pp. 217–225 (2006)

Teunissen, P.J.G., Odolinski, R., Odijk, D.: Instantaneous BeiDou + GPS RTK positioning with high cut-off elevation angles. J. Geodesy 88(4), 335–350 (2013). https://doi.org/10.1007/s00190-013-0686-4

Valeev, V.G.. Kornilov, I.N., Ivanov, V.E.: Improving the accuracy of positioning by GNSS signals at regional level. In: 24th International Crimean Conference Microwave & Telecommunication Technology, 7–13 September 2014 (2014)

Yamamoto, H., Kawasaki, K., Takeuchi, K., Hashimoto, T., Nakao, H.: Effects of current collection noise and obstruction in running on GPS signal reception. In: 8th World Congress on Railway Research, 18–22 May 2008 (2008)

Zhang, Y., et al.: Static and kinematic positioning performance of a low-cost real-time kinematic navigation system module. Adv. Space Res. 63(9), 3029–3042 (2019)

Geomatics for Port Safety and Security

M. Soldani[✉] [ID]

Istituto Nazionale di Geofisica e Vulcanologia, Via di Vigna Murata 605,
00143 Rome, Italy
maurizio.soldani@ingv.it

Abstract. This work shows the results achieved using two prototypes of monitoring and processing systems that are being developed with the aim of increasing the safety and the security in harbours.

The first one has been designed to help port communities (port authorities, pilots) to manage harbour waterside (optimization of ship's navigation and cargo, dock performances, boat moorings, refloating of stranded ships, water quality control). Starting from monitoring the sea level and meteorological parameters in harbours, it can help port communities decide, e.g., when a ship with a certain draft can enter or leave the port, or which the best route to follow is (port safety).

The second system, instead, deals with the monitoring of the Earth's magnetic field in port areas for harbour protection purposes, in particular to detect the possible presence of underwater intruders, e.g. divers swimming in restricted areas (port security).

The processing procedures of both systems are based not on commercial software, but on applications under development by the research team the author belongs to, by using C# and C++ languages and Matlab environment.

Keywords: Port navigation safety · Harbour protection · Underwater detection systems

1 Introduction

During the last years, "anomalous" tidal fluctuations (so-called meteorological tides) have been observed in several harbours, due to hydrostatic compensation following changes in atmosphere weight. A multi-year statistical analysis carried out in Italian ports allowed to obtain, port by port, an estimate of the hydro-barometric transfer factor J_{ph}, that represents the Newtonian correlation between the atmospheric pressure gradient Δp and the consequent sea level variation Δh.

The knowledge of J_{ph} is very useful in harbour waterside management (optimization of ship navigation, dock performance, boats mooring and refloating of stranded ships).

The effects of pressure variations on water depth have been applied to bathymetric maps in several harbours: an expected change of atmospheric pressure can be converted, through J_{ph}, into an expected water depth variation and then into a new bathymetric map. To automate this, a software tool is being developed for dynamic updating bathymetric maps in ports, depending on the sea level measured in real time or on the expected atmospheric pressure. Two threshold levels variable ship by ship, depending on vessel draft, divide the harbour basin into three zones characterized by

C. Parente et al. (Eds.): R3GEO 2019, CCIS 1246, pp. 91–102, 2020.
https://doi.org/10.1007/978-3-030-62800-0_8

different colours (green, yellow and red) that indicate three water depth ranges (respectively deep or allowed for that vessel, shallow or warning, forbidden). By varying the sea level, an area that initially was allowed (green), can become a warning (yellow) or prohibited area (red): this implements what is called a "virtual traffic light" customized for each ship. It is also possible to analyze past events, using sea level measurements acquired during a certain time interval and stored in files.

After this, the paper shows results obtained during several tests performed to develop an anti-intrusion undersea system based on a magnetometer self-informed array; the aim is to detect the presence of underwater threats, such as terrorist divers, in harbours; during tests, divers performed approach runs above the array. The main purpose of magnetic system is to fill the gaps of sonar systems in the boundary of water volume to be controlled (sea bed, docks,...), where acoustic performances deteriorate. Experiments took place in port protection scenarios, characterized by a medium-high environmental magnetic noise that can hide the diver signal (labile, quasi-point-like and kinetic source). The system has two inputs: the environmental magnetic noise and a signal composed by the same noise superimposed on the target magnetic signal; wavelength of diver signal is inside the noise band, therefore frequency filtering is inadequate to avoid noise. So, the system uses the noise as filter for the composed signal to extract the target signal and detect the threat presence; the effectiveness of the procedure is related to the positions of magnetometers: sensors must be so close that they measure the same noise and so far away that only one sensor measures the target signal. To generate alarms when a threat is detected, it has been developed a real-time software application that processes data and turns on a red light and a beep sound when a magnetic anomaly is identified in a certain harbour location.

2   System for Port Navigation Safety

2.1   Meteorological Tides

Tides in harbours are the result of overlapping of different contributions, among which, in Italian ports, the main ones are usually due to the astronomical components (such as the diurnal and semidiurnal ones). While these tidal components are well-known, the significant contribution due to atmospheric pressure variations in ports (the so-called meteorological tide or "inverted barometer" effect when an increase in atmospheric pressure causes a decrease in sea level and vice versa) is currently not foreseeable by deterministic methods (Dobslaw and Thomas 2005; el-Gindy and Eid 1990; Garrett and Majaess 1984; Garrett and Toulany 1982; Le Traon and Gauzelin 1997; Ponte and Gaspar 1999; Tsimplis 1995; Tsimplis and Vlahakis 1994; Wunsch and Stammer 1997).

Futhermore, in the last ten years some anomalous tidal fluctuations have been observed in Italian ports ([1]).

Then, a multi-year study carried out in several ports allowed us to evaluate the hydro-barometric transfer factor J_{ph} from variations of atmospheric pressure

---

[1] data have been measured by means of meteo-mareographic stations belonging to Italian National Tide-gauge Network, managed by ISPRA - Italian Institute for Environmental Protection and Research

(characterized by low-frequency spectral components) to consequent sea level slow fluctuations (Newtonian correlation between atmospheric weight variations and sea level adjustments due to the hydrostatic compensation) (Allen and Denbo 1984; Faggioni, et al. 2013; Merriam 1992).

Many occurrences of this phenomenon have been analysed and for each of them the value of the hydro-barometric transfer factor has been calculated (after a Low Pass filtering to remove high frequency sea level oscillations related to astronomical tides) as:

$$J_{ph} = \Delta h / \Delta p \tag{1}$$

where:

J_{ph} = hydro-barometric transfer factor [cm*hPa^{-1}]
Δh= low-frequency variation of sea level [cm]
Δp = gradient of atmospheric pressure [hPa].

A multi-year statistical analysis performed on all the events that have occurred in several Italian harbours allowed to obtain, for each port, an estimate of the J_{ph} factor. It often assumes, in many ports, values even double compared to the typical 1 [cm*hPa^{-1}] of the offshore. In fact, harbours can be considered as semi-constrained basins that as such amplify the phenomenon just described, because the horizontal component of compensation displacement is inhibited towards the coastline (Faggioni, et al. 2006).

Figure 1 and 2 show, respectively, the atmospheric pressure and the sea level acquired in La Spezia harbour (Italy) between 2 and 9 April 2006. Date is referred to Universal Time Coordinates, sea level to 0 IGM (Italian Geographic Military Institute).

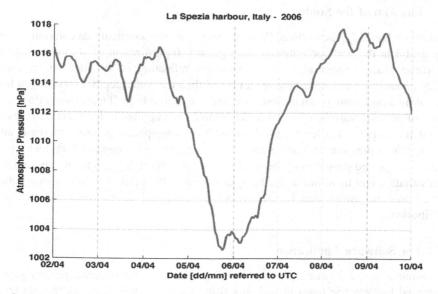

Fig. 1. Atmospheric pressure recorded by ISPRA meteo-mareographic station located in La Spezia harbour (Italy) between 2 and 9 April 2006.

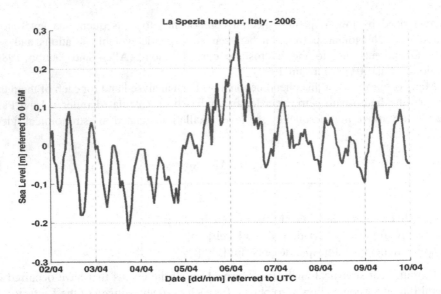

Fig. 2. Sea level recorded by ISPRA meteo-mareographic station located in La Spezia harbour (Italy) between 2 and 9 April 2006.

In this example, a decrease of nearly 15 [hPa] in atmospheric pressure induces an increase of nearly 30 [cm] in low-frequency sea level (high meteorological tide); other possible causes of the phenomenon were absent during the measurement period (e.g. wind effect or storm surges).

2.2   The Aim of the Study

The knowledge of J_{ph} factor (in addition, of course, to astronomical tide components) is very useful in the harbour waterside management (optimization of ship's navigation and cargo, dock performances, boat moorings, refloating of stranded ships, water quality control, …) to forecast the sea level and then the water depth. Obviously, a low tide within a port hinders navigation; vice versa, a high tide facilitates navigation. The effects of pressure variations on water depth have been applied to bathymetric maps in several Italian ports: sea level goes down with an atmospheric pressure increase, and goes up with a pressure decrease; then, pressure variations change the bathymetry of a basin. An expected pressure change can be converted, through J_{ph}, into an expected sea level variation and then into a new bathymetric map. In addition to this, astronomical tide components must then be added to (or subtracted from) the meteorological contribution.

2.3   The Software Application

To automate this, a software program is being developed for dynamic updating geo-referenced bathymetric maps in harbours (Fig. 3 and 4), depending on the sea level measured in real time by means of mareographic stations (or read from files if the analysis is referred to past events), or on the expected atmospheric pressure (measured by barometers and then converted into sea level by means of J_{ph}). This is being done to provide a useful tool to the port community.

Two threshold levels variable ship by ship, depending on vessel draft, divide the bathymetric map of the harbour basin into three zones characterized by different colours (green, yellow and red); these colours indicate three water depth ranges (respectively deep or allowed for that vessel, shallow or warning, forbidden).

For example, for a ship with a draft of 9 [m], we could consider as prohibited (red) the areas with depth less than 9 [m], warning areas (yellow) those in which the depth is between 9 and 12 [m], and allowed areas (green) those where the depth is greater than 12 [m]; so, thresholds could be set at 9 and 12 [m], respectively.

After this, sea level measurements coming from mareographic stations can be used from the software to update the bathymetry and, consequently, to refresh the division of the map into green, yellow and red zones based on the same threshold levels (for the same ship, they remain constant at 9 and 12 [m]).

Therefore, by varying the sea level, an area that initially was allowed (green), can become a warning (yellow) or prohibited area (red) for that vessel: this implements what is called a "virtual traffic light" customized for each ship.

In the dynamic bathymetric map of the port of Livorno (area of about 4.5 [km^2]) shown in Fig. 3 and 4 (thresholds 9 and 12 [m], respectively), the same point (UTM coordinates: easting 604625 [m], northing 4822760 [m], at the center of the white circle) changes from green to yellow light. In fact, its depth decreases from 12.44 to 11.71 [m], due to sea level variation from 13/01/2017 10:10.00 UTC to 14/01/2017 01:30.00 UTC; more generally, the "green channel" inside the white circle becomes narrower.

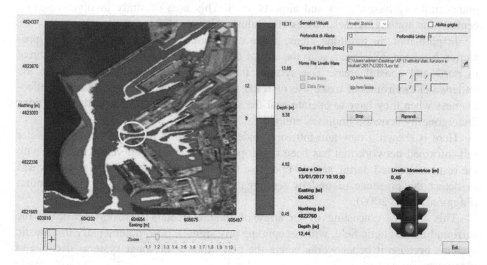

Fig. 3. Dynamic bathymetric map in the port of Livorno (thresholds 9 and 12 [m], respectively) on 13/01/2017 at 10:10.00 UTC.

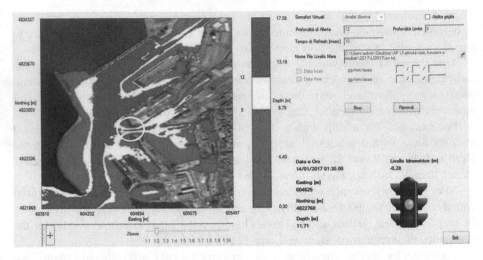

Fig. 4. Dynamic bathymetric map in the port of Livorno (thresholds 9 and 12 [m], respectively) on 14/01/2017 at 01:30.00 UTC.

3 System for Harbour Protection

3.1 The Context

Following the terrorist events that characterized the beginning of this millennium, a technological research topic was born; its aim is to develop systems to defend the so-called critical infrastructures, that are those considered most at risk of attacks (industrial plants, military bases, ports and airports, etc.). This area of study involves research centers, institutions, armies, navies and industries from all over the world.

In particular, in maritime areas, a line of research named harbour (or port) protection has been developed, with the aim of detecting the possible presence of a threat in ports and coastal areas. The systems traditionally used for this purpose in the underwater environment make use of sonar devices, which however lose their effectiveness when they have to operate near the seabed or the docks, due to the reflections undergone by acoustic impulses emitted.

Here is shown a new anti-intrusion underwater system based on a magnetometer self-informed network that has been developed in the last fifteen years, together with the results obtained during several operative tests performed (the goal of the trials was to detect the presence of underwater threats, such as terrorist divers, in harbours) (Faggioni, et al. 2009).

This system, consisting of an array of magnetometers (sensors measuring the surrounding magnetic field, without emitting any signal), is complementary to acoustic systems because it better works where the performance of sonar systems decay, and vice versa.

The main purpose of the magnetic system is therefore to fill the gaps of classical sonar systems, whose performances deteriorate, due to reflections and attenuations, in the boundary of the volume of water to be controlled (sea bed, docks,…).

The magnetic system is usually deployed on the seabed and is able to identify, for example, the presence of a diver swimming near the sensors, distinguishing the signal generated by the diver's equipment ("anomaly") from the environmental magnetic noise ("background") (Faggioni, et al. 2018).

3.2   The Magnetic System

The experiments took place in port protection scenarios, characterized by medium-high environmental noise with a relevant human origin magnetic noise component. Divers performed approach runs near the magnetic underwater array.

Divers are labile, quasi-point-like and kinetic sources: therefore, a processing technique has been developed based on a differential approach to detect labile signals in a high noise environment. In fact, filtering techniques such as those based on the Fourier Transform are inadequate because the frequencies of diver signals (singularities) are inside the noise band, and signal amplitudes are comparable with the noise ones.

Then, the system has two different input signals: the magnetic background field (natural plus artificial) and a signal composed by the same magnetic background field superimposed on the target magnetic signature. The system uses the first signal (background field) as filter for the second one (background field plus the target signature) to detect the target presence by means of a differential technique (Faggioni, et al. 2010). The effectiveness of the procedure is related to the position of magnetic field observation points (reference devices and sentinel device). Sensors must obtain correlation in the noise observations (all the sensors record the same background field, in accordance with the so-called space stability of the magnetic noise) and de-correlations in the target signal observations (only one sensor records the target signature) (Bartels et al. 1992; Cafarella et al. 1992; Chapman 1918; Georgieva et al. 2013; Meloni, et al. 2007).

Recently, operational tests were carried out in the Gulf of La Spezia (Italy). The trials have involved the deployment of five magnetometers. Figure 5 shows the signals generated by a diver equipped with a steel tank (detectable by magnetic sensors). The passage of the diver has been detected by each magnetometer while the diver was swimming forth and back along the array.

The system has proved able also to detect the presence of much weaker magnetic sources, as in the case shown in Fig. 6, where the diver has been equipped with an aluminium tank.

In this case, the pulses in the red ovals have been classified as background noise because all five magnetometers have been "disturbed" in the same way (no alarm). On the contrary, the green pulse in the blue oval has been detected and signaled as an alarm because it has been measured by a single magnetometer and therefore was considered different from the background noise (anomaly).

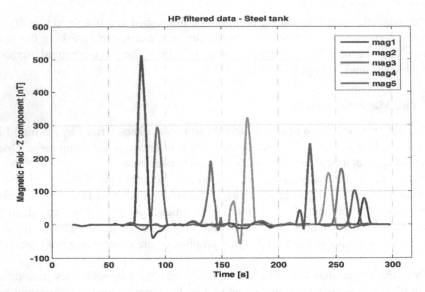

Fig. 5. Signals generated by a diver equipped with a steel tank (after a filtering that eliminates DC component).

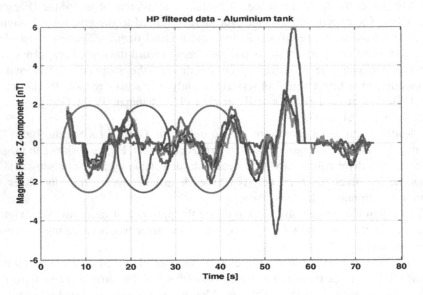

Fig. 6. Signals generated by a diver equipped with an aluminium tank (after a filtering that eliminates DC component).

3.3   The Software Application

To generate alarms when a target is detected, a software program has been developed that processes in real time data acquired by all the magnetometers and turns on a red light and a beep sound when a magnetic anomaly is identified; sensors not alarmed remain green and silent.

Each signal acquired by the sensors is compared with those recorded by all the other magnetometers, to remove environmental background field and detect anomalies generated by the passages of the diver (Telford, et al. 1990; Kanasewich 1981; Faggioni 2018).

Figure 7 shows alarms generated while a diver was crossing the barrier swimming first above the sensors n. 1 and then halfway between n. 2 and n. 3.

In case of multisensorial harbour protection (appropriately integrated systems so that the shadow areas of each one are filled by others), each alarm must be sent to a control station, which collects the alarms received by all the systems employed (e.g. magnetic, acoustic, optical, infrared, electrical, radar, etc.).

The geographic coordinates where each sensor was placed are well-known, so each alarm is georeferenced and can be indicated by a red point on a common picture representing the map of the port, as shown in Fig. 8 and Fig. 9 (sea trial performed in La Spezia harbour, Italy). The yellow line represents the differential GNSS/GPS track of the diver, the red point is the position of the sensor sending alarm, while the green points indicate sensors not alarmed; to record its position, the diver was swimming towing a small buoy with a GNSS/GPS logger; after this, his track was downloaded in post-processing phase.

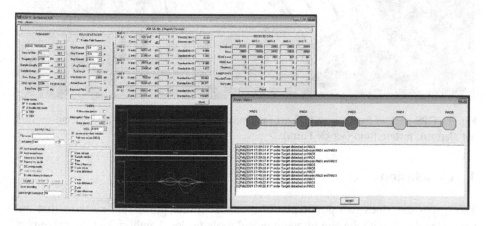

Fig. 7. Alarms generated by a diver.

Fig. 8. Map of La Spezia harbour, Italy (picture from Google Earth).

Fig. 9. GPS track of the diver and array of magnetometers (red: sensor alarmed, green: sensors not alarmed; picture from Google Earth).

4   Conclusions

This paper describes two prototypes of monitoring and processing systems that are being developed with the aim of being useful tools for local authorities to manage port safety and security.

Firstly, the paper highlights the importance of analysis of hydro-barometric inversion for harbour safety. Its applications for harbour waterside management allow us, for example, to improve the effectiveness in maritime works, to help port authorities and pilots decide which the ideal route to follow is for a certain ship, and to optimize ship navigation, dock performance, boats mooring and refloating of stranded ships.

Then, it is shown how experimental tests carried out on the magnetic detection system, in undersea environments with high magnetic noise, has provided extremely positive operational results in detecting intruders transiting in its proximity, in the case of divers equipped both with steel and aluminium tanks. In the context of antiterrorism systems for harbour protection, the magnetic detection system is required to support the acoustic component in peripheral acoustic shadow zones close to the seabed, docks and so on.

In a hypothetical operational scenario, both systems could be integrated in a control room managed by a local authority, to provide useful support to make the best decisions in order to ensure safety and security for the community. A common picture representing the map of the port could show both the hypothetical routes that an incoming/outgoing vessel should follow based on its draft ("virtual traffic light"), and any alarms generated by the passage of an intruder detected by the magnetic system (or by acoustic, optical, infrared, electrical, radar, systems in case of multisensorial harbour protection).

Acknowledgements. The author wishes to thank ISPRA for providing meteo-mareographic data acquired in Italian harbours, in particular in La Spezia and Livorno. These studies were possible thanks to funding from the Italian Ministry of Defence, European Defence Agency (for harbour protection) and several Italian Port Authorities (for port navigation safety), in particular Port Authority of Livorno. He also thanks: Dr. O. Faggioni for its cooperation in these studies; Wass SpA (now Leonardo SpA) and SkyTech Srl for their collaboration in the development of the magnetic system; Dr. D. Leoncini for his contribution in software applications development; Italian Navy for concession of areas, men and naval vehicles to perform several sea trials.

The author also thanks the three anonymous reviewers, whose comments and suggestions helped improve this work.

Part of these activities was conducted when the author was at OGS – National Institute of Oceanography and Applied Geophysics (Trieste, Italy).

References

Allen, J.S., Denbo, D.W.: Statistical characteristics of the large-scale response of coastal sea level to atmospheric forcing. J. Phys. Oceanogr. **14**, 1079–1094 (1984)

Bartels, J., Heck, N.H., Johnston, H.F.: The three-hour-range index measuring geomagnetic activity. Terr. Magn. Atmos. Electr. **44**(4), 411–454 (1992)

Cafarella, L., De Santis, A., Meloni, A.: Secular variation in Italy from historical geomagnetic field measurements. Phys. Earth Planet. Inter. **73**, 206–221 (1992)

Chapman, S.: The diurnal changes of the Earth's magnetism. Observatory **41**, 52–60 (1918)

Dobslaw, H., Thomas, M.: Atmospheric induced oceanic tides from ECMWF forecasts. Geophys. Res. Lett. **32**(10), L10615 (2005)

el-Gindy, A.A.H., Eid, F.M.: Long-term variations of monthly mean sea level and its relation to atmospheric pressure in the Mediterranean Sea. Int. Hydrogr. Rev. **67**(1), 147–159 (1990)

Garrett, C., Majaess, F.: Nonisostatic response of sea level to atmospheric pressure in the Eastern Mediterranean. J. Phys. Oceanogr. **14**, 656–665 (1984)

Garrett, C., Toulany, B.: Sea level variability due to meteorological forcing in the northeast Gulf of St Lawrence. J. Geophys. Res. **87**(C3), 1968–1978 (1982)

Faggioni, O.: The Fourier notation of the geomagnetic signals informative parameters. J. Signal Inf. Process. **9**, 153–166 (2018)

Faggioni, O., et al.: The Newtonian approach in meteorological tide waves forecasting: preliminary observations in the East Ligurian harbours. Ann. Geophys. **49**(6), 1177–1187 (2006)

Faggioni, O., Soldani, M., Cozzani, G., Zunino, R.: Informative signal analysis: metrology of the underwater geomagnetic singularities in low-density ionic solution (sea water). J. Signal Inf. Process. **9**, 1–23 (2018)

Faggioni, O., Soldani, M., Gabellone, A., Hollett, R.D., Kessel, R.T.: Undersea harbour defence: a new choice in magnetic networks. J. Appl. Geophys. **72**(1), 46–56 (2010)

Faggioni, O., Soldani, M., Leoncini, D.A.: Metrological analysis of geopotential gravity field for harbor waterside management and water quality control. Int. J. Geophys. **2013**-Special Issue on Geophysical Methods for Environmental Studies, 12 pp. (2013)

Faggioni, O., Soldani, M., Leoncini, D., Gabellone, A., Maggiani, P.V.: Time domain performances analysis of underwater magnetic SIMAN Systems for port protection. J. Inf. Assur. Secur. **4**(6)-Special Issue on Information Assurance and Data Security, 538–545 (2009)

Georgieva, K., Kirov, B., Nagovitsyn, Yu A.: Long-term variations of solar magnetic fields derived from geomagnetic data. Geomagnet. Aeron. **53**(7), 852–856 (2013). https://doi.org/10.1134/S0016793213070062

Kanasewich, E.R.: Time Sequence Analysis in Geophysics. University of Alberta, Edmonton (1981)

Le Traon, P.-Y., Gauzelin, P.: Response of the Mediterranean mean sea level to atmospheric pressure forcing. J. Geophys. Res. **102**(C1), 973–984 (1997)

Meloni, A., et al.: Systematic magnetic observations in Italy. Publ. Inst. Geophys. Polish Acad. Sci. **C-99**(398), 8 pp. (2007)

Merriam, J.B.: Atmospheric pressure and gravity. Geophys. J. Int. **109**(3), 488–500 (1992)

Ponte, R.M., Gaspar, P.: Regional analysis of the inverted barometer effect over the global ocean using TOPEX/POSEIDON data and model results. J. Geophys. Res. **104**(C7), 15587–15601 (1999)

Telford, W.M., Geldart, P., Sheriff, R.E.: Applied Geophysics. Second edition. Cambridge University Press, New York (1990)

Tsimplis, M.N.: The response of sea level to atmospheric forcing in the Mediterranean. J. Coast. Res. **11**(4), 1309–1321 (1995)

Tsimplis, M.N., Vlahakis, G.N.: Meteorological forcing and sea level variability in the Aegean Sea. J. Geophys. Res. **99**(C5), 9879–9890 (1994)

Wunsch, C., Stammer, D.: Atmospheric loading and the oceanic "inverted barometer" effect. Rev. Geophys. **35**(1), 79–107 (1997)

A Preliminary Study on Attitude Measurement Systems Based on Low Cost Sensors

Fabiana Di Ciaccio$^{(\boxtimes)}$ ⓘ, Salvatore Gaglione ⓘ,
and Salvatore Troisi ⓘ

Department of Sciences and Technologies, Parthenope University of Naples,
80143 Naples, Italy
{fabiana.diciaccio, salvatore.gaglione,
salvatore.troisi}@uniparthenope.it

Abstract. The increasingly use of Autonomous Underwater Vehicles (AUVs) in several context led to a rapid development and enhancement of their technologies, allowing the automatization of many tasks. One of the most challenging tasks of AUVs still remains their robust positioning and navigation, since classical global positioning techniques are generally not available for their operations. Inertial Navigation System (INS) methods provide the vehicle current position and orientation integrating data acquired by the internal accelerometer and gyroscope. This system has the advantage of not needing to either send or receive signals from other systems; however, among the errors the sensors are mainly affected by, the most critical one is related to their drift, which makes the position error growing over time. The attenuation of the effect of these problematics is generally achieved combining different positioning methods, as for example acoustic- or geophysical-based ones. An accurate estimation of the device orientation is anyway necessary to get satisfying results in terms of position and autonomous navigation. In this paper, a preliminary study on the use of smartphone low-cost sensors to perform attitude estimation is presented. With the final aim of developing a cheaper and more accessible underwater positioning system, a first analysis is conducted to verify the accuracy of the attitude angles obtained by the integration of smartphone data acquired in different operative settings. Different filtering methods will be employed.

Keywords: Orientation estimation · Low-cost sensors · Filtering methods

1 Introduction

AUVs have demonstrated versatile capabilities to conduct missions in several fields, as for example oceanographic research, surveillance and defense, demining, underwater energy development, bathymetric data collection, etc., for which high accuracy of measured data is required. Vehicles autonomy stands as one of the most important and at the same time critical point for their development and usage: in the last years, remarkable results have been reached in the field, and the technological development is continuously growing to enhance the vehicles performances.

© Springer Nature Switzerland AG 2020
C. Parente et al. (Eds.): R3GEO 2019, CCIS 1246, pp. 103–115, 2020.
https://doi.org/10.1007/978-3-030-62800-0_9

Being localization and navigation a fundamental part of the autonomy of the AUV, optimizing the algorithms and techniques underlying these processes is crucial. The rapid attenuation of radio signal together with the unstructured nature of the undersea environment makes traditional methods (based on Global Navigation Satellite System, GNSS) not suitable for the AUV control; hence, the design and implementation of navigation systems still constitute one of the most challenging tasks [1]. Modern AUV localization techniques are classified into three main categories: Acoustic Positioning Systems, Geophysical Navigation (GN) and Inertial Navigation System (INS) methods. Ultra-Short Base Line (USBL)-aided buoy is a novel approach to underwater acoustic localization, where the USBL device used to obtain the position of the target is housed in the buoy itself. In this case, Inertial Measurement Unit (IMU) and Differential-GPS (DGPS) are exploited to refer the measures to the current buoy position. Results evidenced that the buoy motion has an effect on the overall accuracy of the localization and particularly the yaw angular rate affects the azimuth measurement [2].

This confirms that the orientation estimation generally provided by inertial systems is fundamental for an accurate positioning process; nevertheless, high accuracy results usually requires high cost instrumentations.

In this paper, the use of low-cost sensors mounted on common smartphones is evaluated as an alternative approach to more expensive INS, in order to further measure the orientation of the device. Several filtering techniques have been tested on data acquired by the gyroscope, accelerometer and magnetometer of an iPhone device. A preliminary evaluation of the proposed method is conducted on the basis of statistical parameters calculated by the analysis of the estimated and ground truth values.

2   Underwater Positioning Systems

The practically impossible use of the GNSS together with the unstructured and hazardous characteristics of the marine environment makes the development of AUVs a very challenging scientific and engineering problems. Different navigation and positioning methods have been studied by researchers, resulting in three main categories of underwater techniques: acoustic, geophysical and INS based methods.

In the first case, localization is achieved by measuring ranges from the Time of Flight (TOF) of acoustic signals (which have a lower absorption rate in the water than radio frequency signals). Three different approaches can be employed, based on the length of the baseline between the transducers: in a long baseline (LBL) system the instruments are more than 100 m spaced over a wide area on the sea floor; in a short baseline (SBL) system, the transducers are placed at the opposite ends of a ship's hull, thus not exceeding 20 m of distance, while for super short or ultra-short baseline (SSBL and USBL) the length among them is smaller than 10 cm. Usually, the system has one transponder and at least three transducers and its deployment depends on the mission: for example, USBL and SBL are more suitable for tracking mission and short-range navigation. Variability of the water characteristics and accordingly of the sound speed, environmental noises and multipath can reduce the performance of these systems, which can also be complex to deploy.

Conventional dead-reckoning (DR) techniques can provide optimal results, especially if combined with geophysical navigation. The latter is based on environmental-observed effects (i.e. terrain topography, gravity anomalies and geomagnetic field variations, acquired by cameras, ranging sonars or magnetometers) and can provide accurate position estimates and low localization errors in the long run with relatively low-cost implementations [3, 4]. One of the implementation of the underwater GN is the terrain-aided navigation (TAN), based on the matching between a set of range measurement acquired by the sensors onboard and a previously acquired digital elevation map (DEM) of the terrain to estimate the vehicle's position. This method is able to mitigate the accuracy drifts of the inertial systems but heavily depends on the need for high-quality geophysical maps before the missions, other than being computationally costly when comparing and matching the map with sensors data.

Simultaneous Localization And Mapping (SLAM) techniques deal with this problem: they allow the AUV to acquire a map of the environment while simultaneously localizing itself basing on the acquisition. The actual methods represent a robust solution for static and limited-size areas reaching sub-metrical precision, but cannot accomplish the task for dynamic, unstructured or large-scale environment [5].

As mentioned before, the use of inertial sensors is typically considered as the central navigation system of AUVs. It contains an inertial measurement unit (IMU) which allows the measurement of linear acceleration and angular velocity by its three orthogonal rate-gyroscopes and -accelerometers respectively. These are integrated to obtain the instantaneous speed and position of the vehicle without the need for external references. Unfortunately, several problems are associated with these sensors: gyroscopes measure angular rate of change and not angular position directly and accelerometers measure more than just linear acceleration (e.g. gravitational acceleration and Coriolis terms); measurements are noisy and biased and body-frame states need to be transformed to the inertial reference frame (e.g. Euler angles) [6]. Moreover, as already stated, the IMU errors increases over time due to the drift of the sensors. The errors accumulation is theoretically linear for heading and velocity and exponential for position [7]. This means that the navigation information provided by the INS can be considered reliable and accurate only within short times, while it is still impossible for a pure inertial navigation system to maintain the high-precision level throughout a mission. That is why external information and measurement constitute an effective improvement to navigation accuracy.

Moreover, even when high-end INS provide high accuracy, their high cost and complexity place constraints on the environments in which they are practical for use, leading to the development and consequent employment of MEMS (Micro Electro-Mechanical Systems) AHRS (Attitude Heading Reference System). Characterized by light weight and small sizes, they integrate a magnetometer to the INS configuration, thus being able to measure the variation of the Earth's magnetic field to estimate the best attitude of the vehicle [8, 9]. Examples of AHRS are smartphones and video game consoles; it should be noted that mobile devices are able to instantly calculate pose estimation using their integrated sensors. In this way, these devices have the potential to be used in several applications beside orientation estimation, like geomatics, augmented reality (AR), etc.

3 Sensors and Algorithms

Today's smartphones incorporate numerous sensors, which may include compass, accelerometer, gyroscope, GPS, camera and sensors of temperature, pressure, proximity, etc. It should be considered that smartphone applications cannot directly access physical sensors embedded into smartphones: the raw signal they measure is processed by the operating system and then made available to the applications in a standardized format (the smartphone sensor). That means that the technical specifications of the sensors cannot be obtained from the manufacturer's data sheet [10], but a general and accurate review of their functioning can be easily found.

3.1 Smartphone Sensor Accuracy

In [10], for example, a sensing application for analyzing accelerometer and gyroscope bias and noise parameters (as starting point) of some of the most common smartphones of the recent years is presented. The iPhone model employed in this experiment is not included in the list, but some general information can be derived from the overall analysis. In particular, an extract by [10] (Table 1) reports the average and the standard deviation of the measured smartphone accelerometer and gyroscope biases.

Table 1. Statistical parameters of the absolute bias values of smartphone sensors [10].

	Accelerometer $[mg_0]$			Gyroscope $[mrad/s]$		
	X	Y	Z	X	Y	Z
Average	14.3	14.6	25.3	9.4	8.7	6.1
StDev	14.2	15.2	25.1	13.6	12.1	8.7

In [11], a static test made through the acquisition of the raw angular velocities and accelerations was performed made to test the stability of the sensors of an iPhone 4. A summary of this test is reported in Table 2, confirming good stability for both the gyroscope and the accelerometer. This result can be projected to the iPhone SE as a really good basis, being its technology surely more advanced than that of its earlier version.

Table 2. iPhone 4 sensors stability performance derived from a static test [11]

	Accelerometer $[g_0]$			Gyroscope $[rad/s]$		
	X	Y	Z	X	Y	Z
RMSE	2.8	2.4	4.2	4.8	3.2	4.3

The low-cost MEMS AHRS sensors of the smartphone are simply strapped to the unit, so that the coordinate frame of each of them has the same directions. This configuration provides much sensitivity to the turning rates but less stability. The raw data acquired by the sensors can have possible errors due to the system design;

moreover, they are affected by thermal and electronic-related noise, usually modelled as additive Gaussian noise. This entails deviations and oscillations around the correct value that can be reduced by prior calibration procedures. However, additional considerations must be made on the sensors [12]. The accelerometer at rest should measure the gravitational acceleration only but, being the sensor very sensitive to vibration and mechanical noise, it will measure the result of many additional forces besides gravity, with consequences on the final estimation. The output of a magnetometer largely depends on the environment additional magnetic fields, which can affect the accuracy of the results. Gyroscope measures the angular rate of change around the three axes in the body frame, which could be integrated to get the angular positions. Unfortunately, even if less sensitive to perturbations and not influenced by external factors, the gyroscope is not free from errors [13]. They are generally caused by the non-perfect symmetricity of the oscillation plane, by the dissipation of the vibration mechanical energy in thermal energy and by the non-linearity of the restoring forces. As an intrinsic characteristic of the gyroscope, these errors accumulate over time, becoming unbounded in magnitude: this is commonly known as gyroscope drift.

The integration of the three sensors can compensate the different errors related to each of them to obtain a complete orientation measurement [14]. The complementary filter, for example, combines the accelerometer good performance in static conditions with those of the gyroscope in dynamic ones. Two filters, a low-pass and a high-pass, are used on accelerometer and gyroscope data respectively [15]. The Kalman filter, also known as Linear Quadratic Estimator (LQE), is the optimal state estimator for any linear stochastic system subject to known normally distributed state and measurement noise. This filter does not only consider the sensor measurements but also the underlying dynamics of the system itself; for these reasons it is widely used to solve many tracking and data prediction tasks. Other implementations as the extended Kalman filter (EKF) and the unscented Kalman filter (UKF) extend these techniques to nonlinear systems [16]. A brief overview on the Kalman filter will be given in the next paragraph to better understand its functioning, while the experiment setup will be analyzed in chapter 4.

3.2   Kalman Filter: An Overview

The Kalman filter is a predictive filter which uses a recursive algorithm to estimate the state of a dynamic system by elaborating sequential measurements. In the discrete time setting, a time-invariant system can be described by a state Eq. (1) and a measurement Eq. (2). In (1) $\vec{x}_t$ is the state vector to be predicted, $\vec{x}_{t-1}$ and $\vec{u}_{t-1}$ are the state and the input vectors at the previous time. A and B are the system matrices, which respectively relate the current states and the inputs to the next states and are assumed stationary over time. The actual measurements can be modelled as in (2): $\vec{y}_t$ is the measure and C is the matrix which relates the system state to the measured one. $\vec{w}_{t-1}$ and $\vec{v}_t$ are the additive process and measurement noise respectively, assumed to be zero-mean Gaussian processes.

$$\vec{x}_t = A\vec{x}_{t-1} + B\vec{u}_{t-1} + \vec{w}_{t-1} \tag{1}$$

$$\vec{y}_t = C\vec{x}_t + \vec{v}_t \tag{2}$$

The Kalman filter equations provide a prediction (3), (4) and an update (5), (6), (7), (8) phases.

$$x_t' = A\vec{x}_{t-1} + B\vec{u}_{t-1} \tag{3}$$

$$P_t' = AP_{t-1}A^T + Q \tag{4}$$

$$S = CP_t'C^T + R \tag{5}$$

$$K_t = P_t'C^T S^{-1} \tag{6}$$

$$x_t = x_t' + K_t\left(y_t - Cx_t'\right) \tag{7}$$

$$P_t = (I - K_tC)P_t' \tag{8}$$

The a-posteriori state estimate x_t is obtained as a linear combination of the a-priori estimate x_t' and a weighted difference between the actual measurement and the prediction, $K_t(y_t - Cx_t')$. The difference in (7) is called measurement innovation or residual and reflects the discrepancy between the predicted measurement and the actual measurement. K is known as the Kalman gain and minimizes the a-posteriori error covariance; P is the error covariance matrix initially set by the user and updated by the filter. Q and R are the covariance matrices of the process and measurement noise respectively. Q indicates the uncertainty about the model dynamics, while R depends mainly on the sensors used in the systems: large values in both the matrices means greater noise levels. As both Q and R greatly affect the final filter performance, a tuning procedure of their values is important, as the true noise statistics are unknown.

4   Experiments and Results

4.1   Coordinate Frames and Smartphone Details

The data collection has been made through the Matlab R2019b Mobile App running on an iPhone SE mobile phone, both in static and dynamic conditions. The orientation is defined by the three angles of Azimuth, Pitch and Roll: to understand and analyse the results of the orientation estimation it is important to point out that Matlab provides measures in a custom body coordinate frame while requiring data in North-East-Down (NED) frame for its underlying functions (Fig. 1). In fact, underwater applications are performed in NED coordinate frame: the positive X-axis points to the North, the positive Y-axis to the East, and the positive Z-axis follows the positive direction of the gravity force. Smartphone data loaded in Matlab is instead expressed in a different body frame, where the positive X-axis extends out of the right side of the phone, positive Y-axis out of the top side, and the positive Z-axis out of the front face of the phone, independently of the actual smartphone orientation. Thus, an appropriate coordinate transformation is needed in order to switch pass from body frame to the NED frame. With this state, the Euler angles are defined as follows: the Azimuth is the angle between the magnetic north to the positive Y-axis, measuring the rotation around the Z-axis of the phone; it will be indicated by θ. The Roll is considered as positive when the Z-axis of the smartphone (laying on a flat surface) begins to tilt towards the positive X-axis and, in the same way, the positive Pitch is defined when the positive Z-axis begins to tilt towards the positive Y-axis. The related angles will be indicated by φ and ψ.

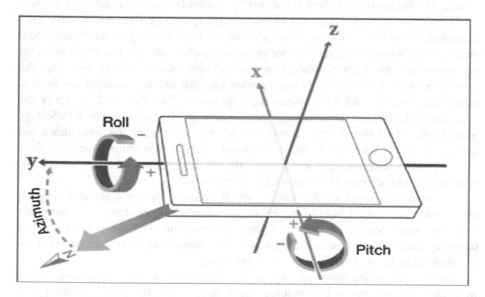

Fig. 1. Coordinates frame required for the use of Matlab built-in functions [17].

4.2   Experiment Setup and Results

Some of the built-in functions of Matlab have been used to combine the sensors measurements. It follows a brief overview [18].

The "ecompass" function combines the accelerometer and magnetometer data and returns a quaternion which can rotate the quantities from the NED frame to a child frame; the orientation angles can be simply obtained applying the "eulerd" function to the quaternion, specifying the correct axis order. The "imufilter" creates a system object characterized by nontunable properties (unless otherwise indicated). These are the sample rate of input sensor data (Hz), the decimation factor, the variance of the gyro signal noise and offset drift ($(rad/s)^2$), the variance of accelerometer signal and of the linear acceleration noise ($(m/s^2)^2$), the decay factor for the linear acceleration drift and the covariance matrix for process noise. Applying this object to the gyro and accelerometer readings, the orientation and angular velocity are computed. This algorithm assumes that the device is stationary before the first call.

The "AHRSfilter" function creates an object which allows to fuse the data provided by accelerometer, gyroscope and magnetometer to obtain orientation and angular velocity. The properties of this filter are the same as the imufilter, with the addition of the variance of the magnetometer signal noise and of the magnetic disturbance noise (μT^2), the decay factor for magnetic disturbance and the expected estimate of the magnetic field strength (μT).

The "complementaryFilter" function, as the previously analyzed filters, returns a System object which is applied to the accelerometer, gyroscope and magnetometer readings to give the orientation of the device. The parameters of this filter are the sample rate (Hz), the accelerometer and magnetometer gains and the output orientation format. The magnetometer input is enabled by default but can be disabled if needed.

The aim of the experiment was to test the smartphone performance in basic configurations, in order to evaluate if the accuracy of the reliability of the results could match a further use of the same device in more complex settings. For this reason, the toy-experiment has been conducted in two different phases. In the first one, the smartphone was placed in a static configuration on a flat surface, avoiding any form of disturbance which could have altered the acquisition. This was made to verify the reliability of the measurements in static mode, where no external noise should affect the acquisition. Stated this, in the second part of, the experiment the smartphone has undergone several rotations on the same flat surface, each time around one of its three axes. Again, to better evaluate and particularly see the response of the sensors, a 90° rotation has been chosen as the most elementary test.

The modalities have been the same for both the phases. Having enabled the sensors, five minutes acquisition have been performed; the resulting readings were automatically sent to the Matlab Drive to be further processed in the desktop version of the software. The orientation parameters given by the smartphone itself were acquired too and then set as the ground truth for the experiment.

The first part of the script allowed the synchronization of the acquisitions, which were then transformed in the required frame to be correctly processed through a coordinates transformation. The orientation angles of Azimuth, Pitch and Roll have then been estimated using each of the Matlab function above mentioned: a first evaluation of their accuracy has been made on the basis of the resulting standard deviation.

At this point, an elementary Kalman filter has been implemented. The state and bias vectors have been initialized as zeroes arrays: the gyro biases will be calculated and subtracted to the state with the aim to reduce the gyro drift. The transformed angular rates of change have been used to get roll, pitch and yaw angles as input vector, while the state update was processed using the results of the magnetometer and accelerometer integration.

As previously said, the Q and R matrices needed a fine tuning, indispensable to obtain the least possible oscillation around the reference values (those directly measured and smoothed by the phone, referred to as ground truth). For this reason, a fuzzy logic-based method has been followed to minimize the standard deviation [19], changing the matrices values and evaluating the parameter variation after each step. This preliminary tuning phase assured a correct estimation of the Euler angles by the Kalman filter.

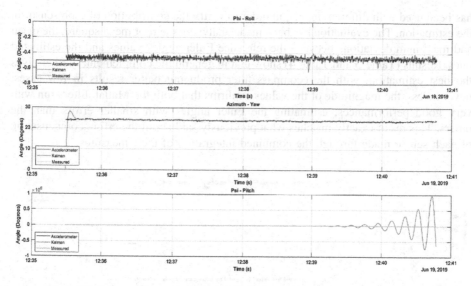

Fig. 2. Kalman filter estimation of the Euler angles. (Color figure online)

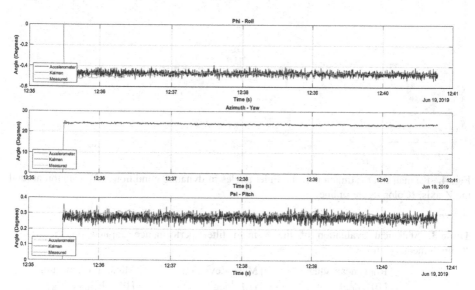

Fig. 3. Kalman filter estimation of the Euler angles after the tuning process.

Figure 2 and Fig. 3 show the results of the finetuning for the static experiment. Although an oscillation in the first part could be tolerated, being due to the normal initial settling of the filter, continued successive fluctuations evidence a wrong tuning, particularly if characterized by abnormal amplitudes as those visible in the third section of Fig. 2, related to the Pitch estimation made by the KF (in red). The enhancement provided by a correct tuning can be seen in Fig. 3, where no excessive oscillations characterize the evaluation trend of the Kalman filter. After the tuning (Fig. 3), the KF has been used with different inputs, in order to verify the contribution of each sensor in the estimation. The evaluation has been made analysing the root mean square, the mean and maximum deviations between the reference Euler angles values and the estimated ones. Results (Table 3 and Table 4) show that in general the complementary filter gives the best estimation, with the ecompass filter producing better results in few cases; nevertheless, the magnitude of the values confirms that both the Matlab filters run with very good performances, estimating the Euler angles with smaller errors than the others. This result exactly matches what previously said about the errors compensation of each sensor made through the combined integration of their measures.

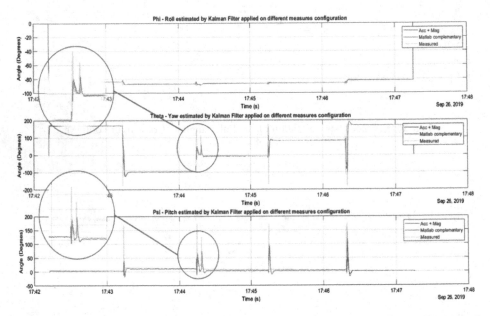

Fig. 4. Kalman filter estimation of the Euler angles in dynamic conditions: 90° rotation around the Z-axis. (Color figure online)

Table 3. Statistical evaluation of the Kalman filter performance applied on the Matlab "Complementary" filter

	Root mean square [10^{-3}deg]	Mean deviation [10^{-3}deg]	Maximum deviation [10^{-3}deg]
Roll (φ)	33.4686	16.9271	571.7200
Azimuth (ϑ)	626.1838	86.8802	379.4724
Pitch (ψ)	22.5467	8.5153	84.9020

Table 4. Statistical evaluation of the Kalman filter performance applied on the Matlab "ecompass" filter

	Root mean square [10^{-3}deg]	Mean deviation [10^{-3}deg]	Maximum deviation [10^{-3}deg]
Roll (φ)	31.6038	7.7425	571.7200
Azimuth (ϑ)	830.8329	101.3869	968.4521
Pitch (ψ)	26.0136	14.8977	58.3436

Figure 4 shows the sensors response to one of the dynamic test made, in which the smartphone has been subjected to a 90° rotation around the Z-axis. The ecompass and the complementary filter plotted in the pictures have quite the same response, as demonstrated by the fact that the black line representing the first function is only rarely visible under the red line of the latter. Moreover, as can be seen in the enlarged sections, both the ecompass and the complementary filters tend to underestimate the true values in the transition phase of the rotation. However, this is compensated by a damping of the operator-induced oscillations, thus satisfying the necessity to reduce as much as possible the fluctuation frequency and their effects on the stability of the measures and of the system in general.

5   Conclusions

In this paper, a preliminary evaluation of different orientation estimation methods based on the use of low-cost sensors is presented. The test is made on data measured by the internal sensors of an iPhone SE (i.e. gyroscope, accelerometer and magnetometer), acquired by the Matlab Mobile application end elaborated with the same software. The registered measurements have been opportunely synchronized and transformed in the coordinates frame required by Matlab to use its built-in integration functions. The experiment has been conducted for two different smartphone settings, aiming at verifying its response during a static acquisition and when subjected to rotations and in general more noisy settings. The data have been integrated using some of the Matlab object filters to give a prior evaluation of this immediate solution; then, a basic Kalman filter algorithm has been structured to integrate the gyroscope measurements with the previously estimated values, to verify if this could enhance the final result. Obviously, the KF needed an opportune tuning process of the measurement and process noise covariance matrix, which in this case has been made following a fuzzy logic-based approach.

Results evidence good performances in both static and dynamic conditions, especially if considering the elementary nature of the experiments specifically targeted at testing easy configurations and solutions.

Further works will be related to a more precise tuning process of the Kalman filter as well as of the Matlab built-in functions, which surely will improve the results.

Moreover, the sensors calibration will be analysed, dealing with their drift and the internal biases of the smartphone, aiming at enhancing the reliability of the estimation. Having said that, these preliminary results can be considered as a good starting point for more elaborated analysis. Orientation estimation stands as one of the key points for an accurate positioning, especially in underwater environments where this not easy task is generally accomplished by the proper integration of different localization systems. INS and acoustic methods already provide optimal results, so the final aim of this study is to lay the foundation for the development of low-cost systems able to provide the same reliability and accuracy of more expensive technology for the orientation estimation as the basis of the overall navigation and localization system.

References

1. Paull, L., Saeedi, S., Seto, M., Li, H.: AUV navigation and localization: a review. IEEE J. Oceanic Eng. **39**(1), 131–149 (2013)
2. Fanelli, F., Monni, N., Palma, N., Ridolfi, A.: Development of an ultra short baseline–aided buoy for underwater targets localization. Proc. Inst. Mech. Eng. Part M: J. Eng. Maritime Environ. **233**(4) (2019). https://doi.org/10.1177/1475090219825768
3. Wang, L., Pang, S.: AUV navigation based on inertial navigation and acoustic positioning systems. In: OCEANS 2018 MTS/IEEE Charleston, pp. 1–8. IEEE (2018)
4. Quintas, J., Teixeira, F.C., Pascoal, A.: AUV geophysical navigation using magnetic data— the MEDUSA GN system. In: 2018 IEEE/ION Position, Location and Navigation Symposium (PLANS), pp. 1122–1130. IEEE (2018)
5. Guth, F., Silveira, L., Botelho, S., Drews, P., Ballester, P.: Underwater SLAM: challenges, state of the art, algorithms and a new biologically-inspired approach. In: 5th IEEE RAS/EMBS International Conference on Biomedical Robotics and Biomechatronics, pp. 981–986. IEEE (2014)
6. Salmony, P.: http://philsal.co.uk/projects/imu-attitude-estimation. Accessed September 2019
7. Bao, J., Li, D., Qiao, X., Rauschenbach, T.: Integrated navigation for autonomous underwater vehicles in aquaculture: a review. Inf. Process. Agric. **7**(1), 139–151 (2020)
8. Ludwig, S.A., Jiménez, A.R.: Optimization of gyroscope and accelerometer/magnetometer portion of basic attitude and heading reference system. In: 2018 IEEE International Symposium on Inertial Sensors and Systems (INERTIAL), pp. 1–4. IEEE (2018)
9. Ko, N.Y., Jeong, S.: Attitude estimation and DVL based navigation using low-cost MEMS AHRS for UUVs. In: 2014 11th International Conference on Ubiquitous Robots and Ambient Intelligence (URAI), pp. 605–607. IEEE (2014)
10. Kos, A., Tomažič, S., Umek, A.: Evaluation of smartphone inertial sensor performance for cross-platform mobile applications. Sensors **16**(4), 477 (2016)
11. Piras, M., Lingua, A., Dabove, P., Aicardi, I.: Indoor navigation using Smartphone technology: a future challenge or an actual possibility? In: 2014 IEEE/ION Position, Location and Navigation Symposium-PLANS 2014, pp. 1343–1352. IEEE (2014)
12. Patonis, P., Patias, P., Tziavos, I., Rossikopoulos, D., Margaritis, K.: A fusion method for combining low-cost IMU/Magnetometer outputs for use in applications on mobile devices. Sensors **18**(8), 2616 (2018)
13. Guo, H., Hong, H.: Research on filtering algorithm of MEMS gyroscope based on information fusion. Sensors **19**(16), 3552 (2019)

14. Madgwick, S.O., Harrison, A.J., Vaidyanathan, R.: Estimation of IMU and MARG orientation using a gradient descent algorithm. In: 2011 IEEE International Conference on Rehabilitation Robotics, pp. 1–7. IEEE (2011)
15. Islam, T., Islam, M.S., Shajid-Ul-Mahmud, M., Hossam-E-Haider, M.: Comparison of complementary and Kalman filter based data fusion for attitude heading reference system. In: AIP Conference Proceedings, vol. 1919(1), p. 020002. AIP Publishing (2017)
16. Hedengren, J.D., Eaton, A.N.: Overview of estimation methods for industrial dynamic systems. Optim. Eng. 18(1), 155–178 (2015). https://doi.org/10.1007/s11081-015-9295-9
17. The MathWorks, Inc. https://www.mathworks.com/matlabcentral/mlc-downloads/down loads/submissions/40876/versions/8/previews/sensorgroup/Examples/html/ CapturingAzimuthRollPitchExample.html. Accessed September 2019
18. The MathWorks, Inc. Homepage. https://www.mathworks.com/. Accessed April 2020
19. Loebis, D., Sutton, R., Chudley, J., Naeem, W.: Adaptive tuning of a Kalman filter via fuzzy logic for an intelligent AUV navigation system. Control Eng. Pract. 12(12), 1531–1539 (2004)

Development and Initial Assessment of a Low Cost Mobile Mapping System

Andrea Masiero[1,2](✉) , Francesca Fissore[2] , Alberto Guarnieri[2] ,
Antonio Vettore[2] , and Ugo Coppa[3]

[1] Department of Civil and Environmental Engineering, University of Florence,
via di Santa Marta 3, 50139 Florence, Italy
andrea.masiero@unifi.it

[2] University of Padova, Interdepartmental Research Center of Geomatics (CIRGEO),
viale dell'Università 16, 35020 Legnaro, PD, Italy
masiero@dei.unipd.it

[3] National Institute of Geophysics and Volcanology, Vesuvius Observatory,
Naples, Italy

Abstract. Mobile mapping system have been used in a wide range of applications during the last decades, most of the times with the goal of quickly and quite reliably acquiring georeferenced spatial information of relatively large areas of interest. Indeed, such kind of systems are often preferred to static surveying techniques when dealing with relatively large areas, where static approaches would require very long surveys. Terrestrial mobile mapping systems are composed by a positioning and mapping system, which is typically mounted on a terrestrial vehicle, such as a car. The use of such systems can be limited by (i) possible restrictions on the area of interest, which might be not well suited for the use of such vehicles, and (ii) by their quite high costs, mostly related to the use of expensive sensors in order to ensure high accuracy and reliability of the acquired geospatial information.

Despite preserving the quality of the produced information imposes quite stringent restrictions on the used sensors, and consequently on their costs, nowadays the recent technological improvements allowed the development of a number of low cost sensors, which can be used in a mapping system instead of their expensive counterparts. In accordance with such consideration, this paper aims at presenting the development of mobile mapping system with low cost sensors, and an initial evaluation of the performance achievable with such system: indeed, the use of low cost sensors typically reduce the quality of obtained results, or restricts the conditions of usability.

To be more specific, this paper presents two versions, one based on stereo vision and the other on mobile laser scanning, of a low cost mobile mapping system recently realized by the University of Padua.

Keywords: Mobile mapping · Low-cost · Inertial Navigation System · LiDAR

© Springer Nature Switzerland AG 2020
C. Parente et al. (Eds.): R3GEO 2019, CCIS 1246, pp. 116–128, 2020.
https://doi.org/10.1007/978-3-030-62800-0_10

1   Introduction

Mobile Mapping System (MMS) is a technology introduced few decades ago to acquire in an efficient way accurate geospatial data from a moving vehicle [1–3]. To this aim, these system are typically composed by an array of integrated and synchronized navigation and spatial data acquisition sensors, such as Global Navigation Satellite System (GNSS), Inertial Measurement Unit (IMU), cameras and laser scanners [2, 4–9].

The rationale at the basis of the development of this kind of system is that of enabling the generation of accurate geospatial information on relatively large areas in a quick and cost-effective way. Such kind of result can be reached by using a moving vehicle acquiring spatial information with a sensor whose position and orientation is well known, thanks to the use of accurate navigation systems. This led to the key idea of *direct georeferencing* of the acquired spatial information [10].

This kind of technology, originally developed using cameras as imaging sensors [11], currently mostly relies on the use of Mobile Laser Scanning systems (MLS) [12, 13]. Furthermore, after the initial development exploiting terrestrial vehicles, more recently such kind of systems have been extended to other terrestrial moving devices [14, 15] and to aerial ones, and in particular to remotely piloted aircraft systems (RPAS) and unmanned aerial vehicles (UAV) [16].

Since their initial development, MMS have been used in a wide range of applications, in particular to provide reliable spatial information on quite large areas, in both the terrestrial and aerial case, such as infrastructure monitoring [17, 18], building and complex structure modeling [19–21], forest monitoring [22].

Despite being on the market for over a dozen years, the typical cost of MMS is greater than 50k dollars. However, the recent technological developments are dramatically influencing the new surveying systems, leading to the realization of new devices, typically improving the performance of previous ones, often at a lower cost. Hence, the aim of this work is that of taking advantage of the recent technological improvements in order to develop a much cheaper MMS. More specifically, the goal is that of limiting the costs of the system sensors to few thousand dollars.

This paper presents the realized system, focusing in particular on the characteristics of the used sensors and on their integration, and an initial performance assessment in terms of precision and accuracy of the acquired geospatial data.

More specifically, the paper will focus on three different aspects:

- The realization of an appropriate modular hardware/software architecture, which should enable the real-time storing and retrieval of the collected sensor data. In particular, the implemented solution can be used for real-time monitoring the acquired data from a web-tool, Sect. 2
- The development of a MMS based on stereo vision (Sect. 3) based on the use of webcams and low cost navigation sensors (Fig. 1).
- The realization of a mobile laser scanning system (Sect. 4) using a cheap Light Detection and Ranging (LiDAR) device, low cost GNSS receivers (usable either in Real-Time Kinematic (RTK) or post-processing) and IMU (Fig. 2).

Fig. 1. Terrestrial vehicle used for mobile mapping. The figure shows the system in the stereo vision configuration.

Since this is an on going project, this work aims at showing the current state of development of such system, where the acquisition and monitoring platform were originally presented in [23].

2   Data Acquisition, Storage and Real-Time Monitoring Platform

This section describes the web platform, developed as an open source tool, realized in order to collect and real-time view all the data from the MMS sensors. It is worth to notice that, since system sensors may be substituted with different or additional ones may be temporarily or permanently added, the acquisition platform has been developed with a modular software architecture, shown in Fig. 3, which enables the independent management of each sensor, hence easing the integration of new ones and the implementation of scripts in different programming languages. It is worth to notice that the implementation of such platform as a web tool enables the real-time retrieval and visualization of the collected data, Fig. 4. The latter can obviously be used also for viewing previously logged data.

The back-end structure of the web tool is written in Python programming language. Its main tasks are: connections and communications between the devices, data acquisition, archiving, and retrieval. After establishing the initial connection with a device/sensor, the system sets the device settings and the data transmission rate, e.g. common settings in the implemented system are: the sample frequency of IMU measurements is 100 Hz, whereas GNSS position estimates are typically acquired at 5 Hz. Webcam images, in the stereo-vision MMS (Fig. 1), acquire images at 0.2 Hz.

Fig. 2. Terrestrial vehicle used for mobile mapping. The figure shows the system in the mobile laser scanning configuration.

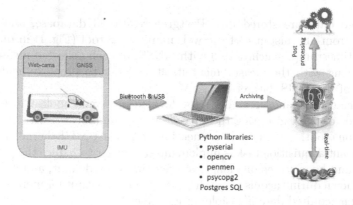

Fig. 3. Architecture of the acquisition, storage, retrieval and monitoring platform.

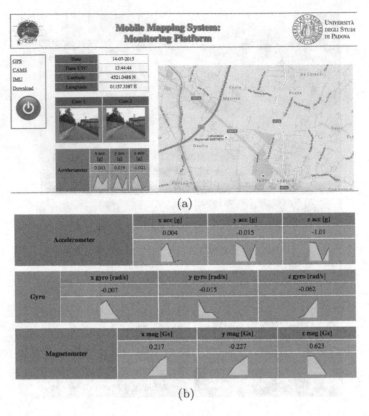

(a)

(b)

Fig. 4. (a) Monitoring platform (usable both in real-time or in post-processing). (b) Inertial sensor data shown in real-time in the monitoring platform.

Collected data are stored in a Postgres relational database, and become retrievable from any instance of the web monitoring tool (Fig. 4) in quasi-real-time. The timestamp, synchronized with GNSS, of each collected measurement is stored along with the measurement itself in order to properly enable post-processing of the MMS dataset.

Data acquisition and archiving is performed on a notebook, which is positioned inside of the van during the survey, and communicates with the sensors either via bluetooth or via cable connection (e.g. via USB/Ethernet port). An energy efficient acquisition task is implemented in order to reduce the power consumption, and hence to enable longer survey times: by default, a quite minimal output is shown during acquisition, whereas graphical output for more accurately checking the acquired data is visible upon request.

In order to facilitate the interaction between the user and the MMS data and to increase the intuitive usage and access, we have decided to develop a web interface with clear panels for each part of the MMS information to be accessed by user.

The web interface, which represents the front-end of the system, is designed with different intuitive panels in order to ease its usage to new users. The modular and open source software approach has been adopted in this case as well, e.g. JQuery, Handlebars, Canvas libraries have been used in the implementation. Real-time monitoring of the acquired is allowed by beans of the interaction with the database through the back-end functionalities.

Data acquired by the different sensors can be seen in a global view (e.g. top of Fig. 4) or independently (e.g. the bottom of Fig. 4 shows an example of graphs of IMU data).

3   Stereo Vision-Based System

The first version of the realized MMS corresponds to a very low cost mobile stereo-vision system, including two cameras, a GNSS and Inertial Navigation System (INS) as positioning system, i.e.: two Logitech c920 webcams, RoyalTek MBT-1100 GNSS receiver and a Microstrain 3DM-GX3-45 IMU.

Logitech c920 webcams allow Full HD video recording (Full HD 1080p in both image and video capture modes). They are provided with automatic low-light correction and USB connection [24].

RoyalTek MBT-1100 is a small and lightweight GNSS receiver (69.5 mm × 23 mm × 20 mm, 38 g), which provides bluetooth connection. It is a C/A code receiver characterized by a position accuracy ranging from 3.0 m (without any aid) to 2.5 m (using Differential Global Positioning System (DGPS)) [25].

Microstrain 3DM-GX3-45 integrates inertial sensors with a GNSS receiver (50-channel u-blox 6 engine). According to Microstrain specifications, typical attitude accuracy (Root Mean Square error (RMS)) for picth and roll is 0.35 deg, whereas it is 1.0 deg for the heading. Typical planar/vertical position accuracy (RMS) is 2.5 m and 5 m, respectively [26].

The positions of the sensors on the van roof rack are shown in the top of Fig. 5.

4   Mobile Laser Scanning System

The mobile laser scanning system developed in this project considers the use of a low cost LiDAR, three GNSS receivers, and an IMU, which shall be properly calibrated [27].

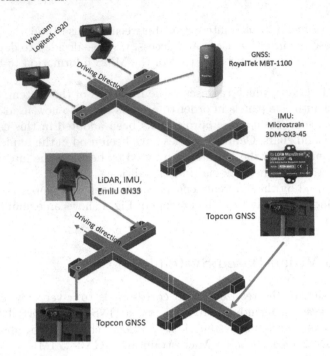

Fig. 5. Sensors on the top of the van in the two system configurations: stereo imaging sensors (top), mobile laser scanning (bottom).

Livox Mid-40 LiDAR (bottom of Fig. 2) is a compact and lightweight laser scanner (8.8 cm × 6.9 cm × 7.6 cm, 760 g). It acquires 100k points/second, with a range precision of 2 cm at 20 m, angular accuracy <0.1°, beam divergence is 0.28° (vertical) and 0.03° (horizontal), and the maximum range is 260 m [28].

Three GNSS receivers are used to compute the position of the van and to preserve the long time consistency of the vehicle attitude estimation. Three configurations have already been tested:

– one Emlid Reach M+, two Topcon HiPer Pro V.
– one Emlid Reach M+, one GeoMax Zenith40, one GeoMax Zenith15.
– one Emlid Reach M+, one Emlid Reach RS+, one Emlid Reach RS2.

In all the considered tests the GNSS receivers worked in Network RTK mode, with Networked Transport of RTCM via Internet Protocol (NTRIP) corrections, however, depending on the specific application, post-processing of the GNSS measurements can be considered as well.

It is worth to notice that, differently from the case of Sect. 3, the usage of GNSS receivers enabling position measurements at centimeter level of accuracy shall increase the overall performance of the mapping system.

Furthermore, despite the system has been currently tested only in the three previously mentioned GNSS configurations, the following one will be developed in the future in order to enable a low cost implementation of the MMS: three

Emlid Reach M+ (cost of $ 300 each, approximately) collecting position samples at 5 Hz, optionally connected to an Emlid Reach RS+ base station ($ 800), if needed [29, 30].

Emlid Reach M+ provides as output a pulse per second signal which is used to synchronize the other sensors.

Finally, a Bosch Sensortec BNO055 chip, is used to acquire inertial sensor measurements (triaxial accelerometer, triaxial gyroscope and triaxial magnetometer) at 100 Hz [31].

Since the accuracy of such sensors is typically not enough to ensure accurate attitude estimates along all the survey duration, information fusion with GNSS measurements and with other sensors shall be used in order to improve the attitude accuracy, e.g. in a Simultaneous Localization and Mapping (SLAM) fashion.

Several sensors have been previously considered in order to improve/compute position/attitude information, e.g. LiDAR [32, 33], radar [34], camera [35, 36].

In particular, in this work an implementation of LiDAR odometry tailored to the specific case of interest is used in order to improve the system attitude estimates. The overall attitude computation workflow is shown in Fig. 6.

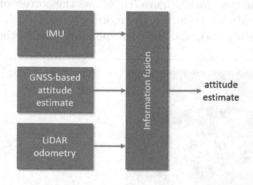

Fig. 6. Attitude computation workflow.

The positions of the sensors on the van roof rack are shown in the bottom of Fig. 5.

5   Initial Results and Discussion

The two proposed MMS solutions are both low cost, even if at a different levels: the first proposed one, Sect. 3, is extremely low cost, however the level of expected accuracy in the acquire information is consequently significantly affected (e.g. position information at metric level of accuracy, quite low quality visual information acquired by the webcams).

Instead, despite being still quite low cost (less than $ 2000, less than $ 3000 when using also a base station), the level of accuracy of the MLS solution is expected to be definitely improved with respect to previous version of the system. The main limitations in this case are related to the use of low cost LiDAR and IMU.

The nominal LiDAR range and angular accuracy (2 cm @ 20 m, and <0.1°) provide a lower bound to the achievable performance: assume the angular accuracy be 0.1°, and that the effects of angular and range error are independent. Then, the combined error at 20 m is approximately 4 cm, and it can be assumed to increase approximately linearly with the distance. Then, the position and in particular the attitude errors contribute to a further increase of the real error level.

Given the above observations, it is clear that the level of mapping accuracy of the overall system may be at centimeter level only for surveys at quite close distances between the vehicle and the surveyed objects, whereas decimeter level of accuracy is expected for longer distances.

Figure 7 shows an initial test of the MLS system conducted on September 26, 2019: the system has been used to map some buildings of the University of Padua. Figure 7(a) shows a satellite view of the test area, and a red solid line corresponding to the van track. Figure 7(b) shows the corresponding point cloud generated with the MLS system. Furthermore, Fig. 8 shows a front view of one of the involved buildings (a), and the corresponding part in the point cloud (b).

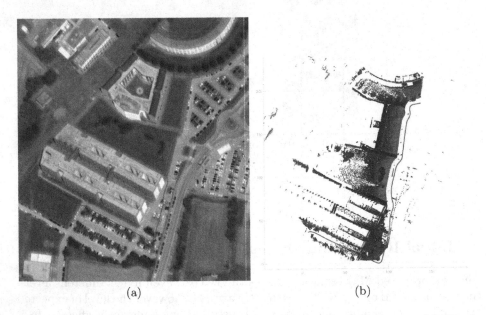

(a)   (b)

Fig. 7. (a) Satellite view of the test area. (b) MLS point cloud of the area (a). Track of the van is shown as a red line in both of them. (Color figure online)

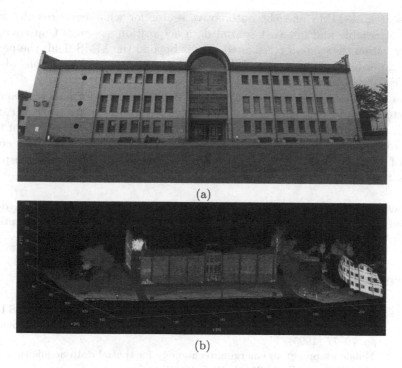

(a)

(b)

Fig. 8. (a) Front view of a University building included in the test area for the MLS system. (b) MLS point cloud of the building in (a).

6   Conclusions

This paper presented the current status of development of a project of the Inter-departmental Research Center of Geomatics of the University of Padua for the realization of a low cost MMS.

Two MMS solutions have been presented, either based on stereo vision or on mobile laser scanning. The first is an extremely low cost solution (< $ 1000), but the generated geospatial information is characterized by meter level absolute position accuracy, whereas the latter is still quite low cost (< $ 2000) with a higher expected surveying accuracy (decimeter level for objects at medium distances from the MMS).

The relatively large error of the stereo vision based system limits its usability to rough mapping at low level of resolution, hence its use is actually excluded to several of the typical geomatics application.

Differently, being the developed mobile laser scanning solution potentially much more accurate with respect to the stereo-vision based, it could be used in a wide spectrum of applications, not necessarily restricted to the geomatics field.

For instance, it is worth to notice that, given the increasing interest in the development of self-driving cars, nowadays there is a strong connection between the research on MMS and the automotive sector for what concerns the availability of reliable and low cost spatial data acquisition systems. Consequently, the interest on the system considered here is beyond the MMS field: the performance improvement of low cost MMSs can have positive repercussions also in other sectors, such as the automotive one.

Clearly, a more in depth assessment of the system performance should be conducted, and, in particular, it will be considered in our future work: a careful analysis of the errors related to the different sensors of the system and of their calibrated interaction should be performed in order to determine the actual effect of such errors on the final system outcome, i.e. the produced geospatial information.

Acknowledgments. The authors acknowledge GEC Software S.r.l., Italian dealer of Emlid Ltd, and its account manager Enrico Iuliano (https://www.strumentitopo grafici.it/) for the supporting us during the development of this project.

References

1. Bossler, J., Toth, C.: Accuracies obtained by the GPSVan [TM]. In: GIS LIS International Conference. American Society for Photogrammetry and Remote Sensing, vol. 1, pp. 70–77 (1995)
2. Li, R.: Mobile mapping: an emerging technology for spatial data acquisition. Photogram. Eng. Remote Sens. **63**(9), 1085–1092 (1997)
3. Schwarz, K.P., El-Sheimy, N.: Mobile mapping systems-state of the art and future trends. Int. Arch. Photogram. Remote Sens. Spat. Inf. Sci. 35(Part B), 10 (2004)
4. Ellum, C., El-Sheimy, N.: Land-based mobile mapping systems. Photogram. Eng. Remote Sens. **68**(1), 13–17 (2002)
5. Piras, M., Cina, A., Lingua, A.: Low cost mobile mapping systems: an Italian experience. In: 2008 IEEE/ION Position, Location and Navigation Symposium, pp. 1033–1045. IEEE (2008)
6. Puente, I., González-Jorge, H., Martínez-Sánchez, J., Arias, P.: Review of mobile mapping and surveying technologies. Measurement **46**(7), 2127–2145 (2013)
7. Tao, C.V., Li, J.: Advances in Mobile Mapping Technology, vol. 4. CRC Press, Boca Raton (2007)
8. Petrie, G.: An introduction to the technology mobile mapping systems. Geoinformatics **13**(1), 32–43 (2010)
9. Tao, C.V.: Mobile mapping technology for road network data acquisition. J. Geospat. Eng. **2**(2), 1–14 (2000)
10. Grejner-Brzezinska, D.A., et al.: On improved gravity modeling supporting direct georeferencing of multisensor systems. Proc. Int. Soc. Photogram. Remote Sens. **35**, 908–913 (2004)
11. El-Sheimy, N.: The development of VISAT: a mobile survey system for GIS applications. University of Calgary (1996)
12. Barber, D., Mills, J., Smith-Voysey, S.: Geometric validation of a ground-based mobile laser scanning system. ISPRS J. Photogram. Remote Sens. **63**(1), 128–141 (2008)
13. Kukko, A., Kaartinen, H., Hyyppä, J., Chen, Y.: Multiplatform mobile laser scanning: usability and performance. Sensors **12**(9), 11712–11733 (2012)

14. Gong, Z., Li, J., Luo, Z., Wen, C., Wang, C., Zelek, J.: Mapping and semantic modeling of underground parking lots using a backpack LiDAR system. IEEE Trans. Intell. Transp. Syst. (2019)
15. Fissore, F., Masiero, A., Piragnolo, M., Pirotti, F., Guarnieri, A., Vettore, A.: Towards surveying with a smartphone. In: Cefalo, R., Zieliński, J.B., Barbarella, M. (eds.) New Advanced GNSS and 3D Spatial Techniques. LNGC, pp. 167–176. Springer, Cham (2018). https://doi.org/10.1007/978-3-319-56218-6_13
16. Lin, Y., Hyyppa, J., Jaakkola, A.: Mini-UAV-borne LIDAR for fine-scale mapping. IEEE Geosci. Remote Sens. Lett. **8**(3), 426–430 (2010)
17. Lin, Y.C., Cheng, Y.T., Lin, Y.J., Flatt, J.E., Habib, A., Bullock, D.: Evaluating the accuracy of mobile LiDAR for mapping airfield infrastructure. Transp. Res. Rec. **2673**(4), 117–124 (2019)
18. Corongiu, M., Tucci, G., Santoro, E., Kourounioti, O.: Data integration of different domains in geo-information management: a railway infrastructure case study. Int. Arch. Photogram. Remote Sens. Spat. Inf. Sci. ISPRS **XLII–4**, 121–127 (2018)
19. Angelini, M., Baiocchi, V., Costantino, D., Garzia, F.: Scan to BIM for 3D reconstruction of the Papal basilica of Saint Francis in Assisi in Italy. Int. Arch. Photogram. Remote Sens. Spat. Inf. Sci. ISPRS **XLII–5/W1**, 47–54 (2017)
20. Alshawa, M., Boulaassal, H., Landes, T., Grussenmeyer, P.: Acquisition and automatic extraction of facade elements on large sites from a low cost laser mobile mapping system (2009)
21. Masiero, A., Fissore, F., Guarnieri, A., Pirotti, F., Visintini, D., Vettore, A.: Performance evaluation of two indoor mapping systems: low-cost UWB-aided photogrammetry and backpack laser scanning. Appl. Sci. **8**(3), 416 (2018)
22. Blomley, R., Hovi, A., Weinmann, M., Hinz, S., Korpela, I., Jutzi, B.: Tree species classification using within crown localization of waveform LIDAR attributes. ISPRS J. Photogram. Remote Sens. **133**, 142–156 (2017)
23. Fissore, F., Pirotti, F., Vettore, A.: Open source web tool for tracking in a low cost MMS. Int. Arch. Photogram. Remote Sens. Spat. Inf. Sci. ISPRS **XLII–2/W8**, 99–104 (2017)
24. Logitech: Logitech c920 HD Pro (2019). https://www.logitech.com/en-hk/product/hd-pro-webcam-c920
25. RoyalTek Ltd: Royaltek bluetooth GPS datalog receiver MBT-1100 user manual v1.1 (2008). http://www.royaltek.com/Upload/DownloadImages/2014040915215263.pdf
26. LORD Sensing: Microstrain 3DM-GX3-45 specifications (2019). https://www.microstrain.com/inertial/3dm-gx3-45
27. Tsai, G., Chiang, K.W., El-Sheimy, N.: Kinematic calibration using low-cost LiDAR system for mapping and autonomous driving applications. Int. Arch. Photogram. Remote Sens. Spat. Inf. Sci. ISPRS **XLII–1**, 445–450 (2018)
28. Livox Ltd: Livox Mid Series User Manual v1.2 (2019). https://www.livoxtech.com/mid-40-and-mid-100
29. Emlid Ltd: Emlid docs (2019). https://emlid.com/
30. GEC Software S.r.l.: Emlid reach m+ (2019). https://www.strumentitopografici.it/emlid-reach-m/
31. Bosch Sensortec GmbH: Bosch sensortec BN055 (2019). https://www.bosch-sensortec.com/bst/products/all_products/bno055
32. Zhang, J., Singh, S.: LOAM: LIDAR odometry and mapping in real-time. In: Robotics: Science and Systems, vol. 2, p. 9 (2014)

33. Li, Q., et al.: LO-Net: deep real-time LIDAR odometry. In: Proceedings of the IEEE Conference on Computer Vision and Pattern Recognition, pp. 8473–8482 (2019)
34. Zahran, S., Mostafa, M., Masiero, A., Moussa, A., Vettore, A., El-Sheimy, N.: Micro-RADAR and UWB aided UAV navigation in GNSS denied environment. Int. Arch. Photogram. Remote Sens. Spat. Inf. Sci. ISPRS **XLII–1**, 469–476 (2018)
35. Nex, F., Remondino, F.: UAV for 3D mapping applications: a review. Appl. Geomat. **6**(1), 1–15 (2013). https://doi.org/10.1007/s12518-013-0120-x
36. Masiero, A., Fissore, F., Vettore, A.: A low cost UWB based solution for direct georeferencing UAV photogrammetry. Remote Sens. **9**(5), 414 (2017)

A Comparison of Indoor Positioning Approaches with UWB, IMU, WiFi and Magnetic Fingerprinting

Ahmed Gamal Abdellatif Ibrhaim Keshka[1], Andrea Masiero[2,3(✉)] [iD],
Mostafa Mohamed Ahmed Mostafa[4], and Antonio Vettore[3] [iD]

[1] Department of Electronics and Communication, Faculty of Engineering,
Zagazig University, Sharkia, Egypt
[2] Department of Civil and Environmental Engineering, University of Florence,
via di Santa Marta 3, 50139 Florence, Italy
andrea.masiero@unifi.it, masiero@dei.unipd.it
[3] Interdepartmental Research Center of Geomatics (CIRGEO), University of Padova,
Viale dell'Università 16, 35020 Legnaro, PD, Italy
[4] Department of Geomatics, University of Calgary, Calgary, Canada

Abstract. Accurate indoor positioning is quite hard to be achieved with a single sensor embedded in the current generation of mobile devices (e.g. smartphones), hence it is commonly accepted that the integration of information from different sensors is a sine qua non condition in order to improve the indoor positioning performance of such devices.

Among the sensors typically used to such aim, it is possible to list inertial, magnetic sensors and radio transreceivers. In particular, pedestrian dead reckoning typically relies on the use of inertial sensor navigation, aided with external information, provided for example from the WiFi radio signal, to compensate the inertial navigation drift. WiFi is used for positioning either exploiting the radio signal strength (RSS) path loss, which can be used to estimate the distance of the device from access points and then trilaterate the device position, or with a fingerprinting approach. The latter has been recently used also for the magnetic field. One of the main issues related to fingerprinting is the long training phase, needed to determine a reliable WiFi/magnetic field model.

In this paper, a set of Ultra Wide Band (UWB) devices has been used to obtain a reference trajectory of a moving pedestrian. In particular, first, the paper compares different approaches used to obtain an appropriate reference trajectory from the UWB measurements, and, then, it investigates the use of UWB positioning to speed up the fingerprinting training phase, showing the characteristics of the WiFi and magnetic datasets collected and processed in this way.

Keywords: Indoor positioning · UWB · IMU · Magnetic field · Fingerprinting

© Springer Nature Switzerland AG 2020
C. Parente et al. (Eds.): R3GEO 2019, CCIS 1246, pp. 129–141, 2020.
https://doi.org/10.1007/978-3-030-62800-0_11

1   Introduction

Nowadays GNSS provides reliable positioning estimates in most of the outdoors conditions of interest. Important exceptions are clearly urban canyons, such as in several city centers and other metropolitan areas, and, more in general, close to high objects, such as mountains, where the GNSS signal is either obstructed or reflected, causing the multi-path phenomena, which significantly degrades the GNSS positioning performance [1].

Thanks to the availability of such reliable positioning systems on the mobile devices of billions of persons all around the World, then, during the last decade, a number of location based services (LBSs), e.g. typically related to commercial activities, spread everywhere exploiting the user location knowledge in order to provide him/her information specifically tailored on his/her own potential needs. The everyday experience of almost any smartphone user experimentally proves that properly exploiting such kind of technology can determine the success of a significant percentage of the commercial activities.

Mostly motivated by the large number of indoor commercial activities and public offices, the interest on indoor positioning systems has continuously increased during the recent years, with the goal of properly extending the availability of location based services also to GNSS-denied environments.

Actually, the current absence of a stand alone indoor positioning system already usable on current smartphones and able to completely substitute the GNSS in indoor environments, and the even higher accuracies required in indoor navigation with respect to its outdoor counterpart, make developing a suitable solution for this task a quite challenging problem.

Despite initially approaches based on single sensors (e.g. WiFi) have been investigated [2–4], nowadays, it is commonly accepted that only a proper integration of the information provided by most of the sensors available on smartphones can lead to a sufficiently robust and accurate navigation solution in indoor environments [5–8].

Furthermore, cooperative positioning, where multiple devices share certain information, has also been investigated to ease the positioning process, in particular when certain of them do not have access to a sufficient amount of information from their own sensors to autonomously compute their own position [9,10].

In most of the cases the tracking algorithm is composed by an inertial sensor-based pedestrian dead reckoning (PDR) approach integrated with external information, such as WiFi and magnetic field fingerprinting, in order to compensate the drift of estimates derived from the inertial navigation system [11]. In particular, given the possibility of acquiring magnetic field measurements at a much higher sample frequency with respect to WiFi RSS in Android phones (which currently represent 85% of the worldwide smartphone market), the use of such information has been proven to be useful to improve a rough device position on a relatively small local neighborhood of the initial rough estimate [12]. Among the different features that can be considered to such aim, the magnetic gradient is probably the most well suited one [13]. In certain cases radio beacons have been used even in the outdoors case to improve GNSS positioning on mobile devices provided with consumer-level GNSS receivers [14]. Furthermore, vision can also be used to significantly improve the positioning performance of mobile devices [15], and it can also be advantageously exploited for mapping purposes [16–18]. However, running vision-based positioning algorithm may be quite computationally expensive, leading to a quite fast run-off of the mobile device battery. According to the latter observation, vision is not included in the approaches considered in this work.

Since fingerprinting training phase is typically quite long, in certain works an RSS path loss model has been integrated with PDR instead [19,20]. Given the simplicity of the path loss model and its higher reliability in open spaces, its use has been investigated also for unmanned aerial vehicles [21], where RADAR and cameras have been considered as well [22].

Actually, in certain cases PDR-based tracks have been used to cope with the fingerprinting training phase, e.g. to ease such phase, typically imposing regular trajectories passing through certain previously well established waypoints [23].

Motivated by the above observation, one of the goals of the project related to this paper is that of assessing the possibility of leveraging the use of a low cost UWB system in order to shorten the duration of the fingerprinting phase. The fast fingerprinting procedure investigated in this paper lets an operator move freely on the area of interest while collecting WiFi RSS and magnetic field samples. Operator's movements are tracked by an UWB positioning system during all the data collection. The user's goal is that of covering as much as possible the area of interest, while acquiring sensor data on a spatially almost continuous trajectory (in particular for what concerns magnetic field data, which are sampled very frequently). Hence, similarly to [23], this method allows to collect information on much more points with respect to standard fingerprinting, which just focuses on a discrete set of locations. On the other hand, the information collected about a single position is clearly less complete with respect to standard fingerprinting. However, differently from [23] an accurate description of the spatial locations of the acquired sensor data is possible while letting the operator move relatively freely, thanks to the use of the UWB system to reliably track his/her position.

This paper aims at assessing the effectiveness of the UWB system to the above described purpose, and hence on the search of the most suitable way to compute a proper UWB-based reference trajectory.

Then, the appropriateness of the collected datasets, whose corresponding positions are computed as described above, for fingerprinting is investigated.

Finally, the positioning performance that can be achieved using such information combined with inertial sensor information is also investigated.

2   Test Area Description

The test area considered in this work involves two corridors of the second floor of a building of the University of Padua. The length of such two parts is approximately 40 m and 12 m, respectively (Fig. 1). It is worth to notice that the passage on such corridors has not been restricted during the tests, hence students freely walked on such area during the tests, as shown in Fig. 1(b), hence the obtained results can be considered as obtained in a real scenario. Figure 2 shows a map of the test area.

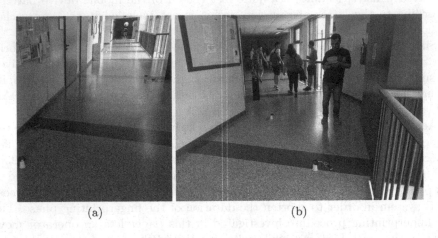

(a)   (b)

Fig. 1. Images of the test area.

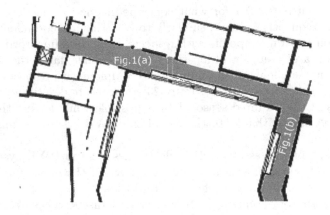

Fig. 2. Map of the test area (gray area). (Color figure online)

3   UWB-Based Reference Trajectory

This work leveraged the use of a set of Pozyx UWB devices to enable accurate positioning on all the test area [24], and hence to compute a trajectory to be used as reference.

UWB positioning is typically based on the use of a network of devices fixed on invariant and known positions, often called anchors, and on one (or multiple) moving device(s), named tag(s), which can measure its (their) distance from the anchors by means of UWB communications, and then assess their own position(s) by means of trilateration. The results of such trilateration assessment can clearly be improved if the UWB ranging error is properly modeled, i.e. calibration of the UWB measurements [25].

Furthermore, an adaptive approach, where the network of UWB nodes can dynamically change, can be considered as well, e.g. smartphones provided with UWB transreceivers freely entering/exiting the area of interest [26].

UWB is often considered as a potentially stand-alone solution, enabling positioning at decimeter level of accuracy. However, it requires the installation of an ad hoc infrastructure of UWB devices, whose number can be quite large in the case of complex buildings. Furthermore, the mobile device to be tracked has to be provided with an UWB transreceiver, which is not common in the current generation of smartphones.

In this work, a set of eleven Pozyx anchors (Fig. 3(a)) were distributed over the area of interest to properly track the position of the tag, which was connected with an Android phone (Fig. 3(b)). The Android phone stored the UWB measurements along with their time-stamps. Furthermore, Android smartphone sensor measurements were collected simultaneously.

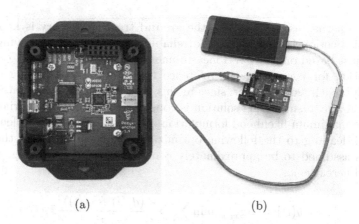

(a)   (b)

Fig. 3. (a) Pozyx anchor. (b) Pozyx rover connected via USB cable with a smartphone.

The position of the UWB anchors is reported in Fig. 4(a) (black circles), along with a schematic map of the area of interest and the ground truth of a short trajectory collected during the tests (green solid line).

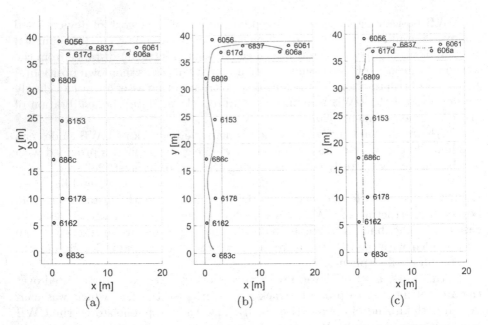

Fig. 4. (a) First part of the reference trajectory (54 s, approximately). (b) Solution of the optimization problem. (c) Filtered solution. (Color figure online)

Despite in the case of Fig. 4(a) the ground truth trajectory is known, the goal of this Section is that of provide reliable estimates of the moving device positions just based on the UWB measurements.

An option for computing the reference trajectory is considering an EKF tracking approach [26], however, since in this case the position estimates can be provided off-line, a smoothing solution is considered as more appropriate.

First, a maximum likelihood formulation of the trilateration problem can be considered, leading to the following optimization functional, where the device altitude is assumed to be approximately constant $\bar{z}$ (2D positioning, which is considered hereafter):

$$\{\hat{x}(i), \hat{y}(i)\} = \arg_{x_i, y_i} \min \sum_i \sum_j \frac{(\hat{d}_j(i) - r_j(i))^2}{\sigma_r^2} \mathbb{I}_j(i) \tag{1}$$

where $[\hat{x}(i) \ \hat{y}(i) \ \bar{z}]^\top$ is the estimated position corresponding to the i-th UWB time sample, $r_j(i)$ is the measurement of the j-th anchor at the i-th UWB time sample, σ_r is the uncertainty on UWB measurements (assumed for simplicity to be zero-mean and Gaussian), $[x_{anch,j} \ y_{anch,j} \ z_{anch,j}]^\top$ is the position of the j-th anchor and $\hat{d}_j(i)$ is defined as follows:

$$\hat{d}_j(i) = \sqrt{(x_i - x_{anch,j})^2 + (y_i - y_{anch,j})^2 + (\hat{z} - z_{anch,j})^2} \tag{2}$$

Finally, $\mathbb{I}_j(i)$ is an indicator function: its value is 1 if the $r_j(i)$ is available, and 0 otherwise.

Actually, the above maximum likelihood trilateration functional can be integrated with a term taking into account of the regularity of the device dynamic, in order to smooth the resulting trajectory.

In this work the following dynamic model was considered, and the corresponding term added to the previous functional to regularize the trajectory:

$$\begin{bmatrix} \hat{x}(t + \Delta t) \\ \hat{y}(t + \Delta t) \end{bmatrix} \approx \begin{bmatrix} \hat{x}(t) \\ \hat{y}(t) \end{bmatrix} + \Delta t \begin{bmatrix} \hat{v}_x(t) \\ \hat{v}_y(t) \end{bmatrix} \tag{3}$$

$$\begin{bmatrix} \hat{v}_x(t + \Delta t) \\ \hat{v}_y(t + \Delta t) \end{bmatrix} = \begin{bmatrix} \hat{v}_x(t) \\ \hat{v}_y(t) \end{bmatrix} + \begin{bmatrix} \hat{e}_{v,x}(t) \\ \hat{e}_{v,y}(t) \end{bmatrix} \tag{4}$$

where $[v_x(t)\ v_y(t)]^\top$ is the 2D device velocity at time t, $[e_{v,x}(t)\ e_{v,y}(t)]$ its variation at time t, and Δt the time interval between two consecutive UWB measurements.

The results obtained minimizing the obtained functional can be seen in Fig. 4(b) for the same trajectory of Fig. 4(a).

It is worth to notice that, despite the obtained trajectory is quite close to the ground truth one, a clear uncertainty on the direction orthogonal to the heading direction is quite visible.

Such behavior is due to the smoothing effect of the regularization term and on the higher estimation uncertainty on such direction caused by the specific UWB anchor network geometry. Similarly to the GNSS case, Fig. 5 shows a map of the geometric uncertainty (geometric dilution of precision, GDOP) along the x and y directions for the bottom part of the test area shown in Fig. 4(b). Figure 5 clearly shows the much higher uncertainty on the x direction on such area with respect to the y one.

Finally, a median filter was used to smooth the static UWB estimates, i.e. those obtained by just optimizing the likelihood (1) separately for each time sample index i. Figure 4(c) shows the obtained results on the trajectory of Fig. 4(a). As shown in Fig. 4(c), the obtained estimate is close to the true one along the corridor while still preserving quite well the original track shape on the corner, i.e. avoiding an extra-smoothing effect.

Given the quite good quality of the trajectory obtained with the median filter, and the much lower computational complexity required by such approach with respect to solving the maximum likelihood optimization problem, the results of the median filter approach are used in the results presented in the following sections.

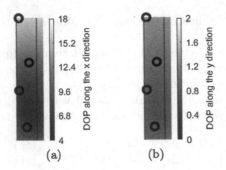

Fig. 5. Geometric DOP along the x (a) and y (b) directions on part of the test area.

4   Fingerprinting

The rationale of the fingerprinting approach considered here is that of exploiting the device positions estimated with UWB trilateration in order to enable free movement data collection. The basic assumptions are in this case: the availability of sufficiently accurate position estimates from the UWB system, and the possibility of collecting enough samples to determine the local characteristics of the magnetic field and of the WiFi RSS. The validity of the latter assumption clearly relies on the sample frequency of the data collection (the higher the better), and on the idea that, despite the values of such physical quantities fluctuate on the area of interest, its behavior is assumed to be in any local spatial neighborhood quite regular.

Given the latter assumption, the statistical characteristics of a quantity on a specific location are computed taking into account of the measurements collected in a neighborhood of such location.

Since this approach can clearly take advantage from measurements taken at high sampling rates, it should be quite well suited for the magnetic field case.

Figure 6 shows the absolute values of the magnetic field collected during three walks on approximately the same trajectory. The estimated positions along the three walks are shown on the left subfigure of Fig. 6, whereas the magnetic field absolute values as a function of the y coordinates are shown on the right.

On the one hand, Fig. 6 shows that the estimated trajectories of the three walks are almost equal: since such trajectories are assumed to be approximately rectilinear, any deviation from a rectilinear line can be considered as an estimate of the positioning error along the direction orthogonal to the heading one. From the figure, it is quite clear that such errors are at decimeter level, as also expected from the previous investigations on UWB positioning.

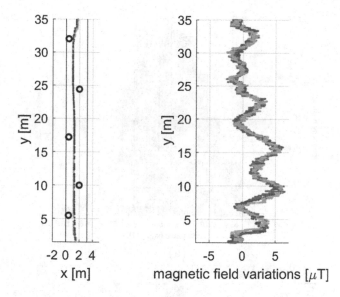

Fig. 6. Estimated device trajectory along three approximately equivalent tracks in the middle of the corridor (left). Variations of the absolute value of the measured magnetic field along such three tracks as a function of the y coordinate of the estimated positions (right).

On the other hand, the figure shows also a clearly repetitive pattern in the magnetic field behavior, which should be useful for positioning purposes.

Then, Fig. 7 compares the distributions of the magnetic field absolute value on a the location at coordinate $y = 7$ m on the center of the corridor collected with standard fingerprinting (e.g. device still on the considered position for a certain time interval) and with the proposed approach, where a spatial neighborhood of 0.6 m has been considered for computing such distribution.

As shown in Fig. 7, the proposed approach allows to approximately determine the magnetic field value corresponding to the peak value of the distribution and to assess the distribution width.

Similar considerations can be repeated for the WiFi RSS case, where, however, the lower sampling rate implies the need of assuming the regularity of such quantity on a larger local neighborhood to determine its distribution characteristics.

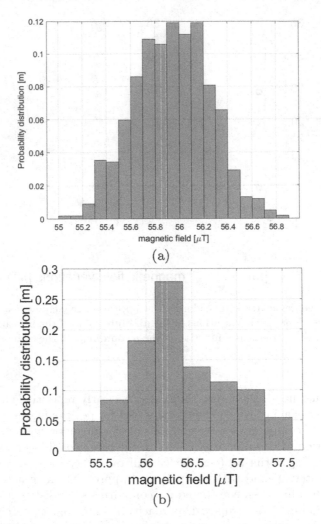

Fig. 7. Distribution of the measured magnetic field values on a fixed position of the corridor, ($x \approx 1.6$m, $y \approx 7$m). Comparison of the distribution computed with the device still on the position for 10 s (a), with that obtained with the device moving, passing three times over the considered location (b).

5   Results

After the model learning phase a short estimated trajectory is shown as validation example in this section.

Figure 8 compares the PDR inertial based trajectory (blue), with the one obtained by integrating also the information about the fluctuations of the magnetic field (red). Furthermore, the reference one is shown as well (green solid line).

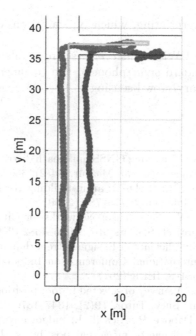

Fig. 8. Comparison of the PDR inertial based trajectory (blue), the one obtained taking into account of magnetic field fluctuations (red), and the reference one (green solid line). (Color figure online)

Despite the plotted trajectory is quite short, the advantage of taking into account of the magnetic field local characteristics is quite apparent.

6   Conclusions

This work considered a partial assessment of the advantages that can be obtained by integrating inertial navigation with other sensor information, and, in particular with a magnetic map properly computed in a previous training phase. A similar approach can clearly be applied also to the WiFi RSS case.

Differently from standard fingerprinting, in this case the training phase has been speeded up by exploiting UWB-based position estimates, and hence dynamically acquiring sensor measurements.

In UWB positioning, the mobile device to be tracked has to be provided with an UWB transreceiver, which is not common in the current generation of smartphones. However, as shown in the initial performance assessment of the results section, the considered approach seems to be quite promising in reducing the fingerprinting training time. Furthermore, such approach allows the operator to move freely in the area of interest, hence potentially acquiring measurements on a spatially much denser set of points (e.g. all points continuously acquired by the device are exploited, hence forming an almost continuous trajectory, differently from standard fingerprinting, which typically considers measurements on a discrete grid).

Finally, in the case UWB transreceivers are available on several mobile devices (or even on standard smartphones), the considered approach can also be considered for voluntary/crowd sensing.

References

1. Xie, P., Petovello, M.G.: Measuring GNSS multipath distributions in urban Canyon environments. IEEE Trans. Instrum. Measur. **64**(2), 366–377 (2014)
2. Bahl, P., Padmanabhan, V.: RADAR: an in-building RF-based user location and tracking system. IEEE Infocom **2**, 775–784 (2000)
3. Casari, P., et al.: The "Wireless Sensor Networks for City-Wide Ambient Intelligence (WISE-WAI)" project. Sensors **9**(6), 4056–4082 (2009)
4. Sakr, M., El-Sheimy, N.: Efficient Wi-Fi signal strength maps using sparse Gaussian process models. In: International Conference on Indoor Positioning and Indoor Navigation (IPIN), pp. 1–8. IEEE (2017)
5. Davidson, P., Piché, R.: A survey of selected indoor positioning methods for smartphones. IEEE Commun. Surv. Tutor. **19**(2), 1347–1370 (2016)
6. Piras, M., Lingua, A., Dabove, P., Aicardi, I.: Indoor navigation using smartphone technology: a future challenge or an actual possibility? In: IEEE/ION Position, Location and Navigation Symposium-PLANS 2014, pp. 1343–1352. IEEE (2014)
7. Dabove, P., Aicardi, I., Grasso, N., Lingua, A., Ghinamo, G., Corbi, C.: Inertial sensors strapdown approach for hybrid cameras and mems positioning. In: IEEE/ION Position, Location and Navigation Symposium (PLANS), pp. 994–1000. IEEE (2016)
8. Wang, C., et al.: Progress on ISPRS benchmark on multisensory indoor mapping and positioning. ISPRS - Int. Arch. Photogram. Remote Sens. Spat. Inf. Sci. **XLII-2/W13**, 1709-1713 (2019)
9. Kealy, A., et al.: Collaborative navigation as a solution for PNT applications in GNSS challenged environments-report on field trials of a joint FIG/IAG working group. J. Appl. Geodesy **9**(4), 244–263 (2015)
10. Seco, F., Jiménez, A.: Smartphone-based cooperative indoor localization with RFID technology. Sensors **18**(1), 266 (2018)
11. Ban, R., Kaji, K., Hiroi, K., Kawaguchi, N.: Indoor positioning method integrating pedestrian dead reckoning with magnetic field and WIFI fingerprints. In: Eighth International Conference on Mobile Computing and Ubiquitous Networking (ICMU), pp. 167–172. IEEE (2015)
12. Binu, P., Krishnan, R.A., Kumar, A.P.: An efficient indoor location tracking and navigation system using simple magnetic map matching. In: IEEE International Conference on Computational Intelligence and Computing Research (ICCIC), pp. 1–7. IEEE (2016)
13. Li, Y., Zhuang, Y., Zhang, P., Lan, H., Niu, X., El-Sheimy, N.: An improved inertial/WiFi/magnetic fusion structure for indoor navigation. Inf. Fusion **34**, 101–119 (2017)
14. Osaba, E., Pierdicca, R., Malinverni, E., Khromova, A., Álvarez, F., Bahillo, A.: A smartphone-based system for outdoor data gathering using a wireless beacon network and GPS data: from cyber spaces to senseable spaces. ISPRS Int. J. Geo-Inf. **7**(5), 190 (2018)

15. Nistér, D., Naroditsky, O., Bergen, J.: Visual odometry. In: Proceedings of the 2004 IEEE Computer Society Conference on Computer Vision and Pattern Recognition. CVPR 2004, vol. 1, pp. 1–652. IEEE (2004)
16. Forster, C., Pizzoli, M., Scaramuzza, D.: SVO: fast semi-direct monocular visual odometry. In: IEEE International Conference on Robotics and Automation (ICRA), pp. 15–22. IEEE (2014)
17. Fissore, F., Masiero, A., Piragnolo, M., Pirotti, F., Guarnieri, A., Vettore, A.: Towards surveying with a smartphone. In: Cefalo, R., Zieliński, J.B., Barbarella, M. (eds.) New Advanced GNSS and 3D Spatial Techniques. LNGC, pp. 167–176. Springer, Cham (2018). https://doi.org/10.1007/978-3-319-56218-6_13
18. Whelan, T., Johannsson, H., Kaess, M., Leonard, J.J., McDonald, J.: Robust real-time visual odometry for dense RGB-D mapping. In: IEEE International Conference on Robotics and Automation (ICRA), pp. 5724–5731. IEEE (2013)
19. Widyawan, P.G., et al.: Virtual lifeline: multimodal sensor data fusion for robust navigation in unknown environments. Pervasive Mob. Comput. 8(3), 388–401 (2012)
20. Masiero, A., Guarnieri, A., Pirotti, F., Vettore, A.: A particle filter for smartphone-based indoor pedestrian navigation. Micromachines 5(4), 1012–1033 (2014)
21. Masiero, A., Fissore, F., Guarnieri, A., Pirotti, F., Vettore, A.: UAV positioning and collision avoidance based on RSS measurements. ISPRS - Int. Arch. Photogram. Remote Sens. Spat. Inf. Sci. 40(1), 219 (2015)
22. Mostafa, M., Zahran, S., Moussa, A., El-Sheimy, N., Sesay, A.: Radar and visual odometry integrated system aided navigation for UAVs in GNSS denied environment. Sensors 18(9), 2776 (2018)
23. Kuang, J., Niu, X., Zhang, P., Chen, X.: Indoor positioning based on pedestrian dead reckoning and magnetic field matching for smartphones. Sensors 18(12), 4142 (2018)
24. Pozyx Labs: Pozyx positioning system (2015). https://www.pozyx.io/
25. Retscher, G., Gikas, V., Hofer, H., Perakis, H., Kealy, A.: Range validation of UWB and Wi-Fi for integrated indoor positioning. Appl. Geomat. 11(2), 187–195 (2019). https://doi.org/10.1007/s12518-018-00252-5
26. Sakr, M., Masiero, A., El-Sheimy, N.: LocSpeck: a collaborative and distributed positioning system for asymmetric nodes based on UWB ad-hoc network and Wi-Fi fingerprinting. Sensors 20(1), 78 (2020)

Sea Tide Analysis Derived by PPP Kinematic GPS Data Acquired at David-Drygalski Floating Ice Tongue (Antarctica)

Luca Vittuari[1] ⓘ, Marco Dubbini[2] ⓘ, Leonardo Martelli[1],
and Antonio Zanutta[1(✉)] ⓘ

[1] Dipartimento di Ingegneria Civile, Chimica, Ambientale e dei Materiali,
Bologna University, 40136 Bologna, Italy
{luca.vittuari,leonardo.martelli,
antonio.zanutta}@unibo.it
[2] Dipartimento di Storia Culture Civiltà, Bologna University,
40136 Bologna, Italy
marco.dubbini@unibo.it

Abstract. One of the most important ice-stream of the Victoria Land (VL) is the David Glacier, which produces 100 km long floating sea-ward ice tongues in the Ross Sea, the Drygalski Ice Tongue (DIT). The ice-tongue slides down into the sea increasing its velocity rates and together with ice-stream movement sometime produce characteristic ice-quakes. This paper shows the effects of the sea tidal variation on both horizontal and vertical components of movement at a portion of DIT. Ocean tide is usually modelled by a series of harmonic coefficients (amplitude and phase), which are estimated through several systems of measurement. For the study area, these data are made available by the Antarctic Tide Gauge (ATG) database. Moreover, tidal data recorded by a multiparameter underwater tide gauge, which was installed at Mario Zucchelli Station (MZS), the Italian Antarctic Base, in February 2006, are being processed again.

The kinematic Precise Point Positioning (PPP) processing was adopted for the analysis of 24 days of acquisition performed with a GPS receiver located in the initial part of DIT, about 46 km seaward from the Ice Fault David Cauldron. The analysis of harmonic tidal components has shown that PPP solutions show correct values of diurnal and semi-diurnal tidal components and therefore can provide valuable information in the coastal area covered by ice tongues.

Keywords: Tide analysis · Kinematic precise point positioning · Glacier mechanics · Antarctica

1 Introduction

Antarctica is a continent almost entirely covered by ice and therefore particularly sensitive to climate change. The Antarctic ice coverage includes continental glaciers and marine ice shelves, which influence Earth's energy balance through their high albedo. For this reason, the decrease in the volume of the ice mass would lead to an increase in the global temperature.

C. Parente et al. (Eds.): R3GEO 2019, CCIS 1246, pp. 142–154, 2020.
https://doi.org/10.1007/978-3-030-62800-0_12

Glacier dynamics depend on several effects (bedrock and ice surface topography, snow accumulation, fault alignments in the bedrock, dry or wet basal condition, ice temperature, weather conditions, etc.). When the ice flows are fed by very large drainage basins, such as those of the plateau areas of Eastern Antarctica, the flows become very fast and concentrate towards the coast in narrow "rivers of ice", which are called ice-streams.

The Drygalski Ice Tongue (DIT), 75°30′ S, 163°50′ E, is the seaward eastward extension of the David Glacier into the Ross Sea. It is about 100 km long and 14–24 km wide, and it is fed by the David Glacier and the Larsen Glacier, along the coast of Victoria Land (VL), more than 100 km far from Mario Zucchelli Station (MZS), the Italian base in Antarctica (Fig. 1). The David-Drygalski Glacier and DIT are the most important glaciers of VL.

In Terranova Bay there is a large area of open water produced by very strong katabatic winds (polynya), which persists throughout the winter. The David Glacier is the most massive drainage glacier for Talos Dome and Dome C in the East Antarctica sector. From Transantarctic Mountains start strong winds that blow downslope, driving the sea ice eastward. The dominant ice drift pattern in the area is northward, so DIT prevents the Terra Nova Bay from being repopulated with sea ice.

The DIT evolution was monitored and studied for glaciological and geophysical purposes [1, 2], and oceanographic ones [3–6].

Remote sensing and past geodetic GPS surveys showed that the terminal part of the DIT is characterized by high superficial velocities, up to 700 m/year [7–12].

In general, the fluctuation of the ice sheets depends on the processes in the sub-glacial environment. The extension variation of the ice shelf affects tides and alters the speed of movement of glacial tongues [13–16].

The study of the behaviour of the Antarctic ice balance is important for understanding the variation of the global marine level, which affects the flow of ice from the continent to the ocean.

Furthermore, DIT acts as a blocking feature to the upper sea, forcing surface current. The local ocean circulation is affected by tidal excursion, which plays a role on in terms of pumping and local supercooling [5].

Shear seismicity along the ice-bed interface is a function of the sliding motion of glaciers, the flow speed and is affected by the tide behaviour [17–24]. The DIT is in hydrostatic equilibrium year-round, but falling tide behaviour produces acceleration of the Ice Tongue.

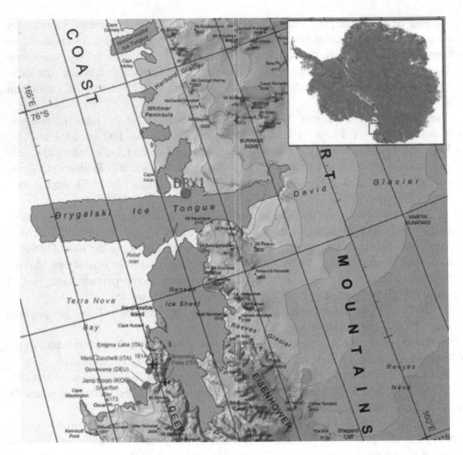

Fig. 1. Map shows the Drygalski Ice Tongue (DIT). DRY1 is the GPS station located in the initial part of DIT (modified from "Map 16: Victoria Land, Edition 3", Polar Geospatial Center, USA). The location of the tide gauge of Cape Roberts is off the map, 170 km far southward DIT.

Tidal observations are the basic water level readings, usually coming from tide gauges, which are instruments that allow most accurate analysis.

Satellite altimetry is a remote sensing suitable technique for measuring tidal changes.

Ice Cloud and Land Elevation Satellite (ICESat) have been running since 2003 using the GLAS Geoscience Laser altimeter System [25]. The system provides water level in Antarctica with accuracy greater than 20 cm [26].

The research purposes are to show the effects of the sea tidal variation on both horizontal and vertical components of movement at a portion of DIT.

Ocean tides in the area of the DIT were obtained using a single GPS receiver and compared with those obtained from the tide gauge placed near MZS [27]. In Antarctica this technique was previously adopted successfully by several authors [19, 28–31].

King and Aoki [32] presented a similar approach to obtain tidal observations on floating ice using a single GPS receiver and processing GPS data based on the Precise Point Positioning. In this case, there is no need for a GPS reference station that acquires continuously and the method provides quite similar precision allowing of diurnal and semi-diurnal tidal constituents, which can be assimilated into numerical tide models.

GNSS data processing and tidal analysis procedures are described in Sects. 2 and 3.

2 GNSS Data Processing

During the 2005–06 Austral Summer (21st Italian Expedition to Antarctica) two GPS antennas (DRY1 and ICF1) were installed on the Drygalski Ice Tongue [19]. The collected dataset resulted in 24-h 15-s GNSS data in compressed RINEX format. The observation periods were 24 and 34 days respectively. Only the point DRY1 was located downstream of the grounding line of the David Glacier, and therefore was reprocessed in this analysis. For the installation of the geodetic GPS station on the ice, an aluminium tube of 13 cm diameter and 3 m long was used, and driven in the ice of about 1 m. To fix the antenna on the top of the pole was used an aluminium adaptor designed to allow the self-centering of the geodetic antenna. A solar panel was used as power supply for the GPS receiver for several days.

Dual-frequency GPS daily observations were analysed firstly by Danesi et al. [19]. In this case, a differential approach was used, adopting the kinematic module TRACK of GAMIT-GLOBK post processing software [33]. Vice versa, in this study a PPP approach was adopted using the Bernese GNSS software, Version 5.2 [34, 35], to calculate the kinematic position of DRY1 GPS antenna.

The CODE products such as satellite orbits, 30-s clocks, and Earth orientation parameters (EOP) were used in the calculation along with the IGS products for the atmosphere modelling. The solution discussed in this paper was calculated using 900 s as the observable sampling interval and does not take into account the atmospheric tidal loading (ATL) corrections.

In Fig. 2 is reported the comparison between the differenced post processing approach, obtained at the time of the measurements using the module TRACK of GAMIT-GLOBK post processing software, and the new PPP processing using the Bernese GNSS software, Version 5.2. The time series are quite similar and the processing following a PPP approach using the Bernese GNSS software furnish a cleaner solution.

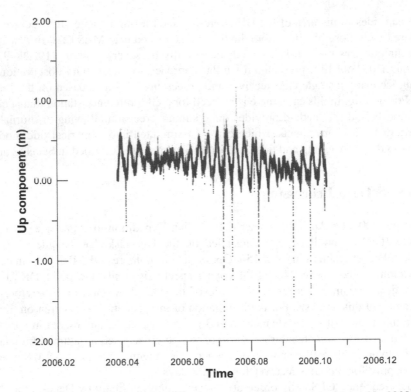

Fig. 2. Comparison between the differentiated post processing approach obtained in 2008 at the time of the measurements using the module TRACK of GAMIT-GLOBK post processing software (red points), and the new processing made in 2019 following a PPP approach using the Bernese GNSS software, Version 5.2 (blue points). (Color figure online)

Considering that 10 years have passed between the differentiated solution and the PPP solution, and that in recent years considerable improvements in analysis methods and in the quality of ancillary products (ephemeris, clocks, PCV models, etc.) have been achieved, we can still consider of good quality the kinematic differentiated solution obtained using a reference station at a distance of over 100 km. Despite the many outliers, now absent in the undifferentiated analysis, the amplitudes and the phases of the signals were also identified in this first analysis. The actual precision achievable using the PPP kinematic approach in the same conditions of those described in this study can be considered at 5 cm level [32].

3   Tidal Analysis

The water level variation is mainly a function of the gravitational interactions between earth, moon and sun. Tidal frequencies are characterized by defined parameters. The purpose of tidal analysis is to reproduce significant and stable absolute tidal parameters representing the tidal regime of the observation place. These parameters are called tidal constants to indicate their stability over time.

The quality of the parameters is also a function of the quantity of data and their temporal extent. The water level changes at both tidal and non-tidal frequencies. Sea level can be modified due to weather conditions, such as evaporation, solar radiation, wind and atmospheric pressure changes. These effects must be added to those derived from the astronomical ones.

The aim of the tide analysis is to separate these two components and to estimate predictable water level. In this study the calculated tidal parameters have a relative non-absolute meaning: they were estimated using a short series of GNSS data collected on DIT (DRY1 24JD), [19].

The closest tidal gauge to DRY1 is placed at Mario Zucchelli Station (MZS), [36]. It is maintained by the Italian Geodetic Observatory in Antarctic (IGOA) in the frame of the Italian National Program for Antarctic Research (PNRA, Programma Nazionale di Ricerche in Antartide). The harmonic tidal parameters used for the comparison were extracted from Goring, Pyne [27].

For the analysis and prediction of water levels in tidal waterways the World Tides and World Current 2013, program described in: John D. Boon Marine Consultant, LLC [37], were adopted.

This analysis permits the evaluation of a water level time series into its tidal harmonic components, relative to the Mean Sea Level (MSL), using a selective least squares harmonic reduction, and employing up to 36 tidal constituents. This program adopts HAMELS method (Harmonic Analysis MEthod of Least Squares) [37] to analyze the level time series, which achieves a progressive reduction in variance adding harmonic specific astronomical terms to a general least squares model [37].

After the evaluation of tidal harmonic constants using measured observations, prediction of the astronomical tide is produced. Differences between predicted and observed tides make it possible to detect residuals signals mainly due to non-tidal effects.

In Table 1 are shown the estimated values of amplitude and phase of sea-tide components: forecast value at MZS and the estimated ones from the PPP time series.

In Fig. 3 are reported the vertical movements derived by the PPP analysis of 24 days acquired at DRY1, compared with the forecast sea tide signal derived by the same dataset.

Table 1. Forecast ocean-tide described by 8 principal harmonic components included in the ATG database for MZS, and estimation of the same parameters from PPP time series observed at DIT.

Tidal Components	Forecast sea-tide derived by ATG database for MZS		Observed PPP at DIT	
	Amplitude (cm)	Phase ° (Greenwich)	Amplitude (cm)	Phase ° (Greenwich)
Q1	4.1	146.0	2.8	108.2
O1	18.3	169.6	10.8	189.7
P1	6.0	204.8	1.8	187.9
K1	16.8	204.2	9.9	226.4
N2	4.4	228.8	3.4	178.8
M2	6.9	336.3	4.0	354.8
S2	5.9	304.7	5.1	342.0
K2	2.5	329.1	1.3	181.1

4 Results

The diurnal declinational tides K1 and O1 are the most important tides which occur once a day. In the Ross Sea as well as in the coasts between 65° W to 140° E there is a tide cycle per day, the lunar phases do not affect the tides. This confirm Thiel et al., [38], who firstly showed that the Ross Sea tide is diurnal and the solar component is predominating. Tides amplitude in the Ross Sea reduces every 13.66 days, corresponding to the Moon's crossing of the equator [27].

Robinson et al. [39] demonstrated that the amplitudes of the diurnal tidal constituents in the Ross Sea are larger than in the adjacent Southern Pacific Ocean, indicating the existence of a diurnal resonance related to the shape and depth of the sea.

The tidal levels observed are given by the sum of the astronomical effects due to the motion of the Moon and the Sun and to the weather contribution, which can play an important role that can change the sea level.

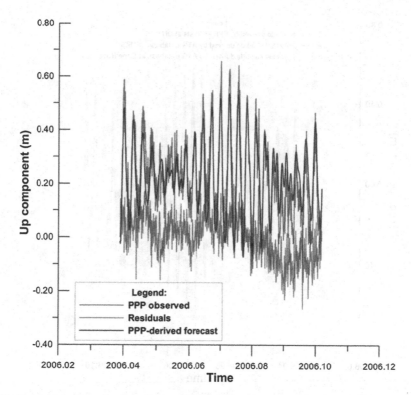

Fig. 3. Comparison between observed PPP time series at DIT and forecast sea-tide, computed by Q1, O1, P1, K1, N2, M2, S2, K2 harmonic coefficients estimated intrinsically by PPP time series. The residuals show the differences between the forecast signal and the observed one.

While the astronomical tide is predictable, the weather effects that produce variation in air pressure and wind induced effects are not easily predictable. Their presence is highlighted by the differences found between the expected and the observed tides (derived by GPS data).

Two main results are pointed out by this experiment:

1. The right amplitude and phase of sea tide response of the ice tongue, which is reduced in amplitude with respect to forecast waited signals (Fig. 4 and Fig. 5); DRY1 GPS station is located about 30 km seaward with respect to the estimated position of the grounding line. In this position, considering the elevation of the GPS point above sea-level, the submerged thickness of the ice is roughly 600 m at the DRY1 position. Due to ice thickness and lateral friction with respect to the rocky walls in which it expands inside a fjord, the amplitude of observed ice-tide at DRY1 is reduced.

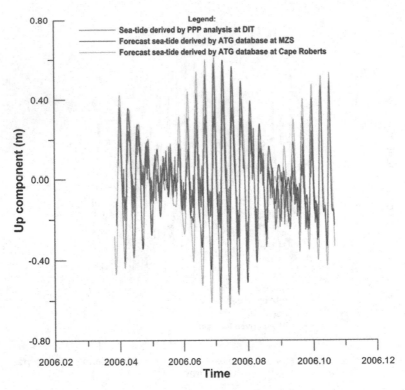

Fig. 4. Comparison between sea-tide observed by means of PPP time series acquired at DIT and the forecast sea-tide, computed by published Q1, O1, P1, K1, N2, M2, S2, K2 harmonic coefficients in ATG database for two sites: MZS (about 100 km Northward of DIT) and Cape Roberts (about 170 km Southern DIT).

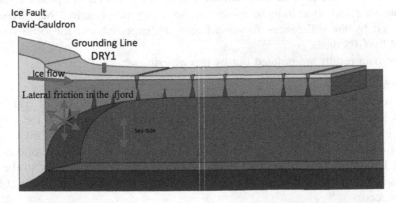

Fig. 5. Scheme of a float ice-tongue, derived by [40], introduced to point out a possible interpretation of Fig. 4, where two tide gauges located the first Northward and the second Southward with respect to DIT show amplitudes of sea-tide greater than the values observed at DRY1.

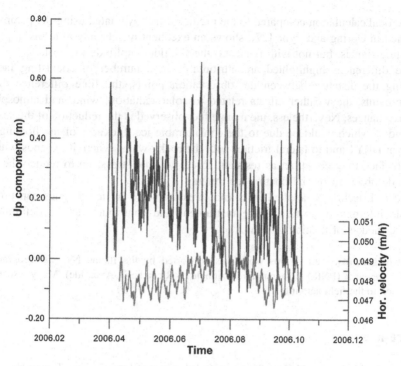

Fig. 6. Analysis of the horizontal velocity of the ice-tongue at DRY1, with respect to the phases of the vertical amplitude of sea tide. As can be clearly point out by the figure, the horizontal ice velocity increases with the increment of the tide amplitude. This effect could be interpreted with a minor friction of the glacial mass coming from the David, due to the greater elevation of the floating ice near the grounding line.

2. Horizontal velocity of ice flow increases and decreases seaward, as a response of tide amplitude changes (corresponding to the Moon's crossing of the equator). In particular, in Fig. 6 can be observed a delay of about 1–2 days between the high tide observed in the maximum amplitude tide phase with respect to the higher horizontal velocity of the ice.

5 Conclusions

In this paper the tidal harmonic constants were determined using post-processed GPS observations according to the PPP procedure and to a standard differentiated approach. The PPP technique is very effective because GPS base station is not required, and this option is particularly useful for acquisitions in remote areas, such as Antarctica, where the number of GNSS permanent stations is limited.

The differences between the predicted and the observed tides were analyzed. The PPP derived elevation time series confirms the diurnal characteristic of the sea tide in the DIT area, with small semidiurnal component.

The tidal calculation compared to the predicted tide evaluated using the parameters published in Goring and Pyne [27], shows an excellent match only in terms of phases of the tide signals, but not with regard to the sea tide amplitude forecast.

The differences highlighted are attributable to a number of coexisting factors, including the distance between the observation points, the time difference of the measurements, the weather effects related to solar radiation, wind, and atmospheric pressure changes. Nevertheless, the main effect observed is the reduction of the sea tide amplitudes, which could be due to the considerable ice thickness of the floating ice-tongue at DRY1 and to lateral friction with the rocky walls, where it expands within a fjord. In fact, they could act as resistant forces to tidal stress, up to reduce the tidal amplitude observed on the floating ice tongue

The PPP technique applied in coastal areas covered by ice tongues can provide valuable information as tide gauge instrument and contributes to the definition of dynamic models of floating glaciers.

Acknowledgements. Part of this work was supported by the Italian National Program for Antarctic Research (PNRA, Programma Nazionale di Ricerche in Antartide). Many researchers contributed to the field activities.

References

1. Frezzotti, M., Mabin, M.C.G.: 20th century behaviour of Drygalski Ice Tongue, Ross Sea. Antarctica. Ann. Glaciol. **20**, 397–400 (1994). https://doi.org/10.3189/172756494794587492
2. Van Woert, M.L., et al.: Satellite observations of upper-ocean currents in Terra Nova Bay. Antarctica. Ann. Glaciol. **33**(407–412), 2001 (2001). https://doi.org/10.3189/172756401781818879
3. Budillon, G., Spezie, G.: Thermohaline structure and variability in the Terra Nova Bay polynya. Ross Sea. Antarct. Sci. **12**(04), 493–508 (2000). https://doi.org/10.1017/S0954102000000572
4. Cappelletti, A., Picco, P., Peluso, T.: Upper ocean layer dynamics and response to atmospheric forcing in the Terra Nova Bay polynya. Antarctica. Antarct. Sci. **22**, 319–329 (2010). https://doi.org/10.1017/S095410201000009X
5. Stevens, C., et al.: The influence of the Drygalski Ice Tongue on the local ocean. Ann. Glaciol. **58**, 1–9 (2017). https://doi.org/10.1017/aog.2017.4
6. Jendersie, S., Williams, M., Langhorne, P.J., Robertson, R.: The density-driven winter intensification of the Ross Sea circulation. J. Geophys. Res. Oceans **123**, 7702–7724 (2018). https://doi.org/10.1029/2018JC013965
7. Berthier, E., Raup, B., Scambos, T.: New velocity map and mass-balance estimate of Mertz Glacier, East Antarctica, derived from Landsat sequential imagery. J. Glaciol. **49**(167), 503–511 (2003)
8. Frezzotti, M.: Glaciological study in Terra Nova Bay, Antarctica, inferred from remote sensing analysis. Ann. Glaciol. **17**, 63–71 (1993)
9. Frezzotti, M., Capra, A., Vittuari, L.: Comparison between glacier ice velocities inferred from GPS and sequential satellite images. Ann. Glaciol. **27**, 54–60 (1998)

10. Frezzotti, M., Tabacco, I., Zirizzotti, A.: Ice discharge of eastern Dome C drainage area, Antarctica, determined from airborne radar survey and satellite image analysis. J. Glaciol. **46**, 253264 (2000)
11. Rignot, E.: Mass balance of East Antarctic glaciers and ice-shelves from satellite data. Ann. Glaciol. **34**, 217–227 (2002)
12. Stearns, L.A.: Dynamics and mass balance of four large East Antarctic outlet glaciers. Ann. Glaciol. **52**(59), 116–126 (2011). https://doi.org/10.3189/172756411799096187
13. Bamber, J.L., Alley, R.B., Joughin, I.: Rapid response of modern day ice sheets to external forcing. Earth Planet. Sci. Lett. **257**, 1–13 (2007)
14. Lugli, A., Vittuari, L.: A polarimetric analysis of COSMO-SkyMed and RADARSAT-2 offset tracking derived velocities of David-Drygalski glacier (Antarctica). Appl. Geomatics **9**, 1–10 (2016). https://doi.org/10.1007/s12518-016-0181-8
15. Rignot, E., Casassa, G., Gogineni, P., Krabill, W., Rivera, A., Thomas, R.: Accelerated ice discharge from the Antarctic Peninsula following the collapse of Larsen B ice shelf. Geophys. Res. Lett. **31**, L18401 (2004). https://doi.org/10.1029/2004GL020697
16. Rott, H., Müller, F., Nagler, T., Floricioiu, D.: The imbalance of glaciers after disintegration of Larsen-B ice shelf, Antarctic Peninsula. Cryosphere **5**, 125–134 (2011)
17. Anandakrishnan, S., Voigt, D.E., Alley, R.B., King, M.A.: Ice stream D flow speed is strongly modulated by the tide beneath the Ross ice shelf. J. Geophys. Res. **30**, 14 (2003). https://doi.org/10.1029/2002GL016329
18. Bindschadler, R.A., King, M.A., Alley, R.B., Anandakrishnan, S., Padman, L.: Tidally controlled stick–slip discharge of a west antarctic ice. Science **301**(5636), 1087–1089 (2003)
19. Danesi, S., Dubbini, M., Morelli, A., Vittuari, L., Bannister, S.: Joint geophysical observations of ice stream dynamics. In: Capra, A., Dietrich, R. (eds.) Geodetic and Geophysical Observations in Antarctica. Springer, Heidelberg (2008). https://doi.org/10.1007/978-3-540-74882-3_3
20. Goldberg, D., Schoof, C., Sergienko, O.: Stick–slip motion of an Antarctic ice stream: the effects of viscoelasticity. J. Geophys. Res. Earth Surf. **119**(7), 1564–1580 (2014)
21. Kamb, B.: Sliding motion of glaciers: theory and observation. Rev. Geophys. **8**(4), 673–728 (1970)
22. Lipovsky, B.P., Dunham, E.M.: Tremor during ice-stream stick slip. Cryosphere **10**(1), 385–399 (2016)
23. Lipovsky, B.P., Dunham, E.M.: Slow-slip events on the Whillans ice plain, Antarctica, described using rate-and-state friction as an ice stream sliding law. J. Geophys. Res. Earth Surf. **122**(4), 973–1003 (2017)
24. Lipovsky, B.P., et al.: Glacier sliding, seismicity and sediment entrainment. Ann. Glaciol. **60** (79), 182–192 (2019). https://doi.org/10.1017/aog.2019.24
25. Fricker, H.A., Padman, L.: Tides on Filchner-Ronne ice shelf from ERS radar altimetry. Geophys. Res. Lett. **29**, 12 (2002). https://doi.org/10.1029/2001GL014175
26. Brenner, A., DiMarzio, J., Zwally, H.: Precision and accuracy of satellite radar and laser altimeter data over the continental ice sheets. IEEE Trans. Geosci. Remote **45**(2), 321–331 (2007)
27. Goring, D.G., Pyne, A.: Observations of sea level variability in Ross Sea, Antarctica. NZ J. Marine Freshwater Res. **37**, 241–249 (2003). https://doi.org/10.1080/00288330.2003.9517162
28. Aoki, S., Ozawa, T., Doi, K., Shibuya, K.: GPS observation of the sea level variation in Lutzow-Holm Bay. Antarctica. Geophys. Res. Lett. **27**(15), 2285–2288 (2000)
29. Aoki, S., Shibuya, K., Masuyama, A., Ozawa, T., Doi, K.: Evaluation of seasonal sea level variation at Syowa station, Antarctica, using GPS observations. J. Oceanogr. **58**(3), 519–523 (2002)

30. Capra, A., Gandolfi, S., Lusetti, L., Stocchino, C., Vittuari, L.: Kinematic GPS for the study of tidal undulation of floating ice tongue. Bollettino di Geodesia e scienze affini **2**, 151–175 (1999). ISSN 0006-6710

31. King, M., Nguyen, L.N., Coleman, R., Morgan, P.: Strategies for high precision processing of GPS measurements with application to the Amery ice Shelf. East Antarctica. GPS Sol. **4** (1), 2–12 (2000)

32. King, M., Aoki, S.: Tidal observations on floating ice using a single GPS receiver. Geophys. Res. Lett. **30**(3), 1138 (2003). https://doi.org/10.1029/2002GL016182

33. Herring, T., King, R.W., McClusky, S.C.: Introduction to GAMIT/GLOBK, Release 10.6. Department of Earth, Atmospheric, and Planetary Sciences Massachusetts Institute of Technology (2015)

34. Dach, R., Lutz, S., Walser, P., Fridez, P.: Bernese GNSS Software Version 5.2. User manual. Astronomical Institute, University of Bern, Bern Open Publishing (2015). https://doi.org/10.7892/boris.72297. ISBN 978-3-906813-05-9

35. Danesi, S., Bannister, S., Morelli, A.: Repeating earthquakes from rupture of an asperity under an Antarctic outlet glacier. Earth Planet. Sci. Lett. **253**, 151158 (2007). https://doi.org/10.1016/j.epsl.2006.10.023

36. Capra, A., et al.: VLNDEF project for geodetic infrastructure definition of Northern Victoria land, Antarctica. In: Capra, A., Dietrich, R. (eds.) Geodetic and Geophysical Observations in Antarctica. An Overview in the IPY Perspective. Springer, Heidelberg (2008). https://doi.org/10.1007/978-3-540-74882-3_3

37. Boon, J.D.: Secrets of the tide: tide and tidal current analysis and predictions, storm surges and sea level trends. secrets of the tide: tide and tidal current analysis and predictions, storm surges and sea level trends, pp. 1–210. Woodhead Publishing (2004). https://doi.org/10.1016/c2013-0-18114-7

38. Thiel, E., Crary, A.P., Haubrtch, R.A., Behrendt, J.C.: Gravimetric determination of ocean tide, Weddell and Ross seas. Antarctica. J. Geophys. Res. **65**(2), 629–636 (1960)

39. Robinson, E.S., Neuberg, H.A.C., Williams, R.T., Whitehurst, B.B., Moss, G.E.: Provisional cotidal charts for the southern Ross Sea. Antarct. J. U.S. **7**(4), 48 (1977)

40. Bassis, J., Ma, Y.: Evolution of basal crevasses links ice shelf stability to ocean forcing. Earth Planet Sci. Lett. **409**, 203–211 (2015). https://doi.org/10.1016/j.epsl.2014.11.003

Photogrammetry and Laser Scanning

A Procedure to Obtain a 3D Model in Bim and Structural Analysis Software

Domenica Costantino[1]([✉]) [iD], Massimiliano Pepe[1] [iD],
Marcello Carrieri[2], and Alfredo Restuccia Garofalo[2]

[1] DICATECh, Polytechnic of Bari, 70126 Bari, Italy
domenica.costantino@poliba.it
[2] AESEI s.r.l. Spin off - Polytechnic of Bari, 74015 Martina Franca, TA, Italy

Abstract. A reliable survey of the building geometry is a basic tool for the knowledge of the structure and the correct setting of numerical computational models. An accurate procedure of the method was applied to the build of the 3D model of church of San Nicola Montedoro in Martina Franca (Italy). In this case study, the survey of the church was performed using integrated geomatics techniques: TLS (Terrestrial Laser Scanner), terrestrial and UAV (Unmanned Aerial Vehicle) photogrammetry. In this way, it was possible to obtain an accurate and detailed geometric point cloud of the object. Subsequently, the 3D mesh model was generated from the point clouds. An adequate procedure of simplification and regularization of the meshes allowed to export and subsequently to import them into BIM (Building Information Modeling) software and structural analysis. In addition, a suitable procedure was implemented to produce a model based on Finite Element Method from a simplified model of polysurface mesh, which allowed quantifying the distortions of the building, through the knowledge of the details of each element, becoming the basis for subsequent analysis of the same.

Keywords: Scan-to-BIM · Point cloud · FEM

1 Introduction

The Scan-to-BIM process, for a renovation or extension works, enables digital analysis and management of buildings or constructions. The Scan task can be realized both with Image Based Method (IBM), i.e. by the use of passive sensor, such as digital camera, or by the use of the active sensors, such as the Terrestrial Laser Scanner (TLS) [1]. Two types of TLS are essentially used for the survey in the Architecture, Engineering and Construction (AEC) field: time-of-flight and phase modulation laser scanners, which allow the survey of even large surfaces with a level of detail with an accuracy of few millimeters and a relatively wide range of action [2]. Using both active and passive sensors, at the end of the Scan process, it is possible to obtain a dense point cloud that describes the geometry of an object or structure and, of consequence, to produce a 3D model [3, 4]. Therefore, the correct survey of building geometry is a basic tool for the structure knowledge and efficient setting of the numerical computational models.

© Springer Nature Switzerland AG 2020
C. Parente et al. (Eds.): R3GEO 2019, CCIS 1246, pp. 157–169, 2020.
https://doi.org/10.1007/978-3-030-62800-0_13

To obtain a model that can be imported into BIM (Building Information Modeling) or FEM (Finite Element Method) software, over the years several methods have been proposed by different authors [5, 6]. Recently, Costantino et al. (2019) [7] have described a method that allowed quantifying the deformations of the building under investigation, through the knowledge of each element details, starting from the survey and subsequently 3D modelling. Compared to previous work realized on the Montedoro church in Martina Franca (Italy), in this paper has been implemented a different procedure to carry out the FEM model.

2   Method

The steps that allow transforming from cloud point to model for BIM or structural analysis are:

1. 3D survey by geomatics techniques (3D point cloud);
2. 3D modelling (3D mesh);
3. BIM construction and structural analysis.

The first step, i.e. the construction of the 3D point cloud of the structure under investigation, can be realized by the integration of the terrestrial and aerial surveys.

In particular, the terrestrial survey can be performed by TLS or IBM method to produce a point cloud of the lower and inner part of the structure while through a photogrammetric survey by UAV to build the point cloud of the upper part of the structure. To build 3D models with IBM method, several methods were implemented based on mage matching approach. Actually, the Structure from Motion (SfM) approach and Multi View Stereo (MVS) have become quite popular in photogrammetry thanks to ability to determine the parameters of external orientation without any a priori knowledge of the approximate positions for cameras and 3D points and, at same time, to produce dense point cloud [8, 9]. In addition, the automation of processes implemented in commercial software based on these algorithms allows producing three-dimensional models quickly and easily. The several datasets can be integrated into a single point cloud to be later modelled into additional software to create and management the meshes.

In the second step, the mesh generated from point cloud is generated in dedicate software. However, the mesh obtained in this way is very heavy and present different problems, such as intersections, no-manifold edgings, holes, etc. This mesh model is unsuitable to be imported on software of structural analysis and BIM (e.g. FEM Midas GTS NX and Autodesk REVIT, used in this procedure). Therefore, the mesh must be reduced, preserving the precision and details of the survey. The mesh correctness must be checked and moreover the relevant problems must be solved in automatic and manual procedures such as problems of edges, no-manifold, zero length edges etc. At the end of the procedure, the regular geometric mesh can be converted into polysurface mesh (NURBS - Non Uniform Rational Basis-Splines). This means that the meshes are converging and not intersected with each other and will not have holes.

The surface obtained in this way, can be exported in two format: Parasolid (10 to 24) (*x_t;*.xmt_txt;*.x_b;*xmt_bin) file for subsequent processing into Midas GTX FX structural software and in *.sat format to be imported into BIM REVIT software. In REVIT the new model is ready in few seconds and can be easily handled, in contrast with to what happens with point cloud. The model thus realized allow building vertical, horizontal support planes and vaulting structure, for the parametric objects (families) of REVIT. The BIM model is, therefore, ready for further processes. Indeed, the model imported into Midas GTS NX can be divided into some section basic on the referring position of each material with different rheological mechanics. The subdivision can be realized by automatically closing the sections in order to obtain closed and distinct volumes (FEM mesh of three-dimensional finite elements). Consequently, the conditions of external, internal, deadweight (structural elements weight), and accidental loads constraint have been assigned and the static analysis has been carried out to verify the procedure.

3 Brief History of San Nicola in Montedoro Church

The church of San Nicola in Montedoro (Fig. 1) is one of the oldest in the town of Martina Franca in the province of Taranto (Italy) and presumably dates back to the fourteenth century, the period of Angevin foundation of the city. Located in the Montedoro district, hence "San Nicola di Montedoro".

The church preserves its original structure, despite the internal transformations of the seventeenth century. Over the centuries the church has undergone several changes, the most significant occurred in the seventeenth century. The structure is characterized by a modest rectangular hall; the stone floor covers an area of about 35 m² (5.2 m × 6.7 m). Late medieval architectural elements visible especially outside: the simplicity of the external facade is embellished only by the roof with raised pitches that intersect and form two gables with cladding made with the typical "chiancarelle". The portal, slightly ogival, is surmounted by a lunette and a small radial rose window, while on the tympanum of the main facade stands a graceful bell tower.

The interior consists of a single room and has two baroque altars in stone. On the walls are visible paintings, made on two layers. Among the saints who can be recognized are St. Nicholas, St. Augustine and St. Scholastica, St. Anthony Abbot, St. Francis of Paola, Our Lady of the Rosary and a Massacre of Innocents.

Fig. 1. View of the outside of the Church of San Nicola in Montedoro

4 Integrated Survey of the Church of San Nicola in Montedoro

The survey of the church was carried out through the use and integration of active and passive sensors, terrestrial and aerial. In particular, the external façade was surveyed using TLS, the inner part using DLSR with fish-eye lens and the upper part of the building (the roof and other architectural elements not visible through a terrestrial survey) through the use of a camera mounted on UAV (aerial) platform.

4.1 TLS Survey

Regarding the generation of the model for the external part of the church, the survey was carried out by the TLS survey using FARO FocusS 350 instruments whose main features are reported below (Table 1).

FARO FocusS 350 is specially designed for outdoor applications. HDR imaging and HD photo resolution (overlay up to 165 megapixel color) ensure true-to-detail scan results with high data quality. In order to cover the entire external surface of the church, three acquisition stations were built.

The scans were aligned and referenced by a control point whose coordinates were determined with a previous topographical survey. The topographic survey, performed by a total station, allowed to determine the coordinates of the control points in a local reference system.

The points thus determined were necessary to record and align the different datasets in a single reference system. To this end, the topographic survey was carried out through the establishment of a 3 vertex polygonal from which the GCPs and CPs were surveyed on natural elements recognized inside and outside the Church. The representation of external facades is shown in the Fig. 2.

Table 1. Main features of FARO FocusS 350 TLS.

Feature	Description
Ranging unit	Unambiguity interval
	614 m for up to 0.5 mil pts/sec 307 m at 1 mil pts/sec 153 m at 2 mil pts/sec
Range	90% Reflectivity (white) 0.6–350 m
	10% Reflectivity (dark-gray) 0.6–150 m
Range noise	2% Reflectivity (black) 0.6–50 m
Max. measurement speed (mil. pts/sec)	@10 m 90% (white) 0.1 mm
Ranging error (mm)	@10 m 10% (dark-gray) 0.3 mm
Angular accuracy	@10 m 2% (black)
3D point accuracy	Up to 2

Fig. 2. 3D point cloud of the church exterior

4.2 Photogrammetric Survey

For the interior of the church, since there are also frescoes of great historical and cultural value and considering the rather restricted environment, a photogrammetric survey was carried out by DSLR Nikon D5000 camera with a calibrated fisheye lens (focal length 10 mm).

The fish-eye is a wide-angle photographic lens that allows to observe a wide scene [10]. This type of lens was used successfully in photogrammetry field, as shown in

Kannala and Brandt, 2006 [11] especially in narrow space. This lens produces many distortions in the image (Fig. 3).

Fig. 3. Image acquired with fisheye lens

For this reason, it is necessary a camera calibration, i.e. the determination of radial and tangential distortions. This task was performed in Agisoft Lens, which allowed determining the internal orientation parameters and the radial and tangential distortions coefficients. Subsequently, in Agisoft Photoscan software, the processing of the image was performed a point cloud of the of the church's interior was obtained (Fig. 4).

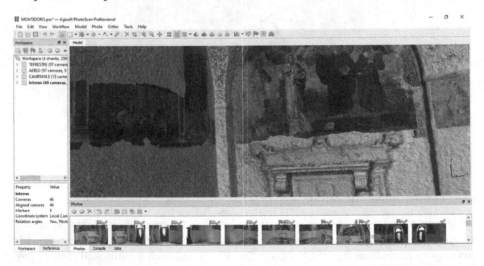

Fig. 4. 3D point cloud of the interior of the church in Agisoft Photoscan environment

In Table 2, it is possible to note the accuracy achieved in the photogrammetric process evaluated on several GCPs (Ground Control Points) which were determinate by traditional topographic survey. In particular, 4 GCPs were used as Control Points (Id points: 201, 203, 205 and 210) while 2 as Check Points (Id points: 202 and 204). The root mean square error achieved on Control Points was 0.003 m while on the Check Points was 0.009 m.

Table 2. Spatial coordinates of the GCPs and relative error.

ID points (#)	X (m)	Y (m)	Z (m)	Error (m)
201	1.844	1.844	1.804	0.003
202	1.877	1.877	1.804	0.012
203	1.391	1.391	2.492	0.004
204	−1.624	−1.624	2.476	0.004
205	−2.547	−2.547	2.600	0.002
210	−0.734	−0.734	0.613	0.004

4.3   UAV Photogrammetry Survey

The aerial survey was carried out using a quadcopter UAV [12, 13]. In particular, a Parrot Anafi drone was used. The take-off weight of this drone is about 400 g with an autonomy flight of 25 min in normal conditions without wind and with a scheduled flight. This system is equipped with a Sony Sensor ® 1/2.4" 21MP (5344 × 4016) CMOS, which allows to obtain, thanks also to a 3-axis stabilizer, clear and detailed images. The Anafi allows a rotation of 180°, i.e. a rotation from −90° (nadir) to +90° (zenith).

The distance between the UAV and the building was really close (range interval from 3 m to 8 m) due to the presence of many obstacles in the old town where the church is located. This mean that the images have a great geometric resolution. In the photogrammetric survey, a high overlap of the images was carried out. In addition, it was possible to capture the entire building by varying the angle of inclination of the camera; this made it possible to obtain a converging network with a high degree of overlap, as shown in the following Fig. 5.

Fig. 5. 3D point cloud of the upper part of the church

A total amount of 97 images were acquired. In order to build the photogrammetric model of the upper part of the church, the post processing of the images was performed in Agisoft PhotoScan software. Taking into account 5 GCPs, root mean square achieved in the alignment step of the process was of 0.009 m. Subsequently, the dense point cloud was built.

4.4   3D Model of the Entire Structure

The integrated survey was performed in order to obtain the 3D point cloud model of the building under investigation. Indeed, the photogrammetric (aerial and terrestrial) and the terrestrial laser scanner survey were connected; the 3D point cloud were aligned and then georeferenced both in the same reference system. This task was performed using 3D Zephyr software. The connection of the different datasets was possible thanks to the topographic network that allowed determining control points (both internal and external to the structure) in a single reference system. The 3D point cloud of the Church is shown in the Fig. 6.

Fig. 6.   3D point cloud of the church

5   BIM of the Structure

The point cloud obtained from the integrated survey was processed to produce a mesh surface in Geomagic Studio software. However, the imported mesh is not very manageable and too heavy to be exported to GTS (FEM software). It was therefore necessary to reduce it using semi-automatic tools. A substantial reduction of 90% has been made, which has however allowed not losing details of the survey. Subsequently, this mesh was reduced and repaired by manual and automatic procedures in order to eliminate any intersections and overlaps between meshes. The resulting mesh surface was imported in Rhinoceros software for the transformation into NURBS surface. The new 3D model was exported in ACIS format (*.sat); in this way, the model can be

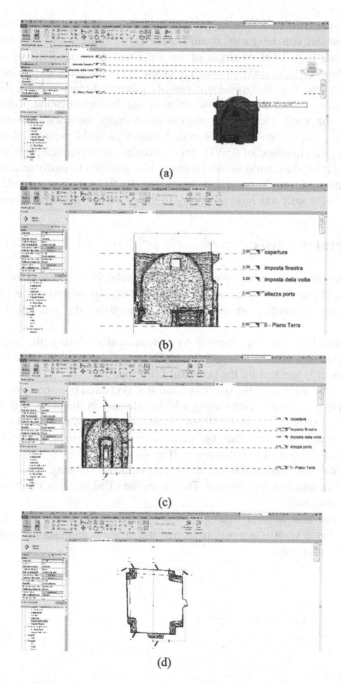

Fig. 7. Design in Revit software; a) view of the NURB geometric model and the parametric vault (in blue) adapted to the existing vault; b) Profile and determining plans for creating BIM objects; c) façade elevation with horizontal plane; d) horizontal section of the roof.

imported into the BIM REVIT software. The surface created is quickly opened by the BIM program and can be easily manipulated with rotations and translations [14]. Considering the high level of detail of the imported geometry, it was possible to identify, in clear way, the areas on which to create the plans and sections. In fact, three lateral sections and four horizontal sections are generated (views: base, door height, vault set, window, cover) that cut the object allowing the identification of the thickness of the walls, the vault, etc. All the objects were easily measurable. Since that the sections were precisely delineated, it was possible to build support planes for the parametric objects (families) of REVIT. By sectioning the horizontal plane (set view of the vault) and from the central vertical section, it is possible to easily create planes, to hook the parametric vault generated inside the REVIT environment dedicated to families. The BIM wall was built according to the procedure described above (Fig. 7).

6 Structural Analysis

The model described above is also exported in parasolid format (*.x_t) for subsequent processing in Midas GTS NX structural software. The imported model is divided into different portions according to the position occupied by the individual geometric elements.

The subdivision was implemented by automatically closing the sections, thus obtaining closed and distinct volumes. In the FEM environment the three-dimensional geometric model is meshed by the powerful GTS module.

The generated mesh is, now, structured and it was created in a semi-automatic way. The structuring was defined considering a higher density in the areas with the highest concentration of stress (perimeter walls of the attack vault) and sparser along the walls.

The geometric elements thus obtained were assigned materials with different mechanical and rheological characteristics (Fig. 8).

The subdivision was implemented by automatically closing the sections, thus obtaining closed and distinct volumes. Therefore, the FEM mesh of the building under investigation was built.

The external and internal constraint conditions and the loads were defined and assigned. In this way, it was possible to perform a static analysis to verify the correctness of the procedure.

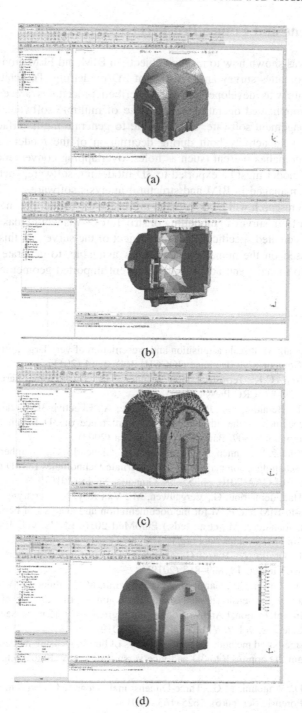

Fig. 8. Processing in Midas software - Solid (mesh) in GTS NX for structural analysis: general perspective view (a), bottom perspective view (b); c) Application of constraints and loads; d) Static analysis: results of deformations

7 Conclusions and Future Prospects

In the paper, it was shown how to manage objects in BIM and FEM environment, after performing a geomatics survey and subsequent 3D modelling. To achieve this aim a suitable procedure was developed. In the described procedures are evident several manual steps, complicated operation and the use of multiple software. In fact, using point cloud management software, it is possible to generate mesh surfaces that, however, require manual activity both during decimation of the model and during the editing of any anomalies present (such as holes, overlapping convergences, etc.). The generated mesh model must be exported to 3D modelling software, such as Rhino, to be subsequently managed in BIM and structural analysis software.

In future, the research will be oriented to minimize the use of intermediate software for the transition from survey to modelling of structures. This would make it possible to generate families created specifically for the subject of the survey. In this way it would be desirable, based on the numerous geometries available, to generate a library that would be easy to manage and adapt to the different imported geometries.

References

1. Callieri, M., et al.: Multiscale acquisition and presentation of very large artifacts: the case of Portalada. J. Comput. Cult. Heritage (JOCCH) 3(4), 1–14 (2011)
2. Petrie, G., Toth, C.K: Terrestrial laser scanners. In: Topographic Laser Ranging and Scanning, pp. 29–88. CRC Press (2018)
3. El-Hakim, S.F., Beraldin, J.A., Picard, M., Vettore, A.: Effective 3D mode ling of heritage site. In: Proceedings of the 4th International Conference of 3D Imaging and Modeling (3DIM 2003), pp. 302–309, Banff, Alberta, Canada (2003)
4. Hermon, S., Pilides, D., Amico, N., D'Andrea, I.A., Giancarlo, G., Chamberlain, M.: Arc3D and 3D laser scanning a comparison of two al ternate technologies for 3D data acquisition. In: Proceedings of CAA 2010, pp. 55–58, Granada, Spain (2010)
5. Bassier, M., Hadjidemetriou, G., Vergauwen, M., Van Roy, N., Verstrynge, E.: Implementation of scan-to-BIM and FEM for the documentation and analysis of heritage timber roof structures. In: Ioannides, M., et al. (eds.) EuroMed 2016. LNCS, vol. 10058, pp. 79–90. Springer, Cham (2016). https://doi.org/10.1007/978-3-319-48496-9_7
6. Ugliotti, F.M., Osello, A., Rizzo, C., Muratore, L.: BIM-based structural survey design. Procedia Struct.3 Integr. 18, 809–815 (2019)
7. Costantino, D., Carrieri, M., Garofalo, A.R., Angelini, M.G., Baiocchi, V., Bogdan, A.M.: Integrated survey for tensional analysis of the vault of the Church of San Nicola in Montedoro. In: International Archives of the Photogrammetry, Remote Sensing and Spatial Information Sciences, vol. 2/W11, pp. 455–460 (2019)
8. Pepe, M.: Image-based methods for metric surveys of buildings using modern optical sensors and tools: from 2D approach to 3D and vice versa. Int. J. Civ. Eng. Tech. 9(09), 729–745 (2018)
9. Costantino, D., Angelini, M.G.: Three-Dimensional integrated survey for building investigations. J. Forensic Sci. 60(6), 1625–1632 (2015)

10. Alessandri, L., Baiocchi, V., Del Pizzo, S., Rolfo, M.F., Troisi, S.: Photogrammetric survey with fisheye lens for the characterization of the La Sassa Cave. In: International Archives of the Photogrammetry, Remote Sensing and Spatial Information Sciences, vol. XLII-2/W9, pp. 25–32 (2019). https://doi.org/10.5194/isprs-archives-xlii-2-w9-25
11. Kannala, J., Brandt, S.S.: A generic camera model and calibration method for conventional, wide-angle, and fish-eye lenses. IEEE Trans. Pattern Anal. Mach. Intell. **28**(8), 1335–1340 (2006)
12. Pepe, M., Fregonese, L., Scaioni, M.: Planning airborne photogrammetry and remote-sensing missions with modern platforms and sensors. Eur. J. Remote Sens. **51**(1), 412–436 (2018)
13. Alfio, V.S., Costantino, D., Pepe, M.: Influence of image TIFF format and JPEG compression level in the accuracy of the 3D model and quality of the orthophoto in UAV photogrammetry. J. Imaging **6**(5), 1–23 (2020)
14. Angelini, M.G., Baiocchi, V., Costantino, D., Garzia, F.: Scan to BIM for 3D reconstruction of the papal basilica of saint Francis in Assisi in Italy. In: International Archives of the Photogrammetry, Remote Sensing and Spatial Information Sciences - ISPRS Archives, vol. 42(5W1), pp. 47–54 (2017)

Integration of Laser Scanning and Photogrammetry in Architecture Survey. Open Issue in Geomatics and Attention to Details

Gabriella Caroti and Andrea Piemonte

DICI, University of Pisa, Largo Lucio Lazzarino 2, 56122 Pisa, Italy
andrea.piemonte@unipi.it

Abstract. In the last decades, surveying methodologies related to Geomatics applications in the Cultural Heritage field have undergone a constant evolution. The first innovation has surely been the development, in the 1990s, of laser scanning systems. These are able to survey the coordinates of millions of points of architectural objects with sub-centimeter precision and high density. The second breakthrough, starting from the 2000s, is the "second youth" of photogrammetry methodologies. The "new photogrammetry" yielded tools and methodologies able to provide low-cost 3-D models, featuring photo-quality textures, suitable for very high scales reconstructions. Although both methodologies are fairly consolidated, one interesting research topic is the integration of the different methodologies aimed at optimizing results as regards both logistics-costs and attainable precision levels. The paper focuses on the latter topic, showing the methodological approach followed for the outer face restitution for the North transect of the Pisa Cathedral at 1:20 scale, as requested by the staff in charge of maintenance and restoration. In detail, the precision problems for the least accessible parts and for the transitions between orthogonal and parallel surfaces, relative to the average direction of the camera axis, are discussed. Finally, the processing methodology used for restitution at the same scale of the development of curved masonry sections, is presented. While compiling these documents for architecture study and documentation, attained geometric precision and texture resolution are checked, with a particular focus on how segmenting model sections with primitive surfaces can improve these parameters, and as a consequence also the final restitution.

Keywords: Survey · Restoration · Laser scanner · Photogrammetry · Segmentation · Orthophoto

1 Introduction

Architectural surveys have provided a main application field for geomatics methodologies since its very inception [1, 2].

C. Parente et al. (Eds.): R3GEO 2019, CCIS 1246, pp. 170–185, 2020.
https://doi.org/10.1007/978-3-030-62800-0_14

This field collects a wide array of operators (engineers, architects, humanities technicians, craftsmen etc.), all of which require, for different reasons, a representation of the architectural object as a starting point for subsequent planning and executive work [3–5].

A still ongoing challenge in geomatics is to improve versatility of architectural surveys, allowing information related to raw survey geometry to be scaled according to the need of users [6, 7].

An interesting example is provided by the ever-increasing attention that the scientific community and land management specialists pay to BIMs (Building Information Models), in particular those applied to historic and architectural heritage, HBIMs (Heritage Building Information Models) [8].

These multidisciplinary platforms, which link and manage georeferenced information for structure geometries, aim to widen their user base. For this reason, the underlying complexity of information and survey, normally hidden to the end user, should be made available according to specific needs.

This is linked to the main issue in geomatics, i.e. survey precision, which provides a starting point for the planning of any survey, in terms of methodologies, instruments, and logistics arrangements [9, 10].

Starting from a single survey, several representations at different scales, can be generated, but ultimately the scale factor is linked to the precision defined at project planning.

Geometric survey of a structure can provide 3-D documents, i.e. point clouds, either raw or modelled by surfaces (meshes, NURBS) or by vectorization of discontinuity lines. On the other hand, however, photorealistic 2-D documents, associating geometries with images (photoplans, orthophotographs etc.), are highly sought after by operators involved in analysis of stratigraphy, structure decay and restoration [5, 6, 11, 12]. In this field, photogrammetry can exploit its full potential in terms of both geometric precision and image resolution [13, 14].

For correct survey planning, considering both client requests and economic feasibility of surveying operations in terms of cost-to-benefit ratio, the relation between geometric precision and image resolution of the end results must be pondered in all of its facets.

As per the Authors' experience, clients often lack this awareness in their requests, often confusing their need for high image resolution with high geometric precision. Following is a clarifying example.

For restorers, 1:20 is a standard scale for intervention planning. Geomatics engineers combine the request for this scale with the concept of graphic error, which in the 1:20 case results in requiring survey precision equal to, or better than, 4 mm. Achieving this level of precision in the geometric representation of complex architectures is certainly possible but, as a downside, possibly entails very high surveying costs [15]. On the other hand, the request for a 1:20 scale sometimes stems from the need to detect, e.g. on an orthorectified image, 4 mm-sized details, rather than their position or dimension with the precision intrinsic in the scale factor.

Of course, upon stating 1:20 representation of a given object, precision and resolution must match the scale. However, if clients and surveyors reach explicit agreement, it is possible to generate somewhat 'hybrid' documents, with a lower scale (e.g. 1:50) geometric precision and image resolution matching the required scale. In fact, it is comparatively easy and not exceedingly costly to increase the resolution of photographic shoots, such as by using lenses with greater focal length (f) and increasing the number of shoots while keeping the same shooting distance.

The present paper reports the experience of the Authors involving the survey of a large, complex structure requiring typical 1:20 precision and resolution, addressing different issues including the need to integrate graphical documents also in the parts where geometric survey presents operating problems in order to achieve the required precision.

2   Materials

The survey used in this paper as case study refers was performed in July 2018 and it refers to the outer side of the North transept of the Pisa Cathedral (Fig. 1).

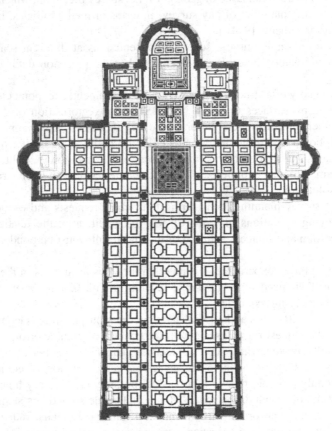

Fig. 1. Pisa Cathedral plan. Red is used for highlighting surveyed parts. (Color figure online)

2.1   The Pisa Cathedral

On the 900th anniversary of the Pisa Cathedral dedication, an ongoing, major effort was started for restoration and clean-up of the outside. A preparatory survey of the North transept and its apse, aimed at the restitution of photorealistic plans at 1:20 scale, was carried out, covering a total of roughly 1700 m^2 (about 500 m^2 for the East and West faces of the transept, about 400 m^2 for its North face – including the apse – and about 300 m^2 for the neighbouring nave sections).

The height from the ground of the top of the cathedral is 30 m, the height from the ground of the transept roofs is 20 m on average and the width is 24 m.

It was necessary to adapt surveying and related activities to the time schedule and the logistics of the large restoration site already in operation, also entailing the need to integrate with the times and requirements of the various processes. For these reasons, only ten days were available for field surveys, it was not possible to use lifting platforms, the area could not be cordoned off and inhibited to tourists, who have free access to Piazza dei Miracoli from as early as 6 am.

2.2   TLS survey

TLS (Terrestrial Laser Scanner) survey has been performed via a Leica Geosystems' C10 ScanStation, whose plate data include a positioning precision of 6 mm for single measurements (1 σ @ max 50 m). The scan density for the survey was about 8 points per cm^2.

Scan positions were mostly set at ground level, due to the unavailability of suitable locations at different elevation on neighbouring buildings or on temporary structures (e.g. scaffoldings or lift baskets). The only exceptions have been provided by two access points to the outside of the tambour supporting the Cathedral dome, located on the roof pitches of the matroneum at the intersection of the transept and the main nave. However, having performed nearly every scan from ground level yielded several projected shadows, due to horizontal overhangs; likewise, horizontal placement constraints for the scan positions resulted in similar shadows in vertical recesses (Fig. 2). In both cases, these projected shadows generated information gaps in the corresponding point clouds, which entailed wider approximation of the mesh model in the areas affected.

On the other hand, in obstacle-free areas the TLS survey was homogeneous for both resolution and precision.

Fig. 2. Pisa Cathedral plan. Red is used for highlighting surveyed parts. (Color figure online)

2.3   Ground-Based Photogrammetry Survey

The photographic campaign met the same logistic issues as TLS survey. Due to the inability of establishing elevated shooting positions, reducing projected shadows to a minimum was achieved by moving the cameras farther away from the survey object.

The camera used in this survey was Nikon's D850 digital SLR, whose 35.9 × 23.9 mm CMOS sensor is capable of 8256 × 5504 pixel resolution. Given the need for shooting from greater distance, a f = 200 mm lens was mostly used: this resulted in a Ground Sampling Distance (GSD) ranging from 1.2 mm to 1.4 mm, fully adequate for the required representation scale, with camera-to-object distance ranging from 55 m to 65 m for the lower and upper sections of the structure, respectively. For some images taken from a closer distance, a f = 50 mm lens was used.

The photographic campaign was carefully planned, as regards time of the day and lighting conditions, in order to keep cast shadows to a minimum. Nevertheless, due to the complexity variety of aspect of the survey object, use of a colour checker (Fig. 3) was mandatory in order to check white balance and exposure, as well to post-calibration of RAW images. The colour checker has routinely been included in the scene every 30 min and at every obvious lighting variation.

Fig. 3. Image with colour checker

2.4   UAV-Borne Photogrammetric Survey

In order to collect data for recessed or otherwise hidden areas, as described in paragraph 2.2 and 2.3, an Unmanned Aerial Vehicle (UAV)-borne photogrammetric survey was also performed. The aircraft used for this purpose was DJI's Phantom 4 Pro equipped with a DJI FC6310 camera, whose 13.2 × 8.8 mm CMOS sensor, capable of 4864 × 3648 pixel, ensured an average GSD of about 2.4 mm at the average UAV-to-object distance of 8 m. The images were acquired following vertical strips.

Obviously, the size of GSD almost doubles its ground-based counterpart. In addition, in spite of fast (1:800 s) shooting time settings, some images were still affected by micro-blurs, with adverse effects on both image quality and precision in the definition of its orientation parameters.

As a consequence, UAV-borne photogrammetry has only been used to reduce the gaps in the ground-based survey of ground–based surveys, which feature far better quality.

3 Methods and Results

TLS and photogrammetry surveys have been suitably integrated and processed in order to achieve the requested geometric precision and photographic resolution and the best possible results in terms of completeness, colour and brightness homogeneity.

Every surveying job exploiting and integrating different methodologies requires homogenization of the different reference systems.

It is well known that, when aligning different surveys, the highest precision can be achieved by placing some targets on the survey object and measure their coordinates by means of traditional surveying (e.g. total station), allowing to plot out a reference system on the survey object.

On the other hand, this procedure is only occasionally feasible on large, complex architectures, and is not cheap in any case. This is also the case for the survey discussed in this paper, for which therefore no supporting traditional survey has been carried out.

In order to homogenize the coordinate systems, the TLS point cloud acted as reference.

3.1 Alignment of Photogrammetry Models

The internal and external orientation parameters of the photograms have been calculated by means of Agisoft's Metashape. Each face of the transept has been separately processed.

Opting to forgo shared targets and sizable overlapping areas between image sets related to different transept faces resulted in the inability to register in a common reference system all the point clouds coming from different projects. As stated above, all point clouds generated in the photogrammetric surveys have been referenced to the TLS-generated point cloud, in order to optimize surveying and processing times.

For each photogrammetric point cloud, some GCPs (Ground Control Points), detected as a first approximation on the referenced TLS cloud, have provided the basis for scaling and georeferencing of the photogrammetric dense point cloud. This has subsequently been exported and processed by JRC Reconstructor software, in order to find the best transformation (rototranslation with scale factor) by means of cloud-to-cloud matching algorithms, resulting in precision of about 4 mm. The coordinates of the GCPs exported along the dense point cloud have then been recalculated and fed back into the Metashape projects, ensuring that every photogrammetric project is framed in the same reference system.

This processing methodology has been applied to all photogrammetric surveys, both terrestrial and UAV-borne, achieving in this latter case a matching precision of about 7–8 mm.

3.2 TLS Model Segmentation

The survey object features some architectural elements whose shape extends in all three dimensions (e.g. capitals, cornices, eave lines), although most of the surface is segmented by planar elements (walls, pilasters, strips etc.).

Definition of these surfaces allows to improve restitution of orthomosaics, particularly in noisy areas or where, due to gaps in the point cloud, the reduction of the geometries following the interpolation implemented by the meshing process is not suitable for the very great representation scale.

The planar surfaces have been detected by interpolating an adequately layered dense point cloud (the one obtained from TLS survey). Figure 4 shows the subdivision of a building section in homogeneous areas as regards the aspect of interpolating plans. Red, green and blue are used for highlighting plans at increasing distance from the camera, while yellow highlights curved portions of the structure, which have been processed separately (see Sect. 3.5). Architectural elements noticeably extending in the three dimensions are excluded from the segmentation.

Fig. 4. Model segmentation

3.3   Generation of Orthophotographs

All the different models available, i.e. the simplified ones generated by cloud segmentation and that generated by direct meshing of the point cloud, have been imported in the relevant Metashape projects. The next step provided the creation of an orthomosaic of the images upon orthorectification against each imported model. All processing has been carried out setting the same bounding box, and exporting the georeferencing file along the orthomosaic.

As regards the use of plans generated by point cloud segmentation for image orthorectification, it is possible to calculate the maximum projection error of outmost points based on its shift from the reference plan. Figure 5 traces this error for images acquired with the Nikon D850 camera (f = 200 mm).

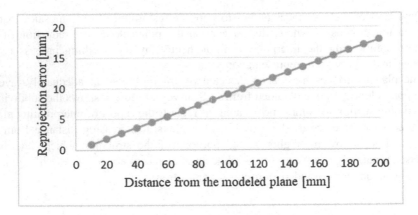

Fig. 5. Maximum projection error on orthophotographs using a plan as 3D model

3.4   Orthophotographs Merge

For the orthophotographs merging a photo editing software (namely Adobe Photoshop) was used. Having generated all orthophotographs by the same bounding box, regardless of the extension of the area actually represented, resulted in perfect image overlap.

Each orthophotograph is placed in a separate layer, which can be associated with a specific subtraction mask for later removal of unwanted areas. In fact, each orthophotograph adequately represents, for size and positioning, only the areas actually laying on the model against which the images have been orthorectified.

All orthophotographs for every section considered have been loaded into the photo editing software.

Figure 6 presents a section of the structure showing the transition between the main body of the building (on the left) and a pilaster (on the right), for which three separate orthophotographs are available. Figure 6a shows the orthophotographs generated by

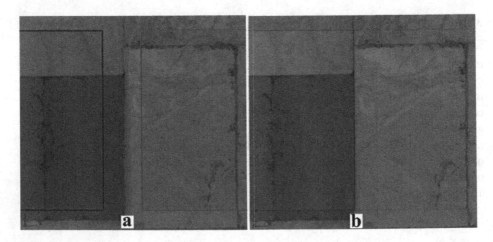

Fig. 6. Orthophotographs merge (Color figure online)

assuming as a model the interpolating plan for the main building body (in blue) and for the pilaster (in red), as well as that generated by the meshing of the entire point cloud (background). The latter matches perfectly those generated via planar models, but, on the other hand, shows an obvious imperfection in the transition between main body and pilaster, due to the inability, for the mesh model, to correctly represent the geometry at this level.

Figure 6b shows the end result of merging the orthophotographs, where the transition zone is correctly represented.

Figure 7 shows a section of the structure featuring cornices extending in the three dimensions. In this case, orthophotographs generated by simplified models (shown in blue and red, same as Fig. 6) are not usable and the mesh model, derived from the entire dense point cloud, must be used instead.

Fig. 7. Orthophotographs merge

3.5 Planar Representation of Curved Elements

Given its curved structure, processing of the apse followed a different approach. The cylindrical shape of masonry surface has been checked in the dense point cloud. Subsequently, the cloud has been segmented in three parts, i.e. one for the masonry, one for the arches and the supporting columns, and one for the pilaster strips found in the upper section [16].

For each of these sections, the interpolating cylinder has been defined in terms of radius and axis (Fig. 8). The latter does not coincide with the vertical due to the sagging of the structure throughout its existence. The radii of three cylinders range from a minimum of 7.91 m to a maximum of 8.52 m, while the axes coincide.

The cylinder interpolating the upper section strips has the been selected in order to project the surface of the entire structure.

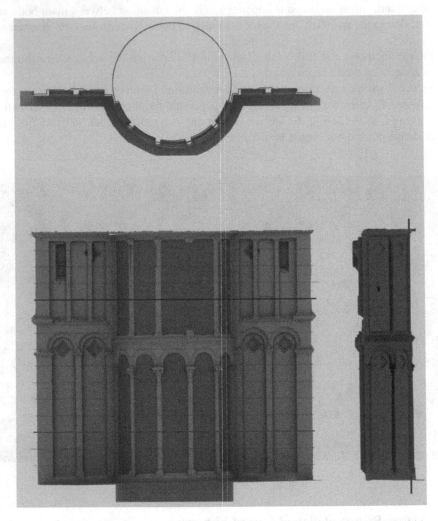

Fig. 8. Cylinder definition for of the apse of the North transept of Pisa Cathedral

3.6 Orthophotographs Equalization for Restoring Purposes

A further processing was performed upon a specific request from the restoration operators. Besides true colour orthophotographs, achieved by including colour checkers in the scene (Fig. 9a), restorers also needed images with different equalization schemes for colour, brightness, contrast and sharpness in order to improve highlighting of any surface discontinuity, as well as particular conditions of oxidization and alteration of the stone faces, for decay analysis and mapping purposes.

The latter processing is directly carried out on the orthophotographs using the equalization tools of the photo editing software (Fig. 9b).

Fig. 9. Colour balancing of orthophotographs for use in restoration works.

4 Conclusions

The methodology used for surveying and processing allowed to obtain 1:20 2-D documents, namely orthophotographs, for both planar (Fig. 10) and curve (Fig. 11) sections.

Fig. 10. North side of north transept orthophotograph.

The stated 1:20 scale has been achieved in terms of both geometry precision and image resolution.

While correct planning of the photographic shoots in itself ensured achievement of the desired image resolution, the required geometric precision has been attained, besides after careful planning, upon adopting some methodological precautions at processing level ensuring full compliance in every area.

In particular, the surveying has been affected by logistics problems, as is frequently the case in complex, extensive surveys.

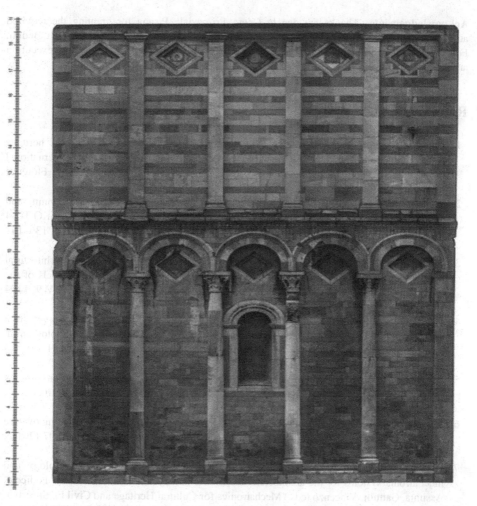

Fig. 11. Apse orthophotograph (cylindrical projection).

As a bottom line, it must be again stressed that image resolution and geometric precision require different surveying and processing strategies in order to achieve the features of the same representation scale.

Mostly due to the widespread availability of extremely user-friendly software packages, the market offers a wide variety of solutions for very high-scale representations in terms of image resolution.

On the other hand, geometric precision for very high scales necessarily requires a rigorous Geomatics approach, also allowing for precise checking of expected versus actual precision.

Acknowledgements. Thanks are due to Opera Primaziale Pisana for granting the required authorizations for the survey of the Pisa Cathedral; technical staff members Andrea Bedini, Federico Capriuoli, Luca Coscarelli and Isabel Martínez-Espejo Zaragoza for survey execution and data processing.

References

1. Croce, V., Caroti, G., Piemonte, A., Bevilacqua, M.G.: Geomatics for cultural heritage conservation: integrated survey and 3D modeling. In: IMEKO TC-4 International Conference on Metrology for Archaeology and Cultural Heritage, pp. 271–276, Florence (2019)
2. Caroti, G., Martinez Espejo Zaragoza, I., Piemonte, A.: Historical data of laser scanning and photogrammetry for the knowledge and memory plan of Cultural Heritage. In: IMEKO TC-4 International Conference on Metrology for Archaeology and Cultural Heritage, pp. 136–141 (2019)
3. Bevilacqua, M.G., Caroti, G., Piemonte, A., Ulivieri, D.: Reconstruction of lost architectural volumes by integration of photogrammetry from archive imagery with 3-D models of the status quo. ISPRS - Int. Arch. Photogramm. Remote Sens. Spat. Inf. Sci. **XLII-2/W9**, 119–125 (2019). ahttps://doi.org/10.5194/isprs-archives-XLII-2-W9-119-2019
4. Tucci, G., Bonora, V., Fiorini, L., Conti, A.: The florence baptistery: 3-D survey as a knowledge tool for historical and structural investigations. ISPRS - Int. Arch. Photogramm. Remote Sens. Spat. Inf. Sci. **XLI-B5**, 977–984 (2016). https://doi.org/10.5194/isprs-archives-XLI-B5-977-2016.Alshawabkeh
5. Alshawabkeh, Y., Haala, N., Fritsch, D.: A new true ortho-photo methodology for complex archaeological application. Archaeometry **52**, 517–530 (2009). https://doi.org/10.1111/j.1475-4754.2009.00484.x
6. Bassier, M., Vincke, S., de Lima Hernandez, R., Vergauwen, M.: An overview of innovative heritage deliverables based on remote sensing techniques. Remote Sens. **10**, 1607 (2018). https://doi.org/10.3390/rs10101607
7. Bevilacqua, M.G., Caroti, G., Piemonte, A., Terranova, A.A.: Digital technology and mechatronic systems for the architectural 3D metric survey. In: Ottaviano, Erika, Pelliccio, Assunta, Gattulli, Vincenzo (eds.) Mechatronics for Cultural Heritage and Civil Engineering. ISCASE, vol. 92, pp. 161–180. Springer, Cham (2018). https://doi.org/10.1007/978-3-319-68646-2_7
8. Bacci, G., et al.: HBIM methodologies for the architectural restoration. the case of the ex-church of San Quirico all'olivo in Lucca, tuscany. ISPRS - Int. Arch. Photogramm. Remote Sens. Spat. Inf. Sci. **XLII-2/W11**, 121–126 (2019). https://doi.org/10.5194/isprs-archives-XLII-2-W11-121-2019
9. Murtiyoso, A., Grussenmeyer, P., Suwardhi, D., Awalludin, R.: Multi-scale and multi-sensor 3D documentation of heritage complexes in urban areas. ISPRS Int. J. Geo-Inf. **7**, 483 (2018). https://doi.org/10.3390/ijgi7120483
10. Chiabrando, F., Sammartano, G., Spanò, A., Spreafico, A.: Hybrid 3D models: when geomatics innovations meet extensive built heritage complexes. ISPRS Int. J. Geo-Inf. **8**, 124 (2019). https://doi.org/10.3390/ijgi8030124
11. Pierrot-Deseilligny, M., De Luca, L., Remondino, F.: Automated image-based procedures for accurate artifacts 3D modeling and orthoimage generation. Geoinformatics FCE CTU **6**, 291–299 (2011). https://doi.org/10.14311/gi.6.36

12. Bevilacqua, M.G., Caroti, G., Piemonte, A., Ruschi, P., Tenchini, L.: 3D survey techniques for the architectutal restoration: the case of St. Agata in Pisa. ISPRS - Int. Arch. Photogramm. Remote Sens. Spat. Inf. Sci. **XLII-5/W1**, 441–447 (2017). https://doi.org/10.5194/isprs-archives-XLII-5-W1-441-2017
13. Carraro, F., et al.: The 3D survey of the roman bridge of San Lorenzo in Padova (Italy): a comparison between SFM and TLS methodologies applied to the arch structure. ISPRS - Int. Arch. Photogramm. Remote Sens. Spat. Inf. Sci. **XLII-2/W15**, 255–262 (2019). https://doi.org/10.5194/isprs-archives-XLII-2-W15-255-2019
14. Rahaman, H., Champion, E.: To 3D or not 3D: choosing a photogrammetry workflow for cultural heritage groups. Heritage. **2**, 1835–1851 (2019). https://doi.org/10.3390/heritage2030112
15. Perfetti, L., Fassi, F., Gulsan, H.: Generation of gigapixel orthophoto for the maintenance of complex buildings. challenges and lesson learnt. ISPRS - Int. Arch. Photogramm. Remote Sens. Spat. Inf. Sci. **XLII-2/W9**, 605–614 (2019). https://doi.org/10.5194/isprs-archives-XLII-2-W9-605-2019
16. Piemonte, A., Caroti, G., Martínez-Espejo Zaragoza, I., Fantini, F., Cipriani, L.: A methodology for planar representation of frescoed oval domes: formulation and testing on Pisa Cathedral. ISPRS Int. J. Geo-Inf. **7**, 318 (2018). https://doi.org/10.3390/ijgi7080318

Integration and Assessment Between 3D Data from Different Geomatics Techniques. Case Study: The Ancient City Walls of San Ginesio (Italy)

Francesco Di Stefano[✉] , Stefano Chiappini , Fabio Piccinini ,
and Roberto Pierdicca

Università Politecnica delle Marche, Dipartimento di Ingegneria Civile,
Edile e dell'Architettura, 60100 Ancona, Italy
{f.distefano, s.chiappini, f.piccinini}@pm.univpm.it,
r.pierdicca@staff.univpm.it

Abstract. The growing availability of complementary geomatics techniques made possible the data collection of a wide variety of objects creating high-quality 3D recordings and representations. Digital photogrammetry proved to be a valuable method to achieve good results in terms of accuracy and quality, exploiting high-resolution images. Mobile Laser Scanners as SLAM devices can produce dense 3D point cloud required to create high-resolution geometric models. In this research project, the data integration from UAV photogrammetry and 'handheld' Mobile Laser Scanner has been tested, performing a comparison, evaluation and assessment of their combined use. The efficiency of this approach has been proved for the survey of the ancient city walls of San Ginesio, close to Macerata (Italy). Given the seismic events that seriously damaged San Ginesio and the Marche Region in 2016, the final output defines a suitable baseline for future analysis and restoration activities. Therefore, it wants to prove the necessity to assess novel methods to perform fast and agile acquisition campaigns for the conservation of the fragile heritage.

Keywords: UAV · MLS · Integration · Assessment · Geomatics · Cultural heritage · Restoration

1 Introduction

Three-dimensional (3D) digitization of Cultural Heritage (CH) sites and artefacts has increased remarkably in recent years. The growing availability of novel, robust and in some cases affordable surveying techniques, made possible the data collection of a wide variety of objects. The purposes are countless, spanning from documentation to preservation, from restoration to valorization [1]. As a result, it is clear that there is not a single method applicable for recording every CH related subject and hence there is a strong demand for making the combination of data, coming from different sensors, more and more straightforward [2]. Toward this end, it is well-known that 3D point clouds can be collected in several ways. Digital photogrammetry proved to be a

C. Parente et al. (Eds.): R3GEO 2019, CCIS 1246, pp. 186–197, 2020.
https://doi.org/10.1007/978-3-030-62800-0_15

valuable method to achieve good results in terms of both accuracy and quality, exploiting high-resolution images. As well, Terrestrial Laser Scanners (TLS), can produce dense 3D point-cloud that is required to create high-resolution geometric models, although the quality of colour information is lower than required [3] or, sometimes, even missing. More recently, we witnessed a revolution with the advent of "handheld" devices exploiting SLAM (Simultaneous Localization and Mapping) [4]. These new systems completely avoid the use of targets and control points. Despite their potential of increasing productivity in 3D digitization projects, data quality still needs to be carefully evaluated. The aforementioned technologies are complementary to one another in creating high-quality 3D recordings and representations. In our research project, the combination of SLAM and photogrammetry has been tested, performing a comparison, evaluation and assessment of their combined use. The efficiency of this approach has been proved for the survey of the ancient city walls of San Ginesio (Italy) representing a challenging benchmark.

2 Related Work

In Conservation and Restoration of CH sites, photogrammetry and TLS are becoming recognized and accepted standard methods. These technologies provide a never-before reached accuracy and completeness of data, they can overcome difficult geometric configurations allowing an almost continuous description of the site features, they considerably reduce time and costs. The integration of adequate methods maximizes the chances to achieve the desired results. TLS and photogrammetry must be understood as complementary methods. On the one hand, TLS is an efficient method to create a geometrically robust base for 3D modelling. However, its main limitation is to be earth-bound. For example, high elements of building façades or city walls or inaccessible roofs tend to be poorly documented from ground surveys. On the other hand, photogrammetry is more flexible. It is easy to record the hard-to-reach areas for example with UAV (Unmanned Aerial Vehicle). An example of investigation on various 3D surveying techniques is represented by the research project for the digital representation of historical porticoes in Bologna, in Italy [5]. Terrestrial photogrammetry and the following image processing were identified as a productive technique for the 3D reconstruction. Same approach was adopted for documenting the current state of conservation of the inner side walls of Avila, in Spain, where the use of drones was inevitable, combining with the close-range photogrammetry carried by reflex camera [6]. Photogrammetry and laser scanner have different approaches to survey a cultural heritage object, so their integration can be a good methodology to enrich the final elaboration of 3D model. The applicability and the combination of both survey system for the data acquisition of vertical structures, complex buildings and difficult accessible architectural parts can provide high precision results. In addition, the topographic acquisition gives more detail defining the reference system for the geo-localization. The experiments done for the survey of the cathedral spire of Milan [7] or of vertical structures in Mantua [8] could represent efficient methodologies. As the last case study describes also this project debates on survey techniques in an emergency context like post-seismic events. The after-earthquake survey has to guarantee time-savings, high precision and security during the operational working steps.

3   Case of Study

San Ginesio is a small town rising on the top of a hill, at 700 m asl, close to Macerata, in the Italian region of Marche. It founded in the 6th century on remains of Roman settlements burned to the ground by Goths and Longobards that, after the fall of the Roman Empire, conquered these lands. In the 10th century some local Lords decided to build a fortress on the highest hill to dominate and so to join forces in an appropriate place. That was the first line of walls was raised up. The most part of walls visible today dates on the 14th century and completed in 150 years. Built in sandstone blocks, it surrounds the entire old village with an irregular plan with edges and protrusions. They characterized by the presence of towers and four main entrance doors [9]. Over the centuries the walls underwent several changes after attacks, so they had a series of interventions and alterations. Nowadays, due to the recent earthquakes (2009, 2016), those hit the central Italy, the walls and the towers have been damaged, with ruins in correspondence of merlons.

4   Data Acquisition

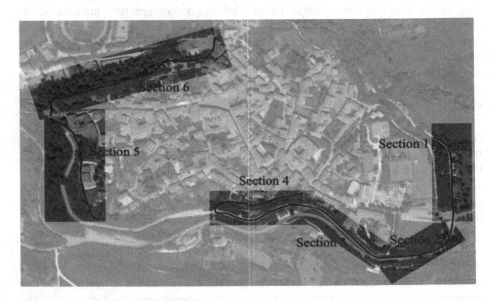

Fig. 1. The sections of the walls for the acquisition phase.

The survey carried out through the town wall of San Ginesio has been dedicated to the search of a methodology that optimizes the time of data acquisition and the following restitution, with less errors of projection. In order to create a complete texturized 3D model of the walls, we decided to use different techniques of acquisition. They include the aerial photogrammetry with UAV and the mobile laser scanner with a SLAM technology. For the combination of the images acquired and the point clouds also a topographic survey was conducted using of Total Station (TS) and setting up a GNSS (Global Navigation Satellite System) network.

In accordance with the methodology and the time of survey based on the instruments used and the accessibility to the site, taking in consideration the situation after the recent earthquake, the visible parts of the walls were divided in six sections (Fig. 1).

4.1   Topographic Survey

The data acquisition was conducted in three days of work, that started with the defining a reference system, realizing an open traverse collecting 123 among control points and ground control points identified on the road surface and on the faces of the walls (Fig. 2). For this survey, a GPT-3105N [10] was used as TS. The targets placed on the ground have been acquired by the GPS HiPer HR [11] with RTK (Real Time Kinematic) method. On top of GNSS (Global Navigation Satellite System) satellite signals an RTK receiver takes in a RTCM (Radio Technical Commission for Maritime Services) correction stream and then calculates your location with 1 cm accuracy in real time. The rate varies between receivers (Base and Rover) but most will output a solution at least once per second.

✕ Targets - GPS   ▲ Support Points - Total Station   ＋ Control Points - Total Station

Fig. 2. Topographic reference network around the walls

4.2   Aerial Photogrammetry

The photogrammetric survey of the walls was performed through a DJI Spark MMA1 drone and its integrated camera [12]. The small UAV is equipped with propeller guards, compulsory to operate in critical scenarios, having a take-off weight of 340 g. Therefore, to operate in the urban area complying with the maximum allowed weight, the aircraft was slightly lightened just below 300 g [13]. Even if the survey was planned in an urban context, respecting the restrictions of a standard urban UAVs acquisition, all ENAC (the Italian Civil Aviation Authority) rules [14] have been followed by the RPAS (Remotely Piloted Aircraft Systems) pilot. The survey had no interference between survey activities and people passage, pledging a safe operating condition, because after the last earthquake (2016) all the urban area was declared as red zone.

For each section of the walls different flights were planned, by varying the grade of the camera and the distance from the object of survey. Photos has been shot with camera in different grades: nadir direction, 30° and 45° from the horizon, and frontal, covering a global field of view of approximatively 180° and guaranteeing a high number of tie points [15]. The survey was carried out considering a constant distance of about 30 m between RPAS camera and the wall, evaluating carefully both the flight time and the global number of shots required to cover all the wall surface, obtaining an average Ground Sample Distance (GSD) of 4 cm. In defining the flight plan, the images have been captured each 12 m in vertical direction and 17 m in horizontal one, in order to guarantee an average overlap of 80% in both directions. At practical level, the overlap considered have been much higher in the flight direction because a manual flight has been carried on and it has been difficult to respect the programmed trajectory and maintain a constant speed in manual driving configuration. Near the high crowns of the trees the integrated proximity sensor was disabled in order to allow an adequate acquisition of the walls.

The average time spent for UAV data acquisition was about 30 min for each section, considering both the interior and exterior sides of the walls.

4.3   SLAM Technology

It was planned also a survey campaign with the mobile laser scanner to obtain 3D point clouds of the walls. Since the scanning has been carried in open area and outdoor environment, KAARTA Stencil 2 [16] was appropriate for this type of survey. KAARTA Stencil 2 is a stand-alone, light weight SLAM instrument, with an integrated system of mapping and real-time position estimation. To realize this type of survey characterized by long paths on foot, the laser scanner was mounted on a small pole held by hand. KAARTA Stencil 2 depends on LiDAR (Light Detection and Ranging) and IMU (Inertial Measurement Unit) data for localization. The system uses Velodyne VLP-16 connected to a low-cost MEMS (Micro Electro Mechanical Systems) IMU and a processing computer for real-time mapping. VLP-16 has a 360° field of view with a 30° azimuthal opening with a band of 16 scan lines. The laser accuracy varies to ±30 mm/±1.2 in. For the analysis different acquisition tests were performed, following closed paths (close-loop) [17] between interior and exterior sides of the wall walking through the entrance doors, representing the limit of each section. In order to acquire the high vertical part of the walls, the LiDAR has been tilted up to ±45° while standing still.

The data acquisitions were captured using the KAARTA Stencil 2 default configuration parameters, set in order to use the instrument in structured outdoor environments. Specifically, these settings include default values for the *voxelSize*, namely the resolution of the point cloud in map file, for *cornerVoxelSize, surfVoxelSize, sorroundVoxelSize*, those indicate the resolution of the point cloud for scan matching and display, and for *blindRadius*, that is the minimum distance of the points to be used for the mapping.

A tracker camera, integrated to the SLAM device, needs to show and save the trajectory made during the acquisition operations. The progress of the scanning was monitored in real time via an external monitor attached with a USB cable.

Table 1 resumes the main characteristics of the resulting products of KAARTA Stencil 2 real-time acquisitions of the sections of the city walls, while in Fig. 3 are showed both the 3D point cloud and the close-loop trajectory of Sect. 4.

Table 1. Characteristics of the real-time solutions of KAARTA Stencil 2

Data	Acquisition time [s]	Trajectory		Point cloud
		N. points	Length [m]	N. points
Section 1	1525	2682	1058	174663563
Section 2	566	2682	922	65356512
Section 3	556	2755	469	57089605
Section 4	992	4874	666	92865392
Section 5	108	533	105	5549475
Section 6	1452	7198	1022	66732560

Fig. 3. The 3D point cloud and the close-loop trajectory (red line) of Sect. 4 carried out with KAARTA Stencil 2 (Color figure online)

5 Data Processing

5.1 Agisoft Metashape

Agisoft Metashape version 1.5.3 [18] is taken into account as reference software for the image elaboration. From the authors experience, no significant changes have been made in comparison with previous versions of Agisoft Photoscan about its use and the obtained results as confirmed preceding tests [19]. The choice of the software used is justified by its good performance on image alignment from different angulations.

In Metashape, for each section of walls a folder of images, previously created, have been imported in order to create a single chunk.

Taking as example the Sect. 4 of the walls, the UAV photogrammetric data have been elaborated. During the image orientation step, 11 photogrammetric reference points (Ground Control Points – GCP) were used as control points for the bundle adjustment, framing the entire data set in the topographic network and minimizing the orientation errors. The selection of the GCP has been a fast operation identifying on the images the targets put in well visible place and so easy to recognize them during the acquisition phase with the drone. The presence of vegetation close to the wall and the buildings, those don't concern with the wall representation, cause the burdening of the point cloud. After the first alignment the points projecting these elements have been deleted, in order to simplify the dense cloud creation process. The average alignment residual computed on the GCP after the bundle adjustment is 2.2 cm, while on the check points it is approximately 1.6 cm (Table 2).

Table 2. Parameters referring to dense cloud processing of Sect. 4

Data	N. cameras	N. points	N. GCP	N. check points	Error GCP [m]	Error check point [m]
Section 4	264	20931657	11	11	0,022	0,016

The resulting photogrammetric dense cloud of Sect. 4, obtained through the photogrammetric and Structure from Motion (SfM) workflow using the Batch Process tool and setting up automatic saving at the end of each operation, is shown in Fig. 4.

Fig. 4. Dense cloud of Sect. 4 processed by Agisoft Metashape

5.2 CloudCompare

At the end of the acquisition phase with KAARTA Stencil 2 the information about the configuration setting, the 3D point cloud, the estimated trajectories are stored in a folder created automatically by the mobile laser scanner processer every operation of survey. In case of elaboration of 3D point cloud made by mobile laser scanner, it's correct to talk about post-processing. The most used open source software for the point cloud analysis, also suggested by KAARTA producers, is CloudCompare [20], that can be downloaded free from internet.

The 3D data, saved in.*ply* (Polygon File Format) format, can be opened in CloudCompare that allows these main functions: registration and alignment of point cloud, manual or automatic cleaning and the final sharpening. Adopting some filters, as the SOR (Statistical Outlier Removal) one, the software tries to make a first cleaning of the loaded point cloud. Then operations of resampling, setting the medium space of 0.2 m between points, and shading by EDL (Eye Dome Lighting) tool, the point cloud becomes lighter and clearly visible.

Since a GNSS system was not integrated with KAARTA Stencil 2 and the mobile laser scanner can't identify the targets placed on the ground used for the aerial photogrammetry, the georeferencing of the point cloud was realized in two ways. The unique method is to select control points on the vertical surface of the walls. So a first solution was to use the Control Points taken by the TS. The second one consisted on identifying some points, easily to search, from the dense cloud built in Metashape and georeferenced with the GPS coordinates. In both cases the control points has been imported in CloudCompare for the alignment of the 3D point cloud.

6 Results

6.1 Integration of 3D Data

KAARTA Stencil 2 has a strong potentiality to generate a higher number of points composing the 3D point clouds. The maximum value of points can be changed in the configuration setting of the parameters before the survey campaign. KAARTA Stencil 2 used for this work, doesn't product good quality of colour information of 3D point cloud or take good resolution images. But the advantage of using the mobile laser scanner at the ground level allows to enrich the point cloud in areas or spaces difficult to acquire with the drone, for example the passage under the arches opening along the path of the walls or objects under the crown of high trees. In these last cases a reflex camera was adopted to complete the photogrammetric survey. Instead, the higher parts of the walls, where the ground-based laser scanner can't reach, the UAV survey is able to compensate for this gap. It's clear that the aforementioned technologies may be complementary to one another in creating complete high-quality 3D representations.

Thanks to CloudCompare software, we tested the combination of processed 3D data gathering together the point clouds from SLAM and UAV surveys and then it could be possible to evaluate and assess this integration.

6.2 Assessment

In order to assess the quality and the correspondence to reality of 3D point clouds, two procedures have been followed: first, the evaluation of the distance between the clouds thus processed, and second the georeferenced dense cloud obtained with the photogrammetry was computed as reference cloud. To this end, the CloudCompare software has been used, which allows these estimates to be performed [21]. Once we have both clouds overlapped, the difference between the reference cloud and the KAARTA Stencil 2 map can be estimated using the distance Cloud-to-Cloud (C2C) tool. The C2C tool exploits the Nearest Neighbour algorithm to compute the Euclidean distance between each point of the compared cloud and the nearest point of the reference cloud [22]. The point clouds have been filtered computing the linearity feature with the identification of the local radius set to 0.3 m. Then, by using the histogram of scalar field, we selected the range of linearity close to 0 value that shows only plan surfaces. In this way we have deleted objects showing elements of curvature that could falsify the distance C2C assessment, like vegetations or the hill slope. Finally, the C2C tool was launched by setting the points distant from the reference model in a range value from 0 to 50 cm as outliers, since the errors that interest us are lower than this limit. From the results of the point clouds assessment it emerges the very small difference between the KAARTA Stencil 2 map and the reference cloud, showing that the point cloud generated by the mobile laser scanner has a short deviation (Fig. 5). In fact, due to the lack of GCP on the façade of the wall, there is a greater discrepancy on the vertical surfaces that are far from the targets detected on the ground, causing a loss of accuracy in the absolute orientation of the cameras. In Table 3 are reported the statistical parameters derived from the analysis with C2C tool, such as: average distance, Root Mean Square Error (RMSE), maximum distance computed and number of the compared points of the segmented point clouds.

C2C absolute distances

0.499999
0.468761
0.437522
0.406283
0.375044
0.343805
0.312566
0.281327
0.250089
0.218850
0.187611
0.156372
0.125133
0.093894
0.062655
0.031417
0.000178

Fig. 5. C2C absolute distance computation analysis of vertical surfaces (Sect. 4) between point clouds of UAV photogrammetry and KAARTA Stencil 2

Table 3. Statistical results from the distance comparison between point clouds of UAV photogrammetry and KAARTA Stencil 2

Data	Avg. Distance [m]	RMSE [m]	Max distance [m]	Point cloud
				N. points
Section 4	0,12	0,10	0,50	4716333

7   Conclusion

The steps of this work involved many research tasks, taking into account the diversity of the data coming from different sensors. The considered techniques (hardware and software) are thus reported with their advantages and disadvantages. In detail, the Mobile Laser Scanner KAARTA Stencil 2 has been used, whilst the UAV photogrammetric survey was performed by DJI Spark MMA1 with a GSD of 4 cm. The ground reference of the survey has been defined by the classical topographical approach (done with TS and GNSS) with the aim to geo-reference the 3D cloud points. For the image processing, Agisoft Metashape has been used, also to build the mesh and to create the orthophotos. Once georeferenced both point clouds from UAV photogrammetry and Mobile Laser Scanner, their integration has been tested on CloudCompare. Therefore, we made a comparison between the point clouds to evaluate the data accuracy and to assess the distance C2C. From this comparison between the point clouds a sufficient centimetric distance was verified to obtain the expected results.

In order to have an accurate absolute orientation of the cameras, it is not only necessary to limit oneself to the ground targets but also to detect targets on high vertical surfaces. In this way we could build a point cloud with a greater detail of precision and accuracy.

It is finally important to remark that the 3D model of the walls was achieved with the accuracy related to the output scale of 1:200 and with a detail and complexity useful for future analysis and restoration activities. In fact, given the seismic events that seriously damaged San Ginesio and the Marche Region in 2016, emerged the necessity to assess novel methods to perform fast and agile acquisition campaigns: providing restorers and public administrations to the conservation and demonstrating that we are still in time to document our valuable CH before other dramatic events may occur.

So, the main contribution of this paper lies on defining a baseline, useful for other researchers dealing with the combination of different acquisition solutions for CH subjects. According to the new strategy in the restoration standards for architectural documentation it is possible to state that the approach in the present research allows to obtain 3D model that fits the need for the knowledge with analysis of the architectural heritage, and eventually collecting all data in an information management system like HBIM implementation, as future work.

Acknowledgements. Our thanks to the team of Restoration course at the Engineering Faculty of Università Politecnica delle Marche, to give us the opportunity to have carried out this survey and for the fruitful collaboration, and the San Ginesio Municipality for providing base material useful to plan the acquisition campaigns.

References

1. Bayram, B., Nemli, G., Özkan, T., Oflaz, O.E., Kankotan, B., Çetin, İ.: Comparison of laser scanning and photogrammetry and their use for digital recording of cultural monument. Case study: byzantine land walls-Istanbul. Int. Arch. Photogramm. Remote Sens. Spatial Inf. Sci. **II-5/W3**, 17–24 (2015)
2. Bitelli, G., Dellapasqua, M., Girelli, V.A., Sanchini, E., Tini, M.A.: 3D geomatics techniques for an integrated approach to cultural heritage knowledge: the case of San Michele in Acerboli's church in Santarcangelo di Romagna. Int. Arch. Photogramm. Remote Sens. Spatial Inf. Sci. **XLII-5/W1**, 291–296 (2017)
3. Kadobayashi, R., Kochi, N., Otani, H., Furukawa, R.: Comparison and evaluation of laser scanning and photogrammetry and their combined use for digital recording of cultural heritage. Int. Arch. Photogramm. Remote Sens. Spatial Inf. Sci. **35**, 401–406 (2004)
4. Makkonen, T., Heikkilä, R., Tölli, P., Fedorik, F.: Using SLAM-based handheld laser scanning to gain information on difficult-to-access areas for use in maintenance model. In: Proceedings of the 34th ISARC, Taipei, Taiwan (ISARC 2017), pp. 887–892 (2017)
5. Remondino, F., Gaiani, M., Apollonio, F., Ballabeni, A., Ballabeni, M., Morabito, D.: 3D documentation of 40 km of historical porticoes – the challenge, Int. Arch. Photogramm. Remote Sens. Spatial Inf. Sci. **XLI-B5**, 711–718 (2016)
6. Aliberti, L., Iglesias Picazo, P.: Close-range photogrammetry practice: graphic documentation of the interior of the walls of Avila (Spain). Int. Arch. Photogramm. Remote Sens. Spatial Inf. Sci. **XLII-2/W15**, 49–53 (2019)
7. Fassi, F., Achille, C., Gaudio, F., Fregonese, L.: Integrated strategies for the modeling very large and complex architectures. Int. Arch. Photogramm. Remote Sens. Spatial Inf. Sci. **XXXVIII-5/W16**, 105–112 (2011)

8. Achille, C., et al.: UAV-based photogrammetry and integrated technologies for architectural applications—methodological strategies for the after-quake survey of vertical structures in Mantua (Italy). Sensors **15**, 15520–15539 (2015)

9. Turismo, S.G. http://turismo.comune.sanginesio.mc.it/alla-scoperta-del-comune/la-storia/. Accessed 10 June 2019

10. Topcon. https://www.topconpositioning.com/it/all-products. Accessed 14 Jan 2019

11. Topcon. https://www.topconpositioning.com/it/gnss-and-network-solutions/ricevitori-gnss-integrati/hiper-hr. Accessed on 14 Jan 2019

12. DJI. https://www.dji.com/it. Accessed 25 May 2019

13. Carnevali, L., Ippoliti, E., Lanfranchi, F., Menconero, S., Russo, M., Russo, V.: Close-range mini-UAVs photogrammetry for architecture survey. Int. Arch. Photogramm. Remote Sens. Spatial Inf. Sci. **XLII-2**, 217–224 (2018)

14. ENAC Regolamento. https://www.enac.gov.it/sites/default/files/allegati/2018-Lug/Regolamento_APR_Ed2_Em4_180704.pdf. Accessed 25 May 2019

15. Azzola, P., Cardaci, A., Mirabella Roberti, G., Nannei, V.M.: UAV photogrammetry for cultural heritage preservation modeling and mapping Venetian Walls of Bergamo. Int. Arch. Photogramm. Remote Sens. Spatial Inf. Sci. **XLII-2/W9**, 45–50 (2019)

16. KAARTA Stencil 2. https://www.kaarta.com/products/stencil-2-for-rapid-long-range-mobile-mapping/#Specs. Accessed 27 Mar 2019

17. Paolanti, M., et al.: Semantic 3D object maps for everyday robotic retail inspection. In: Cristani, M., Prati, A., Lanz, O., Messelodi, S., Sebe, N. (eds.) ICIAP 2019. LNCS, vol. 11808, pp. 263–274. Springer, Cham (2019). https://doi.org/10.1007/978-3-030-30754-7_27

18. Agisoft. https://www.agisoft.com. Accessed 02 May 2019

19. Malinverni, E.S., Chiappini, S., Pierdicca, R.: A geodatabase for multisource data management applied to cultural heritage: case study of Villa Buonaccorsi's historical garden. Int. Arch. Photogramm. Remote Sens. Spatial Inf. Sci. **XLII-2/W11**, 771–776 (2019a)

20. CloudCompare User Manual. http://www.cloudcompare.org. Accessed 15 Apr 2019

21. Malinverni, E.S., Pierdicca, R., Bozzi, C.A., Bartolucci, D.: Evaluating a SLAM-based mobile mapping system: a methodological comparison for 3D heritage scene real-time reconstruction. In: METROARCHEO, IEEE 4th International Conference on Metrology for Archaeology and Cultural Heritage, Cassino, Italy, 22–24 October 2018, pp. 260–265 (2018)

22. Bronzino, G.P.C., Grasso, N., Matrone, F., Osello, A., Piras, M.: Laser-visual-inertial odometry based solution for 3D heritage modeling: the Sanctuary of the Blessed Virgin of Trompone, Int. Arch. Photogramm. Remote Sens. Spatial Inf. Sci. **XLII-2/W15**, 215–222 (2019)

Dynamic Measurement of Water Waves in a Wave Channel Based on Low-Cost Photogrammetry: Description of the System and First Results

Serena Artese[1]([✉]) [ID], Michele Perrelli[2] [ID], Giuseppe Tripepi[1] [ID],
and Francesco Aristodemo[1] [ID]

[1] Department of Civil Engineering, University of Calabria, 87036 Rende, Italy
{serena.artese,giuseppe.tripepi,
francesco.aristodemo}@unical.it
[2] Department of Mechanical, Energy and Management Engineering,
University of Calabria, 87036 Rende, Italy
michele.perrelli@unical.it

Abstract. The paper describes the development of a hardware/software system for the space-time detection of the free surface of water, produced by the movement of waves, and of the relative mass transport.

The first tests of the system were performed using the wave channel of the *Laboratorio Grandi Modelli Idraulici* of the Department of Civil Engineering of the University of Calabria, equipped with hardware/software tools for generating and measuring water waves.

The first version of the system designed and developed uses three cameras positioned appropriately, so as to cover the entire length of the generated waves. The acquisitions of the video cameras are synchronized via software using an ad-hoc code.

Raspberry pi 8 MP cameras were used, mounted on as many Raspberry Pi microcomputers, and full HD videos (1920 × 1080) were acquired. The management features of the processors made it necessary to set up an ad-hoc code for the synchronization of the frames.

The free surface is represented as Dense Digital Surface Model using Dense Image Matching techniques. Due to the size of the wave channel, in the perspective of use for large lengths, low-cost cameras were used, with lenses characterized by high distortions.

Keywords: Photogrammetry · DIC · SIFT · Water waves · Wave channel

1 Introduction

Photogrammetric techniques for wave measurements have been used since two decades. Two or three cameras with calibrated lenses are used, generally positioned in a known position and with a known orientation, in order to get both internal and external parameters. A stereo apparatus for laboratory wave channel was proposed by Tsubaki and Fujita [1]. They projected an irregular model pattern onto the water surface; the captured area was 18 cm by 14 cm and the standard deviation of the results was approximately 16% of wave height. Wanek and Wu [2] used a trinocular stereo imaging system, covering a 3 m by 2 m area of a lake surface, in order to resolve problems due to specular reflection and to provide additional constraints on image matching. Cobelli et al. [3] used a fringe projection technique, applied to a channel 1.5 m long, 0.5 m wide and 0.15 m high. They declared a vertical resolution of 0.2 mm, but didn't take into account the reflection of light below the water surface.

For the surface surveying, the Particle Tracking Velocimetry, used since 1990 as a tomographic technique [4], is a promising method, not yet fully exploited [5]. The problems regard density, dimensions and colors of particles.

Recently, the problems related to refraction have been dealt with in depth [6], while unmanned aerial vehicles [7] have been used for the surveying of the water level.

As regards the image processing, several techniques have been proposed, mainly based on Scale-Invariant Feature Transform (SIFT) and Digital Image Correlation (DIC) [8–11].

Terrestrial Laser Scanner (TLS) is a consolidated technique for dynamic measurements of surfaces subject to deformations [12].

The first applications of Terrestrial Laser Scanner (TLS) for water waves measurements regard the coastal zones and date back to 2000. More recently, Tamari et al. [13] describe the results obtained by using a near-infrared Lidar for monitoring the water level of turbid reservoirs.

The use of TLS applied in a laboratory wave flume is relatively new. For this reason, some parameters influencing the accuracy of results are still under investigation. Harry et al. [14] described an experimental setup and a unique method for measuring wave parameters. Blenkinsopp et al. [15] showed that a single LiDAR instrument can replace large arrays of wave gauges, with higher spatial resolution. Streicher et al. [16] stressed the need to correct the measurements for the penetration of laser beam in the water before its reflection.

All these techniques have big operating limits especially with daylight. It was therefore chosen to develop a system to be tested in different lighting conditions.

Among the issues involved, the following are particularly important: (a) calibration of the camera array (geometric, chromatic and temporal); (b) the large incidence angles of the rays reflected in the presence of waves, which reduce the precision of the matching process; (c) the correction of the effects due to the imperfect synchronization of laboratory equipment and images acquired by the cameras.

The structure of the paper is as follows: Sect. 2 describes the design and the setup of the acquisition system; Sect. 3 deals with the determination of the intrinsic and extrinsic parameters of the cameras and with the code set up for synchronization; Sect. 4 describes the first test with moving water and the relevant results.

2   The Design and the Set-up of the Acquisition System

The goal of the project is to set up a flexible, cost-effective and easy-to-use experimental apparatus for 3D measurements of water waves in a laboratory flume provided with a piston-type wavemaker moved by a servo-controller hydraulic actuator and able to generate regular, irregular and tsunami waves.

The width of the channel is 1 m and the length of the generated waves can reach several meters. Taking into account the field of view of the low-cost cameras to be used and to exploit their resolution, the overlapping area of two cameras is approximately two meters. For the detection of longer waves, therefore, an array of cameras must be used. Therefore, the experimental apparatus should be provided with a series of low-cost digital cameras, in order to obtain 3D wave measurements by photogrammetric techniques.

The design of the experimental apparatus was performed in order to have: (a) the set-up of an effective hardware/software low-cost system; (b) the accurate space-time registration of data obtained by cameras; (c) 3D modelling of surface elevation of water waves in undisturbed and disturbed conditions with a precision comparable or better than the ones obtained by the wave probes (1–2 mm) and; (d) the reconstruction of fluid particle trajectories at the free surface.

The calibration of the system is made through the application of an analytical solution for non-linear periodic waves.

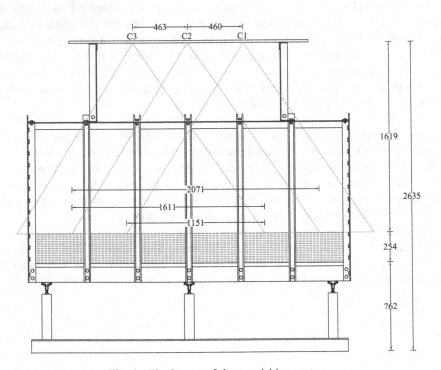

Fig. 1. The layout of the acquisition system.

Regarding the selection of cameras, the criteria for the choice were essentially: (1) low cost, (2) possibility of high frame rate, (3) high resolution. For our aims, a lower resolution (i.e. 1280 × 720 pixels) and 60 fps could be in general sufficient. For the first test, a train of waves with a period of 1 s had to be acquired, therefore it was possible to adopt a reduced transfer rate of 30 frames per second, thus allowing a higher resolution (1080p, full HD).

The layout was designed for obtaining a full trinocular coverage. With reference to Fig. 1, we can observe that a wave with a length up to 2 m can be acquired by stereo pairs. For the central zone, 1.15 m wide, each point of the water surface will be within three overlap areas, i.e. in a position covered by three cameras. This ensures that each point belongs to three stereo pairs. For long waves, an array with more cameras should be used. This choice allows to resolve problems due to specular reflection on the water surface and to provide additional constraints on image matching.

As regards the cameras mounting, it was realized with a metallic portal, equipped with spherical joints in order to allow positioning and orientation of cameras. The portal is independent of the structure frames of the wave channel (see Fig. 2). Furthermore, in this way the cameras are not affected by the micro vibrations of the channel due to environmental disturbances.

Fig. 2. View of the laboratory wave channel equipped by a piston-type wavemaker.

The wave channel is 41.0 m long, 1.2 m deep and 1.0 m wide. It is equipped with a piston-type wavemaker driven by a hydraulic actuator to generate different kinds of waves and a rubble mound breakwater to dissipate the incident waves in the final part (see, for more details, [17, 18]). The adopted instruments to measure the surface elevation are resistance wave gauges placed along the flume and before the measurement area of the cameras. The frequency sampling of the wave gauges is 100 Hz.

3   The Internal and External Calibration of the Cameras and the Code for Synchronization

The camera used for the acquisition system is a Raspberry Pi Camera Module v2®. It is a very low-weight and small camera, that can be directly connected to a Raspberry Pi 4 microcomputer via a dedicated 15-pin MIPI Camera Serial Interface. The microcomputer manages video acquisition, synchronization and recording. Each camera is housed in a case, which allows the locking to an external structure. The microcomputers are also housed in customized cases, while for the connection between camera and microcomputer, a 15-pin cable 1 m long was used during the tests. The main characteristics of the camera are shown in Table 1.

Table 1. Hardware specification Raspberry Pi Camera Module v2.

Hardware specification	Module v2
Still resolution	8 Megapixels
Video modes/transfer rate (frames per second - fps)	1080p/30 fps, 720p/60 fps and 640 × 480p 60/90 fps
Sensor	Sony IMX219
Sensor resolution	3280 × 2464 pixels
Sensor image area	3.68 × 2.76 mm (4.6 mm diagonal)
Focal length	3.04 mm
Horizontal field of view	62.2°
Vertical field of view	48.8°

Fig. 3. The 2D pattern drawn on a flat board.

The use of low-cost cameras involves a very accurate calibration of lenses and sensors in order to guarantee the requested accuracy. Further problems are due to the variation of lighting along the flume. Moreover, the waves imply very different angle of incidence of the reflected beams for adjacent cameras; this causes errors in the matching procedures used to obtain dense surface modeling.

The three camera array was calibrated using a 2D pattern drawn on a flat board (see Fig. 3).

A customized version of Matlab Camera Calibration Toolbox® was exploited, adapted for the use of the pattern shown in Fig. 3, to compute the reprojection errors and obtain intrinsic and extrinsic parameters of the cameras.

Table 2 shows the intrinsic parameters of the three cameras used for the tests: focal length, principal point, distortion coefficients, skew coefficient and their relevant uncertainties. Focal length and principal point coordinates units are in pixels.

The 5-vector kc contains both radial and tangential distortion coefficients; in detail, the first, second and fifth entries are the coefficients of the 2nd, 4th and 6th order radial distortion term, while the third and the fourth entries are the coefficients of the tangential distortion.

Table 2. Calibration results.

Intrinsic camera parameters	Camera 1 (dx)	Camera 2 (center)	Camera 3 (sx)
Focal length fc	1505.77; 1507.12	1510.98; 1512.11	1513.02; 1515.45
Principal point cc	979.95; 537.63	963.71; 542.49	943.68; 526.67
Skew coefficient αc	0.000000	0.000000	0.000000
Distortion coefficients kc	0.143740; −0.256818; 0.000822; 0.002226; 0.000000	0.182430; −0.361047; 0.000201; 0.001755; 0.000000	0.171611; −0.319664; −0.003568; −0.002526; 0.000000
Focal length uncertainty	6.67; 6.60	5.18; 5.20	5.55; 5.46
Principal point uncertainty	8.24; 5.89	5.39; 5.15	6.06; 5.02
Skew coefficient uncertainty	0.000000	0.000000	0.000000
Distortion coefficients uncertainty	0.007189; 0.015909; 0.001330; 0.002454; 0.000000	0.007084; 0.022400; 0.001420; 0.001491; 0.000000	0.007642; 0.021529; 0.001537; 0.001672; 0.000000
Image size	1920; 1080	1920; 1080	1920; 1080

Taking into account 30 images acquired for each camera, the extrinsic parameters are: (1) three series of thirty 3×3 rotation matrices Rc; (2) three sets of thirty 3×1 translation vectors Tc. A custom code was used to obtain, from the extrinsic parameters, the orientation of the second and third cameras with respect to the first.

Since the camera mounting portal is independent of the frames of the wave channel structure, the central position of the lens and some points on the joints of the channel frame, visible in the videos, have been surveyed in order to obtain the orientation of the cameras with respect to the channel. For this purpose, a Leica TS30 total station was used, positioned on the scaffold that houses the computer, the monitors and the operator who performs the acquisitions.

Before the application on the wave channel, after the calibration phase, stereo measurements were performed on laboratory targets, in order to evaluate the accuracy of the system. For a set of 10 points, a standard deviation of 0.2 mm was obtained for the 3D coordinates, at an average distance of 2 m.

In order to acquire images and video from investigated area, three Raspberry pi 8 MP cameras were used, connected on as many Raspberry Pi microcomputers. To get and store the digital images a custom python script was designed. A correct 3D reconstruction of the phenomenon is possible only thanks to a good synchronization of acquisition process. To obtain this result, one of GPIOs of the Raspberries has been configured as input and controlled by a push button connected to them in parallel mode, as shown in Fig. 4.

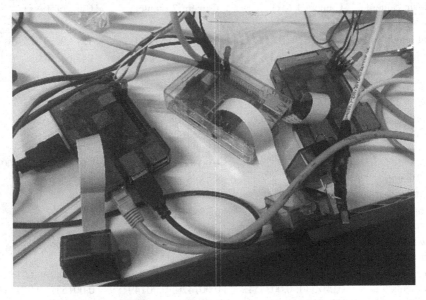

Fig. 4. Raspberry configuration.

Since the initialization process of the pi cameras does not take the same time on each Raspberry, this push button has two main functions: starts the cameras initialization procedure and triggers the image acquisition process after cameras are ready to acquire the image.

In fact, when the user pushes the trigger for the first time, every Raspberry starts the procedure of initialization of its own camera and advises the user with a double green flash light when this process was correctly performed and the camera is ready to stream the image. When all Raspberries have finished this process, by pushing again the trigger, the user can start the simultaneous acquisition of full HD videos with a maximum misalignment of 0.01 s between the corresponding frames of the three cameras. For the data processing, a Dell XPS 13 9360 Notebook was used.

Below the workflow of the acquisitions operations (see Fig. 5).

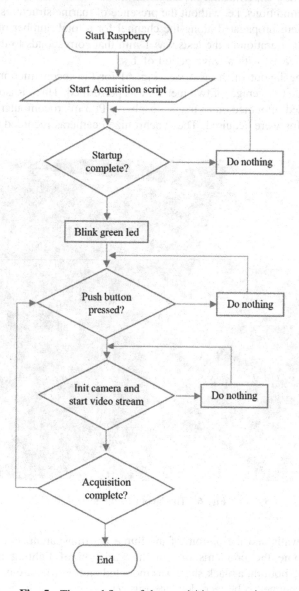

Fig. 5. The workflow of the acquisitions operations.

Matlab scripts, based on SIFT and DIC techniques were used to obtain the water surface model for each pair of frames. Details on the scripts can be found in [8] and [10].

4   The First Acquisitions with Moving Water

The first tests of the experimental investigation in the wave flume were characterized by undisturbed conditions, i.e. without the presence of marine structures. In particular, regular waves were propagated along the channel for a total number of 10 tests. For regular waves, the duration of the tests was 1 min that corresponds to the propagation of a train of 60 waves with a wave period of 1 s.

Regarding the layout of the test (see Fig. 6) for the reconstruction of the water surface, a trinocular coverage, of two meters, was performed. Three Raspberry pi 8 MP cameras were used, mounted on as many Raspberry Pi 3 microcomputers, and full HD videos with 30 fps were acquired. The synchronized cameras recorded a 30 s video.

Fig. 6. The layout of the test.

The lateral walls and the bottom of the flume are transparent. For this reason, in order to overcome the problems due to the variation of lighting and the strong reflections on the bottom, a black sheet was mounted on the structure in order to screen the part of the channel to be recorded (see Fig. 7).

About 4000 colored balls with a diameter of 6 mm were used as irregular pattern (see Fig. 8).

Fig. 7. The black sheet used for screening the part of the channel to be filmed.

Fig. 8. View of the colored balls used to create an irregular pattern.

With reference to the synchronization of the acquisitions of cameras, a clock has been used, with a display showing the hundredth of a second. The clock has been positioned near a wall of the flume and falls in the field of view of all the cameras. In this way it was possible to check the time synchronization of the acquired videos.

Once the acquisitions are finished, the video frames have been extracted.

Using the SIFT and DIC algorithms, it was possible to reconstruct the 3D modelling of surface elevation of water waves. Since the acquired wave has a length greater than the triple overlap zone, two 3D models with an overlap zone have been joined to obtain the whole wave model. Below are the results, taking into account for the centerline of the wave flume and leading to a 2D analysis.

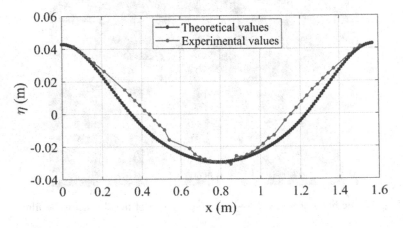

Fig. 9. Comparison between the theoretical shape of the wave (blue points) and that derived from photogrammetric measurements (red points). (Color figure online)

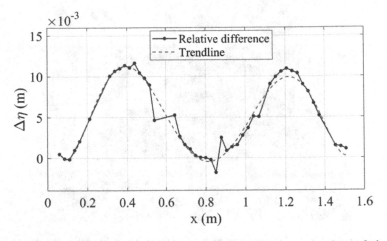

Fig. 10. The relative difference between theoretical and experimental values of the surface elevation (blue points). The dashed red line is the trendline. (Color figure online)

We can observe, in Fig. 9, some differences between the shape of the theoretically obtained wave related to a 3rd order Stokes wave [19], and that derived from photogrammetric measurements. In the figure, the ordinate η is the displacement of the wave surface points with respect to the flat surface of the calm water before the test. In particular, the order of the non-linear Stokes wave has been deduced from the number of harmonics of the experimental power spectrum measured by the resistance wave gauge placed just before the area of the photogrammetric measurements. The representative wave differs in the slope. Indeed, the theoretical one shows a more curved shape compared to the experimental one. The relative differences $\Delta\eta$ are almost negligible in correspondence with the crest and trough and the resulting wave height, i.e. difference between crest and trough, is almost the same. The relative difference reaches the maximum near the zero-crossing points (see Fig. 10). This phenomenon, to be investigated later in the research, could be related to an insufficient accuracy of the calibration parameters.

5   Conclusions and Future Tests

Experiments were performed in undisturbed conditions.

The results are substantially in accord to the ones obtained analytically adopting a 3rd order Stokes wave theory.

Successively the experiments will be performed in the presence of a cylindrical structure where large deformations occur in the near field [20]. Furthermore, the apparatus will allow the tracking of floating particles in order to obtain their trajectories for complex flow fields especially induced by wave-structure interaction, i.e. highly non-linear and breaking waves.

In the second phase of the research the use of a Terrestrial Laser Scanner is programmed, in Line Scanner mode, whose scans will be synchronized to the photogrammetric acquisitions using the timestamp provided by the instrument.

A GPS clock will be used to synchronize the TLS acquisitions with videos and laboratory instruments.

Acknowledgements. We thank the technical staff of the *Laboratorio Grandi Modelli Idraulici* of the Department of Civil Engineering of the University of Calabria for the support during the tests.

References

1. Tsubaki, R., Fujita, I.: Stereoscopic measurement of a fluctuating free surface with discontinuities. Meas. Sci. Technol. **16**(10), 1894 (2005)
2. Wanek, J.M., Wu, C.H.: Automated trinocular stereo imaging system for three-dimensional surface wave measurements. Ocean Eng. **33**(5), 723–747 (2006)
3. Cobelli, P.J., Maurel, A., Pagneux, V., Petitjeans, P.: Global measurement of water waves by Fourier transform profilometry. Exp. Fluids **46**(6), 1037 (2009)
4. Maas, H.G.: Digital photogrammetry for determination of tracer particle coordinates in turbulent flow research. Photogram. Eng. Remote Sens. **57**(12), 1593–1597 (1991)

5. von Larcher, T., Williams, P.D.: Modeling Atmospheric and Oceanic Flows: Insights from Laboratory Experiments and Numerical Simulations, vol. 205. Wiley, New York (2014)

6. González-Vera, A.S., Wilting, T.J.S., Holten, A.P.C., van Heijst, G.J.F., Duran-Matute, M.: High-resolution single-camera photogrammetry: incorporation of refraction at a fluid interface. Exp. Fluids **61**(1), 1–19 (2019). https://doi.org/10.1007/s00348-019-2826-y

7. Kohv, M., Sepp, E., Vammus, L.: Assessing multitemporal water-level changes with UAV-based photogrammetry. Photogram. Rec. **32**(160), 424–442 (2017)

8. Genovese, K.: An omnidirectional DIC system for dynamic strain measurement on soft biological tissues and organs. Opt. Lasers Eng. **116**, 6–18 (2019)

9. Pan, B.: Digital image correlation for surface deformation measurement: historical developments, recent advances and future goals. Meas. Sci. Technol. **29**(8), 8200 (2018)

10. Solav, D., Moerman, K.M., Jaeger, A.M., Genovese, K., Herr, H.M.: MultiDIC: an open source toolbox for multi-view 3D digital image correlation. IEEE Access **6**, 30520–30535 (2018)

11. Wu, J., Cui, Z., Sheng, V.S., Zhao, P., Su, D., Gong, S.: A comparative study of sift and its variants. Meas. Sci. Rev. **13**(3), 122–131 (2013)

12. Artese, S., Zinno, R.: TLS for dynamic measurement of the elastic line of bridges. Appl. Sci. **10**, 1182 (2020)

13. Tamari, S., Mory, J., Guerrero-Meza, V.: Testing a near-infrared Lidar mounted with a large incidence angle to monitor the water level of turbid reservoirs. ISPRS J. Photogram. Rem. Sens. **66**(6), S85–S91 (2011)

14. Harry, M., Zhang, H., Lemckert, C., Colleter, G., Blenkinsopp, C.: Remote sensing of water waves: wave flume experiments on regular and irregular waves. Coasts and Ports 2011: diverse and developing. In: Proceedings of the 20th Australasian Coastal and Ocean Engineering Conference and the 13th Australasian Port and Harbour Conference. Engineers Australia (2011)

15. Blenkinsopp, C.E., Turner, I.L., Allis, M.J., Peirson, W.L., Garden, L.E.: Application of LiDAR technology for measurement of time-varying free-surface profiles in a laboratory wave flume. Coast. Eng. **68**, 1–5 (2012)

16. Streicher, M., Hofland, B., Lindenbergh, R.C.: Laser ranging for monitoring water waves in the new Deltares Delta Flume. In: Scaioni, M., Lindenbergh, R.C., Oude Elberink, S., Schneider, D., Pirotti, F. (eds.) ISPRS Annals of the Photogrammetry, Remote Sensing and Spatial Information Sciences. ISPRS Workshop Laser Scanning 2013, vol. II-5/W2, Antalya, Turkey, 11–13 November 2013. ISPRS (2013)

17. Tripepi, G., Aristodemo, F., Veltri, P., Pace, C., Solano, A., Giordano, C.: Experimental and numerical investigation of tsunami-like waves on horizontal circular cylinders. In: Proceedings of 36th International Conference on Ocean, Offshore and Arctic Engineering, Trondheim, Norway, vol. 7A, pp. 1–10 (2017)

18. Tripepi, G., Aristodemo, F., Meringolo, D.D., Gurnari, L., Filianoti, P.: Hydrodynamic forces induced by a solitary wave interacting with a submerged square barrier: Physical tests and δ-LES-SPH simulations. Coast. Eng. **158**(103690), 1–17 (2020)

19. Dean, R.G., Dalrymple, R.A.: Water Wave Mechanics for Engineering and Scientists. Prentice-Hall, New Jersey (1984)

20. Aristodemo, F., Tripepi, G., Meringolo, D.D., Veltri, P.: Solitary wave-induced forces on horizontal circular cylinders: Laboratory experiments and SPH simulations. Coast. Eng. **129**, 17–35 (2017)

3-D Survey of Rocky Structures: The Dolomitic Spire of the Gusela del Vescovà

Michele Monego⑩, Vladimiro Achilli, Massimo Fabris$^{(\boxtimes)}$⑩, and Andrea Menin

Laboratory of Survey and Geomatics, Department of Civil, Environmental and Architectural Engineering, University of Padova, Via Marzolo, 9, 35131 Padua, Italy
massimo.fabris@unipd.it

Abstract. In the mountain environment, the presence of fractures or degradation in the rock mass could represent an important risk both for the safety of population and for the anthropic structures that have a productive, touristic and/or historical importance. For this reason, the monitoring is a primary action of control and risk mitigation. In this work a 3-D survey of the Gusela del Vescova' Dolomitic Spire was performed for the morphometric definition of its rocky elements using Terrestrial Laser Scanning (TLS) and Structure from Motion (SfM) applied to drone-captured imagery; the georeferencing was executed using classical topographic and GNSS methodologies. Results provides information about the state of the structure after 18 years from the first measurement (2001–2019) of the main fracture and models obtained with the two methodologies, allowing the evaluation of advantages and disadvantages of the techniques for the survey in extreme environment conditions. The comparison between the models, together with GCP's errors estimate, allowed to evaluate the final 3-D models: in this case SfM model shows a better global quality in terms of completeness and photo-realistic representation, with high accuracy that is comparable to the TLS models. This survey provides the first complete 3D high resolution representation of the spire: an up-to-date geometrical and photographic dataset that allows accurate measures, the definition of the cracks pattern and represents the base for further future studies and monitoring of the deformations.

Keywords: 3-D survey · Terrestrial Laser Scanning (TLS) · Structure from Motion (SfM) · Dolomitic spire

1 Introduction

The 3-D survey of complex elements in high mountain environment required the acquisition of high precision and high-resolution data using compact, easily transportable and lightweight instruments due to the difficulty of movement along trails or mountaineering routes.

In north-eastern Italy, the Dolomites mountain group in wide areas represents this type of environment, hardly accessible if not through long approaches.

© Springer Nature Switzerland AG 2020
C. Parente et al. (Eds.): R3GEO 2019, CCIS 1246, pp. 211–228, 2020.
https://doi.org/10.1007/978-3-030-62800-0_17

The geomorphology of the Dolomites is characterized by the presence of spires, cusps and rocky peaks: these mountains in 2009 were inserted in the UNESCO World Heritage Site.

Certainly, the Dolomitic spire named "Gusela del Vescovà" (Fig. 1, Fig. 2), in the "Parco Nazionale delle Dolomiti Bellunesi" located in Veneto Region (North-Easter Italy), is an element of great interest not only for its morphology but, above all, for its historical-monumental significance for the Belluno city. The high frequentation of the area for alpinism and trekking suggests a periodical control that, if could not prevent the occurrence of sudden events, could be important to detect significant displacement and report the related danger.

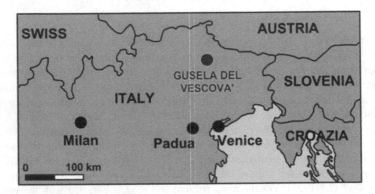

Fig. 1. Geographic position of the Gusela del Vescovà located in the "Parco Nazionale delle Dolomiti Bellunesi" (Veneto Region, North-Easter Italy).

Fig. 2. The west side of the rocky spire (in the red rectangle) and the summit of Mt. Schiara in the background. (Color figure online)

The monitoring of this structure requires, however, to identify the most suitable techniques and to consider some acceptable limitations brought by a set of instruments that have to be reduced as much as possible. The access to the upper part of the monolith, for direct measurements (i.e. geological compass) or the installation of sensors (i.e. extensometers, inclinometers), is substantially to be excluded and would require an expensive and complicated logistics.

In this work the geomatic survey of the Gusela del Vescovà spire has been performed: various attempts to perform the measurement have been tried during the last 4 years but the bad weather conditions (sudden and unexpected fog, wind or rain due to the particular position and altitude) always closed the campaigns without results: only in the summer of 2019 the survey has been successfully performed. In order to describe the status of the structure, the identification of the crack pattern, and provide data to plan future monitoring, we applied the most suitable geomatic methodologies and evaluated the results of each one. Two approaches were used: TLS technique for the acquisitions of point clouds from the ground, and SfM acquiring images of the spire from drone. Data were used to obtain the first 3D high resolution description of the spire representing the base for future monitoring activities. During the survey was performed a repetition of the topographic measurements related to the main fracture, almost vertical, that characterize the Dolomitic spire: a first survey was performed in 2001 acquiring the coordinates of artificial points located in the two portions of the crack that divides the Gusela del Vescovà. The comparison of the measurements has provided information about the behavior of the structure in last 18 years, that brought to the current situation.

2 Geological Aspects

The Gusela del Vescovà is a rocky spire located at 2.320 m a.s.l. in the western side of the Mount Schiara (2.565 m a.s.l.). This mountain belongs to the group of Dolomiti Bellunesi that, thanks to their peculiarity and naturalistic value, constitute since 1988 the "Parco Nazionale delle Dolomiti Bellunesi", an area of 32.000 ha with altitude extension from 400 m to more than 2.500 m a.s.l.

The Schiara group and all the Dolomiti Bellunesi represent the south-eastern district of Dolomite Alps shaping an orographic, environmental and morphological transitional system between the pre-alps region and the Dolomite area strictly speaking. From the tectonic point of view, the M. Schiara is set on a big anticline fold (Coppolo-Pelf) and its geology is characterized by considerable thickness of sedimentary carbonatic formations that variably crop out along its sides as highlighted also by the morphology.

The almost vertical southern face shows the transition from "Dolomita Principale" to "Dolomia della Schiara" until the Soverzene Formation that goes from the summit to the most of the less steep northern side of the mountain. The saddle where Gusela is placed is constituted by "Dolomia della Schiara" that is modeled, as typically of the dolomitic lithology, by vertical fractures, horizontal discontinuities, ridges, towers and indented profiles. Furthermore, erosion, freeze-thaw cycle and mechanical action connected with the climatic phenomena and the past nivo-glacial systems led the rock mass to conditions of local instability (Fig. 3).

At the foot of the walls of Mount Schiara, where debris accumulate, the debris movement, in conjunction with heavy rainfall, is the main slope phenomenon (debris flow) while in the upper parts the rock falls are the most frequent event.

The object of the study presents a main vertical fracture that passes through its volume and along the whole height, dividing the spike in two similar blocks, as highlighted in Fig. 3 (North and South portions). Other discontinuities affect the structure, some with high angle and some with a pseudo-horizontal development. These could constitute surfaces of weakness of the rock mass, leading to blocks detachments or sliding dynamics at the base.

Fig. 3. The approximated virtual plane of the main discontinuity that divide the structure in two parts (N and S), on the left; the position of the 6 control points along the main vertical crack, on the right.

3   3-D Survey

The geomatic survey has been performed using different techniques that include topographic measurements with total station and GNSS for reference network and control points, laser scanning and 3-D photogrammetry (Structure from Motion) for the 3-D survey.

The choice to add the acquisition of images by drone has been guided from the possibility of overcome the environmental issues while maintaining more than acceptable results, comparable with more structured survey methodologies like TLS, as reported in many works (Fabris et al. 2010; Fabris et al. 2012; Wilkinson et al. 2016, Monego et al. 2017; O'Bannion et al. 2018, Scaioni et al. 2018; Monego et al. 2019; Carraro et al. 2019).

Some preliminary remarks about the peculiarity of the environment are due. First of all, the morphology leads to a difficult access (with an approach of 1.100 m up with via ferrata parts) that constrains to carry only lightweight instruments; this aspect affects the methodological choices and in the survey phase leads to poor positioning possibilities for TLS and terrestrial images acquisition.

Furthermore, the high mountain environment is characterized by other critical aspects like long lasting snow deposits, variable weather conditions (with frequent rains, rapid changes and fog) that bring to a limited surveying time (with no choice of the best light conditions).

In September 2001, a system of control and monitoring of the planimetric deformations was set up with reference to the main crack located in the east face of the spire (Fig. 3): 6 control points of stainless steel screw were positioned by Alpine Guides along the two parts of the Gusela del Vescovà divided by the main vertical fracture.

The main objective is to highlight those changes in position of these points in solidarity with the spire that directly cause possible deformations. The movements that could be detected include both those that can be connected to any existing instability phenomena, and those attributable to temperature or other natural changes. The choice of the methodologies and of the instrument to be used is, first of all, influenced by the environment and its complex access. The more realistic aim was the identification of movement of 2–3 cm. The significance of lower values in the computation of the deformations cannot be considered reliable with these methods.

Control began in September 2001 with repetition of the measurements in September 2002 and in September 2019. The reference topographic network consists of 4 points outside the spire; they have been chosen trying to obtain a correct geometrical configuration, compatibly with the morphological characteristics of the site: the southern face is not approachable because of a vertical wall that descends to the valley for several hundred meters. Four stainless steel benchmarks were used, fixed with resin on stable rock near to the Gusela del Vescovà (points 5000, 6000, 7000, 8000 in Fig. 4).

The instrument used in the three measurement campaigns is a high-class total station Leica models: TCRM1105 in 2001, TC2003 in 2002 and TCR1201 in 2019.

The network has been computed with overabundant measurements. The calculation program also allows to estimate the root mean square (r.m.s.) of the point coordinates. The position of the control points, installed on the sides of the main crack by the Alpine Guides, have been chosen so as to guarantee the stability over time, clear visibility from the points of the network and the possibility of obtain accurate repetitions of the measures. They were positioned by couples (control points 1–2, 3–4, 5–6 in Fig. 3) at three different levels in the upper part of the spire.

The points have been collimated by stationing on two points of the network with angular and distance measurements. The coordinates of the points have been determined by adjusting the overabundant measures, always with the adjustment method for indirect observations.

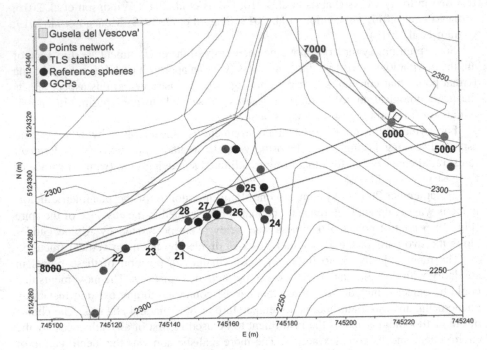

Fig. 4. Planimetry of the surveyed area around to the Gusela del Vescovà: are shown the position of the 4 points of the reference network, the 7 stations of the TLS acquisitions, the 6 reference spheres for the alignment of the TLS scans and the 8 GCPs (Ground Contro Points) for the drone's surveying. All points are located in the North area of the spire and along the East-West direction, without references in the South due to the high slope.

In 2019 the georeferencing was performed by means of GNSS RTK measurements (supported by the Hexagon Smart Net permanent station network) using Leica Viva GS14/CS15 geodetic receivers.

The ConVE software (a coordinates converter developed by the Veneto Region Cartographic Office) has been used for the conversion into the ETRS89/UTM zone 32N cartographic reference system and for the orthometric heights computation.

The coordinates of the control points for the photogrammetric survey were determined with the same methodology.

For the tree-dimensional documentation of the structure, a double approach has been carried out: laser scanning and photogrammetric survey by drone.

With the phase-shift laser scanner Faro Focus 3-D have been executed 7 scans around the Gusela del Vescovà, from the best accessible points (an example of scanning point is shown in Fig. 5).

Two problems (partly already known) about this survey have been revealed during the campaign: the distance between the object and the scanning points could affect considerably the quality of the point clouds acquired with this scanner (that is the only one transportable manually).

Six reference spheres and ten natural points have been used for the scans registration. In this case, acquisitions of the South face of the Gusela del Vescovà were not possible due to the high slope of the ground (Fig. 4).

Fig. 5. The phase of TLS survey with the phase-shift laser scanner Faro Focus 3-D: scanning the west side of the spire.

Together with laser scanning, a photogrammetric survey has been executed, with the lightweight drone Parrot Anafi, in order to create a 3-D model through SfM processing and overcome the limits of the TLS due to the acquisitions from the ground.

A set of 502 aerial images with mean altitude from the take-off point of 67,5 m have been acquired in 4 different flights of 15–20 min, depending on wind conditions that affect the duration of the 4 available batteries. The acquisition configuration is constituted by zenithal, 40° and 80° inclined and side proximal views.

The drone has a 1/2.4″ 21 MP CMOS Sony Sensor (diagonal dimension: 7,834 mm; pixel size: 1,12 × 1,12 μm) and it has been acquired imaged in JPEG "rectilinear" format (4608 × 3456 pixels, 4:3 format, 75.5° HFOV) with 4 mm focal length that correspond to 23 mm (35 mm format equivalent) (Fig. 6) and a mean GSD (Ground Sample Distance) value of 6 mm/pixel. The camera has been auto-calibrated by the software Agisoft Metashape. Our tests on this drone camera have shown that the manual calibration doesn't improve the quality of the results.

Fig. 6. Views of the different configurations used for drone imagery acquisition: zenital (top left), 45° inclined (top right), side proximal view (down left), 80° inclined (down right).

4 Results and Discussion

The network of 4 points was surveyed with classical measurements using the total station in a local reference system and by the GNSS receivers with RTK method: due to the restricted operative time (caused by the difficulties to reach the site and path that requires 5–6 h of round trip via ferrata) and the problematic environmental conditions, in the GNSS survey was measured 3 points of the network. The adjustment of the topographic network provides r.m.s. of the points ranging from 1 mm to 1.6 mm. The accuracy of the RTK positioning was assessed by applying a 7-parameter Helmert transformation to the two reference systems (GNSS and local) which provide an estimation of the precision through its residuals; finally, r.m.s of 12, 13 and 6 mm were obtained for the 5000, 6000 and 8000 points of the reference network.

The processing of the topographic measures and the 6 control points on the spire provides values of planimetric distances between the positions in the years 2001 and 2019, and distance values between the paired point 1–2, 3–4, 5–6: in this case, in fact, are more significant the planimetric deformations because they can lead to the imbalance of the spire and the risk of collapses; moreover, dolomitic spike is on rock soil and then in stable area altimetrically.

The differences in the positions of the control points mostly show values of less than 10 mm, that are to be considered within the precision of the methodology (2-D r. m.s ranging from 7 mm to 10 mm). Only for points 4 and 6 there are values, respectively of 14 and 23 mm, that could be mainly related to the thermal deformations (temperature change rapidly in few hours changing the weather conditions), or could represent a displacement that occurred in south direction so towards the vertical wall of the valley below.

Also the distances between the couple of points show a substantial stability with values between 1 and 7 mm, below the error of the method.

The factors that affect the precision of the measurements, in the specific case of the Gusela del Vescovà, could be related, in most part, to the environment and the morphology: reflector-less measures on points due to the impossibility of reach the summit; positioning of the tripod and measure of the instrumental height; rapid variations in temperature and humidity.

Concerning the 3-D survey, Terrestrial Laser Scanning has not provided the satisfactory results that can produce in more ordinary context (Fig. 7). The limitations in the positioning of the scanner have provided point clouds with insufficient coverage of the upper part of the object on north side (due to the excessive proximity to the base) and insufficient coverage of the South face (due to the impossibility of positioning with a sufficient incidence angle because of the vertical wall).

In this case, the use of the images from the drone has allowed to create a complete 3-D model that, as reported in many works (Wilkinson et al. 2016; Monego et al. 2017; O'Bannion et al. 2018; Scaioni et al. 2018; Monego et al. 2019; Carraro et al. 2019) provides acceptable results for this type of object.

Fig. 7. Global point cloud from TLS that shows some not-surveyed areas in the upper part of the north face (on the left) and a wide area of no data (marked in red) on the South face (on the right). (Color figure online)

The 3-D reconstruction has been performed using the software Agisoft Metashape.

The 502 images have been aligned creating a sparse cloud of the whole scene of 264.734 points (Fig. 8). Selecting a more restricted region of interest a dense cloud of 37 million of points has been produced (Fig. 9).

This constitute the base for the meshing that provide a texturized 3-D model with 3.7 million of vertices and 7.4 million of faces (Fig. 10).

Fig. 8. The sparse points cloud of the spire and the surrounding area from SfM methodology (264.734 points).

Fig. 9. The SfM model (dense points cloud): view of the south-west side (37 million of points).

Fig. 10. The SfM model (textured mesh): view of the south-east side (3.7 million of vertices and 7.4 million of faces).

The GNSS measurements allowed to georeference the network and provide the UTM coordinates of the GCP for the georeferencing and GCP-bundle block adjustment of the SfM model. 5 Points surveyed with Total Station were used as Control Points and other 2 for Check points.

The identification of the markers (35 × 25 cm black/yellow targets) has been done manually on the images. The limit of the GCPs is that it has been possible to position them only at the ground level around the Dolomitic spire.

The related errors are shown in the Table 1, for the 5 GCPs, and in Table 2, for the 2 points selected as Check points, and graphically represented in Fig. 11.

Table 1. RMS on control points.

Point	r.m.s - X (cm)	r.m.s - Y (cm)	r.m.s - Z (cm)	Aver. (cm)	Image (pix)
22	−1.86	−1.19	0.71	2.32	0.43
23	−1.74	1.99	0.06	2.65	0.62
24	−2.59	6.84	0.40	7.33	0.60
25	3.30	−5.55	1.90	6.73	0.41
27	2.94	−2.05	−2.85	4.58	0.87
Aver.	**2.56**	**4.18**	**1.58**	**5.15**	**0.61**

Table 2. RMS on check points.

Point	r.m.s - X (cm)	r.m.s - Y(cm)	r.m.s -Z(cm)	Aver. (cm)	Image (pix)
21	−0.89	2.50	−3.86	4.68	0.62
26	−1.30	−4.87	0.51	5.06	0.60
Aver.	**1.11**	**3.87**	**2.75**	**4.88**	**0.61**

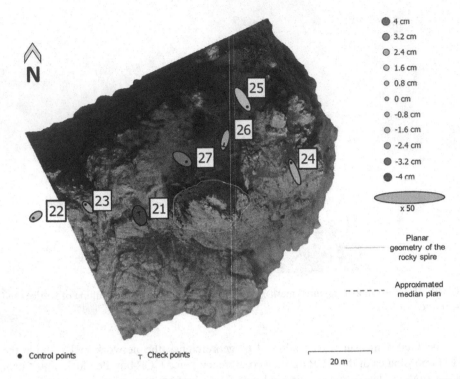

Fig. 11. GCPs locations and estimated error. Z-RMS is represented by ellipse colored. X, Y errors are represented by ellipse shape. Estimated GCPs locations are marked with a dot or crossing.

The entity of the error is conditioned by the positioning at the base of the tower because of the impossibility to locate the targets on the vertical walls at an high height.

The full coverage of the drone imagery is optimal along the rocky structure and at the base could be less redundant so, in order to evaluate the geometrical correctness of the SfM model, it has been compare with a point cloud obtained by TLS.

It has been chosen, as reference, a single scan (in order to avoid inserting the registration error): the one with best coverage is just in front of the North side.

For the comparison it has been used the plugin M3C2 of the free open source software Cloud Compare.

This tool allows to calculate single values of distance between two point clouds setting a reference cloud and a set of core points (at full resolution or at a resampled resolution respect to the original cloud). The core points are generally a sub-sampled version, but the computations are performed on the original raw full data. This option allows to speed up the processing and considers the fact that computation results are generally needed at a lower, more uniform spatial resolution (Lague et al., 2013).

The resulting point cloud could be generated with a resampling that maintain an adequate quality of the representation with a lighter output data.

The other parameters requested by the computation are the normal scale, the projection scale and the max depth (Fig. 12).

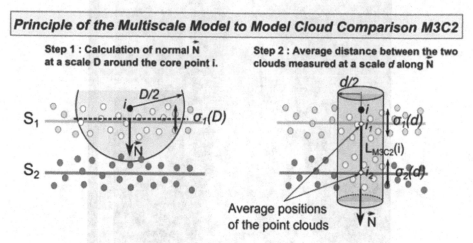

Principle of the Multiscale Model to Model Cloud Comparison M3C2

Step 1 : Calculation of normal $\vec{N}$
at a scale D around the core point i.

Step 2 : Average distance between the two
clouds measured at a scale d along $\vec{N}$

Fig. 12. Principle of the M3C2 algorithm; the two user defined parameters: D (normal scale) and d (projection scale) (Lague et al. 2013).

The normal scale is the diameter of the spherical neighborhood extracted around each core point to compute a local normal. A cylinder oriented following these normals is the volume used as a search region to detect equivalent points in the other cloud.

The diameter of this cylinder is the value of the projection scale while its height (in both directions) corresponds to the max depth value (Fig. 12). Low values in these parameters bring a bigger influence of the local surface roughness (Lague et al. 2013).

The M3C2 parameters used for our computation are: normal scale (D) = 0,05 m; projection scale (d) = 0,1 m; max depth = 0,2 m; core point subsampling = 0,01 m.

The results have shown good correspondence and reliability of the SfM model, that correctly reconstructs the detailed morphology, as highlighted in the green areas (with a mean distance value of 1 mm and standard deviation of 2,5 cm) and with only few and limited shaded parts depicted in red (Fig. 13).

With different tools it has been possible to easily operate measurement of distances that shows an height from the base of 36,92 m, maximum width at the base along major axis of 14,41 m maximum width at the base along minor axis of 8,42 m. Information about the dip values of the surfaces have been extracted from the normals (Fig. 14) and a preliminary geological structural evaluation has been done.

The use of the Compass tool of Cloud Compare has provided a set of orientation values of the main discontinuity plans. This plugin is a structural geology toolbox for the interpretation and analysis of virtual outcrop models. On picking a point on the model, a plane is fitted to all points sitting within the circle (using least squares method), giving an orientation estimate (dip/dip direction).

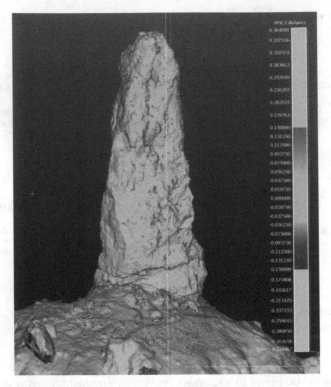

Fig. 13. Point cloud resulting from the comparison. Color scale represents the values of distance between the reference TLS scan and the SfM model. The green areas represent an average distance value of 1 mm (and standard deviation of 2,5 cm). (Color figure online)

These values, plotted on a Stereonet (Fig. 15), has highlighted three main sets of discontinuities (Fig. 16). L1 concerns the main sub-vertical joint (dip: 72°–89°), that cross almost the whole height of the tower. L2 represents a low angle set aligned to the orientation of the stratification, with dip angle of about 45° and prevailing northern dip direction. L3 corresponds to a planar horizontal joint that marks the base of the structure.

These features could be important to study the possible dynamics of slide or detachment of rocky blocks. In fact, these discontinuities represent the principal planes of structural weakness that could be interested in future displacements.

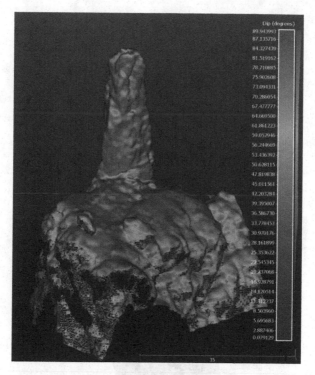

Fig. 14. 3-D view with color scalar field related to the dip values (0–90°) of the surfaces.

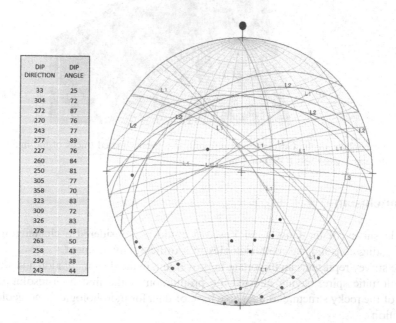

DIP DIRECTION	DIP ANGLE
33	25
304	72
272	87
270	76
243	77
277	89
227	76
260	84
250	81
305	77
358	70
323	83
309	72
326	83
278	43
263	50
258	43
230	38
243	44

Fig. 15. Stereoplot and table of the dip values. 3 main set of planar discontinuities are highlighted: L1 in orange, L2 in green, L3 in blue. (Color figure online)

Fig. 16. Orthophoto of the Gusela (east side) with the approximated traces of the main sets of plans of structural weakness (GSD of 5 mm).

5 Conclusion

The 3-D survey of the Gusela del Vescovà could be considered a challenging case study, testing consolidated methodologies in a difficult environment.

The survey represents an important improvement in the documentation and study of this Dolomitic spire, having allowed the production of the first high-resolution 3-D model of the rocky structure as a reliable base of data for morphological and geological descriptions.

It's due to mark that, despite the laser scanning, most of the time, provides complete models with high accuracy, in this specific case, the SfM has given a more complete model, with a good reliability checked in the comparison TLS-SfM.

This could represent a reference for future comparison in order to detect detachments of rocky blocks or big displacements.

Despite there are no visual evidences of imminent danger, it could be to consider the evaluation of further analysis, with the related issues.

Some possible options could be: an high precision monitoring system (in example, high precision topographic measurements, terrestrial SAR interferometry) with costs and invasiveness that probably don't worth the usefulness of the results; DInSAR analysis, with the cons that only could be detected deformations along the Line Of Sight (LOS); installation of monitoring instrumentations on the discontinuities (crackmeters, deformeters, inclinometers) with the high invasiveness and the setting of a remote control system as onerous aspect.

In conclusion, the detailed morphological knowledge that this geomatic surveys could provide for rocky structures and mountain environments are an essential source of metric information for evaluation of displacements that so frequently occurring in Dolomites. On the other hand, these studies represent an important knowledge in order to evaluate possible interventions and mitigate the risk related to these contexts.

References

Carraro, F., et al.: The 3D survey of the roman bridge of San Lorenzo in Padova (Italy): a comparison between SfM and TLS methodologies applied to the arch structure. Int. Arch. Photogramm. Remote Sens. Spat. Inf. Sci. **XLII-2/W15**, 255–262 (2019)

Fabris, M., Boatto, G., Achilli, V.: 3D laser scanning surveys in the modelling of cultural heritage.In: Meola, C. (ed.) Invited chapter in "Recent Advances in Non Destructive Inspection", pp. 1–32. NovaScience Publishers (2010). ISBN 978-1-61728-082-5 (ebook). ISBN 978-1-61668-550-8 (hardcover)

Fabris, M., Achilli, V., Artese, G., Bragagnolo, D., Menin, A.: High resolution survey of Phaistos Palace (Crete) by TLS and terrestrial photogrammetry. Int. Arch. Photogramm. Remote Sens. Spat. Inf. Sci. **XXXIX–B5**, 81–86 (2012)

Lague, D., Brodu, N., Leroux, J.: Accurate 3D comparison of complex topography with terrestrial laser scanner: application to the Rangitikei canyon (NZ). ISPRS J. Photogramm. Remote Sens. **82**, 10–26 (2013)

Monego, M., Fabris, M., Menin A., Achilli, V.: 3-D Survey applied to industrial archaeology by TLS methodology. Int. Arch. Photogramm. Remote Sens. Spat. Inf. Sci. **XLII-5/W1**, 449–455 (2017). https://doi.org/10.5194/isprs-archives-xlii-5-w1-449-2017

Monego, M., Menin, A., Fabris, M., Achilli, V.: 3D survey of Sarno Baths (Pompeii) by integrated geomatic methodologies. J. Cult. Herit. **40**, 240–246 (2019). https://doi.org/10.1016/j.culher.2019.04.013

O'Banion, M.S., Olsen, M.J., Rault, C., Wartman, J., Cunningham, K.: Suitability of structure from motion for rock-slope assessment. Photogramm. Rec. **33**, 217–242 (2018). https://doi.org/10.1111/phor.12241

Scaioni, M., et al.: Technical aspects related to the application of SfM photogrammetry in high mountain. Int. Arch. Photogramm. Remote Sens. Spat. Inf. Sci. **XLII-2**, 1029–1036 (2018). https://doi.org/10.5194/isprs-archives-xlii-2-1029-2018

Wilkinson, M.W., et al.: A comparison of terrestrial laser scanning and structure-from-motion photogrammetry as methods for digital outcrop acquisition. Geosphere **12**, GES01342.1 (2016). https://doi.org/10.1130/ges01342.1

A Python Customization of Metashape for Quasi Real-Time Photogrammetry in Precision Agriculture Application

Irene Aicardi[1,2] , Stefano Angeli[1(✉)] , Rosario Milazzo[2],
Andrea Maria Lingua[1,2] , and Maria Angela Musci[1,2]

[1] Department of Environment, Land and Infrastructure Engineering (DIATI),
Politecnico di Torino, Turin, Italy
{irene.aicardi,stefano.angeli,andrea.lingua,
mariaangela.musci}@polito.it
[2] PoliTO Interdepartmental Centre for Service Robotics (PIC4SeR), Turin, Italy
rosario.milazzo@studenti.polito.it

Abstract. In this paper, the authors describe a Python customized code based on Agisoft MetaShape processing engine that permits the automatic solution of a complete photogrammetric process from acquisition of the image block by Unmanned Aerial Vehicle (UAV) to final results: Dense Digital Surface Model (DDSM), Digital Terrain Model (DTM) and orthophoto.

Inspired by the old approach on analytical stereo-plotter, the proposed solution is based on a partition of the aerial block in a series of strips that can be transmitted by drones to the processing units during the flight to obtain a "quasi-real-time" solution in a just few minutes at the end of the flight.

The Python code can automatically add images from remote folders creating new Metashape Chunks at the end of each strip; align images of each strip in few seconds using the approximate external parameters of images acquired by drone navigation sensors; recognize coded (and not) markers (GCPs) and make a bundle block solution of each strip; align different chunks in a unique photogrammetric block; solve the final photogrammetric block using camera pose optimization of Metashape with an automatic selection of CPs from the recognized markers; compile and show a report that permits the resulting diagnostic by a skilled user.

The proposed solution has been applied to a precision agriculture environment for automatically surveying a vineyard and recognize the rows and the ground areas for automatic path planning purposes.

Keywords: Path planning · Photogrammetry · Python · Precision agriculture · Real-time · Vineyard

1 Introduction

The image-based survey methods and techniques in the field of Photogrammetry Computer Vision (PCV) are continuously developed to improve effectiveness and efficiency in terms of accuracy, processing time and automatism. Commercial solutions

© Springer Nature Switzerland AG 2020
C. Parente et al. (Eds.): R3GEO 2019, CCIS 1246, pp. 229–243, 2020.
https://doi.org/10.1007/978-3-030-62800-0_18

are consolidated allowing the achievement of correct, controlled and repeatable results using optimized algorithms in continuous development, also in an automatic way.

The automatism requires the definition of a controlled procedure which correctly uses the Structure from Motion (SfM) techniques defining various diagnostic steps at the end of each photogrammetric phase to guarantee the goodness of the results, for example, verifying the photogrammetry block geometry, checking the Ground Control Points (GCPs) geometric configurations, analyzing the accuracy of GCPs and Check Points (CPs) and so on. These steps may be neglected by unskilled users, which use the automatism of SfM technology, causing possible uncontrolled results that may contain significant gross errors and dangerous systematic effects (biases).

For this reason, in this paper it is proposed a strategy to have an automatic imaging process that can return a result in a very short time and that can be directly implemented on board on autonomous ground vehicle computers.

1.1 Precision Agriculture Techniques in Viticulture

The concept of Precision Agriculture (PA) has developed for several years as a management strategy for agricultural activity and several definitions have been proposed [12]. The underlying concept of this activity involves the use of increasingly recent information technologies to collect and process data from different sources (sensors) to improve the analysis and management of resources to manage them more efficient and less expensive. The concept of PA has thus created a technological revolution in agriculture and its production process. This activity allows farmers to help with planning processes and to automate some basic agricultural activities. For example, the planning of the route that the agricultural machine must follow is a fundamental point to have the possibility of making it autonomous in the piloting phase. In this sense, the problem to be addressed does not only concern the movement of the machine from the current position to the desired point, but the choice of the correct path to follow that adapts to the environments [8, 11]. Remote sensing (RS) techniques are widely used in the PA field and it is possible to obtain aerial images mainly in three ways: satellites, airplanes and UAVs. Due to the high cost of the first two methods, especially for small agricultural activities, the development of small sensors and the reduction of their cost, UAVs have increasingly developed and spread over the years [3]. It is demonstrated that UAVs can effectively acquire 3D information [1, 2, 4, 9] with limited costs in different contexts acquiring data useful for structured databases [6].

Route planning is considered a fundamental step for agricultural machines equipped with an autonomous navigation system. As for the vineyards, route planning represents a great challenge due to the land's often hilly morphology. As a first operation, images are acquired to generate an orthomosaic and a digital surface model, which is then used to identify the rows of vines and the inter-row terrain. Autonomous vehicles must, therefore, be equipped with an automatic navigation system and must be able to autonomously select the route based on the specificity of the area and the obstacles present. For agricultural vehicles, route planning for known environments usually involves splitting the area to be covered into small polygonal regions called parcel. Using high-resolution images, the plantation, the borders and the inter-row land become easily distinguishable, giving the possibility to characterize the entire area [10, 13].

2 Methodology

The developed algorithm follows the classic steps of the photogrammetric process, which are, however, managed through a Python code that allows to set the parameters (see Fig. 1).

First of all, the algorithm requires the installation of two modules that contain the functions necessary to work with GeoTIFF files. In order to proceed with the installation, it is necessary to know the Python version used by Metashape, which can be identified by opening python.exe.

The two modules are:

- GDAL (Geospatial Data Abstraction Library), a translator library for raster geospatial data formats;
- Rasterio, which provides clean and fast and geospatial raster I/O.

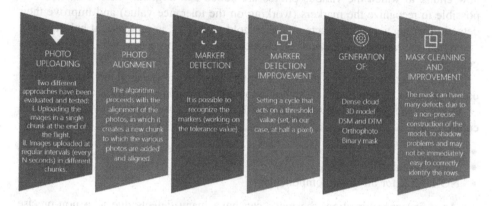

Fig. 1. Workflow schema

The main functions performed by the algorithm are:

1. Photo uploading
2. Photo alignment
3. Marker detection
4. Marker detection improvement
5. Generation of:

   - Dense cloud
   - 3D model
   - DDSM (Dense Digital Surface Model) and DTM (Digital Terrain Model)
   - Orthophoto
   - Binary mask

6. Mask cleaning and improvement

For the photo uploading step, two different approaches have been evaluated and tested:

1. Uploading the images in a single chunk at the end of the flight. However, this procedure excludes the processing during the acquisition phase, which means loss of useful time for the processing. The algorithm on a single chunk loads all the photos into a single chunk without any waiting;
2. Images uploaded at regular intervals (every N seconds) in different chunks and alignment of the images during these intervals. After M intervals in which no photo is acquired, the various chunks are merged (with the tie point merge). In this way there is no loss of useful time. The algorithm in multiple chunks is set up so that it creates chunks of at least 25 photos and, if for 30 s it doesn't get at least 25 photos, it loads the remaining photos in the last chunk created.

Then, the algorithm proceeds with the alignment of the photos, in which it creates a new chunk to which the various photos are added and aligned. After this step, it is possible to recognize the markers (working on the tolerance value) and improve their detection setting a cycle that acts on a threshold value (set, in our case, at half a pixel).

When the images alignment is correct, the code proceeds with the products generation.

The last step is the binary mask generation. This is the base map that the rover will use to generate an automatic and autonomous path planning, based on a binary code.

Initially, the algorithm classifies the mask (considered as a matrix) in three different codes:

- 0 for rows;
- 1 for ground;
- NO DATA for all other components.

As a first approximation, the mask can have many defects due to a non-precise construction of the model, to shadow problems and may not be immediately easy to correctly identify the rows.

For this reason, the mask must be refined following the subsequent steps:

1. The sections with too many 0 (and therefore large areas) are modified since they cannot be rows with NODATA. This step happens considering horizontal and vertical lines with values equal to 0 longer than 50 pixels;
2. The zones between two NODATA points with a distance less than 200 pixels, are placed at NODATA. In this way, it is possible to eliminate the defects of the previous point which are due to the treatment of the images only with horizontal and vertical lines (lines of 0 smaller than 50 pixels or oblique lines);
3. The missing rows are filled by setting the 0 for values which are located between two pixels of rows located:

   - for horizontal and vertical lines no more than 50 pixels apart;
   - for diagonal lines with an angle more than 45° respect to the axes and distant no more than 30 pixels;

- for diagonal lines with an angle more than 22.5° respect to the axes and distant no more than 40 pixels, in order to avoid imperfections due to the treatment for vertical or horizontal lines only.

4. Finally, a final cleaning is performed as in step 2, but with a maximum distance of 350 pixels.

3 Case Study

The activity was carried out at the "Azienda Agricola Ciabot" farm, located in Baldichieri d'Asti (AT), Piedmont, in the hilly area called Basso Monferrato Astigiano. The study area is a vineyard that extends for about two hectares, with an elongated shape, characterized by the presence of two huts between the rows and surrounded by a dense forest. The peculiarity of this vineyard is in the division into different sectors in which different types of grapes are grown (see Fig. 2).

Fig. 2. The case study.

3.1 Data Acquisition

As a first operation, the complete survey of the area was carried out. First of all, 16 plastic markers were placed on the ground to allow a subsequent georeferencing of the digital model. The coordinates of the center of each target have been acquired using a Network Real-Time Kinematic (NRTK) Global Navigation Satellite System (GNSS) technique [5]. The NRTK survey was performed with a Trimble SP80 GNSS receiver, using the real-time correction of the permanent GNSS station in Canelli (AT).

In this case, for the identification of the rows and the inter-row terrain, for route planning purposes, an accuracy of about 2 cm is necessary for the elevation model and orthophoto.

The UAV was chosen according to the size of the study area, flight time and expected output of the survey. Based on this, it was used a DJI Phantom 4 Pro with the following characteristics: focal length: 8.8 mm, CMOS sensor 13.2 × 8.8 mm and pixel size: 2.4 μm.

Because of the characteristics of the camera used, the flight was planned at the distance of 30 m from the ground, to obtain a Ground Sample Distance (GSD) of 8 mm on the object in agreement with the requirements necessary to satisfy the purpose of the survey. A flight (see Fig. 3) with a cross grid scheme was carried out for a total of 470 images acquired.

Fig. 3. UAV flight plan.

4   Algorithm Testing

The next step to data collection was the processing of these data with the commercial software Agisoft Metashape using the Python approach. All acquired images were processed in a single block and also in different chunks, to simulate the download after each acquisition strip, and for the construction of a 3D model (see Fig. 4) to extract orthophoto, DDSM and DTM.

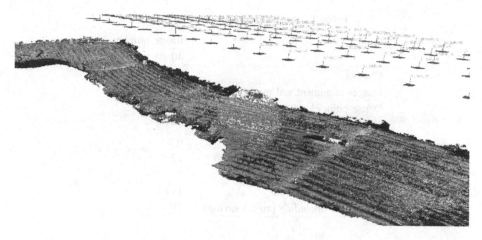

Fig. 4. Result of point cloud generation.

The processing has developed through the following steps [1]:

- alignment and orientation of the cameras (Accuracy: medium, key-point and tie-point without limit using 0 value);
- images georeferencing by GCPs (accuracy about 2 cm);
- point cloud densification with about 40–80 million points (medium quality with mild depth filtering).

From the dense point cloud, mesh (with medium face count and interpolation enabled) and DDSM (see Fig. 5) were generated, and, with a further step, the DTM has extracted into the software thanks to the "Classify ground point" tool that allows to perform an unsupervised classification of the dense point cloud to detect only the points on the ground surface [7]. This classification was performed based on three main parameters:

- Max angle: the maximum slope of the ground within the scene (20°);
- Max distance between the point above the ground and terrain model (0.05 m);
- Cell size of the largest area that does not contain any ground points (1 m^2).

Each of these parameters was chosen according to the features of the area. The outputs of the whole procedure are DDSM, DTM and orthophoto in raster format with a cell size of 0.02 m.

In this processing phase, the camera optimization is not mentioned because it has been tested that with these flight conditions the optimized parameters were similar to the initial ones and therefore it was not considered to save further time (Table 1).

Table 1. Processing time with 40 images.

Phase	Image number
	40
Chunks	1 (40 img.)
Images alignment and marker detection	49 s
Dense point cloud generation	154 s
3D model generation	193 s
DDSM generation	6 s
Ground classification	22 s
DTM generation	5 s
Orthophoto generation	117 s
Total time (including project saving)	10 m

0   25   50   75   100 m

Fig. 5. Orthophoto and DDSM.

5   Results

The tables below summarize the results of some tests that have been achieved considering different numbers of the images and different chunks. The processing parameters were the same for all the tests (see Sect. 4), to have a comparable set of results.

Table 2. Processing time with 60 images and different approaches.

Phase	Image number			
	60	60	60	60
Chunks	1	2 (25 + 35)	2 (30 + 30)	2 (35 + 25)
Images alignment and marker detection chunk I	76 s	25 s	33 s	43 s
Images alignment and marker detection chunk II	–	48 s	45 s	44 s
Chunks merging	–	134 s	142 s	135 s
Dense point cloud generation	201 s	144 s	182 s	182 s
3D model generation	301 s	297 s	296 s	295 s
DDSM generation	32 s	22 s	18 s	19 s
Ground classification	41 s	38 s	39 s	35 s
DTM generation	17 s	17 s	17 s	17 s
Orthophoto generation	188 s	190 s	192 s	188 s
Total time (including project saving)	17 m	18 m	18.5 m	18.5 m

Table 3. Processing time with 80 images and different approaches.

Phase	Image number		
	80	80	80
Chunks	1	2 (40 + 40)	3 (25 + 25 + 30)
Images alignment and marker detection chunk I	110 s	47 s	25 s
Images alignment and marker detection chunk II	–	69 s	28 s
Images alignment and marker detection chunk III	–	–	50 s
Chunks merging	–	239 s	304 s
Dense point cloud generation	272 s	280 s	151 s
3D model generation	379 s	452 s	270 s
DDSM generation	25 s	30 s	16 s
Ground classification	53 s	125 s	31 s
DTM generation	22 s	22 s	12 s
Orthophoto generation	249 s	336 s	170 s
Total time (including project saving)	21 m	30 m	20 m

As can been seen from Table 2 and Table 3, for the sets containing 60 and 80 images respectively, the use of the two approaches by loading images in a single end of flight chunk or loading the images in different chunks every N seconds during the flight allows to obtain processing times very similar to each other except for the case of 80 images divided into two chunks of 40 images each. As regards the second approach, with the division of images into different chunks, it is possible to note that the processing times for the different phases are slightly lower than those concerning the first approach, but unlike this one, it must also take into account the merging time of the different chunks. The advantage offered by the second approach is that it makes it possible to start processing during the flight phase, downloading every N seconds the images to be processed in different blocks separately and not having to wait for the end of the acquisitions. As usually happens in the photogrammetric process we can see how the generation phases of the dense cloud and the three-dimensional model in the form of a mesh are the most time-consuming operations.

The total processing time for each test indicates the sum of the times relating to each phase described and the saving time.

Finally, it is reported in Figs. 6, 7, 8 and 9, the process and the results achieved for the binary mask extraction.

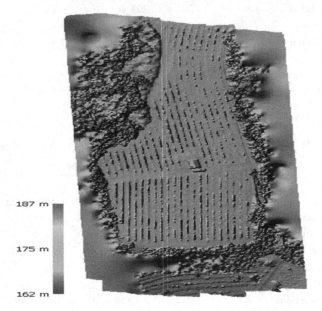

Fig. 6. DDSM extracted with a python algorithm.

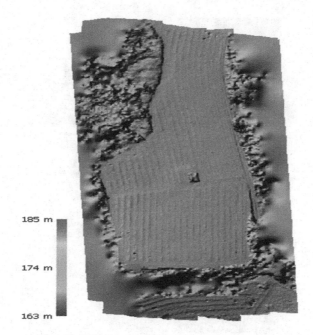

Fig. 7. DTM extracted with a python algorithm.

Fig. 8. First results of the binary mask cleaning: original (left), cleaned (right).

Fig. 9. Focus on the binary mask cleaning: original (left), cleaned (right).

6 Conclusions

In this paper, the processing of a photogrammetric acquisition was presented through the use of a Python algorithm directly usable in the Metashape processing software.

The code was implemented with the idea of speed up the processing time and obtain a (quasi) real time final map of a vineyard for automatic path planning investigations.

The possibility to start the photogrammetric processing on a ground station during the aerial acquisition has been evaluated thanks to the possibility to include multiple chunks in the Metashape photogrammetric software.

In order to evaluate the processing time, different numbers of images and chunks configurations have been evaluated. All the tests showed that with the Python approach it is possible to have a significant reduction in processing times, respect to common Metashape workflow.

The processing in one or more chunks is quite similar, but it the second case it can be started simultaneously with the acquisition of the images themselves. In this way, it is possible to have final data shortly after the flight has taken place.

So, the test demonstrated that it is possible to have a (quasi) real-time result and the aspects that have to be implemented are related to the possibility to directly process the data on the board computer included in the ground vehicle and the data transfer between the two unmanned systems (aerial and ground).

Acknowledgements. The study was carried out within the activities of the PoliTO Interdepartmental Centre for Service Robotics (PIC4SeR) and thanks to the concession of the "Azienda Agricola Ciabot" farm as regards the possibility of operating in the case study area.

Appendix: Python Source Code

a) New chunk creation, images alignment and marker detection

```
for photo in image_list:
    if (os.access((path_photos + "\\" + photo),os.X_OK)):
        photo_set.add(path_photos + "\\" + photo)
chunk=Metashape.app.document.addChunk()
chunk.addPhotos(photo_set)
for frame in chunk.frames:
    frame.matchPhotos(accuracy=Metashape.MediumAccuracy)
chunk.alignCameras()
chunk.detectMarkers(type=Metashape.TargetType.CrossTarget, tolerance=10)
chunk.refineMarkers()
marker_list=chunk.markers
for mark in marker_list:
    projections=mark.projections.keys()
    for camera in projections:
        projection = mark.projections[camera].coord
        reprojection=camera.project(mark.position)
        error=(projection-reprojection).norm()
        if (error<=0.5): |
            if mark.projections[camera].valid==True:
                mark.projections[camera].pinned=True
```

b) Dense cloud generation

```
chunk.buildDepthMaps(quality=Metashape.Quality.MediumQuality,
                filter=Metashape.FilterMode.MildFiltering, reuse_depth=True)
chunk.buildDenseCloud()
```

c) 3D model creation

```
chunk.buildModel(surface=Metashape.SurfaceType.HeightField,
            interpolation=Metashape.Interpolation.EnabledInterpolation,
            face_count=Metashape.FaceCount.MediumFaceCount)
chunk.buildUV(mapping=Metashape.MappingMode.OrthophotoMapping)
chunk.buildTexture(blending=Metashape.BlendingMode.MosaicBlending,size=4096)
```

d) DDSM and DTM generation (including cloud classification)

```
chunk.buildDem(source=Metashape.DataSource.DenseCloudData,
            interpolation=Metashape.Interpolation.EnabledInterpolation)
chunk1.dense_cloud.classifyGroundPoints(max_angle=20.0,max_distance=0.05,cell_size=1.0)
chunk1.buildDem(source=Metashape.DataSource.DenseCloudData,
            interpolation=Metashape.Interpolation.EnabledInterpolation,
            classes=[Metashape.PointClass.Ground])
```

e) **Orthophoto production**

```
chunk.buildOrthomosaic(surface=Metashape.DataSource.ModelData,
                       blending=Metashape.BlendingMode.MosaicBlending)
```

f) **Binary map production**

```
file_dtm=rasterio.open(f2)
dtm=a.read(1,masked=True)
file_dsm=rasterio.open(f1)
dsm=b.read(1,masked=True)
dsm_meta=b.profile
maschera=dsm-dtm
file_maschera=rasterio.open(f3,"w",**dsm_meta)
file_maschera.write(maschera,1)
```

References

1. Aicardi, I., Chiabrando, F., Lingua, A.M., Noardo, F.: 2018: recent trends in cultural heritage 3D survey: the photogrammetric computer vision approach. J. Cult. Herit. **32**, 257–266 (2018)
2. Angeli, S., Lingua, A.M., Maschio P., Piantelli L.: Dense 3D Model Generation of a Dam Surface Using UAV for Visual Inspection Conference on Robotics RAAD 2018. Mechanisms and Machine Science, vol. 67, 29 September 2018. Springer, Cham. https://doi.org/10.1007/978-3-030-00232-9_1
3. Barrientos, A., et al.: 2011: aerial remote sensing in agriculture: a practical approach to area coverage and path planning for fleets of mini aerial robots. J. Field Robot. **28**(5), 667–689 (2011). https://doi.org/10.1002/rob.20403
4. Chiabrando, F., Giulio Tonolo, F., Lingua, A.: UAV direct georeferencing approach in an emergency mapping context. The 2016 central Italy earthquake case study. Int. Arch. Photogramm. Remote Sens. Spat. Inf. Sci. **42**, 2, 247–253 (2019). ISSN 1682-1750. Elettronico
5. Cina, A., Dabove, P., Manzino, A.M., Piras, M.: Network real time kinematic (NRTK) positioning description, architectures and performances. In: Satellite Positioning-Methods, Models and Applications. InTech (2015)
6. Colucci, E., Noardo, F., Matrone, F., Spanò, A., Lingua, A.M.: High-level-of-detail semantic 3D GIS for risk and damage representation of architectural heritage. Int. Arch. Photogramm. Remote Sens. Spat. Inf. Sci. **42**, 4, 177–183 (2018). ISSN 1682-1750. Stampa
7. Grilli, E., Menna, F., Remondino, F.: 2015: a review of point clouds segmentation and classification algorithms. Int. Arch. Photogramm. Remote Sens. Spat. Inf. Sci. **42**, 339 (2017)
8. Kanayama, Y., Hartman, B.I.: Smooth local path planning for autonomous vehicles. In: Proceedings of the IEEE International Conference on Robotics and Automation, vol. 3, pp. 1265–1270. IEEE (1989)
9. Lingua, A.M., Noardo, F., Spanò, A.T., Sanna, S., Matrone, F.: 3D model generation using oblique images acquired by UAV. Int. Arch. Photogramm. Remote Sens. Spat. Inf. Sci. **42**, 4/W2, 107–115 (2017). ISSN 1682-1750

10. Moon, S., Shim, D.H.-C.: Study on path planning algorithms for unmanned agricultural helicopters in complex environment. Int. J. Aeronaut. Space Sci. **10**(2), 1–11 (2009)
11. Nelson, W.: Continuous-curvature paths for autonomous vehicles. In: Proceedings of the IEEE International Conference on Robotics and Automation, vol. 3, pp. 1260–1264. IEEE (1989)
12. Srinivasan, A.: Handbook of Precision Agriculture: Principles and Applications. CRC Press, Danvers (2006)
13. Zoto, J., Musci, M.A., Khaliq, A., Chiaberge, M., Aicardi, I.: Automatic path planning for unmanned ground vehicle using UAV imagery. In: Berns, K., Görges, D. (eds.) RAAD 2019. AISC, vol. 980, pp. 223–230. Springer, Cham (2020). https://doi.org/10.1007/978-3-030-19648-6_26

Innovative Technologies for Coastal Paleo-Landscape Reconstruction and Paleo-Sea Level Measuring

Gaia Mattei(✉) ⓘ, Pietro Patrizio Ciro Aucelli ⓘ,
Claudia Caporizzo ⓘ, Francesco Peluso, Gerardo Pappone ⓘ,
and Salvatore Troisi ⓘ

Department of Science and Technology, Parthenope University of Naples,
Centro Direzionale IS C4, 80143 Naples, Italy
gaia.mattei@uniparthenope.it

Abstract. This paper is aimed at presenting an innovation-technology based approach for reconstructing underwater paleo-landscapes and related paleo-sea levels in coastal archaeological sites of great cultural value. Due to the low operational depth of the investigated area (between −0.5 and −5 m) an Unmanned Vessel Surface was used. It is equipped with instrumentation composed of both acoustic (Single Beam Echo Sounder and Side Scan Sonar) and optical sensors (a suite of cameras). This integrated instrumentation (data-fusion) has allowed acquiring simultaneously a large amount of georeferenced data by means of a Multi-Modal Mapping approach, in order to increase the perception and identification of targets. These innovative techniques have been tested in three different submerged archaeological areas of the Roman time located along the coasts of Campania (Southern Italy), with different operational scenarios. In detail, the port structures (pilae) of the Nisida harbour, and two fishponds located in the Underwater Archaeological Park of Baia have been investigated with the twofold purpose of recreating the ancient landscape and assess the vertical ground movements that have affected the volcanic district of Campi Flegrei in the last 2000 years.

Keywords: Underwater archaeological landscape · Sea level changes · 3D reconstruction

1 Introduction

The underwater sectors of the coastal areas are by nature dynamic environments, strongly modified by wave's action, longshore currents, sedimentary processes, and human activity. Along the Mediterranean coasts, these environments often host underwater archaeological sites, representing important evidence of past coastal settlements, nowadays submerged due to an historical relative sea-level rise of glacio-isostatic origin but probably also related to tectonic and volcano-tectonic ground movements [1–5, 32, 33].

Documenting this underwater cultural heritage is a challenge of great scientific interest, in order to understand the responses of the natural and anthropic environment

© Springer Nature Switzerland AG 2020
C. Parente et al. (Eds.): R3GEO 2019, CCIS 1246, pp. 244–255, 2020.
https://doi.org/10.1007/978-3-030-62800-0_19

to the accelerated trend of sea-level rise due to the ongoing climatic changes. In the last years, the integration between geo-acoustic and optical indirect methods allowed the high-resolution mapping of wide coastal areas, seabed morphologies and underwater archaeological structures by combining remote and direct data.

These methodologies can be also useful to evaluate the local vertical ground movement (VGM) directly influencing sea-level oscillations at medium-short term. In addition, the recent miniaturization of these sensors enables the development of Unmanned Surface Vessels (USV) specifically designed to navigate in very shallow-water sectors.

The acquired data allow the processing of high resolution DTMs and the reconstruction of the submerged archaeological remains morpho-structure. As far as the photogrammetric systems, the 3D elaboration methods and software tools for processing 3D data are cutting-edge instruments for a detailed documentation and protection of underwater cultural heritage. In fact, the 3D or 2D model deriving from photogrammetric data is a relevant information to reconstruct the ancient anthropic and natural landscape [6–9].

These transdisciplinary methodologies are a modern approach to paleo-landscape and paleo-sea level reconstructions, acquiring a large amount of four-dimensional -3D points and time - data that, in the case of archaeological sites, have also a documental value of the cultural and natural heritage [10–12].

This kind of study has a twofold target:

- Protection of the underwater archaeological areas exposed to the wave action after its recent submersion
- Management of the underwater cultural heritage as a witness of the effects of the ongoing climate changes on the ancient settlements as well as on the coastal modifications.

In this paper, we propose a combined approach to the coastal landscape reconstructing, aimed to evaluate the Holocene sea-level variations through the integration of direct surveys, morpho-acoustic and optical measurements, and high-resolution DTM deriving from Lidar data. The submerged archaeological sites here studied are positioned along the coasts of the Naples Gulf densely inhabited since the Greek period, and widely studied due to the volcano-tectonic land mass movements that strongly influenced the Holocene evolution of the natural and anthropogenic landscape [13–24].

2 Methods

In the past, the geoarchaeological surveys were mainly carried out by specialized scuba divers, geologists and archaeologists.

However, in the last years, thanks to the innovative technology applied to the miniaturization of geophysical and optical instruments, the use of USV has had an important development.

This paper contains the results of a technological project of USV (MicroVeGA project) equipped with optical and acoustic sensors conceived to obtain a three-dimensional reconstruction of an underwater archaeological landscape [12, 24–26]. The sensors were installed on-board of a USV designed exclusively for geoarchaeological tasks, in order to realize three-dimensional landscape models.

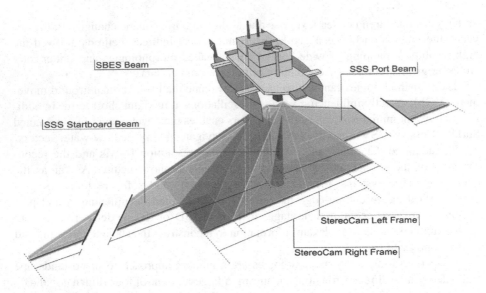

Fig. 1. 3D reconstruction of the beam opening of acoustical and photogrammetric sensors (figure not in scale).

The surveyed data were acquired by using a multi-modal mapping approach that provides the simultaneous use of different sensor types for mapping, localization, and data collection (Fig. 1)

2.1 USV

The Unmanned Surface Vessel (USV) used in this research is a prototype of marine drone designed and engineered by GEAC (Geologia degli Ambienti Costieri) research group of Parthenope University of Naples. This drone was conceived to solve the main operating problems faced during the coastal survey. In fact, it is optimized to navigate in very shallow water sectors, close to the coastline and in presence of submerged archaeological remains.

The challenge of MicroVeGA (Micro Vessel for Geo Application), project has been the integration between professional sensors, low-cost miniaturized sensors and innovative open hardware architecture, to obtain a robust technological solution for the high-definition reconstruction of the archaeological landscape.

The platform is a catamaran-type vessel (Fig. 1) with an overall length of 1.32 m, 0.86 m wide and 0.80 m high. The two hulls are joined by two aluminium crossbars that support a rectangular base of synthetic material (0.70 × 0.80 m) on which the payload is positioned. The operating weight is about 30 kg, although it may vary depending on the operational configuration and the mission profile.

The propulsion is entrusted to two brushless electric motors; the vehicle has a maximum speed greater than 2 Knots, while the speed during the data acquisition phase is less than 1 Knots. Operating autonomy with a battery pack is 2 h. A specific set of sensors and instruments are installed on-board of MicroVeGA USV.

The geo-acoustic sensors installed on-board are:

- A Single-Beam Echo Sounders (SBES) Ohmex with 200 kHz acquisition frequency and 60 meters as maximum measured depth, therefore optimized for coastal bathymetric measurements.
- A Sonar Tritech Side-Scan StarFish 450C, a small instrument (about of 4 kg), optimized for coastal waters with a frequency of 450 kHz CHIRP transmission. The lateral scanning range varies between 2 meters and 150 meters.

The photogrammetric system is composed of three cameras (Fig. 2):

- Two Xiaomi YI Action cameras placed transversally with the vertical axis and with a variable stereographic base chosen in relation to the bathymetry;
- A GoPro Hero 3 camera placed with its axis inclined of about 30 degrees with the seabed to acquire data from non-covered sectors

The low-cost stereovision system consists of two major components: the stereovision system itself and a synchronized triggering sound system for the cameras. The trigger event is generated by the on-board mission software and recorded in the datafile.

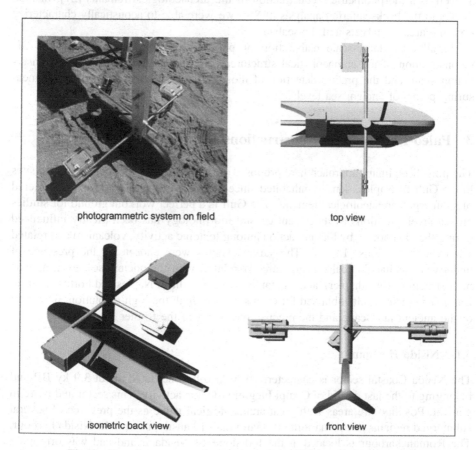

Fig. 2. The photogrammetric system and the SSS installed on-board.

2.2 Marine Surveys and Data Analysis

In this paper, we present the results of several marine surveys carried out in order to test the integrated methodology inspired to the multimodal mapping approach. In this approach, the simultaneous use of several sensors during the same survey is finalized to high-resolution reconstructions of underwater landscapes. In particular, the marine surveys carried out during this research provided two main results, directly related to as many specific planning phases:

1. Extensive morpho-acoustic mapping of the underwater sector by mean of small-scale navigations;
2. High-definition reconstruction of the submerged archaeological structures by means of large-scale navigation.

The small-scale data elaboration was typically applied to the geo-acoustic data. In particular, the bathymetric measurements interpolation provided the high-resolution sea-bottom digital terrain model (seaDTM); instead, the side scan sonar (SSS) data elaboration provided an acoustic and geomorphological characterization of the seabed, as well as a morphometric reconstruction of the archaeological remains [27]. In fact, thanks to the backscattering analysis of SSS we were able to acoustically characterize both the archaeo-targets and the seabed.

Finally, the large-scale elaboration of photogrammetric data provided the 3D reconstruction of the archaeological structures [28, 29], the evaluation of its conservation state, and the precise detection of those structural elements available as measuring points of ancient sea levels.

3 Paleo-Landscape Reconstructions Form Marine Surveys

The transdisciplinary approach here proposed was applied to some archaeological sites in the Gulf of Naples, densely inhabited since the Greek time and nowadays scattered of submerged archaeological remains. The Gulf is a perfect workout ground for studies on sea-level variations as its current coastal morphology has been greatly influenced during the Quaternary by the interaction among tectonic activity, volcanism and related sea-level fluctuations [13, 24]. The surveyed sites were chosen for the presence of underwater archaeological remains directly related with the ancient sea level, as harbour structures (Nisida pier), and fish tanks (Lucullo villa at Naples and Portus Julius at Baia). The main results obtained for each site were both the high-resolution 3D model of the ancient landscape and the precise measuring of the former sea level.

3.1 Nisida Harbour

The Nisida Coastal sector is characterized by a tuff cone dated about 3.9 ky BP and belonging to the last period of Campi Flegrei volcanic activity. This sector and more in general, Posillipo are areas with great archaeological value as the presence of several submerged remains as the maritime Roman villa of Pausilypon and the Nisida harbour. The Roman harbour is located at the footslope of Nisida Island and was originally characterized by two piers in opus pilarum nowadays almost totally destroyed, except for three pilae making up the ancient pier and nowadays submerged.

As shown in Fig. 3, by elaborating of the morpho-acoustic data, the three-dimensional underwater landscape was reconstructed and characterized by discriminating the natural landforms for the anthropic features. Also, the morphology of the all archaeological remains was mapped.

Instead, the large-scale elaboration of photogrammetric data provided the 3D reconstruction of the archaeological structures and the evaluation of its conservation state (Fig. 4). A large part of the upper face of the pila presents a rugged surface due to

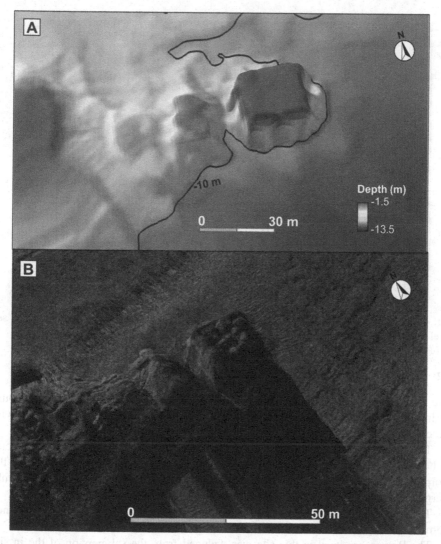

Fig. 3. Geoacoustic data elaboration of Nisida harbour: A) High resolution DTM of the underwater sector; B) SSS mosaic of the same sector in a 3D visualization.

the high erosion degree of the former surface. However, several sectors laying at a depth of −2.6 m and presenting a flat morphology were detected and used as sea level marker. In fact, these small flat elements represent the maximum deepening of the erosive processes and mark the interface between the structures built in subaerial environment and ones built hydraulic concrete not erodible as cast and set underwater [11, 12].

In this sector, a relative sea level during the 1st century BC at −3 m MSL was deduced, and consequently a subsiding trend about of 2 m in the last 2000 years was measured.

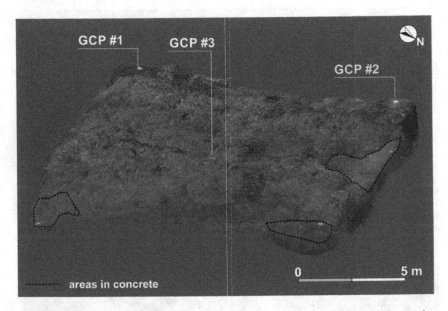

Fig. 4. Photogrammetric data elaboration of the upper part of the submerged *pila*, used as sea level marker at Nisida harbour.

3.2 Baia Fish Tank

The Aragonese Castle of Baia incorporates the remains of a big luxury villa built during the 1st half of the 1st century BC but renovated during the Augustan Age with the construction of its pars maritima [30].

This structure (Fig. 4) is located alongside the tufa seacliff of Miseno coastal sector and belongs to the piscinae in litore constructae [31], as demonstrated also by the morpho-acoustic survey (Fig. 5) that provided a detailed reconstruction of the submerged archaeological structures and the underwater landscape.

The high-resolution model of same collapsed structures - as pillars - was obtained from the photogrammetric data elaboration (Fig. 6).

The Roman sea level in this site was deduced from the submersion of the in situ structures, as the wall reconstructed in Fig. 6 and the well preserved sliding grooves, made of an upper stone with a slot intended for inserting or extracting the gate. These structural elements are the best archaeological sea-level markers, as the top was always located above the highest tide level in order to ensure weather protection.

Furthermore, also, in this case, a relative sea-level at −4.1 m MSL during the 1st century BC was precisely measured in the central sector of the Campi Flegrei active volcano.

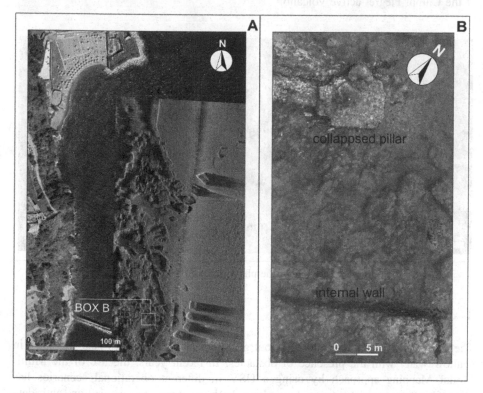

Fig. 5. A) SSS mosaic of Baia fish tank (Datum: WGS84); B) 3D view of the photogrammetric point cloud

3.3   Portus Julius Fish Tank

The ancient Portus Julius is one of the best-known underwater archaeological sites in Italy and it represents a milestone in the marine archaeology [30]. Thanks to the historical sources, the area is well dated and documented so it can be used as a key site in the relative sea level studies.

The port area has developed during two different phases, which caused a continuous variation of the facilities in the period between the 1st century BC and the 1st century AD. The fish tank of Portus Julius is particularly interesting because it represents one of the few examples of fishpond related to commercial activities and not to maritime villas. The existence of a tank within the entry channel can be related to the presence of a fish market or areas intended for the production of the *garum*.

The fish tank was precisely reconstructed by elaborating the photogrammetric data (Fig. 6). In particular, the measurements concerned the most accurate sea-level markers, i.e. the *Cataractae*, closing gates rarely still in situ and located at the access of the canal into the basin or at communication passage between each pool.

Finally, the submersion measurement of the upper part of the closing gate allowed deducing a relative sea level at −3.1 m during the 1st century AD in the central sector of the Campi Flegrei active volcano.

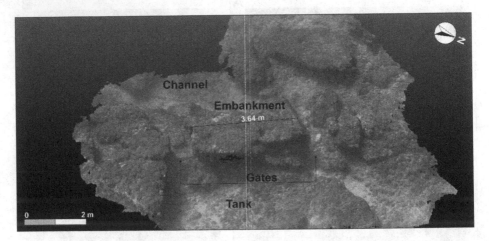

Fig. 6. 3D view of the photogrammetric point cloud

4   Conclusion

The aim of the research was to carry out geoarchaeological surveys near the coast in shallow water with the presence of obstacles. In recent years, the use of the Multi-Modal Mapping approach by using a USV in different operational scenarios has allowed us to acquire strong know-how both in terms of acquisition and data processing.

The main challenge was to synchronize the measurements made by SBES, SSS and stereo-photogrammetric system in the time domain and to carry out the surveys with appropriately spaced navigation lines (grids) in order to obtain an effective coverage of the investigated areas taking into account the different ranges of the sensors installed on-board of the USV. In this sense, the transmission of data in real-time was very useful because it allowed an initial evaluation of raw data directly in the field, thus verifying in real-time both the coverage of the surveyed area and the quality of the data as well.

From this experience, it emerged that the use of synchronized survey techniques in parallel, using different sensors (optical and acoustic) allows a more effective survey and a more effective evaluation of the identified targets. The optical data from the geo-referenced videos are integrated with the acoustic data, making it possible to uniquely identify the location, shape and nature of the archaeological finds identified.

Definitely, the results here presented allowed to evaluating for each site the former sea level and related vertical ground movements affecting the studied coastal sectors in the lasts millennia, as well as to discovering the past human adaptions to natural modifications of the landscape mainly due to the Late Holocene sea-level rise.

This research can be placed in the context of geoarchaeological studies applied to the underwater cultural heritage. This kind of studies plays a fundamental role in understanding the relationship between coastal changes and the history of human settlements. Most of these ancient coastal settlements along the Mediterranean coasts are today submerged mainly due to relative sea level variations occurred over the last millennia.

Then the challenge of the coastal geoarchaeological researches is to study these submerged archaeological structures in order to understand the impacts of the ongoing climates changes on modern populations as well as the effects of Earth processes at the social level.

In conclusion, by the multi-disciplinary approach here proposed, the geoarchaeological study of several underwater archaeological sites in the Gulf of Naples achieved several goals:

- 3-dimensional characterization of the underwater landscape in coastal sectors with archaeological value;
- evaluation of the conservation state of the surveyed archaeological structure as well as the evaluation of erosion processes effects due to wave action by means of a morphometric analysis of the photogrammetric data;
- detailed four-dimensional documentation of a submerged cultural heritage along the Neapolitan coast.

Acknowledgements. In memory of Professor Raffaele Santamaria. Thanks are due to the Neptune's community for the scientific debates that contributed to improve the quality of the paper.

References

1. Vacchi, M., et al.: New relative sea-level insights into the isostatic history of the Western Mediterranean. Quat. Sci. Rev. **201**, 396–408 (2018)
2. Vacchi, M., Marriner, N., Morhange, C., Spada, G., Fontana, A., Rovere, A.: Multiproxy assessment of Holocene relative sea-level changes in the western Mediterranean: sea-level variability and improvements in the definition of the isostatic signal. Earth-Sci. Rev. **155**, 172–197 (2016)
3. Benjamin, J., et al.: Late Quaternary sea-level changes and early human societies in the central and eastern Mediterranean Basin: an interdisciplinary review. Quat. Int. **449**, 29–57 (2017)
4. Alberico, I., Amato, V., Aucelli, P.P.C., Di Paola, G., Pappone, G., Rosskopf, C.M.: Historical and recent changes of the Sele River coastal plain (Southern Italy): natural variations and human pressures. Rendiconti Lincei **23**(1), 3–12 (2012)

5. Pappone, G., et al.: Relative sea-level rise and marine erosion and inundation in the Sele river coastal plain (Southern Italy): scenarios for the next century. Rendiconti Lincei **23**(1), 121–129 (2012)

6. Lo Brutto, M., Dardanelli, G.: Vision metrology and structure from motion for archaeological heritage 3D reconstruction: a case study of various Roman mosaics. Acta IMEKO **6** (3), 35–44 (2017)

7. Nocerino, E., Menna, F., Remondino, F.: Accuracy of typical photogrammetric networks in cultural heritage 3D modeling projects. Int. Arch. Photogramm. Remote. Sens. Spat. Inf. Sci. **40**(5), 465 (2014)

8. Neyer, F., Nocerino, E., Gruen, A.: Image quality improvements in low-cost underwater photogrammetry ISPRS Ann. Photogramm. Remote. Sens. Spat. Inf. Sci. **42**(2/W10), 135–142 (2019)

9. Nocerino, E., Menna, F.: Photogrammetry: linking the world across the water surface. J. Mar. Sci. Eng. **8**(2), 128 (2020)

10. Remondino, F., Rizzi, A.: Reality-based 3D documentation of natural and cultural heritage sites—techniques, problems, and examples. Appl. Geomat. **2**(3), 85–100 (2010)

11. Mattei, G., Troisi, S., Aucelli, P.P., Pappone, G., Peluso, F., Stefanile, M.: Multiscale reconstruction of natural and archaeological underwater landscape by optical and acoustic sensors. In: 2018 IEEE International Workshop on Metrology for the Sea; Learning to Measure Sea Health Parameters (MetroSea), pp. 46–49. IEEE (2018)

12. Mattei, G., Troisi, S., Aucelli, P., Pappone, G., Peluso, F., Stefanile, M.: Sensing the submerged landscape of Nisida Roman Harbour in the Gulf of Naples from integrated measurements on a USV. Water **10**(11), 1686 (2018)

13. Amato, V., et al.: A geodatabase of Late Pleistocene-Holocene palaeo sea-level markers in the Gulf of Naples. Alpine Mediterr. Quat. **31**, 5–9 (2018)

14. Aucelli, P.P., et al.: Ancient coastal changes due to ground movements and human interventions in the Roman Portus Julius (Pozzuoli Gulf, Italy): results from photogrammetric and direct surveys. Water **12**(3), 658 (2020)

15. Aucelli, P., Cinque, A., Mattei, G., Pappone, G.: Historical sea level changes and effects on the coasts of Sorrento Peninsula (Gulf of Naples): new constrains from recent geoarchaeological investigations. Palaeogeogr. Palaeoclim. Palaeoecol. **463**, 112–125 (2016)

16. Aucelli, P., Cinque, A., Giordano, F., Mattei, G.: A geoarchaeological survey of the marine extension of the Roman archaeological site Villa del Pezzolo, Vico Equense, on the Sorrento Peninsula, Italy. Geoarchaeology **31**(3), 244–252 (2016)

17. Aucelli, P.P.C., Cinque, A., Mattei, G., Pappone, G.: Late Holocene landscape evolution of the gulf of Naples (Italy) inferred from geoarchaeological data. J. Maps **13**(2), 300–310 (2017)

18. Aucelli, P., Cinque, A., Mattei, G., Pappone, G., Stefanile, M.: Coastal land-scape evolution of Naples (Southern Italy) since the Roman period from archaeological and geomorphological data at Palazzo degli Spiriti site. Quat. Int. 23–38 (2018)

19. Aucelli, P.P., Cinque, A., Mattei, G., Pappone, G., Stefanile, M.: First results on the coastal changes related to local sea level variations along the Puteoli sector (Campi Flegrei, Italy) during the historical times. Alpine Mediterr. Quat. **31**, 13–16 (2018)

20. Aucelli, P., Cinque, A., Mattei, G., Pappone, G., Rizzo, A.: Studying relative sea level change and correlative adaptation of coastal structures on submerged Roman time ruins nearby Naples (southern Italy). Quat. Int. **501**, 328–348 (2019)

21. Aucelli, P.P., Caporizzo, C., Cinque, A., Mattei, G., Pappone, G., Stefanile, M.: New insight on the 1st century BC paleo-sea level and related vertical ground movements along the Baia - Miseno coastal sector (Campi Flegrei, Southern Italy). In: IMEKO TC4 International Conference on Metrology for Archaeology and Cultural Heritage, MetroArchaeo 2019, pp. 474–477 (2019)

22. Mattei, G., Rizzo, A., Anfuso, G., Aucelli, P.P.C., Gracia, F.J.: Enhancing the protection of archaeological sites as an integrated coastal management strategy: the case of the Posillipo Hill (Naples, Italy). Rendiconti Lincei. Scienze Fisiche e Naturali 31(1), 139–152 (2020). https://doi.org/10.1007/s12210-019-00867-9

23. Mattei, G., Rizzo, A., Anfuso, G., Aucelli, P.P.C., Gracia, F.J.: A tool for evaluating the archaeological heritage vulnerability to coastal processes: the case study of Naples Gulf (Southern Italy). Ocean Coast. Manag. 179, 104876 (2019)

24. Pappone, G., Aucelli, P.P., Mattei, G., Peluso, F., Stefanile, M., Carola, A.: A detailed reconstruction of the Roman landscape and the submerged archaeological structure at "Castel dell'Ovo islet" (Naples, Southern Italy). Geosciences 9(4), 170 (2019)

25. Giordano, F., Mattei, G., Parente, C., Peluso, F., Santamaria, R.: MicroVeGA (micro vessel for geodetics application): a marine drone for the acquisition of bathymetric data for GIS applications. Int. Arch. Photogramm. Remote. Sens. Spat. Inf. Sci. 40(5), 123 (2015)

26. Giordano, F., Mattei, G., Parente, C., Peluso, F., Santamaria, R.: Integrating sensors into a marine drone for bathymetric 3D surveys in shallow waters. Sensors 16(1), 41 (2016)

27. Mattei, G., Giordano, F.: Integrated geophysical research of Bourbonic ship-wrecks sunk in the Gulf of Naples in 1799. J. Archaeol. Sci. Rep. 1, 64–72 (2015)

28. Troisi, S., Del Pizzo, S., Gaglione, S., Miccio, A., Testa, R.L.: 3D models comparison of complex shell in underwater and dry environments. Int. Arch. Photogramm. Remote Sens. Spat. Inf. Sci. 40(5W5), 215–222 (2015)

29. Troisi, S., Baiocchi, V., Del Pizzo, S., Giannone, F.: A prompt methodology to georeference complex hypogea environments. Int. Arch. Photogramm. Remote Sens. Spat. Inf. Sci. 42 (2W3), 639–644 (2017)

30. Miniero, P.: La villa romana nel Castello di Baia: un riesame del contesto, in Mélanges de l'Ecole française de Rome. Antiquité, Roma, pp. 439–450 (2010)

31. Higginbotham, J.A.: Piscinae: Artificial Fishponds in Roman Italy. UNC Press Books (1997)

32. Mattei, G., Aucelli, P.P., Caporizzo, C., Rizzo, A., Pappone, G.: New geomorphological and historical elements on morpho-evolutive trends and relative sea-level changes of naples coast in the last 6000 years. Water 12(9), 2651 (2020)

33. Ascione, A., et al.: Geomorphology of Naples and the Campi Flegrei: human and natural landscapes in a restless land. J. Maps, 1–11 (2020)

Handheld 3D Mobile Scanner (SLAM): Data Simulation and Acquisition for BIM Modelling

Mattia Previtali$^{(\boxtimes)}$ ⓘ, Fabrizio Banfi ⓘ, and Raffaella Brumana ⓘ

Department of Architecture, Built Environment and Construction Engineering,
DABC LAB GIcarus, Politecnico di Milano, Via Ponzio 31, 20133 Milan, Italy
{mattia.previtali, fabrizio.banfi,
raffaella.brumana}@polimi.it

Abstract. Nowadays, the availability of fast data acquisition systems based on mobile and handheld laser scanning platform are increasing in popularity due to their rapidity in data acquisition of large areas. BIM and HBIM based modelling can primary benefit of this new acquisition methods speeding up the so called "Scan-to-BIM" procedure. However, point clouds derived from Mobile Mapping Systems (MMS) compared to traditional static laser scanning acquisition presents some disadvantages: (i) point clouds are more noisy, (ii) generally less dense and (iii) some drift effects can be presents inside the data due to data registration. For those reason, in order to obtain a point cloud to be effectively used for modelling purposes a careful planning of the acquisition has to be taken into account. This paper, presents a methodology for optimal MMS path design according to some predefined target in terms of point density and point cloud completeness. In order to optimize the scanning path a simulation is carried out to define the best scanning configuration. In this paper the developed methodology is tested on a real case study: the outdoor of the main pavilion of the Politecnico di Milano – Polo Territoriale di Lecco.

Keywords: SLAM · MMS · BIM · Data simulation · Data quality

1 Introduction

In the last decade advances in Geomatics Science allowed the development of a wide set of sensors and techniques to be used to collect 3D data of large sites [1]. Specifically, RGB digital cameras and Terrestrial Laser Scanner (TLS) are widely used in a wide range of applications: Cultural Heritage documentation [2], slope stability analysis [3], reverse engineering [4] among the others. In addition, Airborne Light Detection and Ranging systems (LiDAR) can be effectively used for surveying and modelling of extensive sites. Nowadays, the availability of fast data acquisition systems based on mobile laser scanning platform are increasing in popularity due to their rapidity in data acquisition of large areas. Mobile Mapping Systems (MMS) can be either boarded on vans or carter-based, mainly used for civil engineering applications, or backpack and handheld. The main advantage of the latter is the possibility to use such systems both for surveying indoor and outdoor offering a suitable solution in

© Springer Nature Switzerland AG 2020
C. Parente et al. (Eds.): R3GEO 2019, CCIS 1246, pp. 256–266, 2020.
https://doi.org/10.1007/978-3-030-62800-0_20

terms of accuracy, and flexibility. In particular, MMS based on SLAM (Simultaneous Localization and Mapping) technology are becoming more and more popular for their flexibility and portability especially compared with traditional static laser scanning systems. MMS can mainly impact on BIM and HBIM based modelling. Indeed, the so called "Scan-to-BIM" process can benefit from the time reduction of the data collection phase. The possibility to scan an area simply walking through it can open new perspectives in the field of massive cost effective documentation of both cultural heritage sites and large real estate assets management. Even if SLAM-based MMS are increasing in popularity some aspects needs to be highlighted. Indeed, compared with Terrestrial Laser Scanning (TLS), point clouds acquired with SLAM based systems are more noisy, generally less dense and some drift effects can be present in path estimation. For these reasons, in order to obtain a point cloud to be effectively used for HBIM modelling purposes a careful planning of the acquisition has to be taken into account.

Indeed, in the HBIM modelling phase the choice of a Level of Geometry (LOG) implies a range of accuracy and tolerance that has to be met. A transparent choice of accuracy allows to define the model adopted by the different LOGs and to support the adoption of the proper Grade of Generation among different options (GOG1-10) in function of the point clouds geometry and of the scales chosen by the different actors [5].

In this perspective, the acquired point cloud has to guarantee the possibility to respect such constraints and the acquisition has to be planned consequently. In the most cases, planning the instrument standpoints, when using static TLS, is a task that is empirically based on the user experience. However, due to the previously listed reasons in the case of MMS a more robust method has to be designed. A deep preliminary analysis may contribute to save time in the field optimizing the scanning path and to guarantee a better coverage of the surfaces to be recorded. This paper presents a methodology for scanning path optimization based on target values of point cloud density and completeness. The method is based on a simulation of the scan acquisition starting from an approximate geometry of the area to be surveyed. Starting form this initial model selection of the best MMS path can be chosen form a set of alternatives. An operator, even with low survey skills, can perform the survey guaranteeing the predefined requirements by simply follow the outcome path. In this paper the developed methodology is tested on a real case study: the outdoor of the main pavilion of the Politecnico di Milano – Polo Territoriale di Lecco. For this site the comparison between simulated data and real data, acquired with the ZEB HORIZON system, shows a good matching, proving that the proposed method can be an effective tool for MMS path planning and allowing a good estimate of the scanning density and coverage.

A comparison with a TLS data set of the same building is also presented allowing for a discussion about pros and cons of the two data sets.

2 Related Works

Optimal scan planning is a topic that has been widely studied. Scan planning can be carried out in order to fulfil different requirements that has to be taken into consideration according to the specific aim of the survey. Scanning accuracy is not only affected by the scanner's typology (e.g., time of flight, phase shift or triangulation based) and specifications, but also a large set of parameters play fundamental role. Among others, key aspects to be considered are the scanning configuration and conditions. For example, scanning geometry, i.e. the relative location and orientation of the TLS with respect to the scanned surface, significantly influence the local incidence angle and consequently not only the local point density of the laser points but also measurement accuracy [6]. Another factor playing an important role is data completeness and the cost in terms of time, especially for large sites.

For those reason a good planning of the scan location is of primary importance for a successful survey. In the case of TLS the main aim of scan planning is to define the scan positioning in a way that can satisfy the requested level of detail and data coverage. In literature, this problem has mainly addressed in the case of indoor scan planning and robot navigation [7]. The problem of scan optimization was also addressed in more general cases of indoor or outdoor environments. Low [8] presents a specific metric for plan optimization in the case of indoor environment. Blaer and Allen [9] present a two-step procedure. In the first step a 2D map is used to plan a set of initial acquisition. Those acquisitions are then used to refine the scan location. Nagatani et al. [10] focus on outdoor scan planning of large buildings by using a mobile robot. Ahn and Wohn [11] are addressing the issue of scan planning optimization for cultural heritage recording, mainly buildings. The proposed method is an interactive one and integrates some heuristics. The developed tools support the user defining the next best position in a feasible region.

In the case of SLAM-based sensors problems concerning path planning, i.e., driving to a predefined goal state, and active exploration, i.e., exploration an unknown environment by actively minimizing uncertainty in the map, are widely addressed [12]. They are mainly focusing on robot systems while a lower amount of works focuses on the problem of path optimization in the case of handheld laser scanning. This task is however of fundamental importance to assist low-skilled operators in the acquisition activity in order to derive model with a level of detail (point cloud density) and completeness in the case of architectural survey.

3 Methodology

The methodology implemented in this work is based on previous results obtained for TLS and presented in [13]. Figure 1 represents the general workflow of the methodology.

The input of the presented methodology is an approximate model of the area that has to be covered by the survey. In the case of outdoor survey either OpenStreetMap or Google Maps 3D data can be used to derive the 3D model of the area. In particular, in

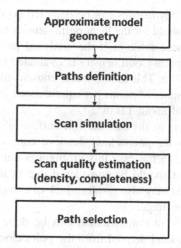

Fig. 1. Workflow presented for optimal path planning.

the case of OpenStreetMap the Open Source converter OSM2World can be used. In the case of indoor an approximate plan of the area can be used.

Starting from the plan a first set of possible paths can be derived by using for example Generalized Voronoi Diagram [14] or similar approaches. To select from the different alternatives the optimal path a simulation step is here performed.

Indeed, starting from the approximate 3D model a simulation of the scan can be performed. In order to operate this task, the software (Heidelberg LiDAR Operations Simulator -HELIOS - https://www.geog.uni-heidelberg.de/gis/helios.html) developed at the University of Heidelberg (GIScience Research Group), Germany, has been used here [15].

The main input for the simulation in HELIOS are: (i) laser scanner typology and scanner parameters, (ii) definition of the area to be scanned, and (iii) definition of the scanning positions/paths. Firstly, the software requires the definition of the scanning platform (TLS, Aerial Laser Scanning - ALS or MMS) and the definition of the characteristics of the scanner (e.g., range accuracy, beam divergence, pulse frequency, etc.). In a scanning project several scanners can also be used and/or scanning parameters can be changed between different scans.

Once the simulations are carried out they are analysed in order to identify the ones that satisfy the scan quality measure both in terms of data density and point cloud completeness.

The evaluation of point density is important to guarantee that the recorded point cloud has a sufficient resolution to reconstruct all the details of the investigated site. According to this concept, the point density should be locally evaluated on the surface within a prefixed diameter around each point, as proposed in [16]. In this paper we are mainly focusing on evaluation of point cloud density of building elements, which are in the majority of cases planar like facades, for a "Scan-to-BIM" procedure. For this reason, we are considering as neighbouring points only points belonging to the same plane (i.e., having the same normal direction). And for this reason neighbouring is measured only in a circle. This metrics can be depicted on the approximate model of the object. A minimum threshold for the local point density can be established to check whether this parameter is acceptable or if the analysed path has to be discarded. In particular, in this work the point cloud density is evaluated taking into consideration a circle of radius equal to 0.57 m. This dimension is chosen since the point cloud density is generally evaluated as number of points per square meter on a flat surface: a circle of radius 0.57 m has an area of about 1.0 m^2.

Point completeness refers to the fact the full surface of the investigated object is surveyed and represented in the point cloud. Lack of completeness is typically due to occlusions during scanning. In the case this problem is due to the incomplete acquisition. On the other hand, it should be considered that in the reality the presence of moving objects or vegetation may also result in lack of completeness, which cannot be foreseen during the planning stage.

The evaluation of the point completeness can be done by comparing the rough model of the site with the model derived from the point cloud. A voxel representation can be efficiently used for the comparison. The entire area to be surveyed can be discretized into voxels and evaluate can be considered as scanned (i.e., the voxel contains a minimum amounts of user-defined points) or not-scanned. The choice of the voxel size and the threshold for used occupancy can be defined according to the LOG defined for the "Scan-to-BIM" process. The higher the LOG and smaller is the dimension of the voxel size and higher the occupancy threshold.

4 Experimental Section

This section presents some tests addressing the present method for optimal path definition comparing simulated data and real data acquired with MMS ZEB-HORIZON (GeoSLAM). A further comparison is carried out between MMS data and TLS point cloud.

4.1 MMS Data Simulation and Acquisition

The presented workflow was tested a couple of case study: the outdoor of the main pavilion of the Politecnico di Milano – Polo Territoriale di Lecco (Fig. 2). The pavilion is 'H shaped' with the long side of approximately 62 m and the shorter side of approximately 42 m. The instrument selected for the test was the MMS ZEB-HORIZON (GeoSLAM). This specific system was selected since it has a maximum range of 100 m, and for it can survey elements positioned further apart (e.g., benches, info point desk, etc.). Some technical data of ZEB-HORIZON are reported in Table 1.

The ZEB_HORIZON system is composed by two elements: scanner head and datalogger/battery. The elements are connected through one data cable. Once started the instrument has to be positioned on a stable horizontal flat position for 1 min, like a bench or a table. After an initial calibration, generally within 1 min, the scanner head starts rotating and it is ready to survey. At this stage the scanner head can be picked up and starting the acquisition. Data are collected at a walking speed. The acquisition path

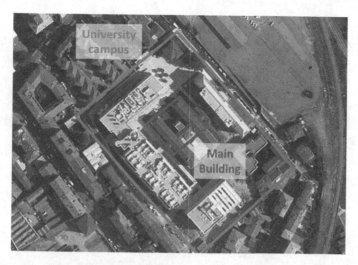

Fig. 2. The Politecnico di Milano – Polo Territoriale di Lecco campus (blue) and the building used as case study for simulation and scanning with ZEB HORIZON (red). (Color figure online)

Table 1. ZEB-HORIZON technical data.

ZEB-HORIZON	
Maximum range	100 m
Data logger carrier	Backpack or shoulder strap
ZEB HORIZON payload	3.7 kg
Scanner points per second	300,000
Relative accuracy	1–3 cm
Raw data file size	100–200 MB a minute

should be planned in a way such that the starting point of the scan coincide with the last one, forming this way closed loops.

SLAM registration is achieved by either uploading to the GeoSLAM Cloud (via an internet connection) or processed locally using the software package GeoSLAM Desktop. Once registered the resulting LAS file can be post processed directly in most commercial or open source packages.

In the specific case study only one half of the building was surveyed and in order to form a closed loop an internal corridor was used. As simplified input model a Google Maps 3D was used while for input paths a set of them was chased combining both models derived by Generalized Voronoi Diagram (red path in Fig. 3) and manually selected paths (green path in Fig. 3). An examples of paths is presented in Fig. 3, for the sake of clarity only few of them are presented.

The simulated point clouds are checked for point cloud density and completeness.

Point cloud density represents the percentage of points having a number of neighbours lower than 100,000 in a circle with radius 0.57 m.

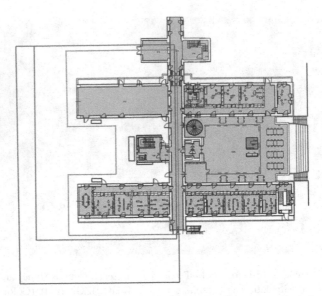

Fig. 3. Examples of paths (red, green and blue) used for the scan simulation. (Color figure online)

The point completeness is computed subdividing the input scene into voxels of size 0.10 m and computing if they are occupied or not by simulated scan points.

Point cloud density target was set at 75%. It means that 75% of points in the point cloud has at least 100,000 neighbouring point in a circle with radius of 0.57 m. Point cloud completeness was set at 80%, meaning that at least the 80% of the building façade had to be surveyed by the point cloud. Two paths among the tested ones. According to those criteria only two paths fulfilled both criteria: red and green in Fig. 3. For the real data acquisition with ZEB-HORIZON the red path was chosen since it is shorter and presents less obstacles than the green one. For those reasons it is easier for a human operator.

Table 2 presents a comparison between the simulated and the real data. The comparison is carried out by using the software CloudCompare v2.10.2 (www.cloudcompare.org). As it can be observed the simulation data shows a good matching with the real acquisition data proving the viability of the presented method to predict in a sufficiently accurate way the point density and completeness of a MMS acquisition following a predefined path. Figure 4 presents some graphic representation of the simulation (Fig. 4a–b) and of the acquired data (Fig. 4c).

Table 2. Point cloud quality evaluation for the simulated data and the real data

	Simulated data	Real data
Point density	79.92%	77.71%
Point completeness	80.03%	81.92%

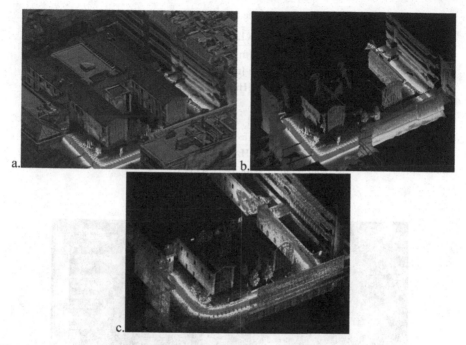

Fig. 4. MMS data simulation and acquisition: (a) the simulated point cloud overlaid to the rough model of the façade; the simulated data (b) and the real data obtained by ZEB HORIZON (c), point clouds are colorized according to data density. (Color figure online)

4.2 MMS and TLS Data Comparison

A second test was carried out comparing data acquired with ZEB HORIZON and data acquired with Faro Focus X130 (Table 3). In particular, 5 scans of the area were carried out. The registration error of the scans can be evaluated, taking into consideration residual of Ground Control Points (GCP) measured with a total station, in the order of ± 3.0 mm. The comparison between MMS and TLS data was carried out taking into consideration two parameters:

- Point cloud distance: TLS point cloud was used as a reference and cloud to cloud distance was evaluated for each point
- Density: point cloud density was computed as the number of neighboring points in a circle of 0.10 m.

Results of the comparison are reported in Fig. 5. In particular it can be observed that the point cloud density obtained with MMS is approximately one order of magnitude lower with respect to the one obtained with TLS.

In order to increase it the scan with MMS should be carried out at smaller walking velocity and/or the distance between the scanner head and the building façade has to be reduced. As a second aspect the point cloud distance comparison showed an average

Table 3. Parameters of the laser scanner used in the test

FARO FOCUS X130	
Range accuracy [m]	0.002
Beam divergence [rad]	0.00019
Pulse frequency [Hz]	100,000
Pulse length [μs]	4
Wavelength [μm]	1550
Vertical scan angle [°]	360
Scan frequency [Hz]	120
Scan rotation velocity [°/sec]	10

Fig. 5. Point cloud density - a detail of (a) TLS data, (b) MMS data.

distance between the two point cloud of approximately 5.0 cm in accordance with the technical data of the two instruments (Table 4). The comparison is carried out by using the software CloudCompare v2.10.2 (www.cloudcompare.org).

Table 4. Statistics on results obtained for point cloud distance comparison

Statistics on discrepancies	
Mean [cm]	5.1
Standard deviation [cm]	12.2
Median [cm]	4.2
Mean Absolute Deviation [cm]	9.7

5 Conclusions

In this paper, an automatic methodology to optimize the scan path of MMS for architectural surveying is presented. The methodology aims at optimizing the scan path according to some specific criterions, data density and completeness. Although the problem of scan planning has been mostly considered for TLS and mainly for indoors, the planning of an acquisition with MMS combining both indoor and outdoor is of major interest for its connection with "Scan-to-BIM" procedure. Indeed, today the reduction of the acquisition time is of major interest in the "Scan-to-BIM" activities.

The time needed for an extensive and accurate surveys of building blocks (indoor and outdoor) with TLS can require a significant amount of time (hours or days). The versatility and flexibility of MMS allow to survey the same area in a few hours. The presented methodology was tested on a real case study: the main pavilion of the Politecnico di Milano – Polo Territoriale di Lecco.

In particular, simulated data were compared with a real acquisition carried out using the same path as for the simulation. From the result we can conclude that the presented methodology is suitable for predicting in a sufficiently accurate way the point density and completeness of a MMS acquisition. This allows to study in advance the best path to accomplish, according to specific criteria defined for the survey requirements. In this way a low skilled operator can perform the survey following the derived path.

Acknowledgements. Research leading to this results is partially funded by Regione Lombardia - Bando "Smart Living: integrazione fra produzione servizi e tecnologia nella filiera costruzioni-legno-arredo-casa" approvato con d.d.u.o. n.11672 dell'15 novembre 2016 nell'ambito del progetto "HOMeBIM liveAPP: Sviluppo di una Live APP multi-utente della realtà virtuale abitativa 4D per il miglioramento di comfort-efficienza-costi, da una piattaforma cloud che controlla nel tempo il flusso BIM-sensori – ID 379270".

References

1. Ramos, M.M., Remondino, F.: Data fusion in cultural heritage-a review. Int. Arch. Photogramm. Remote Sens. Spat. Inf. Sci. **40**(5), 359 (2015)
2. Bentkowska-Kafel, A., MacDonald, L.: Digital Techniques for Documenting and Preserving Cultural Heritage. ISD LLC (2018)

3. Salvini, R., Riccucci, S., Gullì, D., Giovannini, R., Vanneschi, C., Francioni, M.: Geological application of UAV photogrammetry and terrestrial laser scanning in marble quarrying (Apuan Alps, Italy). In: Lollino, G., Manconi, A., Guzzetti, F., Luino, F., Culshaw, M., Bobrowsky, P. (eds.) Engineering Geology for Society and Territory - Volume 5, pp. 979–983. Springer, Cham (2015). https://doi.org/10.1007/978-3-319-09048-1_188

4. Galantucci, L.M., Piperi, E., Lavecchia, F., Zhavo, A.: Semi-automatic low cost 3D laser scanning systems for reverse engineering. Procedia CIRP **28**, 94–99 (2015)

5. Brumana, R., et al.: Generative HBIM modelling to embody complexity (LOD, LOG, LOA, LOI): surveying, preservation, site intervention—the Basilica di Collemaggio (L'Aquila). Appl. Geomat. **10**(4), 545–567 (2018)

6. Boehler, W., Vicent, M.B., Marbs, A.: Investigating laser scanner accuracy. Int. Arch. Photogramm. Remote Sens. Spat. Inf. Sci. **34**(Part 5), 696–701 (2003)

7. Fujimoto, K., Beniyama, F., Moriya, T., Nakayama, Y.: Reconstruction of 3D indoor model by scalable sensing using mobile robot. In: Three-Dimensional Image Capture and Applications 2008, vol. 6805, p. 68050I. International Society for Optics and Photonics (2008)

8. Low, K.L.: View Planning for Range Acquisition of Indoor Environments, p. 0985. University of North Carolina at Chapel Hill (2006)

9. Blaer, P.S., Allen, P.K.: View planning for automated site modeling. In: Proceedings 2006 IEEE International Conference on Robotics and Automation, ICRA 2006, pp. 2621–2626. IEEE (2006)

10. Nagatani, K., Matsuzawa, T., Yoshida, K.: Scan-point planning and 3-D map building for a 3-D laser range scanner in an outdoor environment. In: Howard, A., Iagnemma, K., Kelly, A. (eds.) Field and Service Robotics. STAR, vol. 62, pp. 207–217. Springer, Heidelberg (2010). https://doi.org/10.1007/978-3-642-13408-1_19

11. Ahn, J., Wohn, K.: Interactive scan planning for heritage recording. Multimed. Tools Appl. **75**(7), 3655–3675 (2015). https://doi.org/10.1007/s11042-015-2473-0

12. Meng, Z., Sun, H., Qin, H., Chen, Z., Zhou, C., Ang, M.H.: Intelligent robotic system for autonomous exploration and active SLAM in unknown environments. In: 2017 IEEE/SICE International Symposium on System Integration (SII), pp. 651–656. IEEE (2017)

13. Díaz-Vilariño, L., Frías, E., Previtali, M., Scaioni, M., Balado, J.: Scan planning optimization for outdoor archaeological sites. In: 2nd International Conference of Geomatics and Restoration, GEORES 2019, vol. 42, no. 2, pp. 489–494. Copernicus GmbH (2019)

14. Garrido, S., Moreno, L., Blanco, D., Jurewicz, P.: Path planning for mobile robot navigation using voronoi diagram and fast marching. Int. J. Robot. Autom. **2**(1), 42–64 (2011)

15. Bechtold, S., Höfle, B.: Helios: a multi-purpose lidar simulation framework for research, planning and training of laser scanning operations with airborne, ground-based mobile and stationary platforms. ISPRS Ann. Photogramm. Remote Sens. Spat. Inf. Sci. **3**(3) (2016)

16. Fugazza, D., et al.: Combination of UAV and terrestrial photogrammetry to assess rapid glacier evolution and map glacier hazards. Nat. Haz. Earth Syst. Sci. **18**, 1055–1071 (2018)

Processing of 3D Models for Networking of CH in Geomatics

Andrea Scianna[1]([⊠]) [iD] and Marcello La Guardia[2] [iD]

[1] ICAR-CNR (High Performance Computing and Networking Institute - National Research Council of Italy) at GISLab c/o D'Arch, Polytechnic School of University of Palermo, Viale delle Scienze, Edificio 8, 90128 Palermo, Italy
andrea.scianna@icar.cnr.it
[2] ICAR-CNR (High Performance Computing and Networking Institute - National Research Council of Italy), at GISLab,
Via Ugo La Malfa 153, Edificio 8, 90146 Palermo, Italy
marcellolaguardia87@libero.it

Abstract. In recent times the possibility of reconstruction of complex 3D Cultural Heritage (CH) environments has opened new scenarios for touristic and scientific aims. The different needs for networking or conservation purposes of CH lead to study proper structuring of 3D models. In light of this, a scientific approach has been developed in order to test the networking capabilities, comparing different loading configurations of 3D environments with multiple combinations of 3D models inside them, considering different solutions. This experimentation has been based on WebGL-HTML5 technologies and allowed to discover the true balance between performances of proposed system, the quality of visualization, and the quality of information (geometric and semantic ones) characterizing the 3D visualization of the virtual environment. The present work analyzes all of these parameters in order to find the best combination for the implementation of these models into a virtual 3D Geographic Information System (GIS) environment, based on WebGL technologies and accessible via web. This study could be considered a basic step for the development of interactive geospatial information platforms for the virtual fruition of CH.

Keywords: WebGL · Cultural heritage · 3D model · Networking · CH conservation

1 Introduction

Today, the world of CH needs increasingly new technologies in order to achieve new solutions in the conservation field, but also for sharing cultural information on web, as well finalized to valorization of CH. The development of laser scanning and photogrammetric technologies have given the opportunity of acquiring big data information in a short time during archaeological surveys, generating heavy point clouds for every small area detected, offering the possibility of achieving new ways of representation and visualization of cultural sites (Vacca et al. 2012; Scianna et al. 2019). Considering the laser scanning technology, for example, it has been used also for the creation of close-range datasets for the documentation of objects within museum

© Springer Nature Switzerland AG 2020
C. Parente et al. (Eds.): R3GEO 2019, CCIS 1246, pp. 267–281, 2020.
https://doi.org/10.1007/978-3-030-62800-0_21

collections (Gillespie et al. 2014). At the same time photogrammetric solutions allow by now the 3D reconstruction of large monumental complexes (Masiero et al. 2019; Scianna and La Guardia 2018, 2019).

If on the one hand these technologies guaranteed the acquisition of an exhaustive level of information, sometimes also useful for risk analysis and conservation purposes (Alicandro et al. 2019; Pepe et al. 2019), on the other hand, the huge dimension of these big data strongly limited their management. In fact, an exhaustive representation of 3D models has to take in account hundreds of thousands of polygons, and for this reason requires the use of specific manipulation tools, like repairing and simplification procedures (Nooruddin and Turk 2003). Hence in these years the research of better methods for the simplification of big data information has taken on primary importance.

Before starting the simplification process, once eliminated the main clusters from a point cloud, is important to focus on the needed level of detail (LoD) of the final model (see Fig. 1). For example, if the final 3D model will be used for CH conservation purposes, aimed, for example, to further restoration operations, the model shall contain a big number of polygons. This kind of model could be useful for the conservation but not for sharing online information, because the huge number of polygons strongly compromise the web navigation. In fact, if the model would be used for networking, focused to simple and interactive navigation, the LoD should be lower or, anyway, variable between suitable ranges, saving only the necessary information, in order to give the perception of the CH at different scales of exploration.

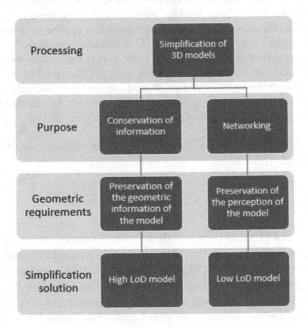

Fig. 1. The different approaches to simplifying the 3D CH models.

At the same time an excessively simplified geometric 3D model, with a small number of polygons, couldn't satisfy needs of online users due to low visualization quality. For this reason, the use of a good quality texture, and generally of surface signals (texture maps, bump maps, environment maps, surface reflections) represents a fundamental tool for reproducing realistic, but at the same time lighter, CH models (Qu and Meyer 2008). The use of a lighter model not only increases the processing speed, simplifying the access to shared online information, but also eliminates possible browser crashes.

Considering this field, not only the simplification procedures, but also the choice of the best file format to use for the implementation of the model in a 3D GIS environment play a relevant role. For instance, in some recent applications, 3D models have been delivered using the X3D file format, because it offers data compression and reduces the downloading times (Koutsoudis et al. 2015). Instead, in this case of study, the 3D model has been generated using .obj format, developed by Wavefront Technologies, because it offers to users a simple way of describing and manipulating 3D objects, allowing manual setting of many options such as texture tessellation, associated with a . mtl file (Willèn 2011). In this work different examples of simplification will be compared, matching different models of CH acquired considering different solutions.

2 Networking of CH: The WebGL Choice

In recent times new experimentations have been carried out regarding the sharing on web of CH models, providing interesting results (Guarnieri et al. 2010), in order to solve loading time issues and web-browser crashes. From these studies emerges that every loaded model should be processed and simplified properly, in terms of numbers of polygons and reduction of the texture resolution. Within this scenario, the skill of users on managing different types of devices (as pc, tablet, smartphone, etc.) plays a fundamental role on the diffusion of mobile web applications based on 3D data, and takes into account important aspects as 3D graphics as well as user interaction and visualization (Koutsoudis et al. 2015).

Until few years ago, in order to display high resolution 3D models, users needed specialized 3D software and suitable graphics cards, strongly limiting the sharing of CH 3D models. Instead, in recent times, the new development of JavaScript libraries totally integrated into all the web standards of browsers, as WebGL (Web-based Graphics Library), and the increasing development in other computer graphics techniques provided the opportunity to share an entire dataset directly within a webpage. These achievements allow to explore 3D models in interactive way (Gillespie et al. 2014). The development of WebGL standards makes available the accelerated graphics pipeline through web-browsers, before unusable. These new technologies almost eliminated the dependency on specific hardware capabilities, in order to achieve efficient rendering rates (Congote et al. 2011).

Many studies and specific frameworks have been developed for visualizing 3D models with elevated streaming performance using WebGL technologies (Potenziani et al. 2015). For these reasons the choice of this solution has become, recently, very useful for sharing online 3D CH interactive models, giving the possibility of visualizing

not only the CH itself, but also the entire landscape around it (Scianna et al. 2016).
Recent developments on WebGL libraries offer, also, the possibility of inserting 3D
models into virtual georeferred earth representations (Globes) (Scianna and La Guardia
2018). The globe solution allows the construction of a multi-dimensional GIS (Pirotti
et al. 2017), providing geographic features to the 3D virtual environment. These new
technologies, anyway, suffer some limits regarding the weight of the model to be loaded.
Indeed, if the model is strongly detailed, with a several number of polygons, browser
can't load correctly the webpage, going to crash. In order to exceed these limits, it's
necessary to differentiate the simplification procedures to follow, according to the final
use of the model (conservation or networking purposes).

3   Simplification Processing for Conservation Purposes of CH

In order to describe the state of art on simplification of 3D models finalized to conservation, it has been taken into account different CH model examples. In particular, it
has been considered a point cloud of a Greek column, generated by a laser scanner
survey, and a photogrammetric reconstruction of a Corinthian capital, in order to take
into account examples coming from different technologies (see Fig. 2).

Starting the simplification phase, the bigger challenge has been the maintenance of
the necessary LoD, and, at the same time, the achievement of a smaller and more
manageable model. The two considered solutions followed different data processes,
considering the different ways of point clouds acquisition. In particular, considering the
point cloud of the Greek column, generated from a laser scanner survey, it has been
simplified using CloudCompare and Blender, both open source software tools. Instead
the point cloud of the Corinthian capital, generated from a photogrammetric reconstruction, has been simplified using Agisoft Photoscan.

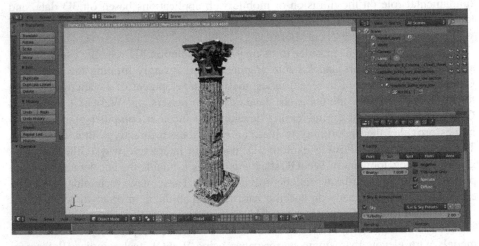

Fig. 2. The models of the column and the capital generated after the simplification processing.

Anyway, to achieve the goal of conservation of a cultural good, the final simplified model needs to contain all the fundamental information, necessary to ensure the preservation of geometries and, also, allowing a hypothetical reconstruction of the archaeological finding.

For this reason, in order to guarantee the conservation purposes of CH, it's necessary to arrange only the needful simplification processes useful to obtain a more manageable model (see Table 1). Indeed, in this experimentation, triangle meshes have been transformed to quads, in order to maintain substantially the original geometry, but, at the same time, to generate a lighter model. Finally, the quality of the result obtained after simplification is substantially similar for both the column and the capital. This research highlights that for the conservation of CH models it's not necessary a laser scanner acquisition of geometry, in fact, a close-range photogrammetry restitution could be exhaustive for this purpose.

The same workflow could be followed for the 3D printing of the model, in order to obtain a real 3D scaled replication, useful for reconstruction of CH or musealization of copies, offering a multi-sensorial form of access to CH (Neumuller et al. 2014).

Instead, as written later, the simplification procedure necessary for the networking results more complex, because the web-browsing of 3D models requires lighter objects to load.

Table 1. The comparison between the two examples of CH model simplification for conservation.

	Greek column (laser scanner survey)	Corinthian capital (photogrammetric reconstruction)
weight of the model (KB)	158.137	25.463
number of faces	1.938.842	191.049
weight of the simplified model (KB)	2.875	2.327
number of faces of the simplified model	51.394	18.215

4 Simplification Processing for Networking of CH Models

In this work, the web publication of 3D models has been developed using .html templates linked with WebGL libraries. The simplification solutions necessary for the web publication of 3D models, and the relative LoDs should be diversified according to the different cultural good to represent. In detail, the procedures are strongly different considering a virtual interactive representation of a single 3D CH model (as in the case of a statue or an archaeological finding present in a museum), or a virtual immersive representation of a 3D model inserted into the surrounding environment (e.g. the case of a virtual navigation into an archaeological site or ancient city). These two possibilities are directly connected with performances of the navigation system.

The interactive web navigation of a 3D CH scene necessarily needs a size limit, according to the capabilities of the web-browser. For this reason, the maximum weight accepted for every loaded model strongly depends on the total number of elements (elementary models) inside the scene and their size. The choice to follow arises between two possibilities: a scene of large number of less detailed and lighter models, or a scene with few heavy models (or only one) with a higher LoD.

In particular, if the focus of the 3D representation, to be included in webpage, consists only in a single cultural good, like a statue, or an archaeological finding, it's necessary to obtain a more detailed model, in order to share it on the web. Instead, if the aim of the networking is to recreate the entire 3D environment of an archaeological site, offering the user a realistic virtual tour, it is necessary to load more models; in this last case, due to size limits of the scene, the LoD of every element must be necessary reduced.

Considering the loading times on web-browsing, in order to represent a single cultural good, the weight limit of the model can't exceed 20–25 MB, over that dimension, the web-browser could crash or not respond; instead, for the representation of an entire environment of an archaeological area, every single model should weight not over 1–2 MB. Studying these two different approaches regarding networking of CH, it is fundamental to establish different procedures of modeling, according with the size and the LoD required.

Another important aspect to take care during simplifying operation for the networking is the maintenance of texture information (see Fig. 3). In fact, if the mesh is exported and simplified (reducing the number of polygons using specific algorithms) into an editing software, like Blender, the 3D model loses texture mapping. For this reason, if the texture mapping needs specific coordinates – e.g. in presence of fronts of historical buildings, detailed ortophotos of terrains or statues -, it's better to simplify meshes with the same acquisition software (considering laser scanner or photogrammetric acquisition). In this case, the simplified model could be anyway modified by an editing software like Blender, duplicating, translating and deleting elements, but maintaining the original texture mapping. Instead, if it's not required a specific texture mapping, for example on walls, vegetations, or any mesh that represents a generic element, the best solution is to simplify the model working on the editing software, like Blender, in order to obtain a better result. Following this last solution, the texture could be recreated with the editing software, painting the surfaces with images of reference or inserting image patterns. In this last case, the use of patters is faster than manual painting operation, but the visual result on the web navigation is strongly different. In fact, during web visualizations of 3D models, images lose any dimension calibration managed by editing software. Instead the manual painting operation creates a real coordinate reference, that remains in the networking visualization.

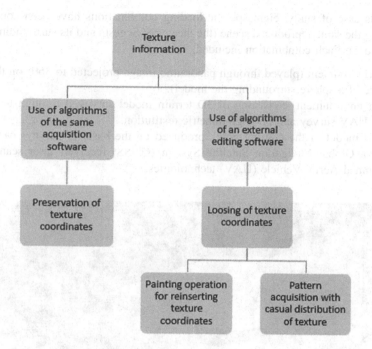

Fig. 3. Different texture simplification approaches.

5   Test and Comparisons of Networking Performances Between Different 3D Models

To thoroughly study the relationship between the different loading times on networking and the complexity of the 3D WebGL model displayed in the browser, different loading configurations of models have been studied, in order to consider all the variables that can come into play in this crucial phase.

In particular, different tests have been performed focusing on the impact of every variable (like the number of models that compose the scene, the overall weight, the quality of the texture associated) that could influence loading times of 3D models.

Such combinations are useful to ascertain what are the factors that produce the greatest impact on loading times. The experimentation has been performed considering the 3D model visualization of the greek theater of Segesta and its surroundings, located in the province of Trapani (Italy).

This test could be useful for the future development of 3D environments containing multiple elements or models, each one having its own identity. In particular, the implementation of semantic and geometric information for every 3D model contained into the environment is the base for the construction of a 3D GIS (Ellul and Altenbunchner 2013) useful for CH valorization, but also for improving virtual simulation of natural disasters (Kilsedar et al. 2019).

In this case of study, eight specific loading combinations have been considered, containing the same reproduced scene (the theater of Segesta and its surroundings) (see Fig. 4 and 5). Each combination included:

- a far environment (played through panoramic image projected to 360° on the inner surface of a sphere surrounding the model).
- a near environment, consisting of 3D terrain model surveyed through the use of aerial UAV survey and photogrammetric restitution.
- the 3D model of the cultural good, produced on the basis of surveys carried out using a Global Navigation Satellite System (GNSS) receiver, laser scanner and Unmanned Aerial Vehicle (UAV) technologies.

Fig. 4. The models considered in the scene for test.

Fig. 5. A browser visualization of the 3D tested scene.

The tests have been implemented using Chrome web-browser and a laptop with these main features: 16 GB RAM, Intel Core i7 1.80 GHz 2.40 GHz processor, GeForce GT 740M graphic card.

With regard to networking, the speed of navigation and loading times depend not only on the composition of the WebGL scene (weight, number of faces, texture, etc.) but also on other parameters regarding the relationship between client-side and server-side. In particular, the quality of the 3D interactive navigation depends also on the server performances, the browser capabilities, and the processor benchmarking scores of the client computer. This activity of benchmarking should consist in testing the performance of the pc CPU, in order to compare different pc architectures (not only looking to their specifications). Anyway, the parameters linked to the relationship between client-side and server-side haven't been considered in this work, because it has been used the same server, the same browser and the same client machine for all studied combinations.

The variables considered for the comparison of the uploading time addictions during web-browsing are linked below:

- the weight of the models (KB);
- the number of faces of every model;
- the presence of texture and its resolution;
- the number of elements involved in the scene;

In particular, two different loading solutions have been studied: loading the 3D CH model as a unique element (unified scene), or loading the same model dividing the mesh into five distinct elements (composed scene). Each of these solutions followed different loading combinations. The other 2 variables considered in this experimentation were the LoD of the models (represented by the weight of the models, the number of faces and the texture resolution) and the presence (or absence) of the texture.

Considering the LoD, it has been represented in the tables by the "number of faces", "weight of the model", and also the quality of the texture, considering its resolution. In fact, considering the textured combinations with a high LoD, the texture resolution is 11060×4283 for the far environment and 4096×4096 for the other elements, instead, considering the textured combinations with a low LoD, the texture resolution is 6000×2324 for the far environment and 1024×1024 for the other elements.

All of these combinations have been studied with the aim of finding the differences of speed between these different loading ways, with the purpose of testing multiple loading combinations, considering the number of elements, the LoD and the presence of the texture. In order to consider in this test the variables related to the LoD (weight of the models, the number of faces and the texture resolution) in an exhaustive way, the same scene has been loaded both with a high LoD and a low LoD.

During the test, eight loading combinations have been studied, in order to take in account all of the multiple loading solutions:

- unified textured scene with high LoD;
- composed textured scene with high LoD;
- unified scene with high LoD, without texture;
- composed scene with high LoD, without texture;

- unified textured scene with low LoD;
- composed textured scene with low LoD;
- unified scene with low LoD, without texture;
- composed scene with low LoD, without texture.

6   Analysis of the Results on Networking Solutions

Considering the simplification studied for the networking of CH, different solutions based on WebGL technologies have been compared. In particular, 3D models have been opportunely resized, in order to simplify 3D meshes and textures and comparing loading times during web-browsing, trying different combinations of meshes, textures and LoDs (see Table 2, 3, 4 and 5).

Table 2. Unified and composed textured scene with high LoD.

High LoD textured scene	Unified scene				Composed scene			
	far environment	near environment	unified model	total scene	far environment	near environment	composed model	total scene
weight (KB)	114	18.226	9.173	27.399	114	18.226	11.419	29.645
faces	2.400	250.168	109.284	359.452	2.400	250.168	109.284	359.452
texture resolution	11060x4283	4096x4096	4048x4048	-	11060x4283	4096x4096	4048x4048	-
elements	1	1	1	2	1	1	5	6
processing time (millisec.)	500	4500	4400	**9100**	500	4500	5200	**9500**

Table 3. Unified and composed scene with high LoD, without texture.

High LoD scene	Unified scene				Composed scene			
	far environment	near environment	unified model	total scene	far environment	near environment	composed model	total scene
weight (KB)	114	18.226	9.173	27.399	114	18.226	11.419	29.645
faces	2.400	250.168	109.284	359.452	2.400	250.168	109.284	359.452
texture resolution	-	-	-	-	-	-	-	-
number of elements	1	1	1	2	1	1	5	6
processing time (millisec.)	200	3500	3700	**6600**	200	3500	4000	**6800**

Table 4. Unified and composed textured scene with low LoD.

Low LoD textured scene	Unified scene				Composed scene			
	far environment	near environment	unified model	total scene	far environment	near environment	composed model	total scene
weight (KB)	114	3.572	3.834	7.406	114	3.572	3.794	7.366
faces	2.400	56.985	38.328	95.313	2.400	56.985	38.328	95.313
texture resolution	6000x2324	1024x1024	1024x1024	-	6000x2324	1024x1024	1024x1024	-
number of elements	1	1	1	2	1	1	5	6
processing time (millisec.)	100	1500	1700	**2500**	100	1500	2000	**2700**

Table 5. Unified and composed scene with low LoD, without texture.

Low LoD scene	Unified scene				Composed scene			
	far environment	near environment	unified model	total scene	far environment	near environment	composed model	total scene
weight (KB)	114	3.572	3.834	7.406	114	3.572	3.794	7.366
number of faces	2.400	56.985	38.328	95.313	2.400	56.985	38.328	95.313
texture resolution	-	-	-	-	-	-	-	-
number of elements	1	1	1	2	1	1	5	6
processing time (millisec.)	100	1000	1200	**1800**	100	1000	1300	**2000**

In light of the different loading times acquired during the networking of a virtual 3D scene and analyzing the results obtained from the tables, it's possible to underline the subsequent results (see Table 6 and 7):

- the difference between a unified and a composed 3D CH model loaded in the WebGL scene hasn't relevant effects on loading times. This means that the development of a scene of multiple loaded 3D models represent a nice solution, with the opportunity of characterize every model by different semantic and geospatial information.

– the textured model takes 1/3 over of loading time than the same model without texture. This result shows the strong influence of the texture on loading processing. Anyway, in order to create an immersive 3D CH complex environment navigable on the web, is better to load a textured 3D model with a reduced number of polygons, than an untextured model with more polygons. Indeed, the presence of texture gives a realistic perception of space, that in other ways should be impossible to obtain, because it would require a mesh with too many polygons.

– There is a strong difference on loading times between the simplified model with a low LoD and the more accurate model with a high LoD. Indeed, the number of loaded faces of 3D models and also the resolution of the applied texture strongly influenced loading times. For this reason, the research on finding the true simplification processing is fundamental to improve the quality of sharing interactive navigation 3D CH models on the web.

Table 6. Compared processing times of high LoD scenes.

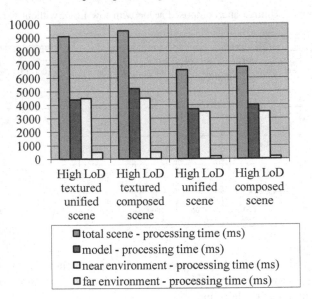

Table 7. Compared processing time of low LoD scenes.

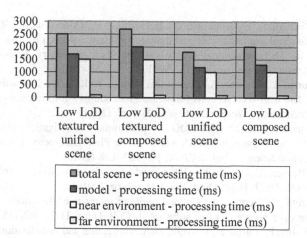

7 **Conclusions and Open Scenarios**

Comparing different loading options and different simplification procedures, it's possible to conclude that the choice of the preferred geomatic processing to follow depends on the final use of the 3D model. There isn't a definitive true workflow, but different combinations of procedures that could change due with different ways of acquisition (laser scanner, close-range photogrammetry) and different requirements of the final product.

In the future, Information and Communication Technology (ICT) procedures could solve many problems caused by the weight of loaded models, in order to allow sharing models on the web with a higher LoD and a more powerful speed of access during web-browsing. Furthermore, with the aim to create a 3D Geospatial Information System, the future studies have to focus the research to the connection of every 3D model loaded in the WebGL environment with an external database, in order to fully manage semantic information for the visualization on the web.

The next step will be the evolution of implementation of semantic information of 3D models, with the development of database structure according to a standard building model type (CH consist in different type of buildings difficult to decompose in simple elements and hence to describe).

The development of technology aimed to speed of access reduction on web through appropriate streaming functions will be an important progress for improving interactive navigation capabilities of 3D scenes. The possibility of access to the model without loading of any apps (that could decompress information) is strategic, but at the same time could be, today, slower.

Furthermore, the study of powerful access modes will be useful to obtain different LoD, according to different uses of 3D models, in order to give the possibility of switching between different visualized levels, also improving the speed of access.

References

Alicandro, M., Candigliota, E., Dominici, D., Immordino, F., Quaresima, R., Zollini, S.: Alba fucens archaeological site: multiscale and multidisciplinary approach for risk assessment and conservation. In: The International Archives of the Photogrammetry, Remote Sensing and Spatial Information Sciences, vol. XLII-2/W11, pp. 47–53 (2019)

Congote, J., Kabongo, L., Moreno, A., Segura, A., Posada, J., Ruiz, O.: Interactive visualization of volumetric data with WebGL in real-time. In: Proceedings - 16th International Conference on 3D Web Technology, Web3D 2011, pp. 137–145 (2011)

Ellul, C., Altenbuchner, J.: LOD 1 Vs LOD 2 – preliminary investigations into differences in mobile rendering performace. In: ISPRS Annals of the Photogrammetry, Remote Sensing and Spatial Information Sciences, vol. II-2/W1, pp. 129–138 (2013)

Gillespie, D., La Pensée, A., Cooper, M.: 3D cultural heritage online; in search of a user friendly interactive viewer. Int. J. Herit. Digit. Era 3(1), 52–68 (2014)

Guarnieri, A., Pirotti, F., Vettore, A.: Cultural heritage interactive 3D models on the web: an approach using open source and free software. J. Cult. Herit. 11(3), 350–353 (2010)

Kilsedar, C.E., Fissore, F., Pirotti, F., Brovelli, M.A.: Extraction and visualization of 3D building models in urban areas for flood simulation. In: The International Archives of the Photogrammetry, Remote Sensing and Spatial Information Sciences, vol. XLII-2/W11, pp. 669–673 (2019)

Koutsoudis, A., Tsaouselis, A., Arnaoutoglou, F., Ioannakis, G., Liakopoulos, V., Chamzas, C.: Creating 3D replicas of medium- to large-scale monuments for web-based dissemination within the framework of the 3D-icons project. In: CAA2015 Proceedings of the 43rd Annual Conference on Computer Applications and Quantitative Methods in Archaeology 2015, vol. 1, pp. 971–978 (2015)

Masiero, A., et al.: 3D modeling of girifalco fortress. In: The International Archives of the Photogrammetry, Remote Sensing and Spatial Information Sciences, vol. XLII-2/W9, pp. 473–478 (2019)

Neumuller, M., Reichinger, A., Rist, F., Kern, C.: 3D printing for cultural heritage: preservation, accessibility, research and education. In: 3D Research Challenges in Cultural Heritage 2014, pp. 119–134 (2014)

Nooruddin, F.S., Turk, G.: Simplification and repair of polygonal models using volumetric techniques. IEEE Trans. Vis. Comput. Graph. 9(2), 191–205 (2003)

Pepe, M., Costantino, D., Crocetto, N., Restuccia Garofalo, A.: 3D modeling of roman bridge by the integration of terrestrial and UAV photogrammetric survey for structural analysis purpose. In: The International Archives of the Photogrammetry, Remote Sensing and Spatial Information Sciences - ISPRS Archives, vol. XLII-2/W17, pp. 249–255 (2019)

Pirotti, F., et al.: An open source virtual globe rendering engine for 3D applications: NASA world wind. Open Geospatial Data Softw. Stand. 2(1), 1–14 (2017). https://doi.org/10.1186/s40965-017-0016-5

Potenziani, M., Callieri, M., Dellepiane, M., Corsini, M., Ponchio, F., Scopigno, R.: 3DHOP Una piattaforma flessibile per la pubblicazione e visualizzazione sul Web dei risultati di digitalizzazioni 3D. Archeomatica 2015(4), 6–11 (2015)

Qu, L., Meyer, G.W.: Perceptually guided polygon reduction. IEEE Trans. Vis. Comput. Graph. 14(5), 1–15 (2008)

Scianna, A., Gaglio, G.F., La Guardia, M.: Augmented reality for cultural heritage: the rebirth of a historical square. In: The International Archives of Photogrammetry, Remote Sensing and Spatial Information Sciences, vol. 42, pp. 303–308 (2019)

Scianna, A., La Guardia, M.: Survey and photogrammetric restitution of monumental complexes: issues and solutions - the case of the manfredonic castle of mussomeli. Heritage 2(1), 774–786 (2019)

Scianna, A., La Guardia, M.: Globe based 3D GIS solutions for virtual heritage. In: The International Archives of the Photogrammetry, Remote Sensing and Spatial Information Sciences - ISPRS Archives, vol. XLII-4/W10, pp. 171–177 (2018)

Scianna, A., La Guardia, M., Scaduto, M.L.: Sharing on Web 3D models of ancient theaters. A methodological workflow. In: The International Archives of the Photogrammetry, Remote Sensing and Spatial Information Sciences - ISPRS Archives, vol XLI-B2, pp. 483–490 (2016)

Vacca, G., Deidda, M., Dessi, A., Marras, M.: Laser Scanner Survey to Cultural Heritage Conservation and Restoration. In: The International Archives of the Photogrammetry, Remote Sensing and Spatial Information Sciences, vol. XXXIX-B5, pp. 589–594 (2012)

Willén, J.: Developing a process for automating UV mapping and polygon reduction. Linkoping University, Department of Computer and Information Science Bachelor's Thesis (2011)

Use of Non-professional UAV Video Sequences for the 3D Modelling of Archaeological Sites by SfM Techniques

Gabriele Bitelli(✉) ⓘ, Federico Artini, Valentina Alena Girelli ⓘ,
Alessandro Lambertini ⓘ, and Emanuele Mandanici ⓘ

Department of Civil, Chemical, Environmental and Materials
Engineering (DICAM), University of Bologna,
Viale Del Risorgimento 2, 40136 Bologna, Italy
{gabriele.bitelli, valentina.girelli,
alessandro.lambertini, emanuele.mandanici}@unibo.it

Abstract. This paper presents two examples of use of amateur video sequences for the 3D modelling of objects in Archaeology. The described case studies refer to the important archaeological sites of Cahuachi (Peru) and Tiwanaku (Bolivia), where the DICAM Dept. of the University of Bologna operated in past years with a surveying activity that involved the application of different geomatic techniques: 3D scanning and image-based surveys of findings and structures, georeferencing of satellite imagery and geophysics works, GNSS surveying, etc.

Within this framework, the paper proposes to investigate the potential of re-using non-professional aerial video sequences of these locations, acquired by means of UAVs (Unmanned Aerial Vehicles) by amateur photographers or simple tourists, freely available on YouTube platform. The aim is obtaining 3D models and mapping of these sites by SfM (Structure from Motion) techniques, after a careful management of the video files and in integration with other geomatic datasets.

In the paper, the two analysed case studies are described, with particular attention to the characteristics of the videos, to the used software and to the solutions adopted for the georeferencing of the obtained products, like 3D models and orthophotos.

Keywords: UAV · 3D modelling · SfM · Cultural Heritage · Video

1 Introduction

The availability of low-altitude digital images, typically acquired today by UAVs, in combination with the potential of the new Multi-View SfM photogrammetric approaches, makes it today possible to create high quality 3D models even for large areas. The applications taking advantage of this possibility are many, including obviously Cultural Heritage, and specifically Archaeology [1–4].

Many archaeological sites, sometimes located in unmapped areas, require to be surveyed in a quick and rigorous way to create large-scale basemaps or to monitor

© Springer Nature Switzerland AG 2020
C. Parente et al. (Eds.): R3GEO 2019, CCIS 1246, pp. 282–295, 2020.
https://doi.org/10.1007/978-3-030-62800-0_22

along the time the progress of excavations. Owning a metric data of good quality would also be essential to document those sites located in areas potentially subjected to natural or anthropogenic risks [5, 6]

Several attempts were made in the past to acquire low-height imagery by balloons or kites [7, 8], but the rapid evolution and diffusion of RPAs (Remotely Piloted Aircrafts) are opening up still relatively unexplored possibilities. The UAVs equipped with cameras are now available at affordable prices and this availability has led to a proliferation of amateur videos shared online, frequently of good quality thanks to the evolution of the sensors mounted on board. A modern UAV camera is able to record a video in the commercially described "4K resolution", equal to 3840 × 2160 pixels. From a 4K recorded video it is possible to extract a finite number of images with more than 8-megapixel resolution each. On the other hand, the big diffusion of social media and other platforms for the sharing of photos and videos, can make possible the creation of a digital photographic collective memory accessible to all, and in some case suitable also for geomatic applications with appropriate approaches [9–11].

In particular, this phenomenon has concerned areas of archaeological interest due to their touristic appeal.

In the paper, the use of non-professional videos acquired by UAV and freely available on internet on YouTube channels is investigated for 3D modelling purposes.

This experimentation is carried out on two of the most important archaeological sites in central South America, Cahuachi (Peru) and Tiwanaku (Bolivia). The two sites have recently been the subject of a surveying activity by the Geomatics group of the DICAM Dept., described in the next paragraph.

The research, here at a preliminary stage, wants to investigate the possibility of using data already freely available on Internet, even if not specifically acquired for mapping purposes, to integrate what was carried out in the field. The paper presents and describes the two study cases and the procedure followed to generate by the videos some final products like 3D models and orthophotos.

In the discussion, attention was given to the different phenomena able to influence the final results: the initial phase of the files management, the solutions adopted for the georeferencing, the software adopted. Bentley ContextCapture has been used as SfM package to process the datasets.

2   The Study Cases and the Surveying Activities of DICAM Dept.

The described study is part of a more complex and extensive research work that DICAM Dept. is carrying out, in particular at the Cahuachi and Tiwanaku sites (Fig. 1), in collaboration with Museo Antonini in Nasca and the ITACA project (ITAlian scientific mission for heritage Conservation and Archaeogeophysics) of the CNR (National Research Council). The goal of the experimentation here described is to enrich the database available about these archaeological sites using amateur photographic material freely available on YouTube platform in a scientific photogrammetric context, with the aim to generate 3D models and mapping of excavation areas.

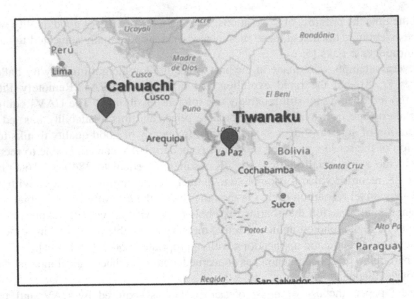

Fig. 1. Location of the two archaeological sites.

2.1 Cahuachi, Peru

The Italian archaeologist Giuseppe Orefici has been excavating at the site of Cahuachi for the past few decades [12].

Cahuachi is one of the most sacred and impressive places in the Nasca culture (Fig. 2). It overlooks some of the Nasca lines and it is the main religious centre of the ancient Peru, and the largest city, in the world, entirely built in adobe, a mixture of clay, sand and straw sun-dried for making bricks.

The city progressed in five different phases during the development of the Nasca civilization and over a period of about 900 years ranging from 450 BC to 450 AD. During this long period, it became an extremely important religious centre and pilgrimage destination by the populations of the Rio Grande Valley.

Thirty-four groups of temples were built there, dedicated to the deities worshiped by the population. The temple and pyramids structures were terraced and characterized by large ceremonial enclosures, with the different levels accessible via impressive staircases.

The area has been investigated in the recent years by using integrated Remote Sensing techniques for the detection of the buried buildings [13].

Fig. 2. The *adobe* Big Pyramid in Cahuachi.

In the archaeological site of Cahuachi, the Geomatics group of the DICAM Dept. conducted some surveying activities in December 2013 with the application of different techniques. GNSS (Global Navigation Satellite System) positioning of some Ground Control Points (GCPs) was performed (Fig. 3), to support the geo-referencing of a GeoEye-1 stereo pair, from which a Digital Elevation Model was extracted, covering the area including Cahuachi, a portion of the Rio Nasca valley and the geoglyphs of Atarca (extension of 60 km^2, spatial resolution of 5 m) [14]. Besides, 3D modelling by close-range photogrammetry was realized for some structures in the archaeological site and some objects preserved in the Antonini museum in Nasca.

Fig. 3. (a) GNSS Master station surveyed with Precise Point Positioning (PPP) method, on the roof of the Antonini Museum in Nasca; (b) rapid-static GNSS positioning of a GCP in the area of Cahuachi.

2.2   Tiwanaku, Bolivia

Tiwanaku, UNESCO World Heritage Site since 1999, is a Pre- Columbian archaeo-logical site located in Bolivia, about 70 km from the capital La Paz and 30 km from Lake Titicaca. The original name of the site is not known, because its founders had no written language, as the term Tiwanaku was assigned by the Incas and means "the city of God".

His dating remains uncertain, though a recent radiocarbon dating estimates that the site was founded around 200–300 BC [15].

Although only an infinitesimal part of this Andean site has been brought to light (it is estimated not more than 3%), it can surprise visitors and experts, considering the magnificence of the engineering realisations, expressions of an extraordinarily evolved civilization (Fig. 4).

Fig. 4. View of the Kalasasaya Temple in Tiwanaku, with GNSS data acquisition.

The Geomatics group of the DICAM Dept. has performed a surveying campaign in Tiwanaku in June 2014.

The activity consisted of rapid-static and kinematic GNSS positioning, to measure respectively the coordinates of some GCPs for high-resolution satellite imagery pro-cessing and to georeference the geophysical profiles acquired by CNR.

Besides, digital photogrammetry and structured-light projection 3D scanning were adopted, with the aim to obtain high detailed 3D model of the Puerta del Sol, one of the most important building in Tiwanaku (Fig. 5), and other finds at the lithic and ceramic Museum.

Fig. 5. 3D scanning of the East side of the Puerta del Sol.

3 Processing of the Non-professional UAV Video Sequences

Regarding Cahuachi, a first 3D model of the site was obtained using an amateur video available on YouTube and uploaded in 2016. The video was acquired by a DJI Phantom 4 and, once downloaded, has a size of 918 M and a total duration of 5 min and 39 s.

In order to extract the images to be processed in the Bentley ContextCapture SfM software, the video was decomposed using the open-source FFmpeg software. The extracted images have a resolution of 3840 × 2160 pixels.

The evaluation of the right extraction interval is a key factor in the processing, in order to obtain a complete and not noisy 3D model of the area. In this case, many tests were conducted, checking the coverage between each extracted image and the subsequent one, choosing an extraction interval of 2 s. The images were then manually skimmed, eliminating those blurred or not relevant for the purpose. The final coverage schema is of course not comparable with the one obtained by a careful photogrammetric planning.

A pre-processing phase was necessary to manually mask the images and delete those areas which could have generated outliers and noise in the extracted point clouds. Of the final set consisting of 170 frames, 167 images were aligned and oriented in the absolute reference system, using as GCPs 5 points measured during the 2013 campaign by GNSS, obtaining an average error equal to about 6 cm and a reprojection error less than 1 pixel (Fig. 6).

Fig. 6. The sparse point cloud and the images acquisition scheme: the detail shows the inhomogeneity in the position uncertainty for the tie points due to the image alignment.

After the alignment phase, in the report it is possible to find the characteristics of the flight: the average altitude is about 190 m and the ground resolution in the order of 5 cm/pixel.

The extraction of the dense point cloud in ultra-high quality required 8 h on a workstation equipped with Intel Core i7-7820X 3.6 GHz CPU and 128 GB of RAM. Two examples of the generated final products are shown in Fig. 7 and Fig. 8.

Fig. 7. Photo-textured 3D model of Cahuachi site.

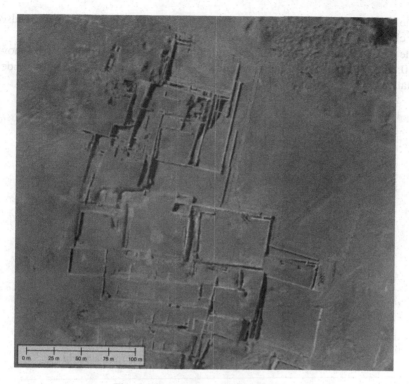

Fig. 8. Orthophoto of Cahuachi site.

Table 1 reports some indicative parameters about the processing and the characteristics of the dense point cloud.

ContextCapture was able to align images and reach good results in term of accuracy thanks to a processing parametrization adaptable to the specific situation. In particular in this case study it was useful to set up conveniently the pair selection mode as exhaustive, advised in cases where the overlap between photos is irregular. Besides, the optical parameters properties were set in multi-pass mode, convenient when aerial triangulation fails, because the initial parameters are far from real values (e.g. unknown focal length or unknown large distortion).

Table 1. The parameters of the photogrammetric processing of the movie concerning Cahuachi site, performed by ContextCapture package.

Aligned images	167
Reprojection error	0.77
Average error on GCPs	6 cm
Dense cloud points	492 million
Dense cloud points spacing	4 cm

The optimal results in terms of interior and exterior orientation affected also the dense cloud extraction.

The dense cloud (Fig. 9) is detailed and complete, as displayed in the area shown in Fig. 10. In particular, walls and other prominence structures are correctly modelled, especially as far as the lateral surfaces are concerned.

Fig. 9. Dense point cloud by ContextCapture for Cahuachi.

Fig. 10. Details of the 3D point clouds of Cahuachi by ContextCapture.

For Tiwanaku archaeological site, three amateur videos were used to create a 3D model of the semi-subterranean Temple and the surrounding area.

All the three videos were found on YouTube, published between 2015 and 2016.

Unlike the movie previously used for Cahuachi, the videos of Tiwanaku showed no details on the drone model or the type of camera and are characterized by lower quality. Their authors also heavily processed the films in the post-editing phase with the addition of superimposed images and joined clips acquired in different weather and light conditions by different equipment. This has complicated the photogrammetric processing, particularly in the phase of images selection and alignment. Table 2 shows the characteristics of the videos.

Table 2. Characteristics of the three videos processed for Tiwanaku site.

	Duration	Frame resolution
Video 1	13 min 36 s	1280 × 720
Video 2	9 min 18 s	1280 × 720
Video 3	5 min 0 s	1920 × 1080

The available GCPs, obtained in the mentioned surveying campaign, having been obtained for the georeferentiation of a larger area by satellite imagery, cannot be suitable for the semi-subterranean Temple: very few points were in fact available.

In order to scale the photogrammetric 3D model obtained by the videos, a point cloud acquired in the framework of a project carried out between 2005 and 2006 by the Center for Advanced Spatial Technologies (CAST) of the University of Arkansas was used [16, 17]; the data were kindly made available on their website. It is a point cloud obtained by means of a terrestrial laser scanning using an Optech ILRIS, which has an accuracy of 8 mm at 100 m (Fig. 11).

Fig. 11. Point cloud of the semi-subterranean Temple in Tiwanaku, acquired by the University of Arkansas [16] and used for georeferencing the UAV 3D model.

The videos were then inserted divided in images, obtaining 3 datasets which were then aligned in a single one, using markers corresponding to points identified in the laser cloud and correspondent to the four corners and the top of Barbado monolith, placed in the centre of Temple.

Figure 12 shows the obtained dense point cloud and the coloured mesh. The photogrammetric cloud of the Temple and surrounding area counts 21 million points, with a point spacing of about 6 cm. The result is satisfactory, even if obviously the cloud by laser scanner results more detailed.

Fig. 12. Point cloud of the Temple obtained processing in ContextCapture the three videos, with superimposed the cloud by laser scanner of the University of Arkansas.

Figure 13 shows a section of the Temple in correspondence of the *Barbado* monolith. The example clearly shows the effect of a non-adequate acquisition by the amateur UAV flight, due to its non-photogrammetric planning and the corresponding areas obstructed with respect to the sensor orientation.

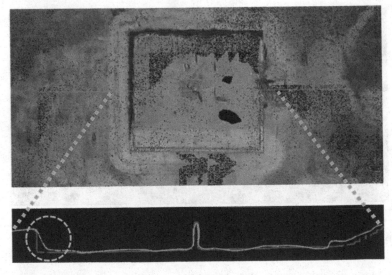

Fig. 13. Section of the photogrammetric point clouds, laser model in red and photogrammetric model in cyan. (Color figure online)

4 Conclusions

The identified procedure considered the extraction and selection of images from amateur video sequences, at the highest possible resolution, and their processing in a SfM approach, with an appropriate geo-referencing in an absolute cartographic system. The experimentation was carried out on two of the most important archaeological sites in central South America, Cahuachi (Peru) and Tiwanaku (Bolivia).

Concerning the site of Cahuachi, the obtained 3D model, including almost the entire ceremonial area, was georeferenced thanks to the GNSS surveys carried out on the site. This model, deriving from images of good quality realized by a semi-professional UAV system, without the need of significant post-production interventions, is of good quality, virtually explorable and measurable, becoming a usable tool for documentation purposes or, if integrated with other surveys of different epochs, useful for mapping the changes that have occurred over the years.

The second model concerns a portion of the large archaeological site of Tiwanaku, the so-called semi-subterranean Templete. The available datasets were characterized by an inferior quality, lower resolution and a stronger lossy compression in the video stream, therefore requiring significant manual editing in the post-production phase. This, combined with a smaller and more discontinuous coverage of the area, has led to a greater difficulty in the images alignment phase and to a less detailed result. The model is measurable thanks to the use, as base for the georeferencing, of a 3D model created by laser scanning in 2005–2006 by the CAST Center from the University of Arkansas. The final products show, on the one hand, how terrestrial laser technology allows, as obvious, to obtain more accurate results, but on the other hand they highlight how a complementary approach, which involves the data fusion between laser and photogrammetric techniques, is particularly effective.

In conclusion, the described experience made it possible to evaluate the contribution that amateur images or video sequences can provide in Cultural Heritage documentation and conservation, and the associated problems. The last are primarily related to several topics:

- a non-professional design of the flight, not specifically aimed at mapping or 3D modelling, producing an inhomogeneous coverage, unwanted occlusions and gaps, not-uniform data quality on the tie points, and then on the final products, due to image alignment problems;
- an incomplete coverage of the area of interest. The problem can be partly compensated by a greater number of available videos. In the last case, they could be however acquired at different dates and conditions, factors that could negatively influence the 3D modelling;
- the need of movie editing to remove unwanted portions, with the risk of breaking the continuity of the ground coverage;
- reduced possibilities to perform internal check on the dataset quality, due to limited data redundancy;
- the quality of the video streams available on the social platforms, sometimes degraded from the original version or modified by post-production activities;

– the quality of the UAV camera and of the stabilization systems, fundamental for modelling purposes; in this sense, the current technological developments are undoubtedly helpful.
– the lack of any metadata information.

On the other hand, it can be stressed the potentiality of aerial UAV-derived images for the documentation of large archaeological sites at low costs. It results particularly useful in mapping of areas that are difficult to reach, or not reachable at all for several reasons.

This approach could also be considered in the framework of collaborative mapping procedures (crowdmapping), useful for rapid mapping of sites in particular situations, or when amateur data are used to reconstruct the 3D geometry and appearance of sites that no longer exist (e.g. destroyed by a war).

Acknowledgements. The authors would like to thank very much Giuseppe Orefici, director of the Antonini Museum in Nasca, Nicola Masini and Rosa Lasaponara from CNR-Italy, the CAST of University of Arizona, and all the authors of the videos.

References

1. Chiabrando, F., Nex, F., Piatti, D., Rinaudo, F.: UAV and RPV systems for photogrammetric surveys in archaelogical areas: two tests in the Piedmont region (Italy). J. Archaeol. Sci. **38** (3), 697–710 (2011). https://doi.org/10.1016/j.jas.2010.10.022
2. Lo Brutto, M., Garraffa, A., Meli, P.: UAV platforms for cultural heritage survey: first results. ISPRS Annals of Photogrammetry, Remote Sensing & Spatial Information Sciences, vol. II-5, pp. 227–234 (2014). https://doi.org/10.5194/isprsannals-II-5-227-2014
3. Fernández-Hernandez, J., González-Aguilera, D., Rodríguez- Gonzálvez, P., Mancera-Taboada, J.: Image-based modelling from unmanned aerial vehicle (UAV) photogrammetry: an effective, low-cost tool for archaeological applications. Archaeometry **57**(1), 128–145 (2015). https://doi.org/10.1111/arcm.12078
4. Cowley, D.C., Moriarty, C., Geddes, G., Brown, G.L., Wade, T., Nichol, C.: UAVs in context: archaeological airborne recording in a national body of survey and record. Drones **2** (1), 1–16 (2018). https://doi.org/10.3390/drones2010002
5. Cherry, J.F., Ryzewski, K., Leppard, T.P.: Multi-period landscape survey and site risk assessment on Montserrat. West Indies. J. Island Coast. Archaeol. **7**(2), 282–302 (2012). https://doi.org/10.1080/15564894.2011.611857
6. Wahbeh, W., Nebiker, S., Fangi, G.: Combining public domain and professional panoramic imagery for the accurate and dense 3D reconstruction of the destroyed Bel temple in Palmyra. In: ISPRS Annals of the Photogrammetry, Remote Sensing and Spatial Information Sciences, vol. III-5, pp. 81–88 (2016) https://doi.org/10.5194/isprsannals-iii-5-81-2016
7. Bitelli, G., Tini, M.A., Vittuari, L.: Low-height aerial photogrammetry for archaeological orthoimaging production. Int. Arch. Photogramm. Remote Sens. Spatial Inf. Sci. **34**(5W12), 55–59 (2003)
8. Bitelli, G., Girelli, V.A., Tini, M.A., Vittuari, L.: Low-height aerial imagery and digital photogrammetrical processing for archaeological mapping. Int. Arch. Photogramm. Remote Sens. Spatial Inf. Sci. **35**, 498–503 (2004)

9. Hartmann, W., Havlena, M., Schindler, K.: Towards complete geo-referenced 3D models from crowd-sourced amateur images. In: ISPRS Annals of Photogrammetry, Remote Sensing and Spatial Information Sciences, vol. III-3, pp. 51–58 (2016) https://doi.org/10.5194/isprs-annals-iii-3-51-2016

10. Bitelli, G., et al.: Metric Documentation of Cultural Heritage: research direction from the Italian GAMHER project. In: The International Archives of the Photogrammetry, Remote Sensing and Spatial Information Sciences, vol. XLII-2/W5, pp. 83–90 (2017). https://doi.org/10.5194/isprs-archives-xlii-2-w5-83-2017

11. Guidi, G., Malik, U. S., Frischer, B., Barandoni, C., Paolucci, F.: The Indiana University-Uffizi project: metrologica! challenges and workflow for massive 3D digitization of sculptures. In: Proceedings of the 2017 23rd International Conference on Virtual Systems and Multimedia, VSMM 2017, pp. 1–8 (2018). https://doi.org/10.1109/VSMM.2017.8346268

12. Lasaponara, R., Masini, N., Orefici, G. (eds.): The Ancient Nasca World. Springer, Cham (2016). https://doi.org/10.1007/978-3-319-47052-8

13. Masini, N., Rizzo, E., Lasaponara, R., Orefici, G.: Integrated remote sensing techniques for the detection of buried archaeological adobe structures: preliminary results in Cahuachi (Peru). Adv. Geosci. 19, 75–82 (2008). https://doi.org/10.5194/adgeo-19-75-2008

14. Bitelli, G., Mandanici, E.: Geomatics applications in Cahuachi and Nasca territory. In: Lasaponara, R., Masini, N., Orefici, G. (eds.) The Ancient Nasca World, pp. 581–591. Springer, Cham (2016). https://doi.org/10.1007/978-3-319-47052-8_23

15. Marsh, E.: A Bayesian re-assessment of the earliest radiocarbon dates from Tiwanaku. Bolivia. Radiocarbon 54, 203–218 (2012). https://doi.org/10.2458/azu_js_rc.v54i2.15826

16. Barnes, A.: Supplemental survey of the templete (Semi Subterranean Temple) in Tiwanaku, Bolivia using the Optech ILRIS 3D. Center for Advanced Spatial Technologies, Fayetteville, AR (2006)

17. Cothren, J., et al.: Fusion of 3-dimensional data at Tiwanaku: an approach to spatial data integration. In: Proceedings of the 36th Annual Conference on Computer Applications and Quantitative Methods in Archaeology, Budapest, 2–6 April 2008 (2008)

Refractory Brick Lining Measurement and Monitoring in a Rotary Kiln with Terrestrial Laser Scanning

Grazia Tucci[✉] , Alessandro Conti , and Lidia Fiorini

GeCO Lab, Department of Civil and Environmental Engineering,
University of Florence, Via di S. Marta, 3, 50139 Florence, Italy
{grazia.tucci,alessandro.conti,lidia.fiorini}@unifi.it

Abstract. Rotary kilns are industrial furnaces used for the continuous processing of raw materials at high temperature, consisting in long steel cylinders lined with refractory bricks and revolved by gears. They are subjected to complex stresses and deformations due to high temperatures and heavy loads, so monitoring and planned maintenance are essential to avoid very expensive unexpected shutdowns and other damages to the exterior shell. The interior of a rotary kiln has been acquired with a terrestrial laser scanner during a maintenance shutdown for checking the wear of the refractory brick lining. Up to now, the refractory lining of the surveyed plant was checked every year taking manual measurements, but this technique produced discontinuous data only. The 3D model has been unwrapped to show the deviation between the current state and the design drawings. The model showed the degradation of the refractories and the thickness of the incrustations in a continuous way on the whole surface. In addition, in this application laser scanning can be considered as a diagnostic imaging technique because degradation patterns can give some indications on the deformation of the steel casing. By selecting some reference points integral to rotating parts, instead to the motionless structures outside the furnace, a permanent reference system has been established to reliably repeat monitoring over time.

Keywords: Rotary kiln · Refractory lining · Laser scanner · Monitoring

1 Introduction

1.1 Rotary Kilns

A rotary kiln is a pyro-processing furnace used to transform ores or other materials at high temperature in a continuous process [1]. Schematically, a rotary kiln is a long, inclined steel cylinder, supported by tyres upon rollers and revolved by girth gears at low speed.

The unprocessed material, fed into the upper end, moves along the kiln, due to the slope and rotation of the pipe, while the thermal process is caused by the counter-current flow of hot gases produced by a burner pipe at the lower end [2]. They are plants used in many industries, mainly for producing cement clinker [3], in metallurgical and chemical processes [4] and for hazardous waste incineration [5].

© Springer Nature Switzerland AG 2020
C. Parente et al. (Eds.): R3GEO 2019, CCIS 1246, pp. 296–310, 2020.
https://doi.org/10.1007/978-3-030-62800-0_23

The inner of kiln is lined by wedge-shaped refractory bricks in annular courses, to insulate the steel shell and outer elements from the high temperature and protect it from mechanical and chemical damages caused by the processed material [6].

Kilns used in diverse fields have specific dimensions, fuel, operating temperatures, rotation speed, slope, lining and other features (Fig. 1).

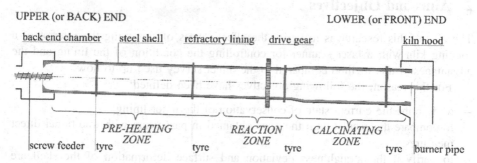

Fig. 1. Schematic drawing of a rotary kiln

1.2 Monitoring and Maintenance

The steel casing of a kiln is designed with decades of almost continuous operating life in mind; therefore, it is very important to protect it from damage and deformation because each shutdown has a major impact on the productivity of the industrial plant. The main condition for the efficient functioning of a rotary kiln is the alignment between all the components and their geometric correspondence to the original design, i.e. the straightness of the rotation axis of the drum, the relative position of the support rollers and tyres, etc. [7]. All the elements operate at very high temperature with heavy loads, so they are inevitably exposed to wear.

The most important parameters for evaluating the operation state of a rotary kiln are the straightness deviation and the surface deformation, the former affects the load distribution on supports and the latter reduces the durability of the lining refractories.

There are several techniques used for tuning up the geometry of kilns based on measures of the external surface of the shell taken with a total station [8] or with a terrestrial laser scanner [9, 10]. If measurements and tuning take place while the plant is operating, the process is called "hot alignment" [11, 12], if they are performed during a maintenance stoppage, it is called "cold alignment" [13].

Other important checks regard the refractory lining, which must be repaired or replaced before the heat could damage the shell and cause a breakdown. It is in the interest of the factory that the refractories degrade in a controlled manner to be replaced during planned maintenance, avoiding damages and unforeseen shutdowns [14].

An indirect evaluation of the condition of the inner lining can be carried out with infrared thermographic inspection, which is also often used for the continuous monitoring the operation of the kilns [15, 16].

Laser scanners have been used to inspect blast furnaces, as far as can be surveyed from the hatch [17]. Customised scanners can be immersed for a short time in operating furnaces up to 1000 °C [18], but they are suitable for quite short vessels only, like the ladles used in the metal industry. To our knowledge, no previous article has examined the use of laser scanners to examine the refractory lining of long furnaces (such as rotary kilns) from the inside, during a scheduled maintenance downtime.

2 Aims and Objectives

The aim of this research is to verify the effectiveness of surveying the interior of a rotating kiln with a laser scanner for controlling the condition of the lining and the advantages of this method compared to the direct survey used up to now.

For this reason, the following objectives have been defined:

– to describe the current state of conservation of the inner lining;
– to compare the results with the ones obtained in past years with traditional direct measures;
– to verify if the straightness deviation and surface deformation of the shell are detectable by the interior lining survey;
– to set up a reliable reference system in order to monitor the condition of the furnace over time.

3 The Case Study

3.1 Description

The surveyed machine is a rotary kiln used to produce barium sulphide. The process reduces barytes using coke as reducing agent [19]. The furnace can be divided in three zones: the upper part, where the raw material is fed, is the pre-heating zone, the central part is the reaction zone and the lower part is the calcinating zone (Fig. 2).

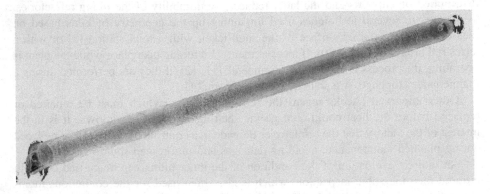

Fig. 2. Point cloud of the interior of the rotating kiln.

The total length is about 50 m and consists of two cylindrical sections connected by a conical transition.

The dimension of the sections and the number of rings of bricks in each section are indicated in Table 1.

Table 1. Nominal dimensions of the sections of the rotating kiln shell and number of brick courses in each section.

Sections	Length	Internal diameter	Brick courses
	m	m	no.
Inlet cap	1.20	2.09	
Upper section	32.74	2.09	142
Conic transition	1.73	2.09–2.39	7
Lower section	14.25	2.39	60 + 2
Outlet opening	0.35	2.39	

The slope is 2%. The interior is covered with trapezoidal refractory bricks of 6 different types and sizes, in a single leaf. In particular, two types of bricks are used for the cylinders, the lower edge is made with two types of special bricks and the conical transition is made with combinations of two other types of bricks. The nominal thickness of the upper section is 140 mm, that of the conical and of the lower sections is 172 mm.

The bricks are arranged in annular rings. Upon visual inspection, groups of rings with different degrees of wear are recognizable (Fig. 3). These correspond to previous partial replacements, since it's not possible to replace single bricks and the repairs must substitute entire rings. Many areas are covered with a layer of slag of varying thickness and consistency. The encrustations are more sizeable in reaction zone, which is situated in the central part.

3.2 Previous Surveys

Until now, the condition of the inner lining has been checked during the yearly shutdown of the machine. Due to the numerous maintenance operations to be carried out, the inspection can only take a few hours, but in this time all useful information to plan the maintenance for the following year must be collected. As this is a tight and at-risk environment, it is compulsory to wear a full personal protective equipment (suit, goggles, mask, helmet, gloves and shoes) and this restricts the movements of the surveyors. The traditional measurement method was inevitably unsystematic and inefficient. Visual checks and direct measurements were carried out every meter with a laser distance meter. Four telescopic rods, arranged on the diameter of the pipe and rotated by 45° each other, were used as a visual reference to measure the distance between opposite points of the lining, so the survey team must be composed by three operators: the surveyor, an assistant for recording measures and another assistant to check the correctness of the direction of the measures from a distance. In such harsh

Fig. 3. Rings of refractories showing different degree of wearing.

conditions, it is difficult to take measures exactly as planned. Moreover, measures are necessarily discontinuous and in order to record information on non-measured intermediate points, written remarks and photographic documentation were taken.

Inside the furnace, there is no permanent reference that allows to determine its attitude and in particular the rotation of the longitudinal axis in relation to the exterior. For this reason, it was difficult to take periodic measurements in exactly the same position for evaluating the aging of the coating over time. In the past, in order to partially overcome this problem, reference lines were engraved on fixed and rotating parts of the drum. The alignment of the reference lines has been used to rotate the kiln approximately in the same position.

4   Survey Operations

4.1   Fieldwork

The survey was carried out on 14th August 2019, during the annual maintenance downtime of the machine. The laser scanner survey team was composed of two operators and the survey lasted about four hours, the same duration as the manual survey. The team that performed the surveys in previous years in the same day carried out manual measurements as above described, in order to verify the differences between the two methods.

In 2019, the scheduled preventive maintenance did not include the complete removal of the furnace end (called "kiln hood"). Therefore, it was possible to access the inside of the furnace only by means of a small manhole. For all these reasons and especially for the limited space available and the need to wear protective equipment, including safety goggles, it was not possible to contemplate the use a total station to set up a topographic control network or to measure targets for scans alignment. Laser scanner is certainly easier to use in this condition, as it requests some simple settings only and automatically acquires all the surfaces in the line of sight at almost 360°.

The survey project was therefore planned considering that the alignment of the scans could only take place with the cloud-to-cloud method.

In addition, the surface covered with inconsistent slag does not allow for a reliable fixing of magnetic targets or the usual flat ones. Some "tilt-and-turn" targets have been placed on the bottom and some small boxes have been glued on the bricks to be used as 3D targets (Fig. 4).

Fig. 4. A scan of the kiln, showing the operators and two boxes used as targets

A Zoller + Fröhlich Imager® 5010c scanner has been used for the acquisition. Its most relevant specifications are listed in Table 2.

The scanner also has an integrated color camera that implements High Dynamic Range (HDR) technology for reproducing a greater dynamic range of luminosity than what is possible with standard digital photography, but in this case the acquisitions of RGB values was not performed, as the overall illumination was very poor and all surfaces were uniformly covered by a greyish dust, so the colour acquisition would had been time-consuming without adding information.

Table 2. Zoller + Fröhlich Imager® 5010c scanner most relevant characteristics.

Type	Phase-shift laser scanner		
Laser class	1		
Laser wavelength	1500 nm		
Max range	187.3 m		
Max data acquisition rate	1,016,000 points/s		
Linearity error	±1 mm		
Vert./horiz. angular accuracy	0.007° rms (0.122 mrad rms)		
Range noise	*Black 14%*	*Grey 37%*	*White 80%*
at 10 m	0.4 mm rms	0.3 mm rms	0.2 mm rms
at 25 m	0.6 mm rms	0.4 mm rms	0.3 mm rms
at 50 m	2.2 mm rms	0.8 mm rms	0.5 mm rms
at 100 m	10 mm rms	3.3 mm rms	1.6 mm rms

Twelve scans were carried out inside the tube (every 4 m approximately) and four scans outside to connect the internal and external surfaces of the kiln. For the connection of the two surfaces, a scan taken from the inside near the manhole also acquired some targets located outside.

All scans have been carried out with the "high resolution" setting (corresponding to an angular step of 0.036° or 6.28 mm at 10 m) and the "normal quality" setting (corresponding to a data acquisition rate of 254 kHz) [20, 21].

Outside, only a part (about 13 m long) of the steel drum is easily accessible and clearly visible, corresponding to the lower section. As already indicated, using a coordinate system integral to fixed elements is unworkable, because it is quite impossible to accurately set the roll of the kiln even with the help of the reference marks engraved on the rotating and motionless parts. In addition, the outer surface reaches high temperatures during operation, so any applied or painted target would be damaged. For this reason, some durable features on the external surface, like eyebolts or welds, have been identified as reference points. Their 3D coordinates will be used for roto-translating any future surveys in the selected local reference system (see 4.2 paragraph) for the monitoring of the machine.

4.2 Data Processing

A cloud-to cloud process has been carried out for the registration of the scans. The point clouds have been manually cleaned removing the operators inside the kiln (as it was not possible to come quickly out) and the bearing elements and surrounding constructions outside. The resulting point model includes more than 492 million 3D coordinates. The best fitting cylinders for the upper and lower portions has been separately calculated using the implementation of the RANSAC algorithm [22] in CloudCompare software [23] to identify the longitudinal axis of the kiln.

The longitudinal axes of the two cylinders are not perfectly aligned (they form an angle of 179.9488°), however the calculation of the best fitting of the two sections may have been influenced by the irregularity and wear of the refractory brick lining and the incrustations layer. It is therefore not possible to determine whether the misalignment is due to an actual straightness deviation of the shell or to the uncertainty of measurement and data processing.

The reference system chosen is right-handed, with the x axis coinciding with the axis of the upper cylinder and the y axis on the vertical plane passing through it (Fig. 5)

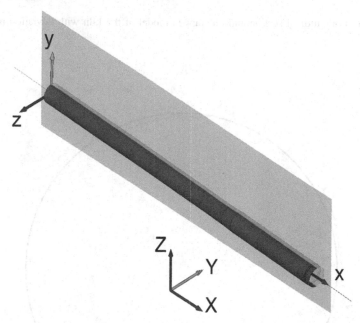

Fig. 5. The kiln reference system (x, y, z) compared to a reference system integral to external fixed objects (X, Y, Z)

It has been also calculated the deviation between the point cloud and an idealised surface of revolution based on existing drawings. Since the original design drawings were missing, a drawing made in 2006 for the maintenance of the cladding was used, which includes overall dimensions, alignment of sections, inclination, laying and dimensions of the various types of bricks, etc.

For better usability, a surface mesh was also modelled and unwrapped for creating a 2D map of deviations (Fig. 6).

In addition, cross sections had been extracted in the same positions where direct measurements had been taken, both to highlight the deviation from the nominal profile and to compare the measures obtained with the scanner and the direct survey (Fig. 7).

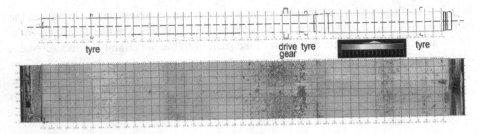

Fig. 6. Longitudinal section and unwrapped model of the kiln with deviation map.

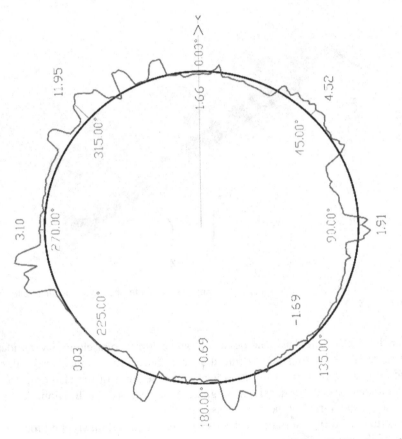

Fig. 7. A transversal cross section: theoretical profile (in black) compared with surveyed profile (in red). Radial deviations in mm, magnification factor ×10. (Color figure online)

5 Results

5.1 Present State of the Refractory Lining

The 3D model clearly represents the inner surface of the kiln, showing the single bricks, their pattern, the state of preservation and the incrustations on the surface.

The pattern does not correspond to the above-mentioned design in just two cases. In one point, two half-brick wide rings have been placed side by side (see rings 150 and 151 in Fig. 8), in another case two rings are bonded up for filling a gap as long as of one and a half bricks, these devices were probably introduced during previous maintenance works.

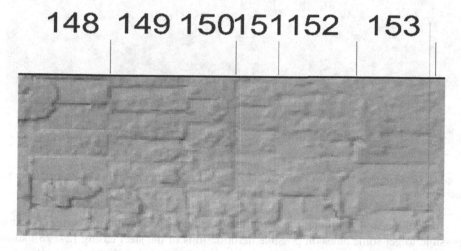

Fig. 8. Half length bricks (rings 150 and 151).

Such anomalies are barely visible on site, therefore had not been highlighted during the manual surveys carried out in recent years.

There are some broken bricks, both isolated or concentrated in some areas, for example immediately before the conical transition between the cylinders, corresponding with the reaction zone and where there is the drive gear outside (see Fig. 4). In the same area there is a considerable erosion of the bricks (more than 5 cm), partly hidden by thick incrustations (Fig. 9).

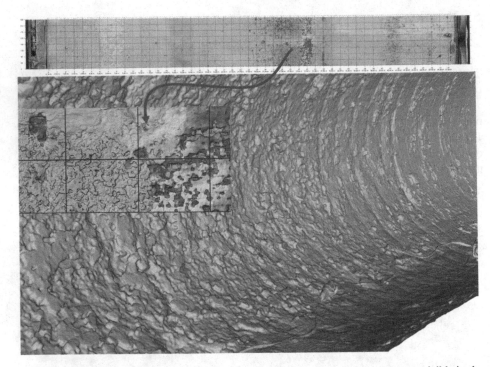

Fig. 9. Detail of the 3D model: slag encrustations and missing or eroded bricks are visible in the reaction zone.

In addition, by examining the lining texture and its degradation patterns, it is also possible to get some clues on possible deformations of the steel casing [24, 25], so in this application laser scanning can be considered like a diagnostic imaging technique. In some points, the bricks are tilted against the axis of the pipe ("spiralling"), which may indicate a relative movement between bricks caused by a loose installation. Elsewhere, the collapse of the bricks head ("spalling") could be a symptom of a shear stress due to the drum ovality (Fig. 10). The opening of the brick joints or single deeply broken bricks can be other effects of ovality (Fig. 11).

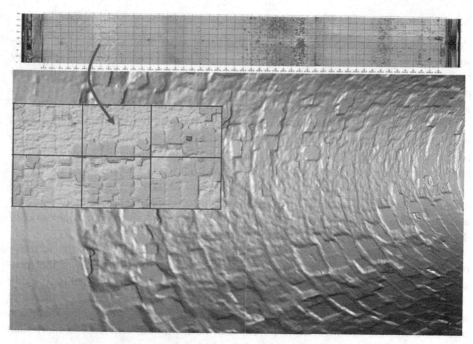

Fig. 10. Collapse of the brick heads ("spalling") due to shear stress probably caused by the ovality of the kiln shell.

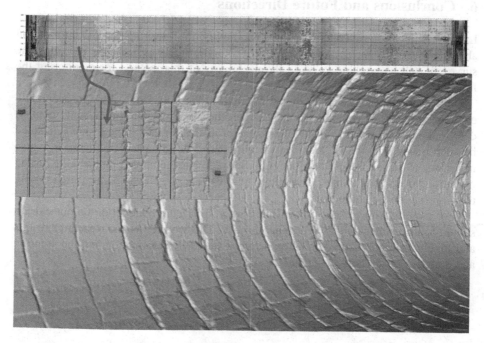

Fig. 11. "Spiralling" and opening of the brick joints probably caused by ovality.

5.2 Comparison with Direct Measures

Compared to the direct measurement method used up to now, when only four measurements were taken for every metre of kiln length, laser scanning samples with a very high resolution the entire surface at the same time. This continuous mesh model produces a very effective visual feedback of the conditions of each part of the lining, while previously it was necessary to add written notes and photographs.

Due to the lack of references, the repeatability of measurements in different epochs was inevitably inaccurate, while the determination of a permanent reference system based on reference points on the outer surface of the casing will allow a reliable monitoring of the entire surface of the refractive bricks coating.

Previously the distance between opposite points of the pipe was measured. Therefore, the thinning of the refractories on the one side could be hidden by the accumulation of slags on the opposite side. Instead, the comparison with a 3D model of the nominal shell surface is not affected by this error.

The main difference between the two survey methods is not primarily the accuracy of the measuring instruments, but rather that, the location and direction of the measurements acquired manually under the above conditions are inevitably roughly determined. A precise comparison between the two series of measurements is therefore not really significant; as an indication, the average difference between the diameters measured with the two methods is 1.4 cm and the maximum difference is more than 4 cm.

6 Conclusions and Future Directions

Laser scanning has proven to be an effective method for acquiring detailed information about the wear of the refractory bricks in a rotary kiln. By periodically repeating the survey, it will be possible to verify the usefulness of this method for monitoring the furnace.

However, the measurement of the internal surface does not allow to accurately evaluate the main geometric parameters of the rotating kiln (alignment, ovality, deformation), but only gives clues of possible problems. In fact, if the casing is affected by such issues, also the measurements acquired will be influenced by them. It is also necessary to be aware of the difference between the geometry of the kiln during operation, loaded and at high temperature, and the one which can be measured during the stoppage of the equipment.

For more accurate results on the lining wear, an accurate model of the outer drum should be made to be used as a reference surface. This would give more accurate results and highlight the possible correlation between the shell deformation and the wearing and damages of the bricks coating.

References

1. Boateng, A.A.: Rotary Kilns. Transport Phenomena and Transport Process. Butterworth-Heinemann, Oxford (2016)
2. Saidur, R., Hossain, M.S., Islam, M.R., Fayaz, H., Mohammed, H.A.: A review on kiln system modeling. Renew. Sustain. Energy Rev. **15**(5), 2487–2500 (2011). https://doi.org/10.1016/j.rser.2011.01.020
3. Saxena, J.P.: Refractory Engineering and Kiln Maintenance in Cement Plants. CRC Press, Boca Raton (2003)
4. Stjernberg, J., Ion, J.C., Antti, M.L., Nordin, L.O., Lindblom, B., Odén, M.: Extended studies of degradation mechanisms in the refractory lining of a rotary kiln for iron ore pellet production. J. Eur. Ceram. Soc. **32**(8), 1519–1528 (2012). https://doi.org/10.1016/j.jeurceramsoc.2012.01.012
5. Jiang, X., Li, Y., Yan, J.: Hazardous waste incineration in a rotary kiln: a review. Waste Disposal Sustain. Energy **1**(1), 3–37 (2019). https://doi.org/10.1007/s42768-019-00001-3
6. Shubin, V.I.: The lining for rotary cement kilns. Refract. Ind. Ceram. **42**(3–4), 130–136 (2001). https://doi.org/10.1023/A:1011380029083
7. Li, X., Shen, Y., Wang, S.: Dynamic modeling and analysis of the large-scale rotary machine with multi-supporting. Shock Vibr. **18**(1–2), 53–62 (2011). https://doi.org/10.3233/SAV-2010-0573
8. Gebhart, W.: Kiln alignment analysis-an overview of the direct method. In: 2000 IEEE-IAS/PCA Cement Industry Technical Conference. Conference Record (Cat. No. 00CH37047), pp. 379–393. IEEE (2000). https://doi.org/10.1109/citcon.2000.848536
9. Kovanič, L., Blišťan, P., Zelizňakova, V., Palkova, J., Baulovič, J.: Deformation investigation of the shell of rotary kiln using terrestrial laser scanning (TLS) measurement. Metalurgija **58**(3–4), 311–314 (2019). https://hrcak.srce.hr/218411. Accessed 10 Jan 2019
10. Bartknecht, F., Siegfried, M., Weber, H.: Sensors solutions and predictive maintenance tools to decrease kiln and conveyor belt downtime. In: 2019 IEEE-IAS/PCA Cement Industry Conference (IAS/PCA), pp. 1–9. IEEE (2019). https://doi.org/10.1109/citcon.2019.8729094
11. Zheng, K., Zhang, Y., Zhao, C., Liu, L.: Rotary kiln cylinder deformation measurement and feature extraction based on EMD method. Eng. Lett. **23**(4) (2015). ISSN: 1816093X
12. Krystowczyk, B.: Dynamical monitoring and correction of rotary machines deformation. Rep. Geodesy (3/74), 115–123 (2005). http://www.geoservex.com.pl/publikacje/d2.pdf. Accessed 10 Jan 2019
13. Mogilny, S.G., Sholomitskii, A.A., Seredovich, V.A., Seredovich, A.V., Ivanov, A.V.: The analysis of methods for determining the geometric parameters of rotating machines. In: Proceedings of the 2nd International Workshop Integration of Point-and Area-wise Geodetic Monitoring for Structures and Natural Objects, pp. 119–130 (2015)
14. Ramanenka, D., Stjernberg, J., Eriksson, K., Jonsén, P.: Modelling of refractory brick furniture in rotary-kiln using finite element approach. In: World Congress on Computational Mechanics (WCCM XI): 5th European Conference on Computational Mechanics (ECCM V), 6th European Conference on Computational Fluid Dynamics (ECFD VI) 20 July 2014–25 July 2014, vol. 2, pp. 1199–1210. International Center for Numerical Methods in Engineering (CIMNE) (2014)
15. Torgunakov, V.G.: 3D simulation in IR thermographic inspection of rotary kilns. Russ. J. Nondestr. Test. **42**(1), 1–11 (2006). https://doi.org/10.1134/S1061830906010013
16. Knopfel, H., Schmidt, D.: Optimized kiln operation by keeping kiln shell temperatures at set point with controlled water cooling. In: 2018 IEEE-IAS/PCA Cement Industry Conference (IAS/PCA), pp. 1–11. IEEE (2018). https://doi.org/10.1109/citcon.2018.8373109

17. Kuo, S.-K., Lee, W.-C., Du, S.-W.: Measurement of blast furnace refractory lining thickness with a 3D laser scanning device and image registration method. ISIJ Int. **48**(10), 1354–1358 (2008). https://doi.org/10.2355/isijinternational.48.1354

18. Lamm, R., Kirchhoff, S.: Optimization of ladle refractory lining, gap and crack detection, lining surface temperature and sand filling of the ladle-taphole by means of a 3D-laserprofile-measurement-system that is immersed in to a hot ladle to evaluate the entire condition. In: UNITECR 2017, Proceedings 2017. http://www.unitecr2017.mundodecongresos.com/abstracts/Paper_rbofbhfxcsxhpgipoispm.pdf. Accessed 10 Jan 2019

19. Du, Q., Mo, H., Tian, L., Yuan, L.: A preliminary control system on a barium sulphide rotary kiln process. In: 2010 International Conference on Measuring Technology and Mechatronics Automation, vol. 1, pp. 286–290. IEEE (2010). https://doi.org/10.1109/icmtma.2010.489

20. Zoller + Fröhlich, Z + F IMAGER® 5010C datasheet. https://www.zf-laser.com/fileadmin/editor/Datenblaetter/Z_F_IMAGER_5010C_Datasheet_E.pdf. Accessed 10 Jan 2019

21. Zoller + Fröhlich, Understanding Imager 5010 accuracy specifications, white paper (2014)

22. Schnabel, R., Wahl, R., Klein, R.: Efficient RANSAC for point-cloud shape detection. Comput. Graph. Forum **26**(2), 214–226 (2007). https://doi.org/10.1111/j.1467-8659.2007.01016.x

23. CloudCompare. Vers. 2.11 alpha. http://www.cloudcompare.org/. Accessed 10 Jan 2019

24. Muhammed, M.A.: A case study of types of failure in refractory bricks lining cement kilns. Kufa J. Eng. **3**(1), 103–123 (2011). http://journals.uokufa.edu.iq/index.php/kje/article/view/2568. Accessed 10 Jan 2019

25. Salman, M.M., Ali, A.M.: The problems of rotary kiln of cement and their remedies. Int. J. Civ. Eng. Technol. **10**(2), 1010–1019 (2019). http://www.iaeme.com/MasterAdmin/Journal_uploads/IJCIET/VOLUME_10_ISSUE_02/IJCIET_10_02_098.pdf. Accessed 10 Jan 2019

Morphological Evolution of Somma-Vesuvio During the Last Century: Integration Between Historical Maps and Airborne LiDAR Survey

Marina Bisson[1]([✉]) [iD], Alessandro Tadini[2] [iD], Roberto Gianardi[1] [iD], and Andrea Angioletti[3]

[1] INGV, Sezione di Pisa, via Cesare Battisti 53, 56125 Pisa, Italy
{marina.bisson, roberto.gianardi}@ingv.it
[2] Laboratoire Magmas et Volcans, Université Clermont Auvergne, CNRS, IRD, OPGC, 63000 Clermont-Ferrand, France
Alessandro.TADINI@uca.fr
[3] Università degli Studi di Pisa, via Santa Maria 53, 56100 Pisa, Italy

Abstract. The eruptive history of a volcano can be investigated by analyzing the changes of its topography through time. This type of analysis can be a useful support to improve studies aimed at volcanic hazard assessment for very densely populated active or quiescent volcanic zones as the Somma-Vesuvio (SV) area. For the first time, in this work the morphological evolution of the SV volcanic edifice from 1876 to nowadays is presented through the reconstruction of topographies obtained from IGM (Italian Geographic Military Institute) historical maps (1876, 1906 and 1929) and remote sensing techniques (e.g. LiDAR). In detail, the multi-temporal morphological analysis has been focused on the Gran Cono area. The main working environment has been the ESRI platform (ArcGIS 10®), but other specific software have been involved to manage the geo-referencing procedures and conversion data (TN-Sharc, IGM-Traspunto/Cartlab). Morphological analyses and volume changes quantification related to the summit portion of the SV edifice from 1876 to nowadays are presented. The morphometric analyses were obtained by using height profiles along the four main direction (N-S, W-E, NW-SE and NE-SW), the changes in volume were estimated elaborating each Digital Elevation Model (DEM) in the area of interest.

Keywords: Cartography · LiDAR · DEM · Somma-Vesuvio

1 Introduction

In order to describe the morphometric changes of any geographic area, the more accurate is the reconstruction of the topography, the more investigations can be done. For this purpose it is necessary to acquire surface elevation points that subsequently are processed to build Digital Elevation Models (DEMs). The main techniques of acquisition are: i) the traditional digitalization of contour lines and height points from available cartographic maps (Tarquini et al. 2007); ii) Aerial Stereo Photogrammetry

© Springer Nature Switzerland AG 2020
C. Parente et al. (Eds.): R3GEO 2019, CCIS 1246, pp. 311–320, 2020.
https://doi.org/10.1007/978-3-030-62800-0_24

(Gwinner et al. 2006); iii) Satellite Stereo Photogrammetry (Beyer et al. 2018); iv) Airborne Laser Scanning (Bisson et al. 2016) and v) the most recent Drone technology (Dering et al. 2019).

In this work we present the morphological evolution from 19th to 21st century of the Somma Vesuvio (SV) volcano, one of the more hazardous volcanoes in the world due to the explosive character of its past eruptions and the high population density of its surroundings. For this study we have reconstructed the DEM of SV at different years by using different typology of data. We have produced the topography of the volcano starting from three historical maps of the Italian Geographic Military Institute (IGM - 1876, 1906 and 1929 years) and by processing the LiDAR (Light Detection and Ranging) data acquired on 2009–2012 surveys. By comparing the historical DEMs with the present day topography (LiDAR DEM), several morphological analyses and volume quantification of the SV summit portion are presented. The morphometric analyses were obtained by using height profiles along the four main direction (N-S, W-E, NW-SE and NE-SW), the changes in volume were estimated by elaborating each Digital Elevation Model (DEM) in the area of interest. The manuscript starts with a short description of the eruptive history of SV, followed by the presentation of the source data, the methods to reconstruct the elevation models of the studied area, the morphological analyses, the most significant results and the relative discussion. Finally, a section that summarizes the main remarks closes the manuscript.

2 Eruptive History of Somma-Vesuvio

SV is a relatively young composite volcano of moderate altitude ($\sim$ 1200 m a.s.l.) located in one of the most urbanized areas of Campania Region (Central Italy - Fig. 1). Its volcanic activity is post-39 ka (Cioni et al. 2008; Santacroce et al. 2008; Sbrana et al. 2020) and includes a wide range of eruption types, from explosive to effusive ones. The oldest part of the volcanic complex is constituted by Mt. Somma (Fig. 1). This edifice grew in the period 39-22 ka BP after mainly effusive activity and was partially destroyed by 4 Plinian eruptions (including the AD 79 Pompeii one) which contributed to the development of the SV summit caldera (Cioni et al. 1999). The Gran Cono edifice (Fig. 1) started to grow within the summit caldera partially after the AD 79 eruption, and more substantially after the AD 472 sub-Plinian eruption (Cioni et al. 1999).

The more recent products (mostly lava flows, pyroclastic fall and flow deposits) were erupted during the last period of activity of the volcano, in the years 1631–1944 (Arrighi et al. 2001). After the last eruption occurred in AD 1944, the volcano is considered quiescent.

Fig. 1. Study area

3   Dataset

This section presents the datasets used to create the 3D digital topography of the SV complex. The data come from different sources and consequently are not characterized by the same spatial resolution and the same errors in x and y. With the aim of making these latter two (i.e. resolution and errors) comparable, we have processed the historical maps according to criteria and rules that assure the lowest possible errors in x and y such as a correct geo-referencing based on the Ground Control Points method, the affine transformation and the RMSE (Root Mean Square Error) threshold. Then, a further co-registration procedure was applied between the historical georeferenced maps and present day cartographies.

3.1   Historical Maps

The historical maps used in this work are referred to the years 1876, 1906, and 1929 and describe either the area surrounding the volcanic edifice or the caldera zone. All the maps were provided from the IGM. In Fig. 2 the 1906 map is shown as example. In all historical maps the geographic reference is reported along the boundary and is expressed in degree according to the Roma 40 Gauss Boaga cartographic system. The scale of the maps ranges from 1:50.000 to 1:10.000. This leads a relative tolerance error in x and y from 5 to 25 m and a spatial resolution from 2 to 10 m.

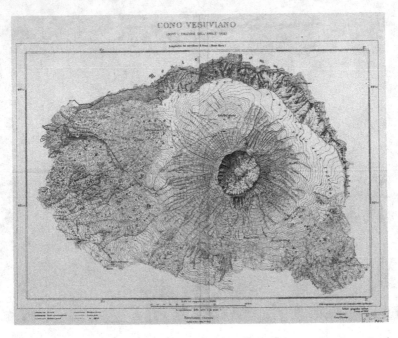

Fig. 2. 1906 IGM map. (The map is provided by IGM in agreement with the authorization n° 0013597 dated 24/09/2019).

3.2 LiDAR Data

For the present-day topography, LiDAR data acquired during the years 2009–2012 by the Province of Naples were processed to classify the ground points and to obtain a very high spatial resolution (1 m) Digital Terrain Model (DTM) with vertical accuracy around ±2 cm (Pizzimenti et al. 2016). The LiDAR is a remote sensing technique able to acquire millions of a surface 3D points by scanning the surface itself with an instrumental system (Infrared Sensor, IMU and GPS) mounted on an aircraft or helicopter. For this study, the source data were organized and elaborated following the procedure described in Pizzimenti et al. (2016). The result consists in a DTM that reproduces with very high detail the morphology of SV after its last eruption occurred in 1944 (Fig. 3). With respect to the total extent of the SV topography, we have focused the analyses on the SV summit caldera area defined in Tadini et al. (2017).

4 Methodology and Analyses

In order to reconstruct the digital elevation models and derive qualitative and quantitative information on the SV morphological changes, we have elaborated the historical maps and LiDAR data by using the GIS ESRI platform as the main working environment. For standardizing the cartographic reference system of each maps in WGS84-UTM-33 N, the Tn-Sharc and CartLab 2.0 software were used as well. In detail the three maps were acquired by scanning the original paper at 300 dpi and the outputs were stored in raster format at 8 bit (grey tones). Subsequently, the three raster maps were geo-referenced by using the Ground Control Points method (De Leeuw et al. 1988). In particular, we have used 8 points located at map boundary or in some features well recognizable both in the historical maps and in the nowadays cartographies. The 8 points were converted from Roma 40 Gauss Boaga in the WGS 84 UTM 33 N cartographic system in order to geo-code the raster maps. The elevation data were then digitalized by developing a dataset of contour-lines and points stored in shapefiles format. By interpolating the datasets according to the Delaunay algorithm (Shewchuk 2002), three

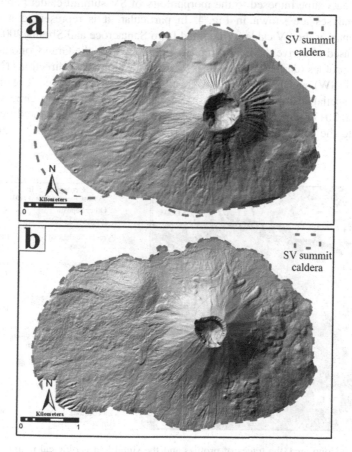

Fig. 3. a) 1906 shaded relief b) LiDAR shaded relief

elevation vector models (ESRI TIN format) were produced and then converted in matrices (ESRI GRID) with a common spatial resolution of 5 meters, a value chosen in order to take into account the scales of relative maps.

The 3 resulting models reconstruct the topography of SV summit caldera zone related to 1876, 1906 and 1929 year. Finally, since the DEMs derived from the historical maps do not cover exactly the same area, we have focused our study on the morphological and volumetric changes in a zone that results common to all DEMs. This zone is represented by the Gran Cono area in according to the definition in Tadini et al. (2017). Figure 3 shows the images of the shaded reliefs derived from the 1906 and LiDAR DEM. From these images, it is possible to observe very clearly some morphological changes of SV between 1906 and 1944. Between these, the most relevant regard the reduction in extent of the crater rim and the several deposits related to AD 1944 eruption as the hot avalanches and the lava flows, both well recognizable on the flanks of the volcano.

4.1 Height Profiles

A series of data superimposed to the morphology of SV summit caldera and useful to the next analyses are shown in Fig. 4. In particular, it is represented a simplified geological map of the SV caldera (modified from Santacroce and Sbrana 2003) and the four traces used to derive the height profiles defined within the Gran Cono area (black circle). The profiles (dashed colored lines) were made along four directions (N-S, W-E, NW-SE, NE-SW) and height points were plotted every 25 meters. The figure also reports the spatial distribution of parasitic effusive vents within the Gran Cono area (Tadini et al. 2017). The height profiles are shown in Fig. 5 and assume different color according to the topography of reference (red-nowadays; yellow-1929; green-1906; blue-1876).

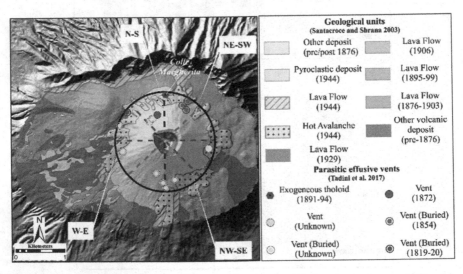

Fig. 4. Gran Cono area, the traces of profiles and the simplified geological map of SV caldera area. (Color figure online)

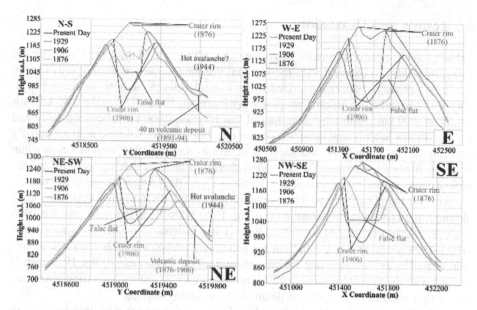

Fig. 5. Height profiles along the main 4 directions. (Color figure online)

In general, all the profiles confirm consistent morphological changes in the Gran Cono summit and interesting modifications in the north and east flanks, whereas the west and south flank do not seem to be affected by significant evidences. However, a more detailed analysis will be treated in the discussion section.

4.2 Volume and Area Changes

The volume and area changes quantification were obtained processing the four SV Gran Cono topographies on ArcGIS software. The calculations were performed inside the black circle (Fig. 4) with a radius of 1 km, trying to eliminate the false flat resulting in the DEM of 1929. For this purpose, we have reconstructed the contour lines of the interior portion of the crater by using the 1906 map. For each Gran Cono topography, the extent of surface and the volume were calculated by Grid format by using default tools present in the software. For each year of reference, Table 1 reports the value of the surface and volume of the Gran Cono edifice.

Table 1. Volumes and 3D Surfaces of the Gran Cono areas through time.

Year	Volume (km^3)	3D Surface (km^2)
Present	0.82	3.82
1929	0.76	3.73
1906	0.74	3.79
1876	0.73	3.69

5 Results and Discussion

Table 1 shows a general increase of volume and 3D surface of the Gran Cono edifice, two results that are coherent with the fact that the time frame considered in this study (1876 to nowadays) was characterized by an intense volcanic activity (Scandone et al. 2008). In particular, the volume progressively increases from 0.73 km^3 to 0.82 km^3 for a total of 0.09 km^3, with more than half of this increase (0.06 km^3) between 1929 and present. In this latter period there has been minor but frequent volcanic activity (mostly intracrateric) in 1929–1944 (Scandone et al. 2008) and the 1944 violent strombolian eruption (Cole and Scarpati 2010), and it therefore appears that the activity in this period deposited more material along the Gran Cono flanks than the previous ones.

Also for the 3D surface we observe an increase from 1876 to present of 0.13 km^2, although the increase is not constant (i.e. the 1929 3D surface is lower than the 1906 one). This could be related to two factors: i) the material deposited in a short time (1906–1929 years) was not sufficient for generating complex morphologies (e.g. erosion channels, gullies, etc.) that increase the extent of 3D surface; ii) the 1929 map is the one with the lowest frequency of isolines (one every 25 m) and elevation points, an aspect that diminishes the level of detail of the resulting surface.

Also the resulting heights profiles (Fig. 5) are in agreement with this increase in volume. In fact, the oldest profile (i.e. the 1876 one) is almost always the one attaining the lowest altitudes along the flanks and highest altitude in the summit crater area (more than 1275 m a.s.l) except for the E part of the crater rim. In this area the present topography is the highest (Fig. 5, profile W-E). The higher elevation of the 1876 crater is explained by the 1906 violent strombolian eruption, which beheaded the upper portion of the edifice (Bertagnini et al. 1991). During the subsequent years, the crater was built mostly to northeast reaching the highest elevation of the present edifice.

With respect to morphometric variations highlighted by the profiles (Fig. 5) we report three main observations:

– In the N-S profile we can see a difference in elevation of around 40 m between 1876 and 1906. This difference could indicate deposits reasonably correlated to the 1891–94 eruptive event. The related deposits outcrop partially in N and NW area of the Gran Cono forming the "Colle Margherita" exhogenous tholoid (Santacroce and Sbrana 2003; see Fig. 4).
– In both N-S and NE-SW profiles are particularly evident the "Hot avalanche" deposits generated by the 1944 eruption (Santacroce and Sbrana 2003; Cole and Scarpati 2010). As described by Hazlett et al. (1991), such peculiar type of debris avalanches took place near the end of the main eruptive phase (although long before the end of the eruption) and were initiated by a seismic crisis that removed 5–10 × 10^6 m^3 of material in the Gran Cono area from elevations >9 00 m a.s.l. These deposits are identified in profiles N-S and NE-SW (Fig. 5) where the height difference between 1906 and 1944 is around 20–25 m. This value is consistent with the thickness of the deposits reported in Hazlett et al. (1991).
– W-E and NE-SW profiles show similar morphologies in the SW flank of the Gran Cono. This could be explained considering that this zone is not particularly affected by the volcano activity post 1876.

6 Concluding Remarks

In order to analyze morphological changes of SV Gran Cono from 1876 to nowadays, this study proposes a comparison between topographies derived from very different sources: historical cartography maps and modern acquisition techniques such as airborne LiDAR. This methodological approach allowed to obtain acceptable results to quantify the morphometry and volume changes despite of the very different accuracy degree of source data. In particular: i) the volume of Gran Cono increased from 0.73 km^3 (1876) to 0.82 km^3 (nowadays), ii) 3D surface increased from 3.69 km^2 (1876) to 3.82 km^2 (nowadays), iii) the thickness of "Colle Margherita" exhogenous tholoid was estimated around 40 m in the outcrop located in N-NW flank, iv) the thickness of 1944 "Hot avalanche" deposits was estimated around 20–25 m.

Since the morphometric analyses, the surface and volume evaluations are in good agreement with the bibliography data and SV volcanic history, this study will be improved by quantifying the planimetric and vertical accuracy of the historical maps. In addition further profiles will be added in specific areas of interest. These new investigations should provide more accurate estimations of the multi-temporal changes in volume and surface of the Gran Cono area.

Acknowledgements. Dr. Marco Bocci from Istituto Geografico Militare (IGM) is greatly acknowledged for kindly allowing the consultation of the IGM archive for the retrievement of historical maps for the Somma-Vesuvio area. We warmly thank R. Mari from "Città Metropolitana di Napoli – Direzione Strutturazione e Pianificazione dei servizi Pubblici di interesse generale di Ambito Metropolitano – Ufficio S.I.T. – Sistema Informativo Territoriale" for kindly providing LiDAR data for DEM implementation. This work was also partly funded by the French government IDEX-ISITE initiative 16-IDEX-0001 (CAP 20-25).

References

Arrighi, S., Principe, C., Rosi, M.: Violent strombolian and subplinian eruptions at Vesuvius during post-1631 activity. Bull. Volc. **63**(2–3), 126–150 (2001). https://doi.org/10.1007/s004450100130

Beyer, R.A., Alexandrov, O., McMichael, S.: The Ames Stereo Pipeline: NASA's open source software for deriving and processing terrain data. J. Geophys. Res. Planets **5**(9), 537–548 (2018). https://doi.org/10.1029/2018EA000409

Bertagnini, A., Landi, P., Santacroce, R., Sbrana, A.: The 1906 eruption of Vesuvius: from magmatic to phreatomagmatic activity through the flashing of a shallow depth hydrothermal system. Bull. Volc. **53**(7), 517–532 (1991). https://doi.org/10.1007/BF00298153

Bisson, M., Spinetti, C., Neri, M., Bonforte, A.: Mt. Etna volcano high resolution topography: airborne LiDAR modelling validated by GPS data. Int. J. Digit. Earth **9**(7), 710–732 (2016). https://doi.org/10.1080/17538947.2015.1119208

Cioni, R., Santacroce, R., Sbrana, A.: Pyroclastic deposits as a guide for reconstructing the multi-stage evolution of the Somma-Vesuvius Caldera. Bull. Volc. **61**(4), 207–222 (1999). https://doi.org/10.1007/s004450050272

Cioni, R., Bertagnini, A., Santacroce, R., Andronico, D.: Explosive activity and eruption scenarios at Somma-Vesuvius (Italy): towards a new classification scheme. J. Volcanol. Geoth. Res. **178**(3), 331–346 (2008). https://doi.org/10.1016/j.jvolgeores.2008.04.024

Cole, P.D., Scarpati, C.: The 1944 eruption of Vesuvius, Italy: combining contemporary accounts and field studies for a new volcanological reconstruction. Geol. Mag. **147**(3), 391–415 (2010). https://doi.org/10.1017/S0016756809990495

Dering, G.M., Micklethwaite, S., Thiele, S.T., Vollgger, S.A., Cruden, A.R.: Review of drones, photogrammetry and emerging sensor technology for the study of dykes: best practises and future potential. J. Volcanol. Geoth. Res. **373**, 148–166 (2019). https://doi.org/10.1016/j. jvolgeores.2019.01.018

De Leeuw, A.J., Veugen, L.M.M., Van Stokkom, H.T.C.: Geometric correction of remotely-sensed imagery usiing ground control points and orthogonal polynomials. Int. J. Remote Sens. **9**(10–11), 1751–1759 (1988)

Gwinner, K., et al.: The HRSC-AX Mt. Etna project: high-resolution orthoimages and 1 m DEM at regional scale. In: Proceedings ISPRS XXXVI, pp. T05–23 (Part 1) (2006)

Hazlett, R.W., Buesch, D., Anderson, J.L., Elan, R., Scandone, R.: Geology, failure conditions, and implications of seismogenic avalanches of the 1944 eruption at Vesuvius, Italy. J. Volcanol. Geoth. Res. **47**(3–4), 249–264 (1991). https://doi.org/10.1016/0377-0273(91) 90004-J

Pizzimenti, L., Tadini, A., Gianardi, R., Spinetti, C., Bisson, M., Brunori, C.A.: Digital elevation models derived by ALS data: Sorrentina Peninsula test areas. In: Rapporti tecnici INGV, no. 361 (2016)

Santacroce, R., Sbrana, A.: Geological map of Vesuvius. SELCA Firenze (2003)

Santacroce, R., et al.: Age and whole rock–glass compositions of proximal pyroclastics from the major explosive eruptions of Somma-Vesuvius: a review as a tool for distal tephrostratigraphy. J. Volcanol. Geoth. Res. **177**(1), 1–18 (2008). https://doi.org/10.1016/j.jvolgeores. 2008.06.009

Sbrana, A., Cioni, R., Marianelli, P., Sulpizio, R., Andronico, D., Pasquini, G.: Volcanic evolution of the Somma-Vesuvius Complex (Italy). J. Maps, 1–11 (2020). https://doi.org/10. 1080/17445647.2019.1706653

Scandone, R., Giacomelli, L., Speranza, F.F.: Persistent activity and violent strombolian eruptions at Vesuvius between 1631 and 1944. J. Volcanol. Geoth. Res. **170**(3–4), 167–180 (2008)

Shewchuk, J.R.: Delaunay refinement algorithms for triangular mesh generation. Comput. Geom. **22**(1–3), 21–74 (2002). https://doi.org/10.1016/S0925-7721(01)00047-5

Tadini, A., Bisson, M., Neri, A., Cioni, R., Bevilacqua, A., Aspinall, W.P.: Assessing future vent opening locations at the Somma-Vesuvio volcanic complex: 1. A new information geodatabase with uncertainty characterizations. J. Geophys. Res. Solid Earth **122**(6), 4336–4356 (2017). https://doi.org/10.1002/2016JB013858

Tarquini, S., Isola, I., Favalli, M., Mazzarini, F., Bisson, M., Pareschi, M.T., Boschi, E.: TINITALY/01: a new triangular irregular network of Italy. Ann. Geophys. **50**(3) (2007). http://hdl.handle.net/2122/3673

GIS and Remote Sensing

Processing Very High-Resolution Satellite Images for Individual Tree Identification with Local Maxima Method

Oscar Rosario Belfiore[1]($\boxtimes$) , Manuel Angel Aguilar[2] ,
and Claudio Parente[3]

[1] Department of Agricultural Sciences, University of Naples Federico II,
Via Università 100, 80055 Portici, NA, Italy
oscarrosario.belfiore@unina.it
[2] Department of Engineering, University of Almería, Ctra. de Sacramento s/n,
La Cañada de San Urbano, 04120 Almería, Spain
maguilar@ual.es
[3] Department of Sciences and Technologies, Centro Direzionale di Napoli,
University of Naples "Parthenope", Isola C4, Naples, Italy
claudio.parente@uniparthenope.it

Abstract. In the last decades, different Remote Sensing (RS) techniques and instruments were developed and utilized to manage and monitor the natural and semi-natural resources. Increasing the number of the sensors with the high spatial and spectral resolution, the remote sensing techniques and the Geographic Information System (GIS), provide more and detailed information, required for the precision agriculture tasks, and support, where possible, the decision-making process. The aim of this study is to develop a chain process, to obtain by using Earth Observation (EO) data, detailed information about the detection of the olive tree crowns. The Individual Tree Crown (ITC) detection process is implemented in a semi-automatic workflow based on Local Maxima Filter (LMF) applied on the Digital Aerial image and WorldView-2 (WV-2) images. The results indicate that the image data characteristics play a fundamental role to detect trees by EO data. For both datasets, the results show a higher accuracy achieved with the NDVI (Normalized Difference Vegetation Index), highlighting the spectral characteristics of the vegetation in the red and InfraRed domain.

Keywords: WorldView-2 · Digital aerial imagery · Orthorectification process · Pan-sharpening · Individual tree crown detection · Local Maxima Filter

1 Introduction

According to Gonzalez et al. [1], the availability of several very high-resolution satellite images (VHRSI) (cell size < 1 m) has increased the opportunities to map automatically different terrain features. Among these, we find the Individual Tree

© Springer Nature Switzerland AG 2020
C. Parente et al. (Eds.): R3GEO 2019, CCIS 1246, pp. 323–335, 2020.
https://doi.org/10.1007/978-3-030-62800-0_25

Crown (ITC) detection and delineation by using Earth Observation (EO) data. One of the earliest studies in this context was introduced in the mid-1980 s, using digital aerial imagery to achieve detailed forest inventory information [2]. Subsequently, several studies were executed to delineate and detect the individual tree crown, considering different vegetation types, by using EO data [3]. A wide range of algorithms was developed to detect single trees [4] and can be grouped into two general categories: i) individual tree crown detection and ii) individual tree crown delineation. Usually, the individual tree crown delineation is performed after the tree detection process, with the aim to reach a greatly [2]. A review of methods for identification of individual tree in optical images is reported by Ardila Lopez [5], describing four main approaches as: Local Maxima, Valley following, Tree modeling and image templates, Segmentation methods. However, the most frequently tested technique is Local Maxima (LM) detection. Considering this technique, it can be assumed that each tree crown is corresponding to a peak intensity in the image, and then the pixel with the maximum brightness can be related at the probable position of each tree in the image [6]. Nevertheless, the LM approach was applied mainly to detect single trees for coniferous forest inventory [7]. This approach is less accurate if applied to detect tree in orchards, commonly characterized with a less density than forests, due to the higher variability that can be found in the optical image concerning shadow, bare soil background and grass [8]. Anyway, in literature can be found several applications about the automatic tree detection to detect single trees in the orchards [9–16]. In this work, a semi-automatic process to detect individual olive tree was proposed, using the Local Maxima Filtering (LMF) on the WorldView-2 (WV-2) and Digital Aerial data.

2 Study Area

This investigation was conducted in the Vesuvian Area (Campania Region), southern Italy. The study site is located in the municipality of Torre del Greco (province of Napoli) in Campania Region. In this Vesuvian area, thanks to the high productivity of the volcanic soils [17], horticulture, orchards, vineyard, and greenhouse floriculture are the main agricultural productions. The analyses were conducted in a young and high dense olive grove, located at the foot of a lava dome (Colle di Sant'Alfonso) (center UTM WGS84 33 N Zone coordinates: E = 449,890.07 m; N = 4,514,314.38 m) (Fig. 1). In this orchard, with an extension of 0.74 ha, 317 trees were planted in 2009 with a square pattern planting (4 m × 4 m) and trained as a single trunk with the crown at about 1 m height.

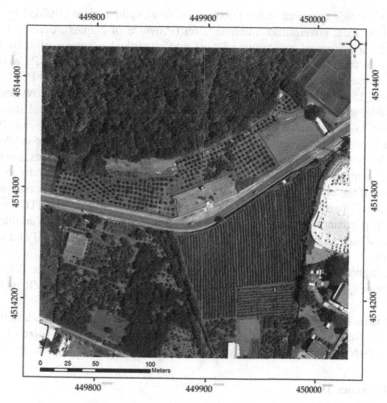

Fig. 1. Olive grove and its location in the selected study area. (Coordinate system: UTM/WGS84-33 N-zone T).

3 Datasets

3.1 Earth Observation Data

In this study, WorldView-2 (WV-2) and digital Aerial imagery were used. The WV-2 data are used in a wide range of applications, such as the production of high-resolution colored orthophoto [18], vegetation mapping [19], coastline identification [20], object-based classification [21, 22]. In fact, the high spatial resolution, as well as availability of eight spectral bands, make WV-2 as a very powerful source of information. In this study WV-2 imagery was acquired on 2015/04/22 and supplied by the provider as Ortho Ready Standard product (ORS2A), which means already rectified using average terrain elevation of the scene (low accuracy) [23]. Using the OrthoEngine tool (Version 2015) (PCI Geomatics) the dataset was orthorectified, with the aim to increase the planimetric accuracy. In details, a combination of 3D Rational Polynomial Function (3D RPFs) and 2D Polynomial Function (2D PFs) was applied [24]. In the first step, the images were orthorectified using 3D RPFs, then the resulting products were submitted to 2D PFs. Ground Control Points (GCPs) and Check Points (CPs) planimetric coordinates in UTM-WGS84 were derived from orthophotos of Campania Region with

0.20 m resolution (nominal scale: 1:5,000), while elevations were obtained by DEM, supplied by local government administration (Province of Naples), derived by lidar data, with a horizontal resolution of 1 m and a vertical accuracy of 0.16 meters (RMSE). In the first step, for the 3D RPFs application, 75 GCPs-15 CPs were considered. Subsequently, to increase the planimetric accuracy a 1st order 2D PFs using 15 GCPs and 15 CPs were performed. This approach allows to obtain low residuals; comparable with WV-2 cell size as well as to avoid other geometrical distortions associable to PFs higher order (i.e. twist with 2nd order). 3D RPFs and 2D PFs algorithms combination permitted to obtain the good results (RMSEGCPs = 0.993 m - RMSECPs = 1.324 m). For both 3D RPF as well as for 2D PF applications, the nearest neighbor algorithm was applied to resample the images, in order not to introduce variations of the initial brightness values. After the orthorectification process, properly performed on panchromatic and multispectral bands, to increase the ITC detection process performance the pan-sharpening was applied using Synthetic Variable Ratio (SVR) of Zhang [25] in order to obtain a final image with the high spatial and spectral resolution.

The higher performance, evaluated by a Visual Quality Assessment (VQA) and Quantitative Quality Assessment (QQA), has been achieved with the SVR method of Zhang.

The latter is the digital aerial imagery, supplied by local government administration (Campania Region), collected in August 2014, characterized by a cell size of 0.20 m for the VIS-NIR multispectral bands, whereas the radiometric resolution is 8 bits.

3.2   Reference Data

To verify the position of each tree a field campaign was conducted in December 2014. Previously, this spatial information was mapped with a visual interpretation of aerial photographs and WV-2 images (Fig. 2). Furthermore, the average crown diameter (ACD$_i$) was calculated of each tree, measuring with a tape measure the major (D$_i$) and the minor diameter (d$_i$) of the crown projected to the ground. The ACD$_i$, using the geometric mean, was estimated for each crown (Eq. 1), and at orchard scale (ACD$_{tot}$) (Eq. 2).

$$ACD_i = \sqrt{D_i \cdot d_i}, \tag{1}$$

$$ACD_{tot} = \frac{\sum_{i=0}^{n} \sqrt{D_i \cdot d_i}}{n}, \tag{2}$$

where, n is the total number of trees in the olive grove.

Deriving the average crown radius at orchard scale (ACR$_{tot}$) from the ACD$_{tot}$, it was possible to set the kernel size (Table 3) required for the application of the Gaussian image smoothing filter and the LM Filter (Fig. 3). More details are reported in the following subsections. The descriptive statistics from the field data are shown in Table 1.

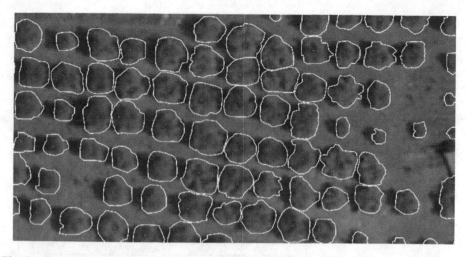

Fig. 2. The results of the visual interpretation of WV-2 and digital aerial data to map each tree crown in the parcel.

Table 1. Descriptive statistics of the tree crown diameter and tree crown radius (in meters) obtained by field measurements.

Min	Max	St. dev	ACD_{tot}	ACR_{tot}
0.9	4.5	0.5	2.7	1.3

4   Methodology

4.1   Individual Tree Crown Detection Process

To optimize the ITC detection, image pre-processing phase is required [26] selecting the best spectral band and enhancing the image data to maximize the tree detection process. In this study, the ITC detection process consists of different steps shown in Fig. (2). Each step is detailed in the following subsection.

4.2   Grey-Level Input Data (GLID)

Different illumination images were considered, with the aim to improve the accuracy of the ITC process [27]. The Grey Level Input Data (GLID) were selected to be used in the ITC detection process (Table 2).

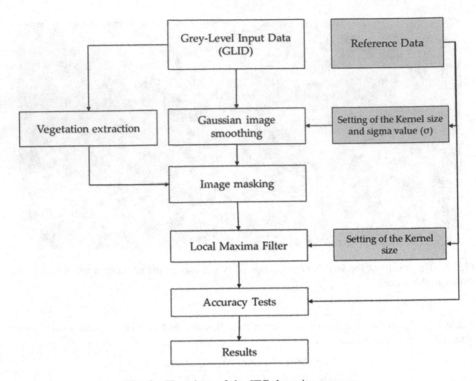

Fig. 3. Flowchart of the ITC detection process.

Table 2. GLID selected for WV-2 dataset and Aerial dataset.

GLID	WV-2	Aerial
Spectral bands	x	x
NDVI [28]	x	x
LCI (Leaf Chlorophyll Index), [29]	x	
CCCI (Canopy Chlorophyll Content Index) [30]	x	
Maccioni et al. [31]	x	
I - (Intensity component) [32]	x	x
PC1(PCA transform) [33]	x	x

4.3   Vegetation Extraction

Subsequently, for both datasets, a vegetation mask was generated, with the aim to remove from the test site no-vegetated area as soil, road, build and other man-made objects. According to Pitkänen [34] thresholding, or commonly, the binarization process is a fundamental step to separate tree crown pixels from the background. To obtain the vegetation mask, the binarization was performed on the NDVI data previously computed by using the classical formula introduced by Rouse et al. [28]. The NDVI map was classified into two classes (vegetation and no-vegetation) using the Maximum

Likelihood algorithm. The threshold values of the histogram of the NDVI image are respectively 0.24 and 0.11 for WV-2 data and Aerial data with an Overall Accuracy (OA) upper to 90% for both datasets.

4.4 Gaussian Image Smoothing

Gaussian smoothing filter was applied for each input data for reducing the noise level in the input image, enhances the tree peaks detection and theoretically minimizes the commission error in the ITC detection process [35]. According to Novotný et al., [36] and Pitkänen [34] the value of the smoothing factor (σ) and the kernel size play a fundamental role to optimize the ITC detection process. Considering the spatial resolution of WV-2 and Aerial data, a conversion of the field measurements to obtain the circle kernel size was performed (Table 3). Finally, tested σ values are 1 and 2, considering the Local Maxima Smoothing Relation (LMSR) as reported in [26]. This relation allows identifying the optimum smoothing factor considering the number of local maxima detected [37].

Table 3. Field measurement conversion to Gaussian kernel size in pixel.

ACR_{tot} (in meters)	Kernel radius (in pixel)	Dataset
1.3	3	WV-2 data
	7	Aerial data

4.5 Local Maxima Filter

The LMF was applied on the previously masked and smoothed images (SI). It allows to detect the individual tree position considering that top of each tree crows produces a local maximum value in the histogram of the optical image. In detail, considering that the local maximum is located probably at the center of the tree crown, applying the Local Maxima Filter, with a specific moving kernel, on the image, the Tree Top (TT) positions can be detected [5]. In this study, the TT detection was achieved using the Focal statistics tool, implemented in the ArcMap software. This spatial analyst tool allows performing a neighborhood operation, where the value for each output cell is a function of the values of all input cells, considering a specified neighborhood around that location. In this study, to detect tree peaks the maximum value was computed, while the neighborhood size was selected using a circle kernel as well as done for the image smoothing process (Table 3). Subsequently, the maximum values detected within each neighborhood were extracted. In detail, to find the hypothetical TT the Conditional Boolean operator (Con) was applied to find those pixels with higher values comparing SI and LMF output raster.

5 Results and Discussion

5.1 Detection Accuracy Tests

According to Ke and Quackenbush, [2], to perform detailed accuracy tests, the correspondence of the detected and reference trees must be evaluated. Therefore, in this study to estimate the accuracy of the ITC detection process, for both aerial and WV-2 images, reference data were generated by visual photointerpretation and on-screen digitizing. This procedure was validated with field survey campaigns, as described in the previous section, to confirm tree locations and estimate the crown diameter. Lamar et al., [38] assert that for ITC detection process the accuracy tests can be performed using the plot level assessment and individual tree level assessment. The Plot Level Accuracy (PLA) allows to estimate the aggregate proportion of rightly detected trees [2], comparing the total number of automatically detected trees with the total number of manually detected trees, reported in the reference data [38]. For the individual tree level assessment, the Accuracy Index (AI) was applied. Introduced by Pouliot et al., [6], this index provides the overall accuracy of the ITC detection process, considering the omission and commission errors. In detail, the omission error refers to those tree crown reference data, where tree top was undetected (Missed–M). Instead, the commission error refers to those tree tops detected out of the boundary of the tree crown reference data or when the tree top was detected as multiple trees, in the single tree reference data (False Positive-FP). Finally, with the aim to achieve a clearer overview and a more accurate quantitative analysis of the results, the specific proportion values of trees detected as Correct (C), Missed (M) (omission error) and False Positive (FP) (commission error), were estimated, as reported in the [39, 40]. For The WV-2 dataset, with a smoothing factor equal to 1, the better performance of the ITC detection process was obtained by the vegetation indices GLID. In details, using the NDVI data, a good level of overall accuracy (AI = 60%) and a low value of the commission error was achieved (FP = 2%). For the other considered GLID, as single WV-2 spectral band, I and PC1, a high value of commission and omission error was recorded. Similar results were obtained also considering a higher value of the Gaussian smoothed factor ($\sigma = 2$). In this case, with NDVI data the overall accuracy achieves a value equal to 53%, but more spectral information was lost. In fact, for each considered GLID, many trees were not detected. For the Aerial datasets, with a smoothing factor equal to 1, the better performance of the ITC detection was achieved by NDVI and NIR GLID, thanks to the spectral characteristics of the vegetation. Particularly, using the NDVI data, the tree detection process achieves an AI = 93% and low values for the omission (M = 4.7%) and commission (FP = 2.2%) error. Similar results were achieved with the NIR band (AI = 90%). However, an overestimation of the detected trees was recorded (FP = 6%) (PLA = 102.2%). This also happens for the other spectral bands of the visible, I image and PC1. In fact, the average values for the missed and false positive trees are respectively equal to 24% and 48%. Using a higher Gaussian smoothing factor ($\sigma = 2$), the better performance is carried out by the NIR band (AI of 94%). Comparable results were achieved also with the NDVI (AI = 92%). However, a higher value of the Gaussian smoothing factor determines a loss of spectral information. In fact, also for the other considered GLID, a higher omission error was recorded.

5.2 Positional Accuracy Tests

As reported in the literature, the positional accuracy can be assessed comparing the coordinates of sample points on a map with the coordinates of the same points obtained from a ground survey or other reference data [41]. This approach can be used to quantify the planimetric accuracy of the tree detected using the LMF [13, 42]. In this study, the centroids of each reference data were extracted, and its (x, y) coordinates were compared with the same coordinates of each TT correctly detected by the LMF. Subsequently, to quantify the discrepancies between reference tree location and TT position, as accuracy measure, the RMSE is considered. Based on the results achieved from the detection accuracy tests, the positional accuracy tests were performed considering those GLID characterized by acceptable values of trees correctly detected. In consideration of the results obtained with the detection accuracy tests, for the WV-2 dataset the vegetation indices GLID are chosen, while for the Aerial datasets NDVI and NIR GLID are selected. As for the detection accuracy, also for the positional accuracy, the tests were performed considering the effect of the different values of the smoothing factor. For The WV-2 dataset, with a smoothing factor equal to 1, the better positional accuracy was obtained with NDVI and LCI GLID (RMSE < 1 m). In details, the NDVI data permit to obtain an acceptable positional accuracy (RMSE = 0.70 m), considering that the cell size of the WV-2 pan-sharpened images is of 0.50 m. Similar results were obtained also with a higher value of the Gaussian smoothed factor ($\sigma = 2$). Therefore, the influence of the smoothing factor can be defined negligible. In fact, with σ equal 2, a slightly better performance was reached for the NDVI, LCI and Maccioni GLID, while for the CCCI GLID a slight worse accuracy was obtained. For the Aerial datasets, the same trend was confirmed, especially for the NIR GLID. In fact, with σ equal 2, a negligible improvement of the positional accuracy was recorded. However, the better performance was achieved by the NDVI GLID. In fact, increasing the smoothing factor ($\sigma = 2$), a better positional accuracy was reached (RMSE = 0.32) and thus comparable with the ground sample distance (GSD) of the Aerial data (0.20 m). In conclusion, the results obtained shown that, the spectral information of the considered GLID play a fundamental role in the ITC detection process. In fact, for both datasets and both accuracy tests, the better accuracy was recorded using vegetation indices as input data of the detection process, especially with the NDVI. In fact, as reported in literature [6], using the vegetation indices in the ITC detection process, permit to enhance the tree peak detection and simultaneously minimize the brightness of the no-tree peaks and soil background pixels. In consideration of the results achieved in both accuracy tests, maybe, in part, explain that the spatial resolution of the digital aerial image (0.2 m), permit to obtain a higher accuracy to detect young olive trees than WV-2 images. In fact, the performance of the ITC detection process is directly related to image scale. In other words, high spatial resolution image is required to allow an acceptable number of pixels to discriminate the tree crown from the soil background [43]. In addition, the lower accuracy, of the detection process, achieved with the WV-2 data, can be influenced also considering the high tree density (number of trees/ha). In fact, as reported in [8], one of the main problems in the ITC detection process is the high tree density, where the adjacent tree crown, appear like a continuous canopy. Regarding the positional accuracy tests, instead the performances are not much influenced by the spatial resolution. In fact, for both datasets were obtained a planimetric accuracy comparable at the cell size of the input data. However, as reported in [42], other factors can be influenced the planimetric accuracy of the individual tree crown position, detected by the LMF method as image acquisition time [8], Sun illumination [44], Sun elevation angle [16] and so on.

6 Conclusions

In this study, the Individual Tree Crown (ITC) detection process was investigated. This semi-automatic process was tested on young olive trees, applying the Local Maxima Filter (LMF) on the Digital Aerial and WorldView-2 (WV-2) images previously orthorectified and pansharpened. The results indicate that image data characteristics play a key role to detect trees by remotely sensed data. In consideration of the spectral information, for both datasets, the results show a higher accuracy achieved with the NDVI, highlighting the spectral characteristics of the vegetation. Another factor affecting tree detection was the spatial resolution of the considered images. In fact, the relationship between tree spacing/tree crown size and the spatial resolution determines different levels of accuracy. In detail, with the Digital Aerial images (cell size = 0.20 m) a higher accuracy was reached, than the WV-2 images, even if pan-sharpened (cell size = 0.50 m). In fact, with the WV-2 data, the small trees were not detected. Furthermore, the high tree density (428 trees/ha) and relative narrow tree spacing (4 × 4 m) determine that the olive tree crown appears like a continuous canopy. In fact, the soil background was not visible, because the trees, with large crown, are closed together. Concerning the positional accuracy tests confirms the reliability of the LMF method, to detect individual tree crown location. In fact, the investigated approach allows to achieve a planimetric accuracy slightly greater than the pixel size.

References

1. González, J., Galindo, C., Arevalo, V., Ambrosio, G.: Applying image analysis and probabilistic techniques for counting olive trees in high-resolution satellite images. In: Blanc-Talon, J., Philips, W., Popescu, D., Scheunders, P. (eds.) ACIVS 2007. LNCS, vol. 4678, pp. 920–931. Springer, Heidelberg (2007). https://doi.org/10.1007/978-3-540-74607-2_84
2. Ke, Y., Quackenbush, L.J.: A review of methods for automatic individual tree-crown detection and delineation from passive remote sensing. Int. J. Remote Sens. **321**(7), 4725–4747 (2011). https://doi.org/10.1080/01431161.2010.494184
3. Heenkenda, M.K., Joyce, K.E., Maier, S.W.: Mangrove tree crown delineation from high-resolution imagery. Photogram. Eng. Remote Sens. **81**(6), 471–479 (2015). https://doi.org/10.14358/PERS.81.6.471
4. Ke, Y., Quackenbush, L.J.: Comparison of individual tree crown detection and delineation methods. In: Proceedings of 2008 ASPRS Annual Conference, 2 May 2008, Portland, Oregon, USA (2008)
5. Ardila Lopez, J.P.: Object-based methods for mapping and monitoring of urban trees with multitemporal image analysis. Ph.D. dissertation, University of Twente Faculty of Geo-Information and Earth Observation (ITC), Twente, Netherlands (2012)

6. Pouliot, D.A., King, D.J., Bell, F.W., Pitt, D.G.: Automated tree crown detection and delineation in high-resolution digital camera imagery of coniferous forest regeneration. Remote Sens. Environ. **82**(2), 322–334 (2002). https://doi.org/10.1016/S0034-4257(02)00050-0

7. Gougeon, F.A., Leckie, D.G.: The individual tree crown approach applied to Ikonos images of a coniferous plantation area. Photogram. Eng. Remote Sens. **72**(11), 1287–1297 (2006). https://doi.org/10.14358/PERS.72.11.1287

8. Masson, J.: Use of very high resolution airborne and spaceborne imagery: a key role in the management of olive, nuts and vineyard schemes in the frame of the common agricultural policy of the European union. In: Proceedings of Information and Technology for Sustainable Fruit and Vegetable Production, 12–16 September 2005, FRUTIC 05, Montpellier, France, pp. 709–718 (2005)

9. Karantzalos, K.G., Argialas, D.P.: Towards automatic olive tree extraction from satellite imagery. In: Geo-Imagery Bridging Continents, 12–23 July 2004, XXth ISPRS Congress, Istanbul, Turkey, pp. 12–23 (2004)

10. Bazi, Y., Al-Sharari, H., Melgani, F.: An automatic method for counting olive trees in very high spatial remote sensing images. In: Geoscience and Remote Sensing Symposium, 2009 IEEE International, 12–17 July 2009, IGARSS 2009, Cape Town, South Africa, pp. II-125–II-128 (2009). https://doi.org/10.1109/IGARSS.2009.5418019

11. Ceylan, N., Unal, E., Masson, J.: A case study of developing an olive tree database for Turkey. Photogram. Eng. Remote Sens. **75**(12), 1397–1405 (2009). https://doi.org/10.14358/PERS.75.12.1397

12. Daliakopoulos, I.N., Grillakis, E.G., Koutroulis, A.G., Tsanis, I.K.: Tree crown detection on multispectral VHR satellite imagery. Photogram. Eng. Remote Sens. **75**(10), 1201–1211 (2009). https://doi.org/10.14358/PERS.75.10.1201

13. Santoro, F., Tarantino, E., Figorito, B., Gualano, S., D'Onghia, A.M.: A tree counting algorithm for precision agriculture tasks. Int. J. Digit. Earth **6**(1), 94–102 (2013). https://doi.org/10.1080/17538947.2011.642902

14. Caruso, T., Rühl, J., Sciortino, R., Marra, F.P., La Scalia, G.: Automatic detection and agronomic characterization of olive groves using high-resolution imagery and LIDAR data. In: SPIE Remote Sensing. International Society for Optics and Photonics, p. 92391F (2014). https://doi.org/10.1117/12.2065952

15. Díaz-Varela, R.A., de la Rosa, R., León, L., Zarco-Tejada, P.J.: High-resolution airborne UAV imagery to assess olive tree crown parameters using 3D photo reconstruction: application in breeding trials. Remote Sens. **7**(4), 4213–4232 (2015). https://doi.org/10.3390/rs70404213

16. Ozdarici-Ok, A.: Automatic detection and delineation of citrus trees from VHR satellite imagery. Int. J. Remote Sens. **36**(17), 4275–4296 (2015). https://doi.org/10.1080/01431161.2015.1079663

17. Shoji, S., Takahashi, T.: Environmental and agricultural significance of volcanic ash soils. Glob. Environ. Res. **6**(2), 113–135 (2002). English Edition

18. Belfiore, O.R., Parente, C.: Orthorectification and pan-sharpening of worldview-2 satellite imagery to produce high resolution coloured ortho-photos. Mod. Appl. Sci. **9**(9), 122–130 (2015). https://doi.org/10.5539/mas.v9n9p122

19. Wolf, A.: Using WorldView 2 Vis-NIR MSI imagery to support land mapping and feature extraction using normalized difference index ratios. In: DigitalGlobe 8-Band Research Challenge, pp. 1–13 (2010). http://www.harrisgeospatial.com/portals/0/pdfs/envi/8_bands_Antonio_Wolf.pdf. Accessed 15 Mar 2018

20. Maglione, P., Parente, C., Vallario, A.: Coastline extraction using high resolution WorldView-2 satellite imagery. Eur. J. Remote Sens. **47**, 685–699 (2014). https://doi.org/10.5721/EuJRS20144739

21. Aguilar, M.A., Bianconi, F., Aguilar, F.J., Fernández, I.: Object-based greenhouse classification from GeoEye-1 and WorldView-2 stereo imagery. Remote Sens. **6**(5), 3554–3582 (2014). https://doi.org/10.3390/rs6053554

22. Figorito, B., Tarantino, E., Balacco, G., Fratino, U.: An object-based method for mapping ephemeral river areas from WorldView-2 satellite data. In: SPIE Remote Sensing, International Society for Optics and Photonics, p. 85310B (2012). https://doi.org/10.1117/12.974689

23. DigitalGlobe. https://mdacorporation.com/docs/default-source/product-spec-sheets/geospatial-services/dg_worldview2_ds_prod.pdf?sfvrsn=4. Accessed 15 May 2018

24. Belfiore, O.R., Parente, C.: Comparison of different algorithms to orthorectify WorldView-2 satellite imagery. Algorithms **9**(4), 67 (2016). https://doi.org/10.3390/a9040067

25. Zhang, Y.: System and method for image fusion. U.S. Patent No. 7, 340, 099, 4 March 2008 (2008)

26. Pouliot, D.A., King, D.J., Pitt, D.G.: Development and evaluation of an automated tree detection delineation algorithm for monitoring regenerating coniferous forests. Can. J. For. Res. **35**(10), 2332–2345 (2005). https://doi.org/10.1139/x05-145

27. Li, Z., Hayward, R., Zhang, J., Liu, Y.: Individual tree crown delineation techniques for vegetation management in power line corridor. In: Computing: Techniques and Applications, 1–3 December 2008, DICTA 2008. Digital Image, Canberra, Australia. IEEE (2008). https://doi.org/10.1109/DICTA.2008.21

28. Rouse Jr., J.W., Haas, R.H., Schell, J.A., Deering, D.W.: Monitoring vegetation systems in the great plains with ERTS. In: Freden, S.C., Mercanti, E.P., Becker, M.A. (eds.) Third Earth Resources Technology Satellite-1 Symposium - Volume I: Technical Presentations. NASA SP-351, pp. 309–317. NASA, Washington, D.C. (1974)

29. Datt, B.: Remote sensing of water content in Eucalyptus leaves. Aust. J. Bot. **47**(6), 909–923 (1999)

30. El-Shikha, D.M., et al.: Remote sensing of cotton nitrogen status using the canopy chlorophyll content index (CCCI). Trans. ASAE (Am. Soc. Agric. Eng.) **51**(1), 73–82 (2008). https://doi.org/10.13031/2013.24228

31. Maccioni, A., Agati, G., Mazzinghi, P.: New vegetation indices for remote measurement of chlorophylls based on leaf directional reflectance spectra. J. Photochem. Photobiol. B **61**(1), 52–61 (2001)

32. Lillesand, T., Kiefer, R.W., Chipman, J.W.: Remote Sensing and Image Interpretation, 7th edn. Wiley, New York (2004)

33. Campbell, J.B., Wynne, R.H.: Introduction to Remote Sensing, 5th edn. Guilford Press, New York (2011)

34. Pitkänen, J.: Individual tree detection in digital aerial images by combining locally adaptive binarization and local maxima methods. Can. J. For. Res. **31**(5), 832–844 (2001). https://doi.org/10.1139/x01-013

35. Gebreslasie, M.T., Ahmed, F.B., Van Aardt, J.A., Blakeway, F.: Individual tree detection based on variable and fixed window size local maxima filtering applied to IKONOS imagery for even-aged Eucalyptus plantation forests. Int. J. Remote Sens. **32**(15), 4141–4154 (2011). https://doi.org/10.1080/01431161003777205

36. Novotný, J., Hanuš, J., Lukeš, P., Kaplan, V.: Individual tree crowns delineation using local maxima approach and seeded region growing technique. In: Proceedings of Symposium GIS Ostrava, pp. 27–39. Ostrava, Czech Republic, 23–26 January 2011

37. Pouliot, D., King, D.: Approaches for optimal automated individual tree crown detection in regenerating coniferous forests. Can. J. Remote Sens. **31**(3), 255–267 (2005). https://doi.org/10.5589/m05-011

38. Lamar, W.R., McGraw, J.B., Warner, T.A.: Multitemporal censusing of a population of eastern hemlock (Tsuga canadensis L.) from remotely sensed imagery using an automated segmentation and reconciliation procedure. Remote Sens. Environ. **94**(1), 133–143 (2005). https://doi.org/10.1016/j.rse.2004.09.003

39. Wulder, M., Niemann, K.O., Goodenough, D.G.: Local maximum filtering for the extraction of tree locations and basal area from high spatial resolution imagery. Remote Sens. Environ. **73**(1), 103–114 (2000). https://doi.org/10.1016/S0034-4257(00)00101-2

40. Wulder, M.A., White, J.C., Niemann, K.O., Nelson, T.: Comparison of airborne and satellite high spatial resolution data for the identification of individual trees with local maxima filtering. Int. J. Remote Sens. **25**(11), 2225–2232 (2004). https://doi.org/10.1080/014311 60310001659252

41. Congalton, R.G., Green, K.: Assessing the Accuracy of Remotely Sensed Data: Principles and Practices, 2nd edn. CRC Press, Boca Raton (2008)

42. Khalid, N., Hamid, J.A., Latif, Z.A.: Accuracy assessment of tree crown detection using local maxima and multi-resolution segmentation. In: IOP Conference Series: Earth and Environmental Science, IOP Publishing 2014, 8th International Symposium of the Digital Earth (ISDE8), 26–29 August 2013, Kuching, Sarawak, Malaysia (2014). https://doi.org/10.1088/1755-1315/18/1/012023

43. Daley, N.M., Burnett, C.N., Wulder, C.N., Niemann, K.O., Goodenough, D.G.: Comparison of fixed-size and variable-sized windows for the estimation of tree crown position. In: Geoscience and Remote Sensing Symposium Proceedings, 6–10 July 1998, pp. 1323–1326, IGARSS 1998. IEEE International, Seattle, Washington, USA (1998)

44. Ke, Y., Quackenbush, L. J.: Individual tree crown detection and delineation from high spatial resolution imagery using active contour and hill-climbing methods. In: Proceedings of 2009 ASPRS Annual Conference, American Society of Photogrammetry and Remote Sensing, 9–13 March 2009, Baltimore, Maryland, USA, pp. 9–13 (2009)

Coastline Extraction from Optical Satellite Imagery and Accuracy Evaluation

Emanuele Alcaras[1](✉) , Angela Errico[2], Ugo Falchi[1] ,
Claudio Parente[1] , and Andrea Vallario[1]

[1] DiST, Università degli Studi di Napoli "Parthenope", Naples, Italy
{emanuele.alcaras, ugo.falchi, claudio.parente,
andrea.vallario}@uniparthenope.it
[2] CIRA - Centro Italiano Ricerche Aerospaziali, Capua, Italy
a.errico@cira.it

Abstract. Different techniques can be applied for shoreline acquisition. Direct survey, based on GNSS (Global Navigation Satellite System) or total station, permits to obtain 3D information that is useful for the correct definition of the coastline also in consideration of the tidal effects. However, the acquisition of long stretches of coast using in-situ survey may be too expensive and time consuming. Additionally, many studies require to reconstruct temporal shoreline dynamics, and, in absence of survey carried out in the past, remotely sensed data may be a valuable source of information. For those reasons, there is a widespread usage of aerial and satellite imagery in many studies needing coastline detection. This research aims to analyze methodological aspects of coastline extraction from optical satellite imagery at medium and high resolution: the evaluation of the results accuracy permits to compare two different approaches based on the multispectral band use. The attention is focused on Normalized Difference Vegetation Index (NDVI) and Normalized Difference Water Index (NDWI), both applied to medium resolution imagery (Landsat 8 OLI) and to high resolution imagery (GeoEye-1). Maximum Likelihood Classification (MLC), one of the most common classification methods in remote sensing based on Bayes' Theorem, is applied to determine a threshold to separate seawater from land. An index based on the direct comparison between the automatic extracted coastline and the manually delineation of it, is used to evaluate the accuracy of the results. Both indices permit to obtain acceptable results reporting accuracy values less than the pixel dimension. However, the accuracy level of NDWI is slightly higher than NDVI.

Keywords: Coastline extraction · NDVI · NDWI · Landsat 8 OLI · GeoEye-1

1 Introduction

Several direct field and remote techniques can be used to achieve coastline position [1]. The field investigation techniques include conventional survey using optical or laser equipment [2, 3] and GNSS receivers [4–6]. The remote techniques comprise Lidar [7, 8], Synthetic Aperture Radar (SAR) [9–11], multispectral images [12, 13]. If defined as the intersection of land and water surfaces, coastline can be easily extracted from low and

© Springer Nature Switzerland AG 2020
C. Parente et al. (Eds.): R3GEO 2019, CCIS 1246, pp. 336–349, 2020.
https://doi.org/10.1007/978-3-030-62800-0_26

medium resolution satellite optical images [14], only by using spectral information because of the different nature (and signature) of the two neighboring element [15]. Sometimes, variations in coastlines are influenced by changes in tides and weather, ocean circulation, as well as anthropogenic activities, such as urbanization [16]. In these cases, more accurate results can be achieved with very high-resolution images (e.g. WorldView-2 images) because of their smaller pixel dimensions and higher number of bands [17]. Particularly, the tidal effects can strongly modify shape and position of the coastline [18]. Therefore, image date and time of acquisition by the sensor are fundamental.

Because manual delineation of coastline using remotely sensed images is particularly intensive and often subjective [19], several automatic coastline extraction methods have been developed in the last decades [20]. Different water indexes to detect the coastline from multispectral satellite images are available in literature. Mainly used for forest studies and agriculture applications, Normalized Difference Vegetation Index (NDVI) gives excellent results in coastline detection [21]. Braga et al. [22] used GeoEye-1 imagery and IKONOS imagery to detect the shoreline in Adriatic Sea area applying NDVI. To better remark water features in contrast with soil and terrestrial vegetation features, Normalized Difference Water Index (NDWI) was introduced by McFeeters [23], using reflected near-infrared radiation and visible green light. Many other researchers investigated on modified NDWI: Liu et al. [24] made an analysis of coastline extraction from Landsat 8 OLI imagery with NDWI. Wolf [25] adapted the index specifically for WorldView-2 and 3 multispectral imageries by using the coastal and near infrared -2 bands. Baiocchi et al. [26] tested the ability to automatically detect the coastline from WordView–2 imagery by applying both NDVI and NDWI, while Saeed and Fatima applied the indices to extract the coastline in Dubai's area [27]. Dai et al. [20] followed Maglione et al. [28] for adopting NDWI index for water classification. Viaña-Borja and Ortega-Sánchez [29] proposed two new indices based on band comparison (shortwave infrared in turn with green and blue) carried out on 621 sets of images. Recently, Hong et al. [30] proposed an automatic sub-pixel coastline extraction based on spectral mixture analysis adopting NDWI, and Wicaksono et al. [31] applied a semi-automatic shoreline extraction from Landsat 8 OLI using NDWI and a modified NDWI.

This paper aims to analyze coastline extraction, from optical satellite imagery at medium resolution (Landsat 8 OLI) and high resolution (GeoEye-1), applying NDVI and NDWI. Firstly, a brief description is given for the methodological approach to Landsat 8 OLI imagery regarding the whole coastline of Campania region (Italy). Secondly, an analogous description is given for the methodological approach to GeoEye-1 imagery concerning Domitian area around Volturno river mouth (Italy). Next, the results of all applications are compared and discussed. Finally, the conclusions are reported in order to remark the relevance of the work and suggest the extension of it. All of the applications are carried out in Quantum GIS 3.8.3 [32].

2   Data and Methods

All the images used in the applications described below are in GeoTIFF format [33], radiometrically pre-processed, referred to World Geodetic System (WGS84) datum and projected using the Universal Transverse Mercator system (UTM).

2.1   Landsat 8 OLI

The satellite named Landsat 8 was launched on February 11, 2013. It carries two sensors: the Operational Land Imager (OLI) and the Thermal Infrared Sensor (TIRS) [34]. All of the spectral bands are reported in Table 1.

Table 1. Characteristics of Landsat 8 OLI images.

Landsat 8 OLI		
Bands	Wavelength (μm)	Resolution (m)
Band 1 - Ultra Blue	0.435–0.451	30
Band 2 - Blue	0.452–0.512	30
Band 3 - Green	0.533–0.590	30
Band 4 - Red	0.636–0.673	30
Band 5 - Near Infrared	0.851–0.879	30
Band 6 - SWIR 1	1.566–1.651	30
Band 7 - SWIR 2	2.107–2.294	30
Band 8 - Panchromatic	0.503–0.676	15
Band 9 - Cirrus	1.363–1.384	30
Band 10 - TIRS 1	10.60–11.19	100*(30)
Band 11 - TIRS 2	11.50–12.51	100*(30)

In this work, bands from 3 to 5 are adopted for the application described in the following section. The study area has an extension of 225 Km^2 (15 km × 15 km) and includes most of Campania Region. Particularly, this area extends within the following

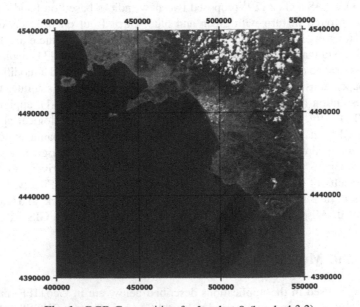

Fig. 1. RGB Composition for Landsat 8 (bands 4,3,2).

UTM/WGS84 plane coordinates - 33T zone: $E_1 = 400,000$ m, $E_2 = 550,000$ m, $N_1 = 4,390,000$ m, $N_2 = 4,540,000$ m. RGB composition obtained with bands 4,3,2, concerning the whole considered scene, is reported in Fig. 1.

2.1.1 NDVI Application

NDVI is typically used to measure the physiological activity of plants, but it permits to distinguish, in addition to vegetation, two other classes: water and bare soil. For Landsat 8 OLI images, it is calculated as follows:

$$NDVI = \frac{Band\,5 - Band\,4}{Band\,5 + Band\,4} \tag{1}$$

The NDVI formula is computed by raster calculator in QGIS, generating a new raster (Fig. 2).

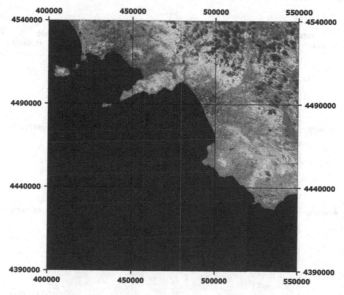

Fig. 2. Landsat 8 OLI imagery NDVI (bands 5, 4).

NDVI values are variable in the range [−1, +1]. Usually, negative values correspond to water, values close to zero correspond to soils and values from 0.2 indicate the presence of vegetated surfaces [35].

Maximum Likelihood Classification (MLC), one of the most common classification methods in remote sensing based on Bayes' Theorem [36], is applied to determine the threshold separating seawater from land. As is known, a pixel with the maximum likelihood is classified into the corresponding class [37]: the likelihood is defined as the posterior probability of a pixel belonging to class k [38]. This method can be applied also in the case of a single band, as well as synthetic band such NDVI in this case.

Particularly, training sites relating these classes are identified using the information included in the Landsat dataset, i.e. panchromatic band (characterized by a higher level of geometric resolution and a larger acquisition spectral range), RGB true color and RGB false color compositions.

2.1.2 NDWI Application

NDWI can enhance open water features by efficiently suppressing and even removing built-up land noise as well as vegetation and soil noise [39]. For Landsat 8 OLI NDWI is expressed as follows:

$$NDWI = \frac{Band\,3 - Band\,5}{Band\,3 + Band\,5} \tag{2}$$

Figure 3 shows the resulting image. It presents a major contrast between water and land than the one obtained with NDVI. The same training sites identified for NDVI classes interpretation are used for NDWI.

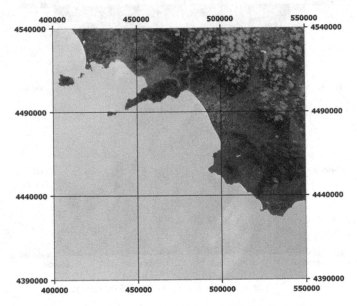

Fig. 3. Landsat 8 OLI imagery NDWI (bands 5, 3).

Similarly to what done for the previous application, MLC is used to determine threshold to separate seawater from land.

2.2 GeoEye-1

GeoEye-1 satellite, formerly known as OrbView-5, was launched on September 6, 2008. It is equipped with high resolution sensors, capable to supply panchromatic and multispectral images [40]. Table 2 reports the characteristics of GeoEye-1 images.

Table 2. Characteristics of GeoEye-1 images.

GeoEye - 1		
Bands	Wavelength (nm)	Resolution (m)
Panchromatic	450–800	0.5
Band 1 - Blue	450–510	2
Band 2 - Green	510–580	2
Band 3 - Red	655–690	2
Band 4 - Near Infrared	780–920	2

The study area has an extension of 2 Km^2 (2 km × 1 km), in the Domitian area of Castel Volturno (Campania Region). Particularly, this area extends within the following UTM/WGS84 plane coordinates – 33T zone: E_1 = 408,600 m, E_2 = 409,600 m, N_1 = 4,541,900 m, N_2 = 4,543,900 m. RGB true color composition obtained with bands 3,2,1 concerning the whole considered scene, is reported in Fig. 4.

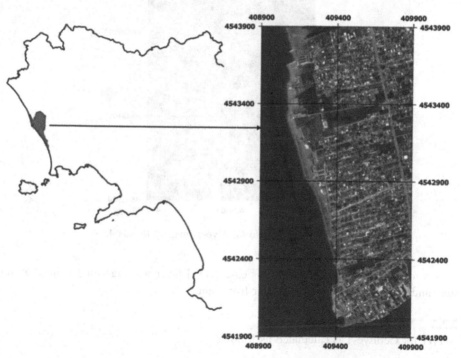

Fig. 4. Study area for NDWI application on GeoEye-1: Domitian area around Volturno river mouth (Castel Volturno).

2.2.1 NDVI Application

NDVI for GeoEye-1 is calculated as follows:

$$NDVI = \frac{Band\,4 - Band\,3}{Band\,4 + Band\,3} \qquad (3)$$

The resulting NDVI layer is shown in Fig. 5.

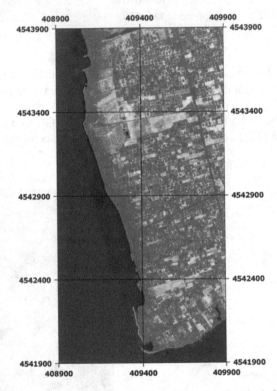

Fig. 5. NDVI applied to GeoEye-1 imagery (bands 4, 3).

As for Landsat 8 OLI, even in this case NDVI layer was classified using training sites and MLC to distinguish seawater from land.

2.2.2 NDWI Application

NDWI for GeoEye-1 is calculated as follows:

$$NDWI = \frac{Band\,2 - Band\,4}{Band\,2 + Band\,4} \qquad (4)$$

Figure 6 reports the resulting image.

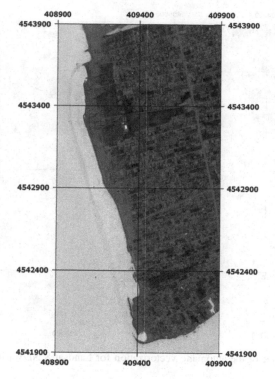

Fig. 6. NDWI applied to GeoEye-1 imagery (bands 4, 2).

In a similar way to what is done in the previous applications, MLC is applied to define the threshold separating seawater from land by using the same training sites identified for NDVI.

2.3   Coastline Automatic Extraction

Starting from NDVI and NDWI re-classed images, the automatic extraction of coastline is carried out. Particularly, GIS function is applied for vectorizing the separation lines between pixels that are differently classified (water/no-water) [41]. Figure 7 and Fig. 8 show particulars of the automatic vectorization for Landsat 8 NDWI and GeoEye-1 NDWI respectively. Figure 9 and Fig. 10 show the entire resulting vector lines (in red) for Landsat 8 NDWI and GeoEye-1 NDWI respectively.

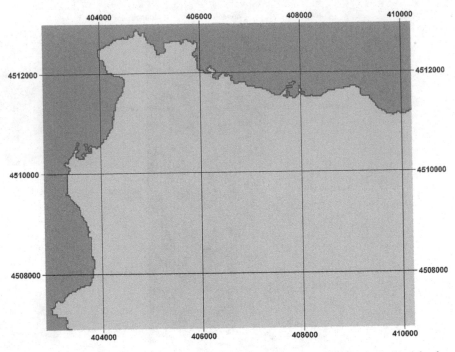

Fig. 7. Particular of the automatic vectorization for Landsat 8 NDWI in Ischia island.

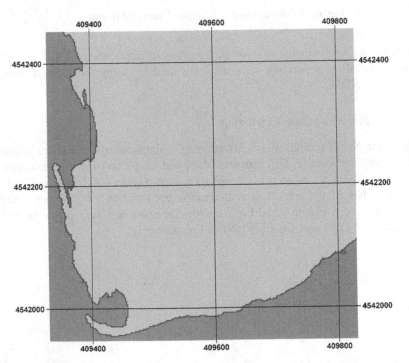

Fig. 8. Particular of the automatic vectorization for GeoEye-1 NDWI in Castel Volturno.

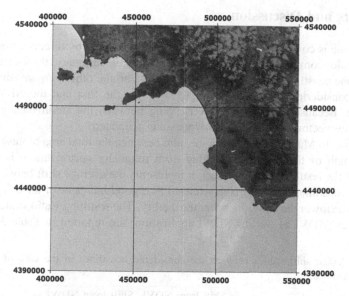

Fig. 9. Coastline extracted from NDWI applied to Landsat 8 OLI imagery.

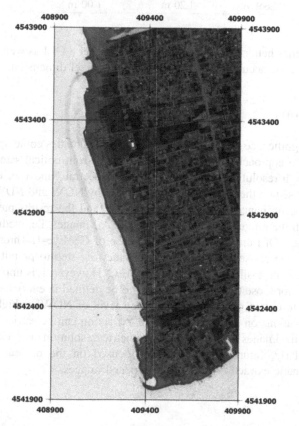

Fig. 10. Coastline extracted from NDWI applied to GeoEye-1 imagery.

3 Results and Discussion

Each coastline is compared with the corresponding obtained by direct vectorization of RGB true color composition based on visual analysis. In summary, three coastlines are achieved: one coastline is manually accomplished, and the other two are automatically extracted, considering the NDVI resulting layer for the first and the NDWI for the second one. Because of the flawed overlapping between the automatically extracted and manually vectorized coastline, polygons are generated.

According to Maglione et al. [12], the ratio between the total area of those polygons and the length of the coastline resulting from manually vectorization, is chosen as indicator of the result accuracy. In fact, it represents the average shift between the two considered coastlines, so it can be considered as a good indicator of the achieved level of quality: the lower the shift, the better the quality. The resulting Ratio values obtained in both cases (NDVI as well as NDWI application) are reported in Table 3.

Table 3. Average shift values between the considered coastlines in the case of NDVI and NDWI applications.

	Shift from NDVI	Shift from NDWI
Landsat 8 OLI	17.02 m	16.84 m
GeoEye-1	1.20 m	1.00 m

NDWI supplies better results than NDVI for Landsat 8 OLI as well as for GeoEye-1. In both cases, the accuracy value is less than the pixel dimension.

4 Conclusions

Given such a significance of coastline acquisition in Geomatics context, this paper aims at analyzing two approaches for coastline extraction from optical satellite imagery at medium and high resolution, both based on multispectral band use. Particularly, the attention is focused on the result exactness supplied by NDVI and NDWI: both indices provide good performance for coastline extraction, and the results present accuracies compatible with the reference scale of the considered images, i.e. medium scale in the case of Landsat 8 OLI and large scale in the case of GeoEye-1. Thresholds to distinguish the reference classes (water/no-water) is the first step to permit automatic vectorization and can be easily carried out using MLC. However, it is impossible to define standard values for those thresholds that need to be defined in every case. Even if both indices permit to obtain good results, accuracy level of NDWI is higher than NDVI. Further investigations on automatic coastline extraction can be carried out using other types of satellite images with different geometric resolution as well as acquisition bands. Particularly, future studies will be focused on the accuracy evaluation of coastline automatic extraction from pan-sharpened images.

Acknowledgements. This work synthesizes results of experiments performed within research activities supported by University of Naples "Parthenope".

References

1. Toure, S., Diop, O., Kpalma, K., Maiga, A.S.: Shoreline detection using optical remote sensing: a review. ISPRS Int. J. Geo-Inf. **8**, 75 (2019)
2. Delgado, I., Lloyd, G.: A simple low cost method for one person beach profiling. J Coast. Res. **20**(4), 1246–1254 (2004). https://doi.org/10.2112/03-0067R.1
3. Gens, R.: Remote sensing of coastlines: detection, extraction and monitoring. Int. J. Remote Sens. **31**(7), 1819–1836 (2010). https://doi.org/10.1080/01431160902926673
4. Gonçalves, R., Awange, J., Krueger, C.: GNSS-based monitoring and mapping of shoreline position in support of planning and management of Matinhos/PR (Brazil). J. Glob. Position. Syst. **11**, 156–168 (2013). https://doi.org/10.5081/jgps.11.2.156
5. Pardo-Pascual, J., et al.: Assessing the accuracy of automatically extracted shorelines on microtidal beaches from Landsat 7, Landsat 8 and Sentinel-2 Imagery. Remote Sens. **10**(2), 326 (2018)
6. Nugraha, W., Parapat, A.D., Arum, D.S., Istighfarini, F.: GNSS RTK application to determine coastline case study at Northern area of Sulawesi and Gorontalo. In: E3S Web of Conferences, vol. 94, p. 1016 (2019). https://doi.org/10.1051/e3sconf/20199401016
7. Stockdonf, H.F., Sallenger Jr., A.H., List, J.H., Holman, R.A.: Estimation of shoreline position and change using airborne topographic Lidar data. J. Coast. Res. **18**, 502–513 (2002)
8. Shaw, L., Helmholz, P., Belton, D., Addy, N.: Comparison of UAV Lidar and imagery for beach monitoring. Int. Arch. Photogramm. Remote Sens. Spat. Inf. Sci. 589–596 (2019). https://doi.org/10.5194/isprs-archives-xlii-2-w13-589-2019
9. Dellepiane, S., De Laurentiis, R., Giordano, F.: Coastline extraction from SAR images and a method for the evaluation of the coastline precision. Pattern Recogn. Lett. **25**(13), 1461–1470 (2004). https://doi.org/10.1016/j.patrec.2004.05.022
10. Nunziata, F., Migliaccio, M., Li, X., Ding, X.: Coastline extraction using dual polarimetric COSMO - SkyMed PingPong mode SAR data. IEEE Geosci. Remote Sens. Lett. **11**(1), 104–108 (2013). https://doi.org/10.1109/lgrs.2013.2247561
11. Bruno, M.F., Molfetta, M.G., Mossa, M., Nutricato, R., Morea, A., Chiaradia, M.T.: Coastal observation through Cosmo SkyMed high resolution SAR images. J. Coast. Res. **75**, 795–800 (2016). https://doi.org/10.2112/SI75-160.1
12. Maglione, P., Parente, C., Vallario, A.: Coastline extraction using high resolution WorldView-2 satellite imagery. Eur. J. Remote Sens. **47**(1), 685–699 (2014). https://doi.org/10.5721/EuJRS20144739
13. Bagli, S., Soille, P.: Morphological automatic extraction of pan - European coastline from Landsat ETM + images. In: International Symposium on GIS and Computer Cartography for Coastal Zone Management, pp. 256–269, October 2003
14. Sharma, R.C., Tateishi, R., Hara, K., Nguyen, L.V.: Developing superfine water index (SWI) for global water cover mapping using MODIS data. Remote Sens. **7**(10), 13807–13841 (2015). https://doi.org/10.3390/rs71013807
15. Boak, E.H., Turner, I.L.: Shoreline definition and detection: a review. J. Coast. Res. **21**(4), 688–703 (2005). https://doi.org/10.2112/03-0071.1

16. McGranahan, G., Balk, D., Anderson, B.: The rising tide: assessing the risks of climate change and human settlements in low elevation coastal zones. Environ. Urban. **19**(1), 17–37 (2007)
17. Palazzo, F., Latini, D., Baiocchi, V., Del Frate, F., Giannone, F., Dominici, D., Remondiere, S.: An application of COSMO-Sky Med to coastal erosion studies. Eur. J. Remote Sens. **45** (1), 361–370 (2012). https://doi.org/10.5721/EuJRS20124531
18. Aguilar, F.J., et al.: Preliminary results on high accuracy estimation of shoreline change rate based on coastal elevation models. Int. Archiv. Photogram. Remote Sens. Spatial Inf. Sci. **33** (8), 986–991 (2010)
19. Liu, H., Jezek, K.C.: Automated extraction of coastline from satellite imagery by integrating Canny edge detection and locally adaptive thresholding methods. Int. J. Remote Sens. **25**(5), 937–958 (2004)
20. Dai, C., Howat, I.M., Larour, E., Husby, E.: Coastline extraction from repeat high resolution satellite imagery. Remote Sens. Environ. **229**, 260–270 (2019). https://doi.org/10.1016/j.rse. 2019.04.010
21. Dominici, D., Zollini, S., Alicandro, M., Della Torre, F., Buscema, P.M., Baiocchi, V.: High resolution satellite images for instantaneous shoreline extraction using new enhancement algorithms. Geosciences **9**(3), 123 (2019). https://doi.org/10.3390/geosciences9030123
22. Braga, F., Tosi, L., Prati, C., Alberotanza, L.: Shoreline detection: capability of COSMO - SkyMed and high resolution multispectral images. Eur. J. Remote Sens. **46**(1), 837–853 (2013). https://doi.org/10.5721/EuJRS20134650
23. McFeeters, S.K.: The use of the Normalized Difference Water Index (NDWI) in the delineation of open water features. Int. J. Remote Sens. **17**(7), 1425–1432 (1996)
24. Liu, Y., Wang, X., Ling, F., Xu, S., Wang, C.: Analysis of coastline extraction from Landsat-8 OLI imagery. Water **9**(11), 816 (2017). https://doi.org/10.3390/w9110816
25. Wolf, A.F.: Using WorldView-2 Vis - NIR multispectral imagery to support land mapping and feature extraction using normalized difference index ratios. In: Algorithms and Technologies for Multispectral, Hyperspectral, and Ultraspectral Imagery XVIII, vol. 8390, p. 83900. International Society for Optics and Photonics (2012). https://doi.org/10.1117/12. 917717
26. Baiocchi, V., Brigante, R., Dominici, D., Radicioni, F.: Coastline detection using high resolution multispectral satellite images. In: Proceedings of FIG Working Week, May 2012
27. Saeed, A.M., Fatima, A.M.: Coastline extraction using satellite imagery and image processing techniques. Red 600, 720 nm (2016)
28. Maglione, P., Parente, C., Vallario, A.: High resolution satellite images to reconstruct recent evolution of Domitian coastline. Am. J. Appl. Sci. **12**(7), 506 (2015). https://doi.org/10. 5721/EuJRS20144739
29. Viaña-Borja, S.P., Ortega-Sánchez, M.: Automatic methodology to detect the coastline from landsat images with a new water index assessed on three different Spanish Mediterranean Deltas. Remote Sens. **11**(18), 2186 (2019)
30. Hong, Z., et al.: Automatic sub-pixel coastline extraction based on spectral mixture analysis using EO-1 Hyperion data. Front. Earth Sci. **13**(3), 478–494 (2018). https://doi.org/10.1007/ s11707-018-0702-5
31. Wicaksono, A., Wicaksono, P., Khakhim, N., Farda, N.M., Marfai, M.A.: Semi-automatic shoreline extraction using water index transformation on Landsat 8 OLI imagery in Jepara Regency. In: Sixth International Symposium on LAPAN-IPB Satellite, vol. 11372, p. 113721 I. International Society for Optics and Photonics, December 2019
32. QGIS 3.8.3. https://qgis.org/downloads/QGIS-OSGeo4W-3.8.3-1-Setup-x86.exe
33. Ritter, N., et al.: GeoTIFF format specification GeoTIFF revision 1.0. SPOT Image Corp, 1 (2000)

34. Du, Z., et al.: Analysis of Landsat-8 OLI imagery for land surface water mapping. Remote Sens. Lett. **5**(7), 672–681 (2014). https://doi.org/10.1109/IGARSS.2014.6946983
35. Giannini, M.B., Parente, C.: An object based approach for coastline extraction from Quickbird multispectral images. Int. J. Eng. Technol. **6**(6), 2698–2704 (2015)
36. Srivastava, P.K., Han, D., Rico-Ramirez, M.A., Bray, M., Islam, T.: Selection of classification techniques for land use/land cover change investigation. Adv. Space Res. **50** (9), 1250–1265 (2012). https://doi.org/10.1016/j.asr.2012.06.032
37. Settle, J.J., Briggs, S.A.: Fast maximum likelihood classification of remotely sensed imagery. Int. J. Remote Sens. **8**(5), 723–734 (1987)
38. Foody, G.M., Campbell, N.A., Trodd, N.M., Wood, T.F.: Derivation and applications of probabilistic measures of class membership from the maximum-likelihood classification. Photogram. Eng. Remote Sens. **58**(9), 1335–1341 (1992)
39. Xu, H.: Modification of normalised difference water index (NDWI) to enhance open water features in remotely sensed imagery. Int. J. Remote Sens. **27**(14), 3025–3033 (2006). https://doi.org/10.1080/01431160600589179
40. eoPortalDirectory, GeoEye-1 - GeoEye-1 (OrbView-5). https://earth.esa.int/web/eoportal/satellite-missions/g/geoeye-1. Access 02 Jan 2020
41. https://docs.qgis.org/2.8/en/docs/user_manual/processing_algs/gdalogr/gdal_conversion/polygonize.html

Using Images Generated by Sentinel-2 Satellite Optical Sensor for Burned Area Mapping

Domenica Costantino[1] (iD), Francesca Guastaferro[2] (iD),
Claudio Parente[3] (iD), and Massimiliano Pepe[1](✉) (iD)

[1] DICATECh, Polytechnic of Bari, via Edoardo Orabona 4, Bari, Italy
massimiliano.pepe@poliba.it
[2] AlmavivA Digitaltec, Centro direzionale, Isola F8, via Francesco Lauria,
Naples, Italy
[3] Department of Sciences and Technologies, University of Naples "Parthenope",
Centro Direzionale di Napoli, Isola C4, Naples, Italy

Abstract. Remote Sensing is identified as an effective and efficient tool for monitoring fire events, and for quantifying fire effects on environment. Satellite images are used both to identify active fires and to analyse their effects, as well as to define burnt areas and map the severity of fires. Fires modify the structure and the reflectance of vegetation as well as the soil properties within the burned area; the produced changes are detectable in the visible, infrared and microwave parts of the electromagnetic spectrum. One of the most useful approach is based on classification of images using the spectral properties of burnt residues. This paper aims to use data obtained from optical sensor mounted on Sentinel-2 platform for mapping areas damaged by fire in a precise and rapid way. Sentinel-2 offers multispectral medium and high spatial resolution images with 13 spectral bands and about 5-day temporal resolution. Two images concerning the same scene in Campania Region but acquired on different dates are considered: pre-fire and post-fire. For each image, the Normalized Burned Ratio Index (NBR) is calculated, which allows to identify the areas affected by the fire and the relative degree of severity. Using change detection techniques, burned map can be identified. The evaluation of the accuracy is carried out using some indexes widespread in remote sensing literature, such as User's Accuracy, Producer's Accuracy, Overall Accuracy and Kappa coefficient. The values obtained in the confusion matrix showed the high quality of the developed method based on the use of the NBR index.

Keywords: NBR (Normalized Burned Ratio Index) · Sentinel-2 · Burned area · Change detection

1 Introduction

Forest fires represent a real and increasing threat throughout the Europe, particularly in Greece, Spain, France, Italy and Portugal, where very severe weather conditions have contributed to increase the number of fires observed in recent decades [1].

Accurate information on the location and extent of a forest area destroyed by a fire is fundamental in order not only to assess the economic losses and environmental

© Springer Nature Switzerland AG 2020
C. Parente et al. (Eds.): R3GEO 2019, CCIS 1246, pp. 350–362, 2020.
https://doi.org/10.1007/978-3-030-62800-0_27

impacts, but also to monitor land use and their changes. Every time it is necessary realized the mapping of forest cover, the estimation of biomass and biodiversity as well as the assessment of impacts of extreme events such as drought on the forest, remote sensing is welcome because it allows having a global coverage [2]. In fact, satellite images consent low cost, rapid and regular coverage of the often extensive and inaccessible areas affected by fire; in addition, they allow collecting data acquired in near-infrared and thermal region of the electromagnetic spectrum [3].

In other terms, remote sensing is a cheap and efficient technique that allows having a global coverage, but also helps to analyse: the location of fires, the intensity of the phenomena, the extent of burned areas and the damage caused [4, 5].

Satellite imagery is used both to identify the active fires as well as to analyse the effects of the same and in particular, to define burnt areas. Burned areas can be mapped through the acquisition of low, medium or high spatial resolution remote sensed imagery. The identification and georeferencing of surfaces covered by fire through remote sensing is based on the recognition of the spectral response of burned vegetation that is typically different from not burnt surface. In general, while the "active fires" are studied by satellite sensors with bands in the infrared (IR) medium (MIR) and thermal (TIR) and with a high temporal frequency [6], the burned areas are studied using the spectral bands of Visible, Near Infrared (NIR) and Shortwave Infrared (SWIR) with different spatial resolution sensors [5, 7, 8].

This paper aims to highlight the use of data obtained from optical sensor mounted on Sentinel 2 platform for mapping areas damaged by fire in a precise and rapid way. Sentinel-2 supplies multispectral medium and high spatial resolution images (10, 20 and 60 m, depending on the native resolution of the different spectral bands) with 13 spectral bands and about 5-day temporal resolution. The download of Sentinel 2 data takes place with a specific level of pre-processing of the images (Level-2A); the granules (also called tiles) have a dimension of 100 km^2 ortho-images in UTM/WGS84 projection. Particularly, the results are obtained with the application of Normalized Burned Ratio Index (NBR) on two images concerning the same scene in Campania Region but acquired on different dates: pre-fire and post-fire. NBR allows to identify the areas affected by the fire and the relative degree of severity. Using change detection techniques, burned map are identified.

The paper is organized as follows. Section 2 resumes the main characteristics of the Sentinel-2 data and their possible usage for burned area detection. Section 3 describes the dataset used for this study and the methodological approach adopted for it; particularly, Normalized Burned Ratio Index (NBR) is introduced and described, while the index values resulting from confusion matrix on test sites, are reported for accuracy evaluation of the final classification. Finally, Sect. 4 presents our conclusions.

2   Sentinel-2 Data and Possible Usage for Burned Area Detection

Developed by the European Space Agency (ESA), the Copernicus Sentinel-2 mission comprises a constellation of two polar-orbiting satellites placed in the same sun-synchronous orbit, phased at 180° to each other (https://sentinel.esa.int/web/sentinel/missions/sentinel-2).

Copernicus is the Earth observation programme developed by European Union, coordinated and managed by the European Commission in partnership with the European Space Agency (ESA), the EU Member States and EU Agencies. Introduced by the Regulation (EU) No 377/2014 in 2014, the Copernicus programme was founded on GME, the previous EU's Earth monitoring initiative established by Regulation (EU) No 911/2010. This programme aims to integrate a vast amount of global data obtained by the Copernicus environmental satellites, air and ground stations and sensors to provide timely and quality information on the health of Earth. In this way, Copernicus make available information on environment and security in order to help public authorities and other international organizations for improving the quality of life for the citizens of Europe. Copernicus counting three components:

- The space part including observation satellites and associated ground segment with missions to monitor land, atmosphere and oceans;
- In-situ measurements including ground-based and airborne data networks to make available information on the Earth surface, atmosphere and oceans;
- Services developed and managed by Copernicus for public usage.

The first component includes two types of satellite missions: ESA's Sentinel missions and Contributing Missions from other space agencies. Each Sentinel mission is based on a constellation of two satellites to monitor land, ocean and atmospheric parameters using radar and super-spectral imaging. The first satellite, Sentinel-1A, was launched on 3 April 2014while Sentinel-1B was launched on 25 April 2016. They carry a C-band synthetic-aperture radar instrument which provides a collection of data in all-weather, day or night, useful for applying Differential Interferometry Synthetic Aperture Radar (DInSAR) for ground deformation detection [9–11]. At present Sentinel-1, Sentinel-2 and Sentinel-3 are operative while Sentinel-4, Sentinel-5 and Sentinel-6 are scheduled for the next years; however Sentinel-5 Precursor (P) satellite is already in orbit to close the gap in continuity of observations between Envisat and Sentinel-5. The Sentinel-2 mission allows to achieve many purposes since that it is able to acquire data of the observed scene in wide swath width (290 km) and high revisit time (10 days at the equator with one satellite, and 5 days with 2 satellites under cloud-free conditions, which results in 2–3 days at mid-latitudes). The coverage limits are from between latitudes 56° south and 84° north. The Sentinel-2 satellites are equipped with the MSI (MultiSpectral Instrument) instrument able to acquire 4 bands in the visible and near infrared with 10 m spatial resolution, 6 infrared bands with 20 m spatial resolution and 3 bands with 60 m resolution of which one in the blue (coastal aerosol) and two in the infrared (See Table 1).

Table 1. Bands, wavelength and spatial resolution in Sentinel-2

Sentinel-2 bands	Sentinel-2A (nm)		Sentinel-2B(nm)		Spatial resolution (m)
	Central wavelength	Bandwidth	Central wavelength	Bandwidth	
Band 1 – Coastal aerosol	442.7	21	442.2	21	60
Band 2 – Blue	492.4	66	492.1	66	10
Band 3 – Green	559.8	36	559.0	36	10
Band 4 – Red	664.6	31	664.9	31	10
Band 5 – Vegetation red edge	704.1	15	703.8	16	20
Band 6 – Vegetation red edge	740.5	15	739.1	15	20
Band 7 – Vegetation red edge	782.8	20	779.7	20	20
Band 8 – NIR	832.8	106	832.9	106	10
Band 8A – Narrow NIR	864.7	21	864.0	22	20
Band 9 – Water vapour	945.1	20	943.2	21	60
Band 10 – SWIR – Cirrus	1373.5	31	1376.9	30	60
Band 11 – SWIR	1613.7	91	1610.4	94	20
Band 12 – SWIR	2202.4	175	2185.7	185	20

Sentinel-2 produces several levels of data, as follow reported [12]:

- Level-0 is compressed raw data. The Level-0 product contains all the information required to generate the Level-1 (and upper) product levels.
- Level-1A is uncompressed raw data with spectral bands coarsely co-registered and ancillary data appended.
- Level-1B data is radiometrically corrected radiance data. The physical geometric model is refined using available ground control points and appended to the product, but not applied.
- Level-1C product provides orthorectified Top-Of-Atmosphere (TOA) reflectance, with sub-pixel multispectral registration. Cloud and land/water masks are included in the product. The ground sampling distance of Level-1C product will be 10 m, 20 m or 60 m according to the band. The final Level-1C product is tiled following a pre-defined grid of 100 × 100km², based on UTM/WGS84 reference frame
- Level-2A product provides orthorectified Bottom-Of-Atmosphere (BOA) reflectance, with sub-pixel multispectral registration. A Scene Classification map (cloud, cloud shadows, vegetation, soils/deserts, water, snow, etc.) is included in the product.

– Level-1C and Level-2A products are made available to users via the Copernicus Open Access Hub, while Level-0, Level-1A and Level-1B products are not disseminated to users.

To detect burned areas, specific indexes have been successfully applied in the last decades using images obtained from sensors mounted on satellite platforms. Indeed, many works were carried out at the beginning of this century based on Landsat 7 ETM + data usage, particularly on the joint use of NIR band between 760–900 nm and a SWIR band between 2080–2350 nm, both presenting pixel size 30 m × 30 m.

Recently, the Copernicus Sentinel-2 mission allowed to obtain a NIR region with different and higher geometric resolutions: the band 8 (NIR) has a resolution of 10 m and the band 8A (Narrow NIR) with a geometric resolution of 20 m. As regards the SWIR region, Sentinel-2 provides two bands with the same geometric resolution (20 m) but with different wavelength. Indeed, the band 11 works with a central wavelength of 1613.7 nm (Sentinel-2A) and 1610.4 (Sentinel-2B) while the band 12 use a central wavelength of 2202.4 nm (Sentinel-2A) and 2185.7 (Sentinel-2B).

Therefore, considering the high geometric resolution achieved by Sentinel-2 bands, it is possible to identify even the small burned areas, as shown in Pepe and Parente, 2018 [13]. On the other side, the availability of multispectral sensors on board different satellites, i.e. Landsat 8 and Sentinel-2, permits to perform high-frequency time series analyses, so to expand the opportunities to perform multi-temporal change detection studies on phenomena characterized by a significant dynamic behaviour (like fires) [14].

3   Data and Methods

3.1   Datasets

The Sentinel-2A datasets used in this study were produced by radiometric and geometric corrections, including ortho-rectification and spatial registration on a global reference system with sub-pixel accuracy.

The Sentinel-2 datasets have been downloaded from ESA website (https://scihub. copernicus.eu/). The datasets used for this experimentation taking into account the conditions of pre and post-fire of the 12th July 2017 are:

– Level 2A:
  – Pre- fire
    • S2A_MSI-
      L2A_20170518T095031_N0205_R079_T33TVF_20170518T095716.SAFE
– Post- fire
  • S2A_MSI-
    L2A_20170806T095031_N0205_R079_T33TVF_20170806T095744.SAFE

As is known, a remote sensing image can be represented in false-colour (or also called "pseudo-colour").

This type of representation is useful to visualize the wavelengths that the human eye does not see (i.e. near infrared and beyond). In fact, false colour images are a representation of a multispectral image created using any bands as the red, green and blue components of the display.

The use of some bands increases spectral separation and can enhance the interpretability of data. There are many different false colour compositions that can distinguish many different functions.

A representation in true-colour and one in the false-colour of the same scene (pre and post fire) are shown respectively in Fig. 1a and in Fig. 1b for pre fire and 2a, 2b and 2c figures for post fire.

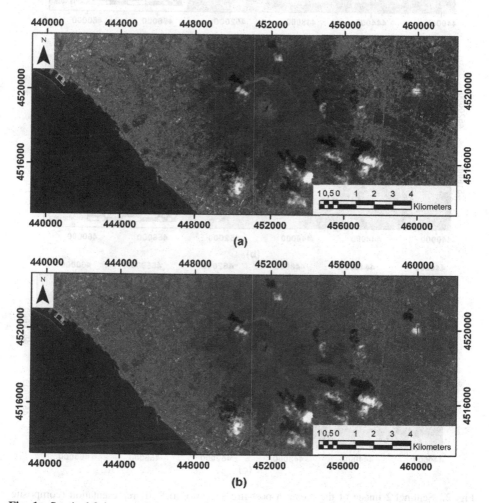

(a)

(b)

Fig. 1. Sentinel-2 image of the scene in pre-fire scenario. a) RGB representation (composite bands 4-3-2); b) False colour representation (composite bands 6-3-2). (Color figure online)

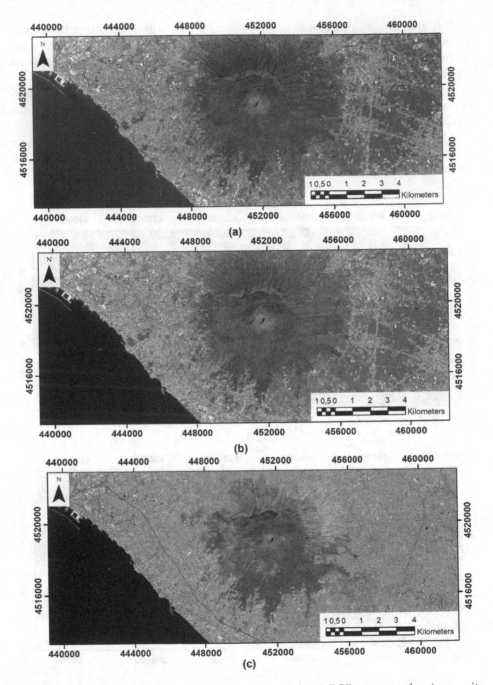

Fig. 2. Sentinel-2 image of the scene in post-fire scenario. a) RGB representation (composite bands 4-3-2); b) False colour representation (composite bands 6-3-2); c) False colour representation (composite bands 12-8-4) (Color figure online)

In Fig. 2b it is possible to note, as the burned areas are easily recognizable with the combination of the Vegetation Red Edge, Green and Blue bands (6-3-2 bands) where burnt areas are in red. Instead, in RGB colour representation (Fig. 2a), burned areas are shown in grey colour.

3.2 Difference Normalized Burn Ratio (dNBR)

In this work, burnt areas are extracted by using differenced Normalized Burn Ratio (dNBR). It is calculated starting from the Normalized Burn Ratio (NBR) index applied to pre and post fire images.

The NBR formula is like NDVI but it combines near-infrared (NIR) and short-wave-infrared (SWIR) bands for its calculation, as shown in the following formula:

$$NBR = \frac{(\rho_{NIR} - \rho_{SWIR})}{(\rho_{NIR} + \rho_{SWIR})} \tag{1}$$

Considering there are two Sentinel-2A MSI NIR bands, the formulation of the NBR index can be obtained as [15]:

$$NBR = \frac{(b8A - b12)}{(b8A + b12)} \tag{2}$$

Another way to calculate the NBR index is [16]:

$$NBR = \frac{(b8 - b12)}{(b8 + b12)} \tag{3}$$

Since bands 12 and 8A both have a resolution of 20 m, band 8A was chosen over band 8, which has a 10 m resolution.

Figure 3 shows NBR index applied to pre and post fire scenario.

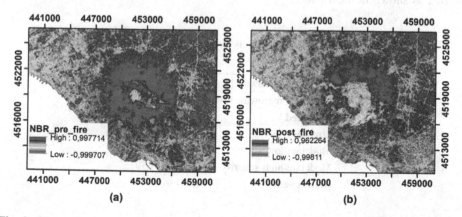

Fig. 3. Thematic map about NBR: a) NBR map in pre-fire scenario; b) NBR map in post-fire scenario. (Color figure online)

3.3 Calculation of dNBR in Pre-fire and Post-fire Scenario

Created pre- and post-fire NBR images, the post-fire image was subtracted from the pre-fire image to create a differenced (or delta) NBR image that indicates burn severity. In other words, change detection analysis was carried out using direct comparison of the NBR images. Particularly, the difference of Normalized Burn Ratio index in the condition of pre and post-fire was used according to the following formula:

$$dNBR = NBR_{pre-fire} - NBR_{post-fire} \tag{4}$$

The resulting image produced by difference of NBR is shown in the Fig. 4.

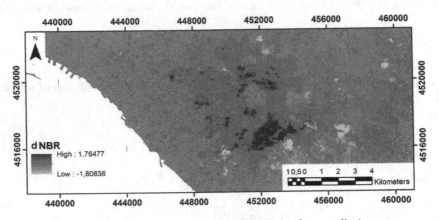

Fig. 4. Thematic map about dNBR. (Color figure online)

Starting from the *dNBR* map, it was necessary to create a severity fire map. The USGS FireMon program, a National Burn Severity Mapping Project of the U.S. Geological Survey, indicates seven severity levels to map the burned areas from dNBR, as shown in the Table 2.

Table 2. Ordinal severity levels range of dNBR (scaled by 10^3)

Severity level	dNBR range
Enhanced regrowth, high	−500 to −251
Enhanced regrowth, low	−250 to −101
Unburned	−100 to +99
Low severity	+100 to +269
Moderate-low severity	+270 to +439
Moderate-high severity	+440 to +659
High severity	+660 to +130

Considering the severity level range suggested by USGS, the dNBR map was reclassified: a new map was created in relation to the severity of burn in 7 classes, as shown in the Fig. 5.

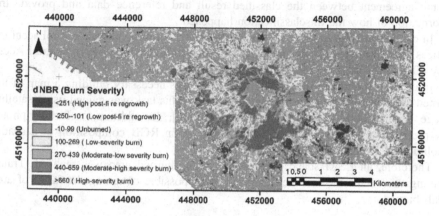

Fig. 5. Thematic map about dNBR (scaled by 10^3) in relation to burn severity. (Color figure online)

In order to identify the pixel burned as a single class, a map reclassification was performed. In other words, a suitable threshold value, among those suggested and indicated in Table 2, was used to distinguish the entire study area in two classes: burned and unburned zones. Since this threshold value may change in relation to the scene, the desired value was obtained by iterative method on some test areas by photointerpretation on colour images with a high geometric resolution. Therefore, pixels with a value greater than those of the threshold (250) are classified as burned pixels (Fig. 6).

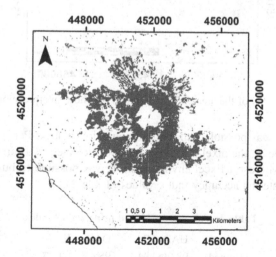

Fig. 6. Map of the area classified burned by the use of remotely sensed images and change detection techniques.

3.4   Evaluation of the Accuracy of the dNBR

To verify the accuracy of the thematic map reported in the previous figure, the confusion matrix technique was applied. This matrix can provide the detailed assessment of the agreement between the classified result and reference data and provide the information of how the misclassification happened.

In order to analyse the quality of the remote sensing index tested, several accuracy indices were used: User's Accuracy (UA), Producer's Accuracy (PA), Overall Accuracy (OA) and Kappa coefficient (k) [17].

In order to calculate these quality indexes, it was necessary building a map of the burned area obtained by photo-interpretation task. This task was gained using satellite image with a high geometric resolution [18–20]. In addition, a further photo-interpretation was carried out on Sentinel images in RGB composition at a spatial resolution of 10 m.

Therefore, an ESRI shape polygon file of the burned area was realized. Transforming this vector file in raster (Fig. 7), it was possible obtaining the raster of area (real) burned.

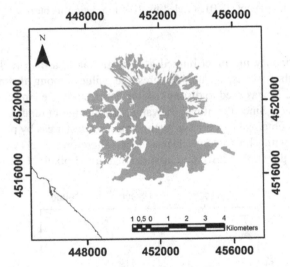

Fig. 7. Map of the area classified burned by photo-interpretation task.

In this way, it was possible building the confusion matrix. Performing in ArcGIS software a compute on the pixel classified in a specific category (burned or unburned), subsequently, in Microsoft Excel environment, it was possible to build the confusion matrix and calculate the accuracy index values (Table 3).

Table 3. Accuracy achieved using *dNBR* index

	UA	PA	OA	K
Burned	98,9%	84,3%	95,4%	89,7%
Unburned	94,4%	99,6%		

4   Conclusions

In this paper it was shown as the use of NBR index applied to post-fire satellite images, allowed to identify the burned area in forest area in reliable way. Indeed, considering this index in pre-fire e post-fire condition, it was possible to build a thematic map of the burned area by the use of "change detection analysis".

According to the USGS FireMon program, seven severity level classes were distinguished in the study area starting from dNBR values. Then, in order to identify the pixel burned, a reclassification was performed calculating a suitable threshold value by iterative method based on photointerpretation: using colour images with a high geometric resolution, some test areas were manually classified in burned/no-burned and used to define the dNBR value separating from each other class. The confusion matrix shows high values (%) of the accuracy indexes and, of consequence, a high degree of reliability of the adopted approach.

As regards the satellite images acquired with Sentinel-2, the high spatial resolution, the multi-spectrality of the images and the high temporal frequency, allowed mapping burnt areas.

References

1. Turco, M., et al.: Decreasing fires in mediterranean Europe. PLoS One **11**(3), e0150663 (2016)
2. Foody, G.M.: Remote sensing of tropical forest environments: towards the monitoring of environmental resources for sustainable development. Int. J. Remote Sens. **24**(20), 4035–4046 (2003). https://doi.org/10.1080/0143116031000103853
3. Flasse, S.P., et al.: Remote sensing of vegetation fires and its contribution to a management fire information system. In: Wildland Fire Management Handbook for Sub-Sahara Africa, Goldammer, J.G., de Ronde, N.C. (eds.) Global Fire Management Center, pp. 158–211 (2004). ISBN 1- 919833-65-X
4. Chuvieco, E., Deshayes, M., Stach, N., Cocero, D., Riaño, D.: Short-term fire risk: foliage moisture content estimation from satellite data. In: Chuvieco, E. (ed.) Remote Sensing of Large Wildfires in the European Mediterranean Basin, pp. 17–38. Springer, Heidelberg (1999). https://doi.org/10.1007/978-3-642-60164-4_3
5. Mitri, G., Gitas, J.: A semi-automated object-oriented model for burned area mapping in the Mediterranean region using Landsat -TM imagery. Int. J. Wildland Fire **13**, 367–376 (2004)
6. Ceccato, P., Flasse, S., Downey, I.D.: An automatic algorithm to detect vegetation fires globally from NOAA-AVHRR. Data Adv. Remote Sens. **4**(4), 84–89 (1996)
7. Tansey, K., et al.: A global inventory of burned areas at 1 km resolution for the year 2000 derived from spot vegetation data. Clim. Change **67**, 345–377 (2004). https://doi.org/10.1007/s10584-004-2800-3
8. Roy, D.P., Boschetti, L., Trigg, S.N.: Remote sensing of fire severity: assessing the performance of the normalized burn ratio. IEEE Geosci. Remote Sens. Lett. **3**, 112–116 (2006)
9. Barreca, G., et al.: An integrated geodetic and InSAR technique for the monitoring and detection of active faulting in southwestern Sicily. Ann. Geophys. **63**, 1–11 (2020)

10. Barra, A., Monserrat, O., Mazzanti, P., Esposito, C., Crosetto, M., Scarascia Mugnozza, G.: First insights on the potential of Sentinel-1 for landslides detection. Geomat. Nat. Hazards Risk **7**(6), 1874–1883 (2016)
11. Devanthéry, N., Crosetto, M., Monserrat, O., Cuevas-González, M., Crippa, B.: Deformation monitoring using Sentinel-1 SAR data. Multi. Digit. Publishing Inst. Proc. **2**(7), 344 (2018)
12. Baillarin, S.J., et al.: Sentinel-2 level 1 products and image processing performances. In: International Geoscience and Remote Sensing Symposium (IGARSS), pp. 7003–7006 (2012). Art. no. 6351959
13. Pepe, M., Parente, C.: Burned area recognition by change detection analysis using images derived from Sentinel-2 satellite: the case study of Sorrento peninsula, Italy. J. Appl. Eng. Sci. **16**(2) 225–232 (2018)
14. Mandanici, E., Bitelli, G.: Preliminary comparison of Sentinel-2 and Landsat 8 imagery for a combined use. Remote Sens. **8**, 101 (2016)
15. Huang, H., et al.: Separability analysis of Sentinel-2A multi-spectral instrument (MSI) data for burned area discrimination. Remote Sens. **8**(10), 873 (2016)
16. Hawryło, P., Bednarz, B., Wężyk, P., Szostak, M.: Estimating defoliation of Scots pine stands using machine learning methods and vegetation indices of Sentinel-2. Eur. J. Remote Sens. **51**(1), 194–204 (2018)
17. Congalton, R.G., Green, K.: Assessing the Accuracy of Remotely Sensed Data: Principles and Practices. CRC Press, Boca Raton (2019)
18. Parente, C., Pepe, M.: Bathymetry from worldview-3 satellite data using radiometric band ratio. Acta Polytechnica **58**(2), 109–117 (2018)
19. Baiocchi, V., Dominici, D., Giannone, F., Zucconi, M.: Rapid building damage assessment using EROS B data: the case study of L'Aquila earthquake. Italian J. Remote Sens. Rivista Italiana di Telerilevamento **44**(1), 153–165 (2012)
20. Pipitone, C., Maltese, A., Dardanelli, G., Lo Brutto, M., La Loggia, G.: Monitoring water surface and level of a reservoir using different remote sensing approaches and comparison with dam displacements evaluated via GNSS. Remote Sens. **10**(1), 71 (2018)

Monitoring Strategies of Displacements and Vibration Frequencies by Ground-Based Radar Interferometry

Giovanni Nico[1] , Giuseppina Prezioso[2]([✉]) , Olimpia Masci[3] ,
and Yuta Izumi[4]

[1] Istituto per le Applicazioni del Calcolo, Consiglio Nazionale delle Ricerche,
70126 Bari, Italy
g.nico@ba.iac.cnr.it
[2] Dipartimento di Scienze e Tecnologie, Università degli Studi
di Napoli "Parthenope", 80143 Naples, Italy
prezioso@uniparthenope.it
[3] DIAN S.r.l, 75100 Matera, Italy
[4] Graduate School of Environmental Studies, Tohoku University,
Sendai, Miyagi 980-8576, Japan

Abstract. In this work we present an overview of ground-based radar inter-ferometry applications, using both real and synthetic aperture configurations, to measure deformations and vibration frequencies of infrastructures and terrain displacement due to geological phenomena. A short introduction to the basic principles of ground-based radar interferometry and the concept of interfero-metric coherence is provided. The interferometric processing of radar data provides the measurement of the Line-of-Sight (LoS) displacement with a sub-millimeter precision. In this paper we show results obtained in the monitoring of landslides, piers, dams, towers and bridges. Results have been obtained by means of a ground-based radar sensor working in the Ku-band with a range resolution of 0.75 m. Furthermore, we provide a review of literature on ground-based radar applications to volcano and glacier monitoring and measurement of vibration frequencies telecommunication and wind towers. The issues of mea-surement precision and artifacts due to propagation in the atmosphere are also discussed.

Keywords: Ground-Based Synthetic Aperture Radar (GBSAR) · SAR interferometry · Displacement · Vibration frequency · Landslides · Bridges · Dams

1 Introduction

Ground-based radar interferometry relies on the application of the principles of radar interferometry to data acquired by a ground-based radar system that observes a scene from the same location at different times. The basics concept is that of Real Aperture Radar (RAR) system which is a stepped-frequency continuous-wave (SF-CW) radar that emits a continuous wave with different progressive frequencies within a given frequency

© Springer Nature Switzerland AG 2020
C. Parente et al. (Eds.): R3GEO 2019, CCIS 1246, pp. 363–374, 2020.
https://doi.org/10.1007/978-3-030-62800-0_28

band. The corresponding echoes, backscattered by the scene, give rise to the raw data. If the radar system is sled along a rail of finite length, changing its position with a constant step, a SAR system is obtained where the SF-CWs, with increasing frequencies, are transmitted, and the corresponding echoes received, at each position of the rail. In the case of a SAR system, the raw data structure consists of a matrix with the number of columns, given by the acquisition positions along the rail, and rows, given by the transmitted frequencies. Recently, it has been demonstrated that the data acquisition time can be reduced and the need for a rail released using a multiple input multiple output (MIMO) arrays [1–3]. Passive Bistatic GBSAR (PB-GBSAR) systems exploit an existing non-cooperative signal (e.g., broadcasting signal, communication signal, or navigation signal) to replace the GBSAR transmitter have been proposed [4, 5]. The main advantage of PB-GBSAR is the possibility to deploy only receiving radar sensors, so simultaneously measuring displacements along different Line-of-Sights (LoS) directions using the same spaceborne transmitter. In this paper, we provide an overview of applications developed using both RAR and SAR ground-based interferometers, emphasizing the enhancements that could be achieved using the most recent MIMO and PB-GBSAR advancements. The structure of the paper is as follows. Section 2 summarizes the basic principles of RAR and SAR interferometry. Section 3 provides an overview of applications of this technique to the measurements of displacements and vibrations frequencies in the monitoring of landslides, dams, piers, retaining walls, bridges and monuments. The precision and accuracy that can be attained by this technique, as well as the impact of propagation delay in the lower troposphere on the displacement and vibration measurements are discussed in Sect. 4. Finally, a few conclusions are drawn in Sect. 5.

2   Ground-Based Radar Interferometry Principle

Ground-based radar interferometry relies on the application of the principles of radar interferometry to radar data. Given two radar datasets S_1 and S_2, acquired at times t_1 and t_2, and co-registered on the same grid, usually corresponding to one of the two images, the interferometric phase is computed as follows:

$$\Delta \varphi_{1,2} = atan\{S_2 \cdot conj(S_1)\} \tag{1}$$

The LOS displacement $D_{1,2}$ of a point P, occurred in the time interval, $[t_1, t_2]$ is related to the interferometric phase $\Delta \varphi_{1,2}$ by the relationship:

$$D_{1,2} = \frac{\lambda}{4\pi} \Delta \varphi_{1,2} \tag{2}$$

where λ is the radar wavelength. The precision of displacement measurements depends on the accuracy of phase measurements and the wavelength. In Ku band, it can be a fraction of a millimeter, if artifacts due to phase propagation in atmosphere are identified and corrected (e.g. [6], where an experiment with a corner reflector mounted on a micrometric screw is described). Radar datasets can be 1D profiles, where target are discriminated based on their range distance with respect to the location of radar. This

1D profiles are obtained using the so-called Real Aperture Radar (RAR) configuration, with static TX/RX antennas. If the couple of TX/RX antennas are moved along a rail, or more TX and RX antennas are mounted along a linear structure as in 1D MIMO radars, we have a Synthetic Aperture Radar (SAR) configuration which can provide 2D SAR images where target are discriminated based on both their range distance and azimuth position, measured along the direction of rail, or linear structure in MIMO radars. For both RAR and SAR configurations, it is possible to use only RX antennas collecting an opportunity signal transmitted e.g. by a telecommunication satellite and scattered by a target in the imaged scene. Such an acquisition configuration can be used to provide Passive Bistatic RAR and SAR images [5].

3 Overview of Ground-Based Radar Applications

This section provides an overview of main applications of ground-based radar interferometry of interest for geomatics and monitoring purposes. Monitoring of bridges was one of the first applications since this technique was developed [7]. The current use of ground-based radar interferometry relies on a RAR configuration to build a time series of displacements. Figure 1 shows two examples, one related to the displacement of the platform of a bridge when a train is crossing it (Fig. 1 (top)), the other measuring the displacements of the fence on the two sides of the bridges (Fig. 1 (bottom)). The main applications of such measurements is in the area of static and dynamic assessment of bridges [6, 8–10]. In particular, an example of static assessment of a bridge is reported in [6]. Concerning the dynamic assessment, Fig. 2 shows the times series of displacements of main structural elements of a bridge and the corresponding spectra of vibration frequencies. The main output of this analysis is the measurement of natural frequencies of bridge. A ground-based radar in RAR configuration has been also used to measure the vibration frequencies of towers [11, 12], including telecommunication and wind towers [13, 14], and for the seismic assessment of dam concrete infrastructures [15]. The use of both RAR and SAR configurations in ground-based radar acquisitions for the dam monitoring has been detailed in [15], where new visualization tools have been described. In particular, acquisitions using SAR configurations allows to map the displacement of dam surfaces instead of measuring displacements in a few points usually on the crown of dam surface [15, 16]. For this specific application of dam monitoring, ground-based SAR interferometry can integrate the information provided by spaceborne SAR interferometry, GNSS and geodetic techniques [17–23]. An example of application of ground-based radar to measure the displacement pattern of a pier during a bollard-pull trial is described in [24]. Figure 3-(a) displays the amplitude maps of the scene. A set of corner reflectors has been deployed on the pier to mitigate the impact of grazing-angle radar acquisitions and materialize a few measurement points. These targets appear as red-colored spots and are characterized by a high interferometric coherence (see Fig. 3-(b)). The coherence is then used to mask out noisy pixels in the interferogram displayed in Fig. 3-(c) and provide the displacement map of Fig. 3-(d). The comparison of radar and levelling measurements points out a root-mean square error lower than 0.1 mm which can also be explained in terms of the different characteristics of radar and levelling measurements. In fact, radar measurements refer to pier portions whose extension depends on the range and azimuth resolution and provide the mean displacement within the interval between two radar acquisitions. In contrast, levelling measurements provide the instantaneous displacement of a mirror, i.e. point-like targets. The deployment of a ground-based radar for the measurement of displacements of façades of building and monuments can be done using a more favourable measurement configuration of that which can be adopted for the pier monitoring as the radar LoS is almost perpendicular to the surface to be monitored.

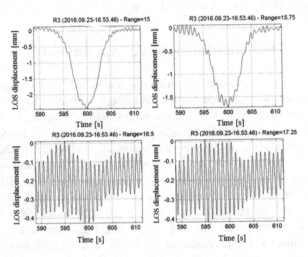

Fig. 1. Displacements by a ground-based radar in RAR configuration: (top) bridge; (bottom) fence.

A few examples of building monitoring are reported in [25–27]. A more advanced monitoring strategy of an archaeological area based on the joint use of ground-based radar and laser scanning is described in [28].

In both applications a pure SAR configuration has been used to map surface displacements. Usually, this configuration is the most suitable to monitor slope stability. For instance, a ground-based radar interferometer has been used to measure slope displacements in open-pit mines (e.g. see [29–31]).

The same SAR configuration, with a vertical baseline between the RX antennas, can also be used to map the terrain surface. In this case, the interferometric phase is used to estimate the height difference of terrain point with respect to the radar location and the relationship (2) is not longer used. More details on the topographic mapping of small areas by means of a ground-based radar can be found in [32–35].

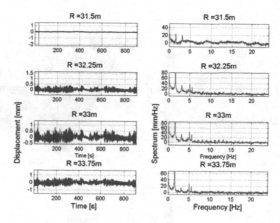

Fig. 2. Displacements and frequency spectra of a bridge by a ground-based radar in RAR configuration.

The landslide monitoring is a further successful application of ground-based radar interferometry, using a SAR acquisition configuration [36–45]. Two monitoring strategies have been used. One strategy is based on a continuous monitoring of the landslide prone area. This approach is used when an emergency is faced and the continuous monitoring is needed to keep under control the mass movement. A second approach consists in the periodic acquisition of radar data, with campaign repeated at time intervals of a few weeks. The duration of each campaign is usually of a few hours. The availability of a good quality Digital Elevation Model (DEM) of the area, before the starting of mass movements, allows to study the morphological changes of slopes both at a short time scale, corresponding to the duration of each campaign, and a long time scale [46]. A key point of this application of ground-based radar is the choice of interferometric couples having a high interferometric coherence. The coherence values of each interferometric couple is real number between 0 and 1. This quantity measures the quality of the interferometric phase. The lower the coherence, the noisier is the interferometric phase and less pixels of the SAR images can be used to estimate the terrain displacement. Coherence decreases in case of slopes covered by dense vegetation or when SAR images with a long temporal baseline are processed. Figure 4 displays an example of matrix summarizing the mean coherence values of the interferometric couples obtained by taking different combination of the acquired SAR images. In the case of the Fig. 4, a time series of 100 images is used to compute the mean coherence values of all interferograms.

The coherence scale has been set to [0.8, 0.9] to emphasize pixels with a coherence higher than 0.8. A tool as the matrix reported in Fig. 4 is useful to identify the interferometric couples with a high SNR, which provide a better estimate of terrain displacements. Other visualization tools useful for the interferometric processing of ground-based radar images of landslide-prone areas are described in [47].

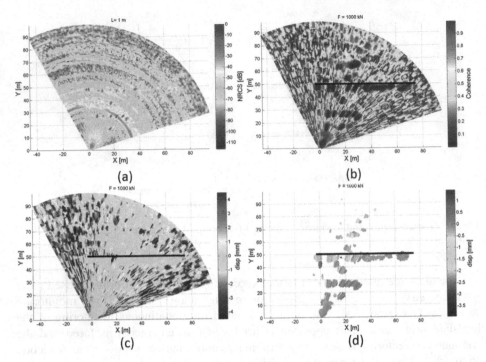

Fig. 3. Displacement measurement of a pier during a bollard pulling trial by means of a ground-based radar: (a) amplitude, (b) coherence, (c) interferogram and (d) displacement maps [24].

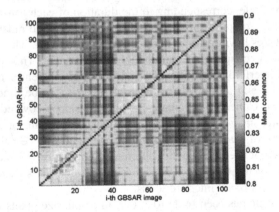

Fig. 4. Summary of mean coherence values of all interferometric couples obtained by combining a time series of N = 100 ground-based radar images.

Figure 5 shows an example of coherence map and corresponding displacement maps of a landslide-in urban area. It can be observed that estimates of displacements are provided only for the pixels having a coherence higher than 0.8.

Monitoring of volcano activity and sinkholes are two further applications of ground-based radar interferometry to the study of geological phenomena. Concerning volcano activity, ground-based radar was able to both measure terrain displacements triggered by volcano eruption [48, 49] and, indirectly, study the conduit pressurization pulses [50, 51]. The use of ground-based radar to measure terrain displacements caused by sinkholes is more difficult due to the unfavorable observation geometry with respect to satellite SAR images. Nevertheless, an example of application of ground-based radar to monitor sinkholes can be found in the literature [52].

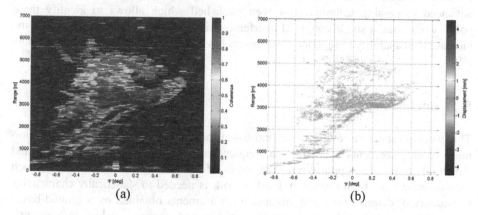

(a)   (b)

Fig. 5. Monitoring of a landslide: (a) coherence and (b) displacement maps.

We conclude this review of applications of ground-based radar interferometry mentioning the use of this technique to study displacement of glaciers [53, 54] and the coherence properties of snow for the mitigation of avalanche risk [55].

4 Precision and Accuracy of Ground-Based Radar Measurements and Impact of Propagation Delay in Atmosphere

The precision of displacement measurements provided by a ground-based radar depends on the phase dispersion and the radar wavelength. The ground-based radars used in the applications described in this paper are mainly working in the Ku band with a wavelength of about 18 mm. This means that the precision of displacement measurements is a fraction of a millimetre, also depending on the interferometric coherence of the moving target. However, the propagation delay of the radar signal in the troposphere is the main phenomenon impacting on the quality of displacement measurements. In fact, this delay strongly affects the accuracy of displacement measurements provided by a ground-based radar.

We can state that the output of a ground-based radar, if not properly processed, provides a means to measure the propagation delay in the troposphere more than the actual displacement of terrain. Different approaches have been attempted to separate the two signals as those published by [56–58].

Another problem related to the use of ground-based SAR interferometry in geotechnical applications is the selection of points of the monitored scene where displacement measurements can be provided with a high precision. Usually, this requires the processing of a long time-series of SAR images in order identify those points and try to disentangle atmospheric artifacts from real displacements. Recently, a new advanced processing technique has been published which allows to identify these points even using a single couple of interferometric SAR images and at the same time increase the capability to separate close targets having different displacement behaviors [59].

5 Conclusions

This work presented a review of ground-based radar results obtained in the measurement of displacements and vibration frequencies with interest in geotechnical and structural engineering applications. The issues of the precision and accuracy of such measurement have been discussed. Further work is needed to statistically characterize the quality of displacement and vibration measurements obtained by a ground-based radar which could provide their actual precision and accuracy values in a specific measurement campaign.

References

1. Tarchi, D., Oliveri, F., Sammartino, P.F.: MIMO radar and ground-based SAR imaging systems: equivalent approaches for remote sensing. IEEE Trans. Geosci. Remote Sens. **51** (1), 425–435 (2012)
2. Anghel, A., Cacoveanu, R., Moldovan, A.S., Savlovschi, C., Rommen, B., Datcu, M.: Bistatic SAR imaging with Sentinel-1 operating in TOPSAR mode. In: Proceedings of the IEEE Radar Conference, pp. 601–605, Belfast, UK (2017)
3. Feng, W., Friedt, J.M., Nico, G., Sato, M.: Three-dimensional ground based imaging radar based on C-band cross-MIMO array and tensor compressive sensing. IEEE Geosci. Remote Sens. Lett. **16**(10), 1585–1589 (2019)
4. Anghel, A., et al.: Compact ground-based interferometric synthetic aperture radar: short-range structural monitoring. IEEE Signal Process. Mag. **36**(4), 42–52 (2019)
5. Feng, W., Friedt, J.M., Nico, G., Wang, S., Martin, G., Sato, M.: Passive bistatic ground-based synthetic aperture radar: concept, system, and experiment results. Remote Sens. **11** (15), 1753 (2019)
6. Di Pasquale, A., et al.: Ground-based SAR interferometry as a supporting tool in natural and man-made distasters. In: Lasaponara, R., Masini, N., Biscione, M (eds.) Proceedings of the EARSeL Symposium 2013, Towards Horizon 2020, pp. 173–186 (2013). ISBN 978-88-89693-34-6

7. Tarchi, D., Ohlmer, E., Sieber, A.J.: Monitoring of structural changes by radar interferometry. Res. Nondestruct. Eval. **9**, 213–225 (1997)
8. Pieraccini, M., Fratini, M., Parrini, F., Atzeni, C.: Dynamic monitoring of bridges using a high-speed coherent radar. IEEE Trans. Geosci. Remote Sens. **44**(11), 3284 (2006)
9. Pieraccini, M., Frattini F., Parrini, M., Atzeni, C., Bartioli, G.: Interferometric radar vs. accelerometer for dynamic monitoring of large structures: an experimental comparison. NDT & E Int. **41**(4), 258–264 (2008)
10. Dei, D., Pieraccini, M., Frattini, M., Atzeni, C., Bartioli, G.: Detection of vertical bending and torsional movements of a bridge using a coherence radar. NDT and E Int. **42**(8), 741–747 (2009)
11. Marchisio, M., Piroddi, L., Ranieri, G., Calcina, S.V., Farina, P.: Comparison of natural and artificial forcing to study the dynamic behaviour of bell towers in low wind context by means of ground-based radar interferometry: the case of the leaning tower in Pisa. J. Geophys. Eng. **11**(5) (2014). Article no. 055004
12. Pieraccini, M., Dei, D., Betti, M., Bartoli, G., Tucci, G., Guardini, N.: Dynamic identification of historic masonry towers through an expeditious and no-contact approach: application to the "Torre del Mangia" in Siena (Italy). J. Cult. Herit. **15**, 275–282 (2015)
13. Artese, S., Nico, G.: TLS and GB-RAR measurements of vibration frequencies and oscillation amplitudes of tall structures: an application to wind towers. Appl. Sci. **10**(7), 2237 (2020)
14. Nico, G., Prezioso, G., Masci, O., Artese, S.: Dynamic modal identification of telecommunication towers using ground based radar interferometry. Remote Sens. **12**(7), 1211 (2020)
15. Di Pasquale, A., Nico, G., Pitullo, A., Prezioso, G.: Monitoring strategies of earth dams by ground-based radar interferometry: how to extract useful information for seismic risk assessment. Sensors **18**(1), 244 (2018)
16. Alba, M., et al.: Measurement of dam deformations by terrestrial interferometric techniques. Int. Arch. Photogramm. Remote Sens. Spat. Inf. Sci. **37**(1374), 133–139 (2008)
17. Wang, T., Perissin, D., Rocca, F., Liao. M.S.: Three Gorges Dam stability monitoring with time-series InSAR image analysis. Sci. China Earth Sci. **54**, 720–732 (2011)
18. Voege, M., Frauenfelder, R., Larsen. Y.: Displacement monitoring at Svartevatn dam with interferometric SAR. In: Proceedings of the IEEE International Geoscience and Remote Sensing Symposium (IGARSS), Munich, Germany, pp. 3895–3898 (2012)
19. Dardanelli, G., La Loggia, G., Perfetti, N., Capodici, F., Puccio, L., Maltese, A.: Monitoring displacements of an earthen dam using GNSS and remote sensing. In: Neale, C.M.U., Maltese, A. (eds.) Proceedings of the SPIE Remote Sensing for Agriculture, Ecosystems, and Hydrology XVI, vol. 9239. SPIE-Int. Soc. Optical Engineering, Bellingham (2014). ISBN 978-1-62841-302-1
20. Yigit, C.O., Alcay, S., Ceylan, A.: Displacement response of a concrete arch dam to seasonal temperature fluctuations and reservoir level rise during the first filling period: evidence from geodetic data. Geomat. Nat. Hazards Risk **7**, 1489–1505 (2016)
21. Pipitone, C., Maltese, A., Dardanelli, G., Lo Brutto, M., La Loggia, G.: Monitoring water surface and level of a reservoir using different remote sensing approaches and comparison with dam displacements evaluated via GNSS. Remote Sens. **10**(1), 71 (2018)
22. Al-Husseinawi, Y., Li, Z., Clarke, P., Edwards, S.: Evaluation of the Stability of the Darbandikhan Dam after the 12 November 2017 Mw 7.3 Sarpol-e Zahab (Iran– Iraq border) earthquake. Remote Sens. **10**, 1426 (2018)
23. Xiao, R., Shi, H., He, X., Li, Z., Jia, D., Yang, Z.: Deformation monitoring of reservoir dams using GNSS: an application to south-to-north water diversion project, China. IEEE Access **7**, 54981–54992 (2019)

24. Nico, G., et al.: Measurement of pier deformation patterns by ground-based SAR interferometry: application to a bollard pull trial. IEEE J. Ocean. Eng. **42**(4), 822–829 (2018)
25. Pieraccini, M., Tarchi, D., Rudolf, H., Leva, D., Luzi, G., Atzeni, C.: Interferometric radar for remote monitoring building deformations. Electron. Lett. **36**(6), 569–570 (2000)
26. Tarchi, D., Rudolf, H., Pieraccini, M., Atzeni, C.: Remote monitoring of buildings using a ground based SAR: application to cultural heritage survey. Int. J. Remote Sens. **21**(18), 3545–3551 (2000)
27. Castagnetti, C., Cosentini, R.M., Lancellotta, R., Capra, A.: Geodetic monitoring and geotechnical analyses of subsidence induced settlements of historic structures. Struct. Control Health Monit. **24**(12), 1–15 (2017)
28. Tapete, D., Casagli, N., Luzi, G., Fanti, R., Gigli, G., Leva, D.: Integrating radar and laser-based remote sensing techniques for monitoring structural deformation of archaeological monuments. J. Archaeol. Sci. **40**(1), 176–189 (2013)
29. Severin, J., Eberhardt, E., Leoni, L., Fortin, S.: Development and application of a pseudo-3D pit slope displacement map derived from ground-based radar. Eng. Geol. **181**, 202–211 (2014)
30. Carlà, T., Farina, P., Intrieri, E., Ketizmen, H., Casagli, N.: Integration of ground-based radar and satellite InSAR data for the analysis of an unexpected slope failure in an open-pit mine. Eng. Geol. **235**, 39–52 (2018)
31. Dick, G.J., Eberhardt, E., Cabrejo-Liévano, A.G., Stead, D., Rose, N.D.: Development of an earlywarning time-of-failure analysis methodology for open-pit mine slopes utilizing ground-based slope stability radar monitoring data, Canadian. Geotech. J. **52**(4), 515–529 (2015)
32. Nico, G., Leva, D., Antonello, G., Tarchi, D.: Ground-based SAR interferometry for terrain mapping: theory and sensitivity analysis. IEEE Trans. Geosci. Remote Sens. **42**(6), 1344–1350 (2004)
33. Nico, G., Leva, D., Fortuny-Guasch, J., Antonello, G., Tarchi, D.: Generation of digital terrain models with a ground-based SAR system. IEEE Trans. Geosci. Remote Sens. **43**(1), 45–49 (2005)
34. Macfarlane, D.G., Wadge, G., Robertson, D.A., James, M.R., Pinkerton, H.: Use of a portable topographic mapping millimetre wave radar at an active lava flow. Geophys. Res. Lett. **33**(3), L03301 (2006)
35. Noferini, L., Pieraccini, M., Mecatti, D., Macaluso, G., Luzi, G., Atzeni, C.: DEM by ground-based SAR interferometry. IEEE Geosci. Remote Sens. Lett. **4**, 659–663 (2007)
36. Casagli, N., Farina, P., Leva, D., Nico, G., Tarchi, D.: Ground-based SAR interferometry as a tool for landslide monitoring during emergencies. In: Proceedings of the IEEE International Geoscience and Remote Sensing Symposium, Toulouse, France, pp. 2924–2926 (2003)
37. Canuti, P., Casagli, N., Farina, P., Leva, D., Tarchi, D., Nico: Some examples of slope movements monitored by ground-based SAR interferometry. In: Proceedings of IW Flows 2003 International Workshop on Occurrence and Mechanisms of Flows in Natural Slopes and Earthfills, Sorrento, Italy, pp. 71–77 (2003)
38. Antonello, G., et al.: A ground-based interferometer for the safety monitoring of landslides and structural deformations. In: Proceedings of the IEEE International Geoscience and Remote Sensing Symposium, Toulouse, France, pp. 218–220 (2003)
39. Leva, D., Nico, G., Tarchi, D., Fortuny-Guasch, J., Sieber, A.J.: Temporal analysis of a landslide by means of a ground-based SAR interferometer. IEEE Trans. Geosci. Remote Sens. **41**(4), 745–752 (2003)
40. Antonello, G., et al.: Ground-based SAR interferometry for monitoring mass movements. Landslides **1**(1), 21–28 (2004)

41. Barla, G., Antolini, F., Barla, M., Mensi, E., Piovano, G.: Monitoring of the Beauregard landslide (Aosta Valley, Italy) using advanced and conventional techniques. Eng. Geol. **116** (3–4), 218–235 (2010)
42. Del Ventisette, C., Intrieri, E., Luzi, G., Casagli, N., Fanti, R., Leva, D.: Using ground based radar interferometry during emergency: The case of the A3 motorway (Calabria Region, Italy) threatened by a landslide. Nat. Hazards Earth Syst. Sci. **11**(9), 2483–2495 (2011)
43. Takahashi, K., Matsumoto, M., Sato, M.: Continuous observation of natural-disaster-affected areas using ground-based SAR interferometry. IEEE J. Sel. Top. Appl. Earth Obs. Remote Sens. **6**(3), 1286–1294 (2013)
44. Nico, G., Borrelli, L., Di Pasquale, A., Antronico, L., Gullà, G.: Monitoring of an ancient landslide phenomenon by GBSAR technique in the Maierato Town (Calabria, Italy). In: Lollino, G., Giordan, D., Crosta, Giovanni B., Corominas, J., Azzam, R., Wasowski, J., Sciarra, N. (eds.) Engineering Geology for Society and Territory - Volume 2, pp. 129–133. Springer, Cham (2015). https://doi.org/10.1007/978-3-319-09057-3_12
45. Lombardi, L., et al.: The Calatabiano landslide (Southern Italy): preliminary GB-InSAR monitoring data and remote 3D mapping. Landslides **14**(2), 685–696 (2016). https://doi.org/10.1007/s10346-016-0767-6
46. Casagli, N., Farina, P., Leva, D., Nico, G., Tarchi, D.: Landslide monitoring on a short and long time scale by using ground-based SAR interferometry. In: Ehlers, M. (ed.) Proceedings of the SPIE Remote Sensing for Environmental Monitoring, GIS Applications, and Geology II, vol. 4886, pp. 322–329. SPIE-Int. Soc. Optical Engineering: Bellingham (2003). ISBN 0-8194-4668-8
47. Nico, G., Kostić, U., Di Pasquale, A.: Tools for the real time visualization and analysis of Ground-based SAR data: application to the monitoring of landslides. Adv. Landslide Res., 59 (2018)
48. Casagli, N., Farina, P., Guerri, L., Tarchi, D., Fortuny, J., Leva, D., Nico, G.: Preliminary results of SAR monitoring of the Sciara del Fuoco on the Stromboli Volcano. In: Proceedings of IW Flows 2003 International Workshop on Occurrence and Mechanisms of Flows in Natural Slopes and Earthfills, Sorrento, Italy, pp. 14–16 (2003)
49. Antonello, G., et al.: SAR interferometry monitoring of landslides on the Stromboli Volcano. In: Proceedings of FRINGE 2003 Workshop, ESA SP-550, Frascati, Italy, p. 78.1 (2004)
50. Casagli, N., et al.: Deformation of Stromboli Volcano (Italy) during the 2007 eruption revealed by radar interferometry, numerical modelling and structural geological field data. J. Volcanol. Geotherm. Res. **182**(3–4), 182–200 (2009)
51. Di Traglia, F., et al.: Groundbased InSAR reveals conduit pressurization pulses at Stromboli Volcano. Terra Nova **25**(3), 192–198 (2013)
52. Intrieri, E., Gigli, G., Nocentini, M., Lombardi, L., Mugnai, F., Casagli, N.: Sinkhole monitoring and early warning: an experimental and successful GB-InSAR application. Geomorphology **241**, 304–314 (2015)
53. Caduff, R., Wiesmann, A., Bühler, Y., Pielmeier, C.: Continuous monitoring of snowpack displacement at high spatial and temporal resolution with terrestrial radar interferometry. Geophys. Res. Lett. **42**(3), 813–820 (2015)
54. Luzi, G., et al.: Monitoring of an alpine glacier by means of ground-based SAR interferometry. IEEE Geosci. Remote Sens. Lett. **4**(3), 495–499 (2007)
55. Martinez-Vazquez, A., Fortuny-Guasch, J.: A GB-SAR processor for snow avalanche identification. IEEE Trans. Geosci. Remote Sens. **46**(11), 3948–3956 (2008)
56. Luzi, G., et al.: Ground-based radar interferometry for lanslide monitoring: atmospheric and instrumental decorrelation sources on experimental data. IEEE Trans. Geosci. Remote Sens. **42**(11), 2454–2466 (2004)

57. Pipia, L., Fabregas, X., Aguasca, A., López-Martinez, C.: Atmospheric artifact compensation in ground-based DInSAR applications. IEEE Geosci. Remote Sens. Lett. **5**(1), 88–92 (2008)

58. Izumi, Y., Zou, L., Kikuta, K., Sato, M.: Iterative atmospheric phase screen compensation for near-real-time ground-based InSAR measurements over a mountainous slope. IEEE Trans. Geosci. Remote Sens., 1–14 (2020). https://doi.org/10.1109/tgrs.2020.2973533

59. Feng, W., Nico, G., Sato, M.: GB-SAR interferometry based on dimension-reduced compressive sensing and multiple measurement vectors model. IEEE Geosci. Remote Sens. Lett. **16**(1), 70–74 (2018)

Multi-scale Remote Sensed Thermal Mapping of Urban Environments: Approaches and Issues

Gabriele Bitelli$^{(\boxtimes)}$ (ID), Emanuele Mandanici (ID),
and Valentina Alena Girelli (ID)

Department of Civil, Chemical Environmental and Materials Engineering
(DICAM), University of Bologna, viale del Risorgimento 2,
40136 Bologna, BO, Italy
{gabriele.bitelli, emanuele.mandanici,
valentina.girelli}@unibo.it

Abstract. Among the applications of Remote Sensing for urban environments, Thermal Mapping is currently one of the most interesting, although still quite limited in usage. Airborne, drone and satellite thermal imagery can in fact provide effective data for different purposes and at different scales. The peculiar characteristics of thermal images, on the other hand, make their use not really straightforward or immediate, and its insertion in an urban GIS must be carefully managed. The paper presents some approaches and solutions adopted for both the mapping of urban heat island at the scale of a whole city and a more detailed study of energy losses from building blocks. These includes geometric and radiometric calibration aspects and the integration of different sources of geomatic and remote sensing data.

Keywords: Thermography · Urban heat island · Heat losses

1 Introduction

Thermal Mapping is currently one of the most interesting applications of Remote sensing in urban environments, although still quite limited in usage due to the complexity of data processing and interpretation.

Airborne, UAV (Unmanned Aerial Vehicles) and satellite thermal imagery can in fact provide effective data for different purposes and at different scales. The range of uses is not limited to management and monitoring in a Smart City perspective (e.g. energy studies), but it can be expanded to the support of new city developments planning or to the tuning of mitigation strategies to remedy situations where citizens suffer from uncomfortable living situations, especially in case of heat waves [5].

The peculiar characteristics of thermal images, on the other hand, make their use not really straightforward or immediate, and its insertion in a urban GIS must be carefully managed. The derivation of accurate values of surface temperatures, indeed, requires complex radiometric and geometric calibration procedures, to compensate the effects of the atmosphere, of the emissivity and of the distortions of thermal cameras.

C. Parente et al. (Eds.): R3GEO 2019, CCIS 1246, pp. 375–386, 2020.
https://doi.org/10.1007/978-3-030-62800-0_29

Furthermore, thermal data can be combined and integrated with other geomatic information, coming from airborne LiDAR or multi/hyperspectral surveys or from terrestrial 3D surveys realized by Mobile Mapping Systems through multisensor platforms.

Airborne or satellite thermal mapping provides a synoptic grid of temperature data even on very large areas and therefore permits analysis at different scale levels on urban building materials, energy losses, surface energy budgets and urban heat island effects. The application depends of course on the pixel size of the images, which can vary from sub-meter to hundreds of meters depending on the type of platform used.

If the interest is towards the energy losses from the building roofs, airborne surveys are the best solution to cover the whole city area with a suitable spatial resolution. If the product must be a city temperature map, we are facing with specific problems, e.g. related to the knowledge of the emissivity of the diverse roof materials or to the photogrammetric approach to realize thermal orthophotos with a good metric accuracy [4].

On the other hand, if the interest is towards a picture of the Urban Heat Inland (UHI), indicative of the rise in the temperature of urban areas in comparison with periurban and rural neighborhoods [20], satellite imagery can provide a good solution, offering also the opportunity to collect multitemporal data [14]. Unfortunately, only few sensors are today available operating in the thermal bands with a sufficient spatial resolution for urban applications. These data can be integrated or calibrated with terrestrial surveys, e.g. realized along transects by using moving vehicles, or by referring to a network of fixed meteorological stations.

The approaches for both energy losses and UHI mapping were developed by the authors in the frame of different research projects, where specific issues related to the processing of thermal imagery and its integration with ground surveys were addressed. The paper will present the approaches adopted, from the city scale to the building scale, the main problems encountered, and the achieved results.

2   City Scale Analyses

The Urban Heat Island effect has been studied since the early seventies [9, 19]. It consists in a rise in the temperature of urban areas in comparison with periurban and rural neighbourhoods of about 1–3 K [25, 26] and up to 12 K under particular conditions. There are many negative effects of UHI, involving discomfort or serious diseases for city dwellers, energy waste for buildings and infrastructures, potential impact on air pollution increase.

Several causes have been identified for the UHI effect [1, 5]. The most obvious one is the change in land use, where vegetable canopies are substituted by urban surfaces that are characterized by different biophysical properties such as emissivity, thermal inertia and conductivity. Thermal mass is higher on artificial surfaces, if compared to natural ones, causing heat storage in daytime and heat release during nights. Furthermore, the geometry of buildings induces complex reflection of radiation [23] and the presence of obstacles for airflows affects the transport of energy and mass (e.g. "urban canyon" effects). Finally, emissions of heat, aerosols and greenhouse gases from human activities affect radiative processes and add waste heat and water vapour to the urban atmosphere. For example, a first attempt to measure the impact of heating and cooling systems on urban microclimate was conducted in the city of L'Aquila (Italy), by comparing Landsat images acquired after the seismic event of 2009, which caused the relocation of the inhabitants in different areas [2].

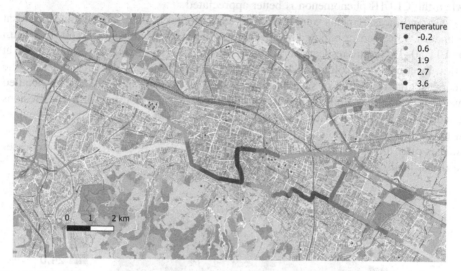

Fig. 1. Example of air temperature transect measured in February 2011 during night through Bologna city and the surroundings.

UHI affects both air and surfaces in urban areas [27]. Air temperature UHI is largest at night, under clear sky and light winds; it can be divided into the CLUHI (Canopy Layer Urban Heat Island, from the ground level to the mean building height), that is essentially a nocturnal phenomenon, and the BLUHI (Boundary Layer Urban Heat Island), observable all over day [21, 24]. Conversely, the SUHI (Surface Urban Heat Island) usually appears more intense by day. CLUHI can be detected with in-situ sensors at standard meteorological height or sensors mounted on mobile vehicles. SUHI, instead, is usually observed by thermal remote sensing. More recently, also sub-surface effects of the UHI in the shallow layers of the terrain were investigated [12], because they can be exploited for innovative geothermal systems [7].

Some experiments were carried out by the Authors in Bologna during specific cold and hot periods. These experiments include both the use of terrestrial sensors mounted on vehicles and the analysis of satellite thermal imagery.

To measure air temperature along some transects starting from the country-side and crossing the city centre, a temperature and humidity datalogger was mounted on top of a slowly moving car, georeferenced during the path. A multiplate shield, realizing a Stevenson screen, was used to protect the sensor from direct heat radiation from outside sources, but allowing the air to circulate freely inside, and a sampling rate of two seconds was set. Since the execution of a transect requires a lot of time (and during this time meteorological conditions can vary significantly), data from one fixed station were used to correct the mobile records.

An example of the results from a winter acquisition (February 2011), where the UHI is clearly visible, is shown in Fig. 1, where the centre of the city shows a significant difference in respect of the suburban areas. The transect was executed at night, when the CLUHI phenomenon is better appreciated.

Ground measurements were performed contemporary to the acquisition of Landsat 8 images. TIRS sensor onboard records images in two thermal bands (10.60–11.19 μm and 11.50–12.51 μm, respectively) at the spatial resolution of 100 metres, resampled at 30 m by a cubic convolution algorithm when delivered in L1T products. Clearly, the coarse spatial resolution of satellite thermal sensors is a serious limitation for detailed analyses, since it is not possible to go beyond the scale of urban districts. Besides Landsat 8, only ASTER and Landsat 7 platforms are still providing thermal images with slightly better resolutions (90 m and 60 m, respectively). In any case, these images offer the opportunity to make synoptic evaluations of environmental processes in urban landscapes [8].

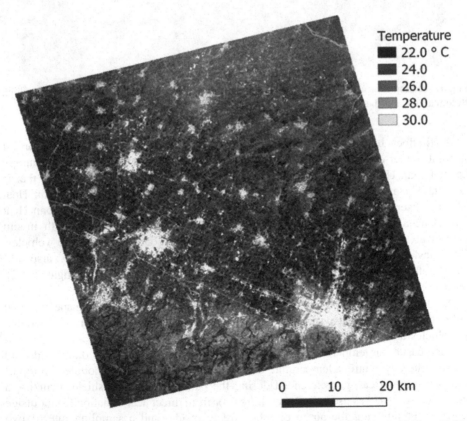

Fig. 2. ASTER image of Bologna and part of the Po valley acquired on July 7, 2017 at 11 PM (local time).

As it can be seen in Fig. 2, the processing of an ASTER thermal image acquired in Bologna in 2017 summer confirm the presence of the UHI phenomenon, with a magnitude in the order of 2 K, especially during nighttime. The image is an AST8s level product; it provides land surface temperatures with a nominal accuracy of 1–6 K, derived from the application of a temperature–emissivity separation algorithm [10].

It is worthwhile to mention that the validation of surface temperature results is always a complex task, also because of the punctual nature of temperature data recorded by traditional ground measuring stations when compared to the areal values coming from remote sensed analysis. A more extended validation, realized by many distributed points acquired in the same conditions, is in fact very expensive and quite complex to be systematically adopted outside of research purposes.

3   District/Blocks Analyses

The study of energy efficiency and heat losses in urban areas involves analyses at a completely different scale; thus, high spatial resolution is required to identify single buildings or, at least, building blocks. Suitable thermal imagery can be obtained in this case through sensors mounted on aircrafts or drones. Regulations and limitations in autonomy of current UAV platforms make the choice of airborne surveys optimal, especially when the analyses must encompass an entire city. In Fig. 3 an example of orthomosaic derived from airborne thermal imagery is shown.

When working at this scale, however, the preprocessing of thermal images becomes more challenging, from the point of view of both geometric and radiometric accuracy. For a correct quantitative evaluation of surface temperatures, indeed, several processing phases are required, which consider the effects of the acquisition geometry, the morphology of the scene, the influence of the atmosphere and of the emissivity of the different materials lying on the ground [17]. To accomplish these calibration tasks, several additional data are required; among them, multi or hyperspectral imagery, digital elevation models, atmospheric measurements and ground surveys.

High resolution multispectral images can be used to produce thematic maps of the roofing and paving materials by classification approaches. This mapping is crucial for an accurate temperature estimation because it provides information to apply correct emissivity coefficient to the observed materials. Indeed, the impact of the emissivity value on the retrieved temperatures can be up to several degrees (Fig. 4) [16]. In case of single-channel thermal sensors, indeed, temperature – emissivity separation algorithms are not applicable, and the derivation of emissivity must rely on external data. An example of map of roofing materials based on a WorldView-2 very-high resolution image of Bologna city is shown in Fig. 5.

Also hyperspectral sensors may be a valuable data source for the classification of materials, since they can provide detailed spectral/spatial signatures for different materials by collecting data in many narrow bands distributed in an almost continuous wavelength range. They can be mounted on both aircraft and satellite platforms [3]. The various types of hyperspectral devices can be distinguished in several ways, including spectral and spatial resolution, number of bands, electronic design and scanning geometry. The acquired hyperspectral data sets must be radiometrically and geometrically corrected. These images allows the collection of the spectral signatures of different roofing and paving materials, which can be used as training for classifications.

Fig. 3. Orthomosaic of aerial thermal images over Bologna city, acquired in March 2017.

The sky-view factor (SVF) is another relevant parameter in urban climate modelling, because it has a strong influence on the exchange of heat in complex structures. In particular, it influences the amount of both downwelling radiation coming from the sky and radiation coming from the surroundings objects, which are reflected by the target surface in the observing direction, thus affecting thermal imaging [17]. Different formulations of the SVF have been proposed in the literature. Basically, it can be expressed as the radiation coming from the visible part of the sky divided by the total radiation from the entire hemisphere [29], or, alternatively, as the portion of visible sky in the entire celestial hemisphere centred on the observation point [28]. The two definitions lead to numerically different sky-view factors, even if the geometry is the same. Regardless the definition used, including the SVF in the preprocessing of the thermal imagery appears to improve significantly the accuracy of the retrieved temperatures [17].

Fig. 4. Natural color (left) and uncalibrated thermal image (right) of roofs. The building marked with a pin has a very low emissivity value, resulting in an exaggeratedly cold apparent temperature.

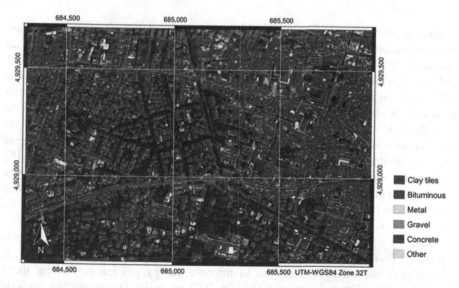

Fig. 5. Example of roofing materials classification over a portion of Bologna city [4].

SVF can be computed starting from digital surface models that can be derived, for example, from LiDAR surveys or from photogrammetry [18]. An example of SVF map is shown in Fig. 6.

Fig. 6. Example of sky-view factor map over a portion of Bologna city [17].

From a geometrical point of view, a significant problem is the mosaicking and orthorectification of hundreds or even thousands of images, when 2D thermal maps are required. Even though the orthorectification of aerial image blocks is a mature and well-established technique for digital cameras operating in the ordinary wavelengths of visible and near-infrared radiation, when coming to thermal cameras some distinctive characteristics of thermal images makes the process more challenging [6]. In fact, the lower dynamic range and geometric resolution, together with poor definition of the discontinuities and small details (e.g. blurred edges), may sometimes cause the failure of commonly used algorithms or, more often, a significant drop in their accuracy [13, 15].

After a complete geometric and radiometric preprocessing, thermal data can be finally used in different contexts; one of the most interesting is within a spatial decision support system (SDSS) to take decisions about energy management and saving and for CO_2 emission reduction in a municipality.

Relatively few works were conducted by municipalities or public administrators to map energy loss of buildings by the processing of thermal remote-sensed imagery, in order to plan cost-effective solutions to improve energy efficiency. Among them, Birmingham City Council commissioned in 2002 an aerial thermographic study in order to identify buildings with poor insulation levels [22] and the Energy Mapping Study of Canadian Urban Institute [11] developed a web-based GIS containing an energy land-use map of buildings in the urban area of Calgary with the aim to support local authorities, householders and the entire community in reducing greenhouse gas emissions and encourage the use of alternative energy systems.

Fig. 7. Example of WebGIS interface built for the European project EnergyCity [4].

Also, a few research projects were carried out about the combined use of thermal remote-sensed data in order to analyse energy use in cities and plan efficient remedial measures of energy efficiency improvement in urban areas. Among them, the Central Europe project "EnergyCity - Reducing energy consumption and CO_2 emissions in cities across Central Europe" explored the simultaneous use of moderate resolution satellite thermal images, sub-metric resolution airborne both thermal and hyperspectral images and ground-based thermographic surveys on seven cities (Bologna, Treviso, Velenje, Budapest, Prague, Ludwigsburg and Munich), with the aim to reduce energy consumption and CO_2 emissions. The project involved a complex flow of processes (Fig. 8), both in the field and in laboratory. Basically, ground surveys (contemporary to the execution of the thermal flight) and ancillary cartographic data were used for geometric correction and radiometric calibration of thermal images. For the accurate derivation of surface temperature, emissivity data were derived from a parallel processing of hyperspectral data, acquired during dedicated flights, targeted to the classification of the major types of roofing materials. Atmospheric attenuation was computed through the MODTRAN radiative transfer code.

One of the relevant final product of the EnergyCity project was the Web-based Spatial Decision Support System (Fig. 7). It was designed to display heat loss maps and CO_2 emission for the seven cities [4]. An indicative energy model was applied. In brief, the model was based on the relative roof temperature derived by thermal images. Roofs were divided into five classes based on their roof temperature.

Aerial surveys provided also information about buildings outline, the perimeter and the covered ground area. The average building height was instead obtained from digital surface models and digital elevation models. These three types of numerical information enabled the computation of the heated volume and the total exposed surface. The specific heating energy consumption was then calculated for the five temperature ranges, considering typical energy consumption values obtained from available building stock databases.

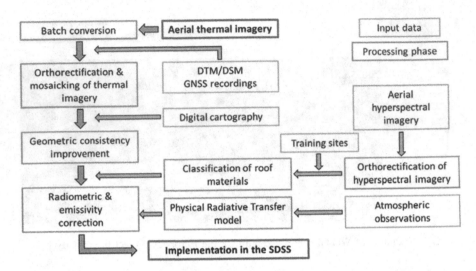

Fig. 8. Workflow for the processing of thermal data adopted in the EnergyCity project.

4 Conclusions

Climate changes and the increasing severity and frequency of heat waves impose to consider with great attention phenomena related to the increasing temperature in urban environments, either in relation to the city dwellers' health and to energy savings and CO_2 emissions reduction.

In this perspective, it is of vital importance to dispose of instruments for temperature monitoring at different scale of analysis. On the one hand, there is an increasing number of solutions proposed for close-range measurements (e.g. by UAV); on the other hand, there is the lack of suitable satellite platforms for diurnal and (mainly) nocturnal imaging with good spatial resolution.

The experiences described in the present paper demonstrate that, beside the acquisition issues, special care is to be taken during the data processing. Temperature retrieval is extremely sensitive to several parameters, which are often poorly known, compared to the traditional use of optical imagery. For this reason, the integration of different techniques seems the most promising way for a better monitoring of the urban context also in the perspective of Smart Cities implementation.

Acknowledgments. Part of the work was performed in the framework of Central Europe project 2CE126P3 "EnergyCity - Reducing energy consumption and CO_2 emissions in cities across Central Europe" (PI T. Csoknyai).

References

1. Arnfield, A.J.: Two decades of urban climate research: a review of turbulence, exchanges of energy and water, and the urban heat island. Int. J. Climatol. **23**(1), 1–26 (2003). https://doi.org/10.1002/joc.859
2. Baiocchi, V., Zottele, F., Dominici, D.: Remote sensing of urban microclimate change in L'Aquila city (Italy) after post-earthquake depopulation in an open source GIS environment. Sensors **17**(2) (2017). https://doi.org/10.3390/s17020404
3. Bitelli, G., Blanos, R., Conte, P., Mandanici, E., Paganini, P., Pietrapertosa, C.: Hyperspectral data classification to support the radiometric correction of thermal imagery. In: Gervasi, O., et al. (eds.) ICCSA 2017. LNCS, vol. 10407, pp. 81–92. Springer, Cham (2017). https://doi.org/10.1007/978-3-319-62401-3_7
4. Bitelli, G., Conte, P., Csoknyai, T., Franci, F., Girelli, V.A., Mandanici, E.: Aerial thermography for energetic modelling of cities. Remote Sens. **7**(2), 2152–2170 (2015). https://doi.org/10.3390/rs70202152
5. Bitelli, G., Conte, P., Csoknyai, T., Mandanici, E.: Urban energetics applications and geomatic technologies in a smart city perspective. Int. Rev. Appl. Sci. Eng. **6**(1), 19–29 (2015). https://doi.org/10.1556/1848.2015.6.1.3
6. Conte, P., Girelli, V.A., Mandanici, E.: Structure from motion for aerial thermal imagery at city scale: pre-processing, camera calibration, accuracy assessment. ISPRS J. Photogramm. Remote Sens. **146**, 320–333 (2018). https://doi.org/10.1016/j.isprsjprs.2018.10.002
7. Focaccia, S., Barbaresi, A., Tinti, F.: Simulation of observed temperature field below a building. Environ. Geotech., 1–39 (2018). https://doi.org/10.1680/jenge.17.00105
8. Gallo, K., Tarpley, J., McNab, A., Karl, T.: Assessment of urban heat islands: a satellite perspective. Atmos. Res. **37**(1), 37–43 (1995). https://doi.org/10.1016/0169-8095(94)00066-M
9. Gartland, L.M.: Heat Islands: Understanding and Mitigating Heat in Urban Areas. Routledge (2012). https://doi.org/10.4324/9781849771559
10. Gillespie, A., Rokugawa, S., Matsunaga, T., Cothern, J.S., Hook, S., Kahle, A.B.: A temperature and emissivity separation algorithm for advanced spaceborne thermal emission and reflection radiometer (ASTER) images. IEEE Trans. Geosci. Remote Sens. **36**(4), 1113–1126 (1998). https://doi.org/10.1109/36.700995
11. Hemachandran, B., Hay, G.J., Kyle, G.D., Chen, G., Powers, R.P.: HEAT – home energy assessment technologies: a web based system for residential waste heat analysis using airborne thermal imagery. In: Proceedings of the 2010 Canadian Geomatics Conference and Symposium of Commission I. ISPRS (2010)
12. Kasmaee, S., Tinti, F.: A method to evaluate the impact of urbanization on ground temperature evolution at a regional scale. Rudarsko-geološko-naftni zbornik **33**, 1–12 (2018). https://doi.org/10.17794/rgn.2018.5.1
13. Khodaei, B., Samadzadegan, F., Javan, F.D., Hasani, H.: 3D surface generation from aerial thermal imagery. ISPRS Int. Arch. Photogramm. Remote Sens. Spat. Inf. Sci. **XL-1-W5**, 401–405 (2015). https://doi.org/10.5194/isprsarchives-xl-1-w5-401-2015
14. Li, Z.L., et al.: Satellite-derived land surface temperature: current status and perspectives. Remote Sens. Environ. **131**, 14–37 (2013). https://doi.org/10.1016/j.rse.2012.12.008
15. Maes, W., Huete, A., Steppe, K.: Optimizing the processing of UAV-based thermal imagery. Remote Sens. **9**(5), 476 (2017). https://doi.org/10.3390/rs9050476

16. Mandanici, E., Conte, P.: Aerial thermography for energy efficiency of buildings: the ChoT project. In: Erbertseder, T., Esch, T., Chrysoulakis, N. (eds.) Remote Sensing Technologies and Applications in Urban Environments, Proceedings SPIE, vol. 10008, p. 1000808. SPIE (2016). https://doi.org/10.1117/12.2241256

17. Mandanici, E., Conte, P., Girelli, V.A.: Integration of aerial thermal imagery, LiDAR data and ground surveys for surface temperature mapping in urban environments. Remote Sens. **8** (12), 880 (2016). https://doi.org/10.3390/rs8100880

18. Mandanici, E., Girelli, V.A., Poluzzi, L.: Metric accuracy of digital elevation models from worldview-3 stereo-pairs in urban areas. Remote Sens. **11**(7) (2019). https://doi.org/10.3390/rs11070878

19. Oke, T.R.: City size and the urban heat island. Atmos. Environ. (1967) **7**(8), 769–779 (1973). https://doi.org/10.1016/0004-6981(73)90140-6

20. Oke, T.R.: The energetic basis of the urban heat island. Q. J. R. Meteorol. Soc. **108**(455), 1–24 (1982). https://doi.org/10.1002/qj.49710845502

21. Parsaee, M., Joybari, M.M., Mirzaei, P.A., Haghighat, F.: Urban heat island, urban climate maps and urban development policies and action plans. Environ. Technol. Innov. **14**, 100341 (2019). https://doi.org/10.1016/j.eti.2019.100341

22. Roberts, S., Starling, G.: Making the most of Birmingham city council's aerial thermographic study. Technical report, Centre for Sustainable Energy (2004)

23. Roth, M.: Effects of cities on local climates. In: Proceedings of the Workshop of IGES/APN Mega-City Project. Institute for Global Environmental Strategies, Kitakyushu (2002)

24. Sen, S., Roesler, J., Ruddell, B., Middel, A.: Cool pavement strategies for urban heat island mitigation in suburban phoenix, arizona. Sustainability **11**(16) (2019). https://doi.org/10.3390/su11164452

25. Stewart, I.D., Oke, T.R.: Local climate zones for urban temperature studies. Bull. Am. Meteorol. Soc. **93**(12), 1879–1900 (2012). https://doi.org/10.1175/BAMS-D-11-00019.1

26. Voogt, J.A., Oke, T.R.: Thermal remote sensing of urban climates. Remote Sens. Environ. **86**(3), 370–384 (2003). https://doi.org/10.1016/s0034-4257(03)00079-8

27. Weng, Q.: Thermal infrared remote sensing for urban climate and environmental studies: methods, applications, and trends. ISPRS J. Photogramm. Remote Sens. **64**(4), 335–344 (2009). https://doi.org/10.1016/j.isprsjprs.2009.03.007

28. Zakšek, K., Oštir, K., Kokalj, Ž.: Sky-view factor as a relief visualization technique. Remote Sens. **3**(2), 398–415 (2011). https://doi.org/10.3390/rs3020398

29. Zhu, S., et al.: Influence of sky temperature distribution on sky view factor and its applications in urban heat island. Int. J. Climatol. **33**(7), 1837–1843 (2013). https://doi.org/10.1002/joc.3660

Correction to: Educational Experiences for Geomatics Scientific Dissemination

Domenico Sguerso📵, Elena Ausonio📵, Bianca Federici📵,
Ilaria Ferrando⁽⊠⁾📵, Sara Gagliolo📵, and Stefania Viaggio📵

Correction to:
Chapter "Educational Experiences for Geomatics Scientific
Dissemination" in: C. Parente et al. (Eds.): *R3 in Geomatics:
Research, Results and Review*, CCIS 1246,
https://doi.org/10.1007/978-3-030-62800-0_5

In the originally published version of the chapter 5, the name of the author Stefania Viaggio was incorrect. The name has been corrected.

The updated version of this chapter can be found at
https://doi.org/10.1007/978-3-030-62800-0_5

Author Index

Printed in the United States
By Bookmasters